Windows Server 2003
Registry

Windows Server 2003 Registry

Olga Kokoreva

A-LIST, LLC
295 East Swedesford Rd.
PMB #285
Wayne, PA 19087
702-977-5377 (FAX)
mail@alistpublishing.com
http://www.alistpublishing.com

This book is printed on acid-free paper.

Windows Server 2003 Registry
By Olga Kokoreva

ISBN 1-931769-21-4

Printed in the United States of America

03 04 7 6 5 4 3 2 1

A-LIST, LLC titles are available for site license or bulk purchase by institutions, user groups, corporations, etc.

Book Editors: Thomas Rymer, Rizwati Freeman

Contents

Introduction

Intended Audience

I became a member of a small team of Windows Server 2003 beta testers when the system was an early beta. Even at that early stage of beta testing, we could see that there were differences between Windows 2000 and its successors, code named "Whistler". It was an amazing experience to see how the system improved with the release of each new beta or Release Candidate. To generalize the common trend, the system became more and more powerful and reliable. However, despite all these improvements, the new system didn't entirely eliminate the features that had existed in Windows 2000; rather, it improved and extended this functionality while adding new tools and features. The new operating system implements all the best features of its predecessor. In this way, Windows Server 2003 continues the Windows 2000 tradition, emphasized by the "Built on NT Technology" slogan displayed at boot time. Windows 2000 had many features in common with the previous version of Windows NT, as do the products of the Windows Server 2003 family. If you examine it carefully, you'll see that it has many features in common with Windows 2000 as well.

Will thousands of users all over the world migrate to the newer version immediately? Some probably will (especially those who get the system with the new hardware), but many others will continue using Windows 2000 while examining this new system and testing existing applications for compatibility. This book is addressed to such readers, including system administrators, technical support personnel, and experienced Windows NT/2000 users.

Aims of This Book

Like many other Windows Server 2003 system components, the Registry is very much like the Windows NT/2000 Registry. However, there are also many differences, some of which are obvious (such as the elimination of the registry size limitation), while others are hardly noticeable. Mostly, the changes in Windows Server 2003 registry are due to the kernel enhancements introduced with this new release of the operating system. Throughout the book, I'll emphasize these differences and draw your attention to them. The Windows Server 2003 registry also contains a large number of new records. This isn't surprising, since each new registry entry corresponds to a new feature introduced with the new release. The registry is a centralized storage area for all the information on the hardware and software system components. Because of this, all new features introduced with Windows XP and Windows Server 2003 must be reflected in the registry.

Can this book be considered a reference describing all registry keys, or a handbook of practical solutions for everyday work? Unfortunately, no, it cannot. I dream about a book like that myself! I also know what a bulky book that would be (if it'd be possible to write at all). My aim isn't quite so ambitious. In this book, I'll describe the important components of Windows NT/2000, Windows XP, and Windows Server 2003 registries, and emphasize the similarities and differences that exist between them. I'll also discuss various techniques of backing up and recovering the registry, and provide essential technical information on other aspects of working with the registry as well. I hope that this book will be useful for system administrators and advanced users who want to improve their knowledge of the Windows NT/2000 registry and get acquainted with the Windows XP and Windows Server 2003 registry.

Quite often, one may hear users say "I hate Windows registry because it is rather cryptic, contains tons of redundant information, and makes the system vulnerable, since Windows can't run without it". If you hate the Windows registry too, I will not try to convince you to love it. After all, most people tend to hate a thing that they can't properly understand. I can also agree that this opinion is partially valid, because the registry actually is cryptic, difficult to understand, and really is required for the system to run. However, from this point of view, a human being is also very far from perfect, since the human body doesn't live without a brain (and even if someone supported this life artificially, how miserable it would be!). What I am really after is helping you understand the registry. Therefore, I didn't try to describe all known registry tips and tricks. Rather, I tried to explain how these tricks work and why they work at all. I think that when you have a sound understanding of the registry architecture, structure, and data types, you'll soon be able to discover such tricks yourselves.

Obviously, my own experiences of working as a technical support specialist have influenced both my methods of work in general and this book in particular. When I begin working with a new operating system, I'm mainly interested in providing a trouble-free environment — various aspects of backing up and recovering the more important system components (the registry, in our case), including non-traditional and rarely used ones. Various aspects of registry backup and recovery, together with methods of eliminating system failures, take priority in this book.

I'm sure that before migrating to the new operating system and experimenting with it, the user needs to study these topics very carefully. Testing backup, restore, and troubleshooting procedures will also be helpful.

The book contains the following chapters:

❏ *Chapter 1* contains an overview of the registry as it existed in all Windows NT-based operating systems. It provides a brief description of registry structure, valid data types, and methods used for storing registry data in Windows NT/2000, Windows XP, and Windows Server 2003. At the same time, it considers some kernel enhancements introduced with Windows XP and Windows Server 2003, which resulted in registry changes — for example, the removal of registry size limitation.

❏ *Chapter 2* is dedicated to various methods of backing up and restoring the registry. Even the most experienced Windows NT/2000 user should read this chapter carefully, since these procedures have changed significantly in the newer release.

❏ *Chapter 3* discusses the user interface of the registry editor (Regedit.exe). Most experienced Windows NT/2000 users should remember that Windows NT 4.0 and Windows 2000 actually included two registry-editing utilities — Regedt32.exe, the more powerful utility with extended capabilities but an old-fashioned interface, and Regedit.exe — the newer utility with an enhanced UI, which lacked, however, some powerful features of Regedt32. In Windows XP and Windows Server 2003, the situation has changed, and there is now only one registry-editing tool — Regedit.exe, which combines the functionality of the two registry editors. Beginners can use this chapter as a brief reference on this tool (which, by the way, Microsoft is positioning as one of the reliability enhancements).

❏ *Chapter 4* looks at the simplest methods of configuring the operating system. This chapter describes both the method of configuring the system using administrative utilities and the method that requires registry editing. Some of the tips provided here also apply to Windows NT and Windows 2000, while others are specific to Windows XP and Windows Server 2003.

❏ *Chapter 5* discusses the problem of storing hardware information in the registry. It also provides basic information on Plug and Play architecture implementation in Windows 2000, Windows XP, and Windows Server 2003, including two new kernel-mode subsystems — Plug and Play Manager and Power Manager. Also covered are the OnNow initiative and the ACPI specification.

❏ *Chapter 6* contains a detailed description of the boot process for all Windows NT-based operating systems, including Windows NT/2000, Windows XP. and Windows Server 2003. It describes the registry's role in the boot process and provides a brief overview of the methods of eliminating boot failures. Special attention is focused on built-in reliability enhancements, including safe mode, Driver Rollback,

Recovery Console, and code signing options such as Windows File Protection, System File Checker, and File Signature Verification.

❑ *Chapter 7* can be used as a brief reference to the registry keys.

❑ *Chapter 8* discusses network settings in the registry for Windows 2000, Windows XP, and Windows Server 2003.

❑ *Chapter 9* has a special place in this book, because it discusses one of the most important topics, namely, various aspects of protecting and securing the registry. Besides universal recommendations suitable for all Windows NT-based operating systems, special attention has been drawn to security enhancements introduced with Windows XP and Windows Server 2003, such as Software Restriction Policies.

❑ *Chapter 10* discusses the problems of managing user working environments, including user profiles and group policies.

❑ *Chapter 11* explores the relationship between Active Directory and the local registry, covering such important topics as Group Policies, Windows Installer technology and Active Directory Class Store — a kind of "super-registry" or "centralized registry".

❑ *Chapter 12* contains recommendations and tips on eliminating the most common problems (including boot failures) by means of editing the registry. It is of special interest for system administrators and technical support personnel.

❑ *Chapter 13* is dedicated to advanced customization and troubleshooting topics.

❑ *Chapter 14* provides a brief overview of the handy third-party registry utilities.

❑ *Chapter 15* provides an overview of automating registry management using Windows Script Host (WSH). Of course, it can't be considered a reference on Windows automation and scripting languages (this topic deserves a special book). However, we will consider the registry-manipulation methods provided by WSH, then create a simple example illustrating their usage, and then produce a small but really useful script.

❑ *Appendix 1* — Internet resources. If I intended to create a reference on the Internet resources dedicated to Windows 2000/XP, it would be a large book indeed! Of course, not all of these resources are equally useful. Because of this, I have included only the most informative and reliable ones in the appendix.

❑ *Appendix 2* — Bibliography. This appendix provides a list of sources where the reader can find supplementary information concerning the topics discussed in this book.

To conclude this brief introduction, I would like to thank all the members of the A-LIST Publishing team for offering me the opportunity to work on this book.

CHAPTER 1

Windows Server 2003 Registry Overview

R is for Rocket.
Ray Bradbury

This book is meant for system administrators, technical support personnel, and advanced users of Windows NT-based systems (Windows NT/2000, Windows XP and products of the Windows Server 2003 family). Most of you already have at least some previous knowledge of the registry. Its prototype already existed in Windows 3.1, and most programmers already knew what the registry is if it comes up in conversation. In the world of Science Fiction (SF) R is for Rocket, according to the classics. To continue this analogy, for most Windows professionals R certainly stands for the Registry. Registry topics became popular with the user community after the release of the Windows 95 operating system. This isn't surprising, since the registry is the most important component of all modern operating systems belonging to the Windows family, none of which can run without it. The registry can be found anywhere in the Windows world — including in Pocket PCs.

 Note

Of course, most computer-literate and advanced users will immediately point out that there is a vast area in the world of operating systems where there is no registry at all — namely, in operating systems other than Windows. Various UNIX and Linux clones are good examples. However, one of the greatest obstacles in the general usage of these operating systems is the fact that they don't support some of the popular Windows applications. If these applications were available, these operating systems would be even more popular than they currently are. There are, of course, different ways of running Windows applications on UNIX and Linux, for example, starting them within an emulator such as Windows Application Binary Interface (WABI), WINE or VMWare. Another approach (which is better one from the standpoint of reliability) involves porting the application's code so that it runs natively. If you choose this approach, you'll have to emulate Windows registry, because Windows applications that are ported to run in UNIX environments still require the equivalent of a registry and the information it contains.

When the system is up and running smoothly, the registry remains in the background and works silently (so silently, actually, that end users might not even notice its existence). However, like the system made famous by the film "Matrix", it is present everywhere in the Windows world and never fails to make this fact evident when something goes terribly wrong. To demonstrate this point, the following question is sufficient: Have you ever received a message informing you that the operating system couldn't be loaded because of registry corruption? An example of such a message is provided below:

```
Windows  could not start because the following file is missing
or corrupt:
\WINNT\SYSTEM32\CONFIG\SYSTEM
You can attempt to repair this file by starting Windows  Setup using
the original Setup floppy disk of CD-ROM.
Select 'r' at the first screen to repair.
```

The example provided above clearly demonstrates that a single error in the system registry (the *System* file mentioned in the messages shown above contains registry information) can influence the whole system configuration and even prevent the operating system from booting. Furthermore, there are some applications, which can only run properly after editing the system registry. For this reason, the importance of understanding the registry and having practical skills to be able to work with it can't be underestimated.

This chapter provides a brief overview of the Windows NT/2000, Windows XP, and Windows Server 2003 registry, describes registry structure and data types, and also covers the methods of registry-data storage used in Windows XP and Windows Server 2003.

So, what exactly is the registry? It is a centralized database that stores all of the settings of the operating system and the applications running on it. This makes the registry similar to various INI files, as well as to files like Autoexec.bat and Config.sys that were used in earlier Windows versions. The registry also stores information about all of the hardware, including Plug and Play devices, Object Linking and Embedding (OLE) data, and file associations. The registry contains all of the data related to the applications that support Plug and Play and OLE, networking parameters, hardware profiles, and user profiles.

To summarize, if there is any hardware or software in the computer system that influences it in some way, you can be certain that the system registry stores information about that component.

History of the Registry

The registry concept itself isn't new to Windows. However, the modern registry is an impressive advance in improving system manageability from a single source — the *registry database*. This database was developed as the basis for all system-wide hardware and software parameters and custom user settings that exist in Windows.

The first successful operating system in the Windows family was Microsoft Windows 3.1. This system had three different types of configuration files:

❑ *System initialization files.* The standard Windows 3.1*x* installation had six system initialization files: Control.ini, Progman.ini, Protocol.ini, System.ini, Win.ini, and Winfile.ini. The Win.ini file contained basic information concerning software configuration, as well as some parameters that were added by applications as the user installed additional programs. In earlier Windows versions, each newly installed application introduced its settings to the Win.ini file. Thus, the file grew rapidly if the user installed a large number of applications. However, the file was limited in size (no more than 64 K). This limitation began causing problems when the file size reached its upper limit. Windows 3.1*x* did not warn the user when the Win.ini file grew beyond this limit and all modifications added to the last sections of the file (beyond the initialization range) were ignored by the system. Because of this, Microsoft recommended that software developers store application-specific information in separate files — so-called private initialization files (private INI files). The System.ini file served as the main storage place for system information related to hardware. The Progman.ini file contained initialization settings for Windows Program Manager and the Winfile.ini file contained Windows File Manager settings. The Protocol.ini file was added with the release of the Windows for Workgroups 3.1*x* operating system. This file stored initialization settings for Windows networks.

❑ *Private initialization files.* These were INI files added by applications that were installed in the system. The files were used for storing application-specific information, including the size and position of application windows and lists of recently used files (the MRUList parameter).

❑ Finally, there was the Reg.dat file, which was the direct predecessor of the Windows 9*x*/ME, Windows NT/2000/XP and Windows Server 2003 registries. This was a hierarchical database that comprised a single-root container structure called HKEY_CLASSES_ROOT. This root structure contained nested structures, which stored the system information needed to support OLE (Object Linking and Embedding) and file associations. This registry database allowed Windows 3.1*x* users to modify the behavior of linked or embedded objects and allowed them to view the list of applications registered in the Windows environment.

In contrast to INI files, which were ASCII text files available for editing by any text editor or word processor, the Reg.dat file was a binary file. To edit this file, the user needed a special application called Registry Editor (Regedit.exe). When the user started the REGEDIT.EXE /v command, this application displayed the Reg.dat file as a hierarchical structure with nested parameters. However, the structure of Reg.dat was far simpler than the structures of the modern registry.

Drawbacks of INI Files

One of the most significant problems related to INI files was their manageability. The standard set of INI files, created during the installation of Windows 3.*x*, didn't present any difficulties. However, as the user installed and deleted applications, the number of INI files constantly grew. This approach had some serious drawbacks:

❑ Editing INI files manually and setting correct values for various application-specific parameters wasn't very difficult for advanced users. However, even experienced users sometimes had to try more than once to obtain the desired result. With regard to beginners, these tasks were sometimes far beyond the scope of their skills and knowledge.

❑ Clear rules for storing INI files didn't exist. Private initialization files could be stored in any directory; they weren't write-protected, and there was always the chance of deletion. As a result, users frequently had to search for the INI files they needed and sometimes these files were hard to find.

❏ INI files didn't provide any support for a multi-user environment. Consequently, the users couldn't customize the settings for computer systems and applications.

❏ INI files didn't support multiple hardware configurations. Because of this, there was no Plug and Play support in Windows 3.*x*.

❏ Each application stored its settings in its own private initialization file. This, of course, was an official recommendation issued by Microsoft and was intended to provide a workaround for the Win.ini size limitation mentioned earlier. On the other hand, this recommendation just produced another limitation, because it restricted the capabilities for sharing information among applications.

▶ Note

Any Windows-compatible application (this is true for both Windows 9*x*/ME, Windows NT/2000, Windows XP and Windows Server 2003) has to meet a set of requirements, one of the most important being the presence of uninstall capabilities. Automatic uninstall capabilities that allow the user to delete an application correctly aren't new. However, implementation of this concept in Windows 3.*x* was far from easy. Modern operating systems that belong to the Windows family store all configuration data in the registry, which makes implementation of uninstall capabilities an easy task.

The Purpose of the Registry

The registry is a successor to INI files, which had serious drawbacks and limitations and, as a result, were so inconvenient to use. Windows NT 3.5 was the first operating system from the Windows family that had a registry that was more or less similar to the modern one (at that time, the registry had 4 root keys: HKEY_LOCAL_MACHINE, HKEY_CURRENT_USER, HKEY_CLASSES_ROOT, and HKEY_USERS). The new component of the operating system took the form of a centralized source of configuration information, which provided the possibility of managing the system environment much more efficiently.

Windows Server 2003 system components that use the registry (Fig. 1.1) are briefly described below.

❏ *Setup programs.* Any time a setup program runs (including Windows Setup program, Windows Installer, and other setup utilities that install software or device drivers), it adds new configuration data to the registry. If the Setup program is developed correctly, it reads the registry information to determine if all the components necessary to complete the installation procedure successfully are present in the system. Because the registry is a centralized storage space for configuration information, all applications can share this information and have broader capabilities of interacting with each other. Any application program carrying the claim "Designed for Windows" has to use the registry and provide a special uninstall utility that allows the user to delete this application correctly (Fig. 1.2). Application-specific information stored in the registry allows the user to perform this procedure correctly without deleting the shared components (DLL, OCX, and so on), which may be needed by other applications.

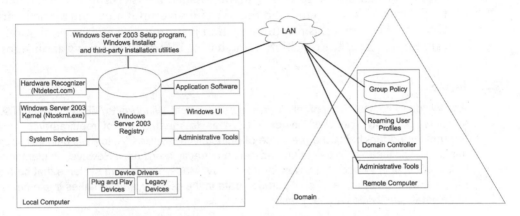

Fig. 1.1. Windows Server 2003 system components that use the registry

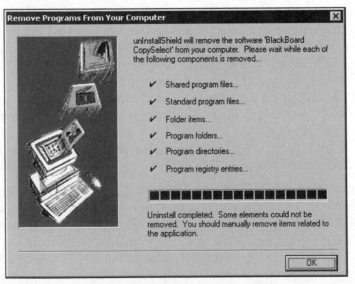

Fig. 1.2. The uninstall utility deletes registry settings that correspond to the application to be uninstalled

❏ *Hardware recognizer.* Each time Windows NT/2000, Windows XP, or Windows Server 2003 starts, the hardware recognizer creates a list of the devices it has detected, and stores the list in the registry. On Intel-based computers, hardware detection is performed by the hardware recognizer (Ntdetect.com) and the Windows NT/2000/XP/Server 2003 kernel (Ntoskrnl.exe).

❏ *Windows NT/2000/XP/Server 2003 kernel.* During the system-boot process, the kernel reads the registry to retrieve information on the device drivers and the sequence in which they should be loaded. The Ntoskrnl.exe program also passes its own information to the registry (for example, data on the system version and build). Microsoft has introduced many enhancements to the Windows XP and Windows Server 2003 kernel, intended mainly to increase system performance and stability. As will be shown later in this chapter, these kernel enhancements also include registry enhancements (the removal of the registry size limit, for example).

❏ *PnP Manager.* This new kernel-mode component was first introduced in Windows 2000. PnP Manager detects and identifies hardware devices using two identifiers: *vendor identifier* (Vendor ID or VID), and *device identifier* (device ID or DID). The combination of these two numbers uniquely identifies the device. Having detected a unique combination of VID and DID, PnP Manager asks the registry to get information about the bus where the device has been detected, and checks to see if the appropriate device driver has been installed. If the device driver hasn't been installed, PnP Manager informs the user-mode PnP subsystem. The user-mode PnP subsystem, in turn, has to detect the appropriate INF file and start the driver-installation procedure.

❏ *Device drivers.* Device drivers exchange boot parameters and configuration data with the registry. This data is similar to the DEVICE= lines in the Config.sys file used to start MS-DOS. The device driver has to provide information on the system resources that it needs, including IRQ and DMA. The system then includes this data in the registry. Application programs and device drivers can read this information from the registry to provide the users with the correct installation and configuration tools.

❏ *Administrative utilities.* Built-in administrative utilities supplied with Windows NT/2000, Windows XP and Windows Server 2003, including Control Panel applets and programs that belong to the Administrative Tools program group, are the most convenient and safest tools that can be used to modify the registry. Registry editors, which will be discussed in detail in *Chapter 3*, are special built-in utilities intended for viewing and modifying the registry. However, they should be used with care and caution.

❑ *User profiles.* Windows NT/2000, Windows XP, and Windows Server 2003 support multiple user profiles. All information related to an individual user name and the user rights associated to it is stored in the registry. *Chapter 10* describes user profiles in more detail. At this point, it is enough to note that the user profile defines custom display settings, networking parameters, printers, and so on. There are three types of user profiles: *local user profiles*, which are created automatically when the user logs on to the local computer for the first time; *roaming user profiles*, created by the network administrator and stored on the server; and *mandatory user profiles* — roaming profiles that are bound to be used. Note that, in Windows XP and Windows Server 2003, mandatory user profiles are included only for backward compatibility with the existing Windows NT 4.0 domains. User profile information is also stored in the registry. To manage Windows 2000 user profiles, double-click on **System** in the **Control Panel** window and go to the **User Profiles** tab. To manage user profiles in Windows XP/Windows Server 2003, start the System applet in Control Panel, go to the **Advanced** tab (Fig. 1.3), and click on the **Settings** button in the **User Profiles** group to open the **User Profiles** window (Fig. 1.4). You can create new user profiles here by copying existing ones. You can also delete user profiles or change their types. Note that, to perform this task, you need to log in to a local computer as the Administrator.

❑ *Hardware profiles.* Unlike INI files, the registry supports multiple hardware configurations. For example, you can create hardware profiles for dock stations (this is essential for laptop users) and removable devices. Each hardware profile is a set of instructions used to specify device drivers that have to be loaded when booting the system. To create new hardware profiles in Windows XP and Windows 2003 Server, double-click on **System** in the **Control Panel** window, go to the **Hardware** tab (Fig. 1.5) and then click on **Hardware Profiles** button. This will open the **Hardware Profiles** window shown in Fig. 1.6. Like in Windows 2000, when you install Windows XP or one of the products of the Windows Server 2003 family, the Setup program creates a standard hardware profile, which includes information on all hardware devices detected at the time of installation.

❑ *Group policies.* Group Policies introduced with Windows 2000 have significantly improved the ability of system and network administrators to configure security and to manage users and computers. Windows Server 2003 and Windows XP include considerable new functionality in this area. More detailed information on this topic will be provided in *Chapter 10*.

❑ *Remote administration tools.* Windows 2000, Windows XP and Windows Server 2003 registry supports remote administration.

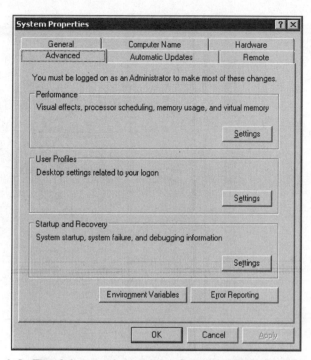

Fig. 1.3. The **Advanced** tab of the **System Properties** window

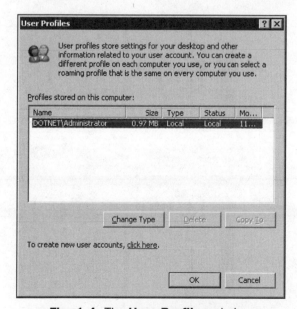

Fig. 1.4. The **User Profiles** window

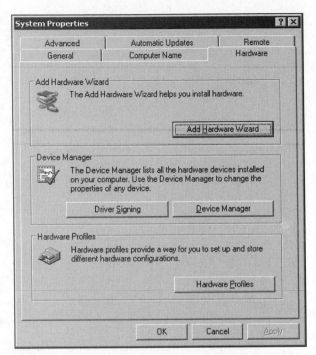

Fig. 1.5. The **Hardware** tab of the **System Properties** window

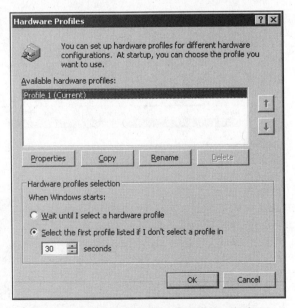

Fig. 1.6. The **Hardware Profiles** window

Registry Structure

For a better understanding of the logical structure of the registry, we will compare this to the file system that exists on the disk. The registry contains *keys*, which are similar to folders, and *values*, which can be compared to the files stored on the disk. Registry keys are container objects that can store both *subkeys* and values. Registry values contain the data (like the files). The top-level keys of this hierarchical structure are called *root keys*.

The convention used to name registry keys and values is also similar to the one used to name files and folders. For example, a typical folder path such as D:\WORK\BHV is comparable to a typical registry path: HKEY_LOCAL_MACHINE\SYSTEM\ CurrentControlSet.

In Windows 2000/XP and Windows Server 2003, the registry comprises the following five root keys: HKEY_CLASSES_ROOT, HKEY_CURRENT_USER, HKEY_LOCAL_MACHINE, HKEY_USERS, and HKEY_CURRENT_CONFIG. This hierarchical registry structure is illustrated in Fig. 1.7.

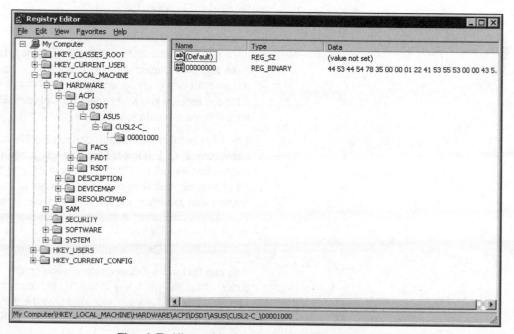

Fig. 1.7. Hierarchical structure of the registry

All of the names of the root keys begin with the HKEY_ string, which indicates that this is a handle that can be used by a program. The handle represents the value used uniquely to identify the resource that can be accessed by a program. Table 1.1 lists the root keys that exist in Windows NT/2000, Windows XP, and Windows Server 2003 registries, the respective abbreviations that are often used to designate these root keys, and provides a brief description.

Table 1.1. Registry Root Keys

Root key	Abbreviation	Description
HKEY_LOCAL_MACHINE	HKLM	Contains global hardware information and operating system data, including bus type, system memory, device drivers and other information used during the system boot process. Information on this key is applicable to all users who log on to the local system. Actually, this key is a placeholder that corresponds to no physical file stored on the disk. Instead, it contains other keys that do: (HKEY_LOCAL_MACHINE\SYSTEM, HKEY_LOCAL_MACHINE\SAM, HKEY_LOCAL_MACHINE\SECURITY, HKEY_LOCAL_MACHINE\SOFTWARE). This key has three top-level aliases — HKEY_CLASSES_ROOT, HKEY_CURRENT_CONFIG, and HKEY_DYN_DATA — a hidden registry key that serves as a placeholder for performance data lookups.
HKEY_CLASSES_ROOT	HKCR	This key contains information concerning filename associations, OLE (Object Linking and Embedding) information associated with COM objects, and file-class associations (this data is equivalent to the registry that existed in earlier Windows versions). Parameters contained in this key are equivalent to those stored under the HKEY_LOCAL_MACHINE\Software\Classes key.
		You can find more detailed information on the HKEY_CLASSES_ROOT key in the *"OLE Programmer's Reference"* manual included with the Windows Platform Software Development Kit (SDK).

continues

Table 1.1 Continued

Root key	Abbre-viation	Description
HKEY_CURRENT_CONFIG	HKCC	Contains the configuration data of the current hardware profile. Hardware profiles are sets of modifications introduced into the standard configuration of services and devices set by the Software and System subkeys of the HKEY_LOCAL_MACHINE root key. The HKEY_CURRENT_CONFIG key contains only changed data.
		Moreover, the data contained in this key is also contained in the HKEY_LOCAL_MACHINE\System\CurrentControlSet\HardwareProfiles\Current key.
HKEY_CURRENT_USER	HKCU	Contains the user profile of the user who is currently logged on to the system, including environment variables, desktop settings, network settings, and application settings.
		This key is a reference to the HKEY_USERS\user_SID key, where user_SID is the Security ID of the user who is currently logged on to the system.
HKEY_USERS	HKU	Contains all active user profiles, including HKEY_CURRENT_USER and the default user profile. Users who can access the server through the network do not have profiles under this key because their profiles are loaded remotely on their workstations.
		Windows NT/2000, Windows XP, and Windows Server 2003 require that each user who logs on to the system have his or her own user account. The HKEY_USERS key contains the \.Default subkey, which is used before any user logs on to the system. It also contains other subkeys associated with the Security ID assigned to the appropriate user.

Registry data are parameters stored within registry keys. Each parameter has its own name, data type, and value. The three parts of the registry entry are also stored in the following order:

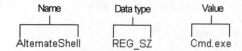

All registry data types defined and used in Windows NT/2000, Windows XP, and products of the Windows Server 2003 family are listed in Table 1.2.

Table 1.2. Registry Data Types

Data type	Description
REG_BINARY	Binary data. Most hardware components use binary information. Registry editors display this information In hex.
REG_DWORD	This data is represented as a 4-byte binary value (double word). Most services and device drivers use this data type. Registry editors display this data using binary, hex, or decimal formats.
REG_EXPAND_SZ	Expandable data string. This text string contains a variable name, which can be substituted by a variable value when called by an application.
REG_MULTI_SZ	Multi-string field. Normally, all values that actually represent lists of text strings have this data type. A NULL character is used as a separator.
REG_SZ	Text string in user-friendly format. Normally, this data type is used for component descriptions.
REG_DWORD_LITTLE_ENDIAN	32-bit number in little-endian format. Equivalent of the REG_DWORD data type. When using the little-endian format, the lowest bit ("little end") appears first when representing the value. For example, the A02B hex value will be represented as 2BA0. The little-endian format is used in Intel processors.
REG_DWORD_BIG_ENDIAN	32-bit number in big-endian format. In contrast to the little-endian format, the highest bit ("big end") appears first when representing the value.
REG_LINK	Unicode symbolic link. This data type is intended for internal use only. The REG_LINK is especially interesting because it allows one registry entry to reference another registry key or registry value. For example, if a registry contains the entry \Root1\Link with the REG_LINK data type and its value is \Root2\RegKey, and the RegKey key contains the RegValue value, then this value can be identified using the following two paths: \Root1\Link\RegValue and \Root2\RegKey\RegValue. Windows NT/2000, Windows XP, and Windows Server 2003 make active use of this method. For example, some of the root keys listed in Table 1.1 are links to the nested keys of other root keys.
REG_NONE	No defined data type.
REG_QWORD	64-bit value.

continues

Table 1.2 Continued

Data type	Description
REG_QWORD_LITTLE_ENDIAN	64-bit value represented using little-endian notation. Equivalent of the REG_QWORD data type.
REG_RESOURCE_LIST	List of hardware resources, which are only used in HKEY_LOCAL_MACHINE\HARDWARE.
REG_FULL_RESOURCE_DESCRIPTOR	Hardware resource handle, which is only used in HKEY_LOCAL_MACHINE\HARDWARE.
REG_RESOURCE_REQUIREMENTS_LIST	List of hardware resources, which is only used in HKEY_LOCAL_MACHINE\HARDWARE.

Registry Data Storage

All Windows NT-based operating systems, including Windows 2000, Windows XP, and products of the Windows Server 2003 family, store registry entries as an atomic structure rather than simply as one large file. The registry is subdivided into components, called *hives,* for their resemblance to the cellular structure of a beehive. The Registry hive is a discrete body of keys, subkeys, and values rooted at the top level of the registry hierarchy.

Note

As with Windows NT/2000, Windows XP/Windows Server 2003 registry also resides on the disk in the form of multiple files called hives, serving as a repository for system configuration data. The registry code has been redesigned for Windows XP and Windows Server 2003, providing enhanced performance, while remaining transparent to applications by using existing registry programming interfaces. Windows XP and Windows Server 2003 registry enhancements are mainly intended to provide performance improvements and will be covered in more detail later in this chapter.

Registry hive data is stored physically in disk files, which in turn are stored in *%SystemRoot%*\System32\Config and *%SystemRoot%*\Profiles*Username* folders (Windows NT 4.0). Windows 2000, Windows XP, and Windows Server 2003 store registry hives in *%SystemRoot%*\System32\Config and *%SystemDrive%*\ Documents and Settings*Username* folders.

At first glance, it might seem that each root key seen while running one of the registry editors is a separate hive. However, this relationship isn't that simple and straightforward. In fact, none of the root keys represent physical hives. Actually, the Configuration Manager — the kernel subsystem that implements the registry —

links hives together, creates the root keys and builds the familiar registry structure displayed by registry editors.

Each physical registry hive is associated with a set of standard supporting files. Table 1.3 lists standard registry hives, existing in Windows NT/2000, Windows XP, and Windows Server 2003 together with supporting files.

Table 1.3. Registry Hives Existing in Windows NT/2000, Windows XP, and Windows Server 2003

Registry hive	Supporting files
HKEY_LOCAL_MACHINE\SAM	Sam, Sam.log, Sam.sav
HKEY_LOCAL_MACHINE\Security	Security, Security.log, Security.sav
HKEY_LOCAL_MACHINE\Software	Software, Software.log, Software.sav
HKEY_LOCAL_MACHINE\System	System, System.alt*, System.log, System.sav
HKEY_CURRENT_CONFIG	System, System.alt*, System.log, System.sav
HKEY_USERS\.DEFAULT	Default, Default.log, Default.sav
HKEY_USERS*User_SID* ·HKEY_CURRENT_USER	*%SystemDrive%*\Documents and Settings\ *Username*\Ntuser.dat, *%SystemDrive%*\ Documents and Settings\ *Username*\Ntuser.dat.log
HKEY_USERS*User_SID*_Classes	*%SystemDrive%*\Documents and Settings\ *Username*\Local Settings\Application Data\ Microsoft\Windows\UsrClass.dat and *%SystemDrive%*\Documents and Settings\ *Username*\Local Settings\Application Data\ Microsoft\Windows\UsrClass.dat.log
(Files that aren't associated with keys)	Userdiff, Userdiff.log, Userdifr**, Userdifr.log**

* Files that were eliminated starting with Windows XP

** Files that were first introduced in Windows XP

 Note

As you can see from this table, some registry files were eliminated with the introduction of the Windows XP and products of the Windows Server 2003 family, while other files were introduced for the first time. This is due to the registry enhancements implemented in Windows XP and Windows Server 2003, which will be covered in more detail later in this book. Also note the difference between HKEY_USERS*User_SID*, HKEY_USERS*User_SID*_Classes and HKEY_CURRENT_USER keys and their respective hives. HKU*User_SID* and HKU*User_SID*_ Classes are hive files containing user-specific settings. The HKU*User_SID* data corresponds to the Ntuser.dat and Ntuser.dat.log files stored under *%SystemDrive%*\Documents and Settings*Username*, while UsrClass.dat and UsrClass.dat.log hives support data under the `HKEY_USERS\User_SID_Classes` registry keys. This separation was first introduced with Windows 2000, in order to support roaming user profiles. If the user has a roaming profile, Windows 2000/XP and products of the Windows Server 2003 family synchronize the Ntuser.dat file with the copy of the user profile stored on network server. On the other hand, the UsrClass.dat file isn't subject to this synchronization (more information on this topic will be provided in *Chapter 10*).

The main difference between physical registry hives and other groups of registry keys is that physical hives are constant registry components. Physical hives aren't created dynamically when the system boots and aren't deleted when someone shuts the system down. However, besides physical hives, there are other important registry structures created and managed entirely in memory — for example, the `HKEY_LOCAL_MACHINE\ Hardware` key, which is created dynamically by the hardware recognizer when the system boots. This key stores information related to physical devices and their assigned resources. Since hardware detection and resource assignment take place during each system boot, it is quite logical not to store this information on disk. Thus, the `HKEY_LOCAL_MACHINE\Hardware` key can't be considered a physical hive. Sometimes, such registry structures are referenced as volatile hives.

All hive files, except for `HKEY_CURRENT_USER`, are stored in the *%SystemRoot%* System32\Config folder.

The `HKEY_CURRENT_USER` hive is supported by Ntuser.dat and Ntuser.dat.log files. Ntuser.dat files contain user profiles, while Ntuser.dat.log files reflect all of the changes introduced to Ntuser.dat file. Windows NT 4.0 stores these files in subfolders of the *%SystemRoot%*Profiles folder (except for the \All Users subfolder). Windows 2000 and its successors store these files in *%SystemDrive%*Documents and Settings*%Username%* folders.

There are four types of files associated with registry hives. All of these file types, with the appropriate filename extensions, are listed in Table 1.4.

Table 1.4. Types of Files Associated to Registry Hives in Windows NT/2000, Windows XP, and Windows Server 2003

Filename extension	Description
None	Contains the registry hive copy.
ALT*	In Windows NT/2000, the ALT files contain the backup copy of the `HKEY_LOCAL_MACHINE\System` hive. The `System` hive is the only hive that has this type of backup copy stored in the System.alt file. As was already mentioned, ALT files were eliminated in Windows XP and Windows Server 2003 because the registry code was redesigned to provide improved algorithms for faster queries, improved reliability, and larger registries.

continues

Table 1.3 Continued

Filename extension	Description
LOG	Contains the transaction log. Any changes introduced to the keys and values make up this hive.
SAV	Contains copies of registry hive files from the time the text-mode part of the installation process was accomplished. There are SAV files for the following registry hives: \Software, \System, \SAM, \Security, and \Default.
	Windows NT/2000, Windows XP, and Windows Server 2003 make backup copies of the registry hives during the installation process. The installation procedure consists of two parts; namely, the text-mode and the GUI-mode part of the installation. When the text-mode part of installation procedure is complete, the Setup program backs up the registry hives to the SAV files. This is done to protect the hives from failures, which may occur during the GUI-mode part of setup. If such a failure occurs, the GUI-mode setup will resume after reboot, and SAV files will be used for rebuilding the registry hives.

*Files that were excluded from Windows XP and Windows Server 2003

Hive Atomicity and Recovery

The registry ensures the atomic nature of individual operations. This means that any modifications made to a registry value (resetting, deleting, or saving) either work or don't work. This mechanism eliminates corrupt combinations of old and new registry values, in case the system stops unexpectedly due to a power failure, a hardware malfunction, or problems with the software. Consider, for example, the case where an application sets a value and the system shuts down unexpectedly while this change is being made. After rebooting the system, this registry entry will either be reset to its previous value or have a new value, but no meaningless combinations of both registry parameters will appear. Moreover, the size and time data for the key containing the affected value will be accurate, whether this value has been changed or not.

Flushing Data

Windows NT-based operating systems save registry data only after a flush occurs. Data flush occurs only after the modified data ages past a few seconds. Furthermore, data flush can be initiated by a direct call from the application, which intentionally flushes its data to the hard disk.

The system performs the following flushing procedure:

1. All changed data are saved to the LOG file of the respective hive, together with information on the exact location of the changed data within a hive. When this is done, the system performs a flush, and all modified data are written to the LOG file.

2. The first sector of the hive file is marked, which means that this file is in a transitional state.

3. The modified data are written to the hive file.

4. Finally, this hive file is marked as completed.

 Note

If the system shuts down unexpectedly while performing this procedure (between steps 2 and 4), it will recover the affected hive. When this hive is loaded during system startup (except for user profile hives, which are loaded when the user logs on to the system), the system will note the marker left in step 2 and it will continue recovering the hive using the changed data saved to the LOG file. Thus, if the hive wasn't in transition, its LOG files aren't used. If the hive was in transition when the system stopped, it can't be loaded without a respective LOG file.

The \System hive is vitally important and is used at the earliest stages of the system boot. This hive includes the HKEY_LOCAL_MACHINE\SYSTEM\CurrentControlSet\ Control key, which contains information necessary for initializing the registry during the boot process. For example, registry entries stored with the HKEY_LOCAL_ MACHINE\SYSTEM\CurrentControlSet\Control\hivelist specify the location of all other registry hives. Thus, if the \System hive is missing or corrupt, it can't be recovered using the procedure described above. Because of this, Windows 2000 and earlier versions use a different flushing process for the hive.

The System.alt file contains a copy of the System hive data. During the flush process, all changes are marked, saved, and then marked as completed. After this process is completed, the same flush process is done for the System.alt file. If there is a power failure, hardware malfunction, or a problem with the software that causes a system shutdown at any stage of this process, the system will try to find the correct information in either the System file or the System.alt file.

The System.alt file is similar to the LOG file, except that, during a boot, the system will switch to using the System.alt file instead of trying to reapply all the changes saved in the LOG file. If the System file isn't marked as being in transition, then System.alt won't be needed.

Note

Windows XP and Windows Server 2003 solve this problem by moving the registry out of the paged pool and using the cache manager to carry out an in-house management of the registry. Therefore, there is no need to use the System.alt file in Windows XP and Windows Server 2003.

Registry-Size Problem

When we discussed the drawbacks of INI files earlier in this chapter, we mentioned the problems caused by the Win.ini size limitation. The Windows NT/2000 registry seemed to solve this problem, but it still remained limited in size. At the same time, there was a steady trend among registry consumers to use the registry like a database, which constantly increased the demands made on registry size. The original design of the registry kept all of the registry files in the paged pool, which, in the 32-bit kernel, is effectively limited to approximately 160 MB because of the layout of the kernel virtual address space. A problem arose because, as larger registry consumers such as Terminal Services and COM appeared, a considerable amount of paged-pool was used for the registry alone, potentially leaving too little memory for other kernel-mode components.

Registry Size Limit in Windows NT/2000

To solve the problem described above, Windows NT 4.0/Windows 2000 allows for the restriction of the size to which the registry can grow. To set the registry size limitation in Windows 2000, use the following procedure:

1. Double-click on **System** in the **Control Panel** window. The **System Properties** window will appear.
2. Go to the **Advanced** tab and click on the **Performance Options** button to open the **Performance Options** window (Fig. 1.8). Click on the **Change** button in the **Virtual Memory** group of options. The **Virtual Memory** window will appear (Fig. 1.9). At the bottom of this window is the **Registry size** group with the **Maximum registry size (MB)** field, allowing the user manually to set the maximum registry size.

Windows NT/2000 registry data loaded to the memory are stored in a paged pool, which is a region in the physical memory used for storing data that can be flushed to the hard disk if not used for a long time. The size limit on the registry is set to prevent the situation where the registry consumes all of the space required by other processes.

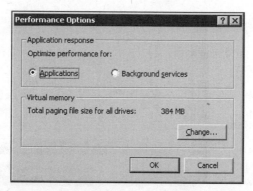

Fig. 1.8. The **Performance Options** window

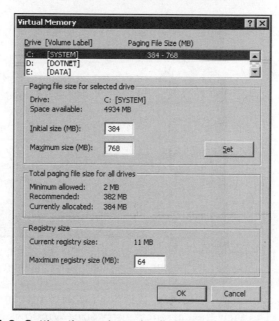

Fig. 1.9. Setting the registry size limitation for Windows 2000

Registry Enhancements in Windows XP and Windows Server 2003

In contrast to Windows NT/2000, in Windows XP and products of the Windows Server 2003 family, the registry size limitation has been removed. The registry code has been redesigned to provide enhanced performance, while remaining transparent to applications by using existing registry programming interfaces.

The new registry implementation delivers two key benefits:

❏ Larger registries
❏ Faster queries

Therefore, neither Windows XP nor Windows Server 2003 provide the user with the option to establish a registry size limit (Fig. 1.10).

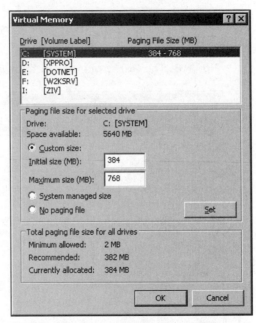

Fig. 1.10. In Windows XP and Windows Server 2003, there is no option for setting the registry size limitation

Thus, in contrast to Windows NT/2000, where you can use the System applet in Control Panel to view the current registry size, Windows XP and Windows Server 2003 don't provide you with this option. However, to discover how much data is actually stored in your registry, you can use the Dureg.exe Resource Kit utility, which can be downloaded from **http://download.microsoft.com/download/ win2000platform/WebPacks/1.00.0.1/Nt5/EN-US/Dureg.exe**. Although this command-line tool is part of Windows 2000 Server Resource Kit, it also works fine with Windows Server 2003. Besides estimation of the amount of data stored in the whole registry, this tool allows you to discover how much data is stored in any registry subtree, key, or subkey, and also enables you to search for all occurrences of a text string in the registry.

The Dureg.exe utility uses the following syntax:

```
dureg [{/cr | /cu | /u | /lm | /a}] [{/s | /d}] [registry_path]
[string to search],
```

where:

/a — this option will calculate the size of the entire registry.

/cr *registry_path* — this option will evaluate the size of the HKEY_CLASSES_ROOT root key. To evaluate the size of specific subkey within this key, it is necessary to specify a registry path (*registry_path* parameter).

/cu *registry_path* — this option will evaluate the size of the HKEY_CURRENT_USER root key. Include a registry path to calculate the size of any subkey within this subtree.

/lm *registry_path* — calculates the size of HKEY_LOCAL_MACHINE root key. To evaluate the size of any subkey within this subtree, specify the path to that key (*registry_path*).

/u *registry_path* — this option will calculate the size of HKEY_USERS root key. Include a registry path to find the size of any key within this subtree.

/s *string* — use this option to find any text string within the registry.

 Note

The Dureg.exe utility counts data, not space. Because the space any data occupy varies with the storage method and amount of free space available, the size of data and size of space consumed are not equal. Also, Dureg.exe does not account for fragmented free space in the registry.

Let us consider the registry enhancements mentioned above in more detail.

❑ *Larger Registries.* Windows XP and products of the Windows Server 2003 family support larger registries than previous versions of the kernel, which were effectively limited to about 80 percent of the total size of the paged pool. The new implementation is limited only by the available system disk space. This problem was solved by moving the registry out of the paged pool and using the cache manager to carry out the management of the mapped views of the registry files. The mapped views are mapped in 256K chunks into system cache space instead of into the paged pool.

❑ *Faster Queries.* Another issue that affected registry performance in earlier versions was the *locality problem*. Related cells are spread through all of the registry files. Accessing certain information, such as attributes of a key, could degenerate into page-faults, which lower performance. In Windows XP and Windows Server 2003, the registry uses an improved algorithm for allocating new cells that keeps related cells in closer proximity — for instance, keeping cells on the same page or nearby pages which solves the locality problem and reduces the page faults incurred when accessing related cells. A new hive structure member tracks freed cells instead of relying on linked freed cells. When future cells are allocated, the freed cell list and a vicinity argument are used to ensure that they are put in the same bin as the hive.

Windows XP and products of the Windows Server 2003 family improve the way the registry handles large data. In earlier versions, prior to Windows XP and Windows Server 2003, if an inefficient application increased a value steadily by small increments, it created a sparse and wasteful registry file. Newer versions of the Microsoft Windows operating systems solve this problem with a large cell implementation, where cells larger than 16K are split into increments of 16K chunks. This reduces fragmentation when the data length of a value is increased within a certain threshold.

When You Should Edit the Registry

The best answer to this question is: "Only in an emergency". You definitely should not get in the habit of editing the registry any time a problem arises. In any case, minor problems should not be solved by editing the registry. Microsoft has made significant efforts to develop powerful and flexible graphical administrative tools to help users carry out everyday tasks related to system configuration and troubleshooting. All users are recommended to try solving problems using these tools and to proceed with editing the registry only when all other methods have failed.

However, there is always a chance that all of the methods of configuring the system using Control Panel applets or resetting device settings using Device Manager will fail. If this is the case, you will need to know how to work with the registry and how to edit it using the registry editor.

Some actions related to customizing applications can be performed only by editing the registry directly. For example, if you need to open Windows Explorer when the user double-clicks on **My Computer**, or to enable built-in leak detection, you'll need to edit the registry because these tasks can't be achieved using other methods. If you need to edit the registry, do it very carefully and in accordance with the instructions.

The Internet contains many tips related to registry editing. Usually, these tips are related to setting some registry entries. If you decide to modify the registry, don't forget to create a backup copy of the registry before proceeding with these changes.

Alternative Methods of Editing the Registry

Remember that, even in cases where registry editing is absolutely necessary, an unskilled user can create even greater problems when performing this task. For example, errors that occur while editing the registry may lead to problems with loading device drivers or with logging on to the system. Don't edit the registry if you are not absolutely sure that the changes that you are going to make are correct, or if you simply can't afford to lose a significant amount of time for troubleshooting. A single error can mean the need to reinstall your entire operating system.

! Caution

Administrative tools always provide a method of configuring the system preferable to direct registry editing. Using administrative utilities is much safer, because these utilities don't allow you to save incorrect values in the system registry. If you make an error while using one of the registry editors, you won't get a warning, because registry editors don't recognize these errors and don't take any corrective actions.

After you get acquainted with the registry, you may feel tempted to edit it in order to install or configure hardware devices. The registry editor, discussed in *Chapter 3*, is a special tool used for viewing and modifying the registry. However, before proceeding with direct registry editing, try to perform the same task using the administrative utilities. Most hardware-related registry entries are very hard to understand unless you have a working knowledge of the hex format. These settings only affect the hardware devices that use them.

For example, you shouldn't manually edit the registry when installing new hardware, because of the methods the system uses to configure Plug and Play devices. As you'll see in *Chapter 5*, Plug and Play devices now have no default settings. If a device requests a resource that's already in use by another Plug and Play device, the system may change the Plug and Play device settings in such a way as to eliminate hardware conflicts with the new device. If you change the registry settings for Plug and Play devices manually, you'll get constant settings. These settings can't be changed by the operating system if another device requests the same resource.

Installing New Devices

Even if Windows XP or Windows Server 2003 encounters a new device not currently included in the registry and the system has no information on this device, it attempts, first, to detect it. If the new device has been successfully detected and recognized, you will see a small pop-up window in the lower right corner of the desktop informing you that the system has found new hardware (Fig. 1.11). Note that in this case, the system will automatically install the device driver, configure the device settings and, after a few seconds, display another pop-up window, reporting that the newly installed device is ready to use (Fig. 1.12).

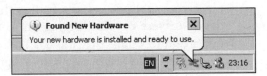

Fig. 1.11. Windows XP and Windows Server 2003 automatically detect new hardware

Fig.1.12. The newly detected device is successfully installed and configured

In contrast to Plug and Play devices, legacy devices developed before the release of Windows 95 have fixed settings. The task of installing and configuring legacy devices is more complicated than installing Plug and Play devices. Always remember one thing though: Before modifying the registry directly, try to achieve the same result using Hardware Wizard. In Windows XP and Windows Server 2003, this program was significantly improved by extending its functionality and introducing a more intuitive user interface, even in comparison to Windows 2000. To install a legacy device in Windows XP or Windows Server 2003, follow the instructions provided below:

1. Open the **Control Panel** window, then double-click on the **Add Hardware** icon, or, alternatively, start the **System** applet to open the **System Properties** window, go to the **Hardware** tab, and click on the **Add Hardware Wizard** button. Any of these methods will open the **Add Hardware Wizard** window. Click on the **Next** button.

2. The wizard will try to detect the new device. If it fails, it will display another window prompting the user to specify if the new device is already connected. The wizard will display a series of screens containing the options available and step-by-step instructions. To install and configure the new device, just follow these instructions, select the required options, and click on **Next** to continue. Beside new device installation, Hardware Wizard allows you to view the list of installed devices and troubleshoot the devices that are not working properly

(Fig. 1.13). To install a new device that is not listed here, select the **Add a new hardware device** option and click **Next**.

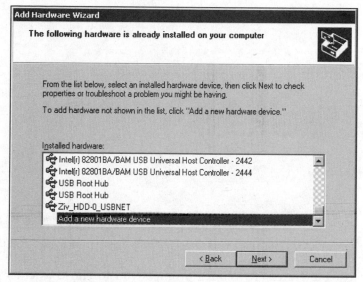

Fig. 1.13. Hardware Wizard enables you to view the list of installed devices and troubleshoot the devices that are not working properly

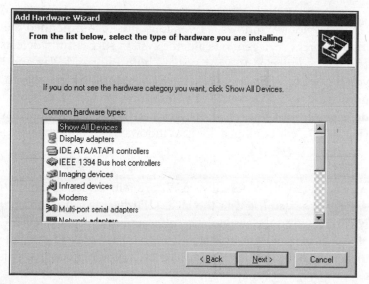

Fig. 1.14. Hardware Wizard provides a list of device classes. Select **Show All Devices** if you don't see the hardware category that you require

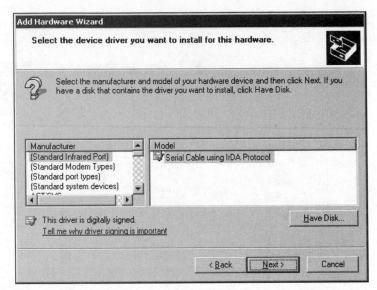

Fig. 1.15. The Windows NT/2000-style list of supported devices

3. Next, the Hardware Wizard prompts you to chose whether you are going to search for the hardware automatically or select an appropriate device from the list. Since Windows XP and products of the Windows Server 2003 family provide enhanced hardware support, even in comparison to Windows 2000, let alone previous Windows NT versions, it is recommended that you select automatic search. As a general rule, the system successfully detects all the hardware correctly connected to your system, both Plug and Play and legacy. Therefore, you'll need to select manually the device from the list only in a worst-case scenario (Fig. 1.14). If you don't find your device in this list, set the **Show all devices** options and click on **Next**. In this case, the next window will open (Fig. 1.15), containing a long Windows NT/2000-style list of all supported hardware.

As was stated above, Hardware Wizard will detect all compatible hardware devices that have been listed in the HCL (Hardware Compatibility List) and are correctly connected to the system. This also applies to legacy devices. If you encounter problems, first make sure that the device you are going to install is included in the Windows XP or Windows Server 2003 HCL, then check that it is usable and connected properly to your system.

This method of installing and configuring new devices is much safer than direct registry editing, because it eliminates the risk of compatibility problems. However, from time to time, you may need to change the settings of the legacy devices by means of direct registry editing. Many advanced users are interested in changing the resource settings for the hardware devices. You already know that the device manager controls these settings automatically when installing a new device or booting Windows. Sometimes, though, you may need to set these parameters manually. For example, this situation can arise in the case where there is a hardware conflict that can't be solved by the configuration manager. Suppose, for example, that there is a conflict between the IRQ and DMA settings for two legacy devices. In such a case, you can also use the Device Manager to solve the problem.

Hardware-related registry keys are discussed in detail in *Chapters 5* and *6*, where you will also find instructions on editing registry parameters and selecting appropriate values.

Other Tools for Changing the Registry

Besides Control Panel applets and other GUI tools provided by Windows XP and Windows Server 2003, there are other tools for changing the registry. These tools are listed below:

❑ You may use the **Options** dialogs present in Windows-compatible applications. As was already mentioned, any Windows-compliant application has to store its settings in the registry and provide the user with graphic tools enabling him or her to change these registry settings.
❑ The registry settings can also be changed using shareware or freeware applications (both Microsoft and third-party). More detailed information on the most popular registry utilities will be provided later in this book.
❑ REG and INF files.
❑ Installation programs.

Summary

This chapter provided a brief description of the Windows NT/2000/XP/Server 2003 registry, as well as an overview of the registry's history, its role, and its capabilities. We've also discussed the place of the registry in the system architecture. Most registry aspects covered in this chapter will be discussed in greater detail later in this book.

CHAPTER 2

Registry Backup
and Recovery

Documents twenty thousand years old?
Things decay, perish, are destroyed
through inefficiency or war.
— But there should be records of the records,
copies, copies of the copies
and copies of the copies of the copies.

I. Asimov
"Foundation and Earth"

Windows Server 2003, Microsoft's newest family of operating systems for servers, provides a vast number of improvements over the previous generation, Windows 2000 Server. Windows Server 2003 is an impressive upgrade integrating two and a half years of improvements on Windows 2000, both evolutionary and revolutionary. The long list of improvements includes dramatic kernel enhancements, along with enhancements to practically every subsystem, including Windows Media Services, Internet Information Services (IIS) and Terminal Services. Besides this, the new Group Policy Management Console and numerous security improvements (which will be covered in detail in *Chapter 9*) are also worth mention. Like its predecessors, Windows Server 2003 presents some important choices for IT, network and security administrators, corporate decision makers, and technical support personnel personally responsible for deploying and supporting Microsoft server solutions.

In fact, Windows Server 2003 is so vast in terms of functionality that it's quite easy to get lost in all of the new features — just remember the well-known Murphy's Law, which states: "To err is human, but to really foul things up requires a computer". Like in any joke, there is an element of truth here, especially when it comes to such serious things as business continuity (don't forget that we are dealing with a server platform) and disaster-recovery planning. Furthermore, this law usually strikes when we least expect it. The complexity of modern computer systems and their use in business-critical processes inevitably raises the following question: Can we trust computers? Most hardware manufacturers and vendors will try to convince you that their products are robust and reliable, and they also are right. We can certainly trust computers insofar as they are designed to avoid or prevent system failures and data loss. In relation to operating systems, even the earlier versions of Windows NT included several built-in features providing fault tolerance, and its successors, including Windows 2000, Windows XP, and products of the Windows Server 2003 family, increase and enhance them even further. Still, despite the efforts of hardware manufacturers and software developers, disasters happen from time to time. Why? The answer to this question is clear — it doesn't make a difference how reliable products are initially. The factors that really count are how you configure and maintain a computer and what precautions you have taken just in case anything goes wrong.

The "Foundation" saga by Isaac Asimov, a famous "historical novel of the future" and the story of the rise and fall of the Galactic Empire, mentions data that actually survived more than twenty thousand years. In all likelihood your data doesn't need to survive that long, but it has, at least, to survive emergency situations. In the real world, having a solid disaster-recovery plan can make the difference between a company that survives and one that doesn't. According to statistics, of the companies that suffer major and permanent data loss:

❏ 90% are out of business within a year
❏ 50% never reopen their doors at all after the disaster

The causes of data loss might be different. According to a report by Ontrack Data International, a research firm based in Minneapolis, they break down as follows:

❏ System malfunction or hardware error (44%)
❏ Human error (32%)

- ❏ Software malfunction (14%)
- ❏ Virus attacks (7%)
- ❏ Natural disasters (3%)

However, when disaster strikes, it doesn't matter what is the cause. Both data loss caused by a natural disaster and that caused by virus attack or by hardware failure produces the same havoc in the organization. Thus, fault tolerance and disaster recovery are matters of primary importance, especially when vital information for a company — such as databases, accounting software and other essential records — are placed on the network.

Today, most companies already understand that simply hoping for the best and expecting that disaster won't strike is the quickest way to ruin the whole business. Therefore, practically every company maintains backups for its data and systems (the best backup strategies and practices, including registry backup and recovery, are the main topic of this chapter). This approach is necessary, since daily backup is an important element of disaster recovery, but it still isn't sufficient. Today's business environment is becoming increasingly vulnerable to computer-system disruptions. Consider, for example, an e-business, where a mere minute of downtime usually results in significant financial losses! This is where Disaster Recovery Planning becomes indispensable. Only a thorough Disaster Recovery Plan can help you avoid losing data or, at least, minimize the loss and survive the disaster.

The process of evaluating the risks of major data and operational loss, and planning ahead to prepare for failures by minimizing those risks, is known formally as *Disaster Recovery Planning* (DRP). A properly developed disaster-recovery plan can save thousands of dollars by protecting information and computer operations and preventing downtime and losses in productivity.

In other words, practices such as ensuring fault tolerance, performing regular backups of systems and data, and implementing properly developed and tested disaster-recovery plans are much like insurance. Still, there are some people, businesses — even large companies - that mistakenly believe that they can do without them. This is the worst mistake that they can make!

▶ *Note*

Failing to implement a disaster-recovery plan is a form of corporate negligence. The development and implementation of such a plan is a strategic, moral, and even legal obligation to one's company. Of course, legal issues related to disaster-recovery planning represent the most confusing part of the whole process of creating an effective plan and they are often underestimated and misunderstood. Although there are no specific laws stating categorically that your company must have a disaster-recovery plan, there exist several legal precedents that can be used to hold companies responsible to those who have been negatively affected by a company's inability to recover from a disaster. Note also that not only corporations, but individuals as well can be held liable for professional negligence if they are found to have failed to take reasonable measures given special knowledge, skills, and abilities. Of course, disaster-recovery planners can't be expected to be lawyers, but they need at least to understand the potential legal consequences of a failure by their company to implement an effective disaster-recovery plan and to be aware of the areas where disaster-recovery planning and the law intersect. For this reason, it is highly recommended — particularly for large companies — to include a legal expert lawyer in any team of contingency-plan developers. Liability insurance also should not be overlooked. If the worst should happen, liability insurance wouldn't prevent your or your company from ending up in court but at the least, it will cover damages and help to pay the costs of litigation. Thus, the basic idea is simple: by paying proper attention to disaster-recovery planning, you are not only protecting the interests of your company, but its long-term future as well.

Basic Steps in Disaster-Recovery Planning

The disaster-recovery planning process may vary from organization to organization, but the basic steps that must be performed in all cases are listed below:

❑ *Establish a planning committee.* The top management of the organization must be involved in the development of the disaster-recovery plan. Management should be responsible for coordinating the disaster-recovery plan and ensuring its effectiveness within the organization. Adequate time and resources must be committed to the development of an effective plan, with the resources under consideration including financial considerations and the effort of all personnel involved. The planning committee should include representatives from all operational areas of the organization. This is essential, since it is common that separate plans exist for each department, and these plans must be coordinated. Failure to do this can result in multiple demands on the same resource, incompatible strategies, time delays, and, in the worst case, the failure to properly carry out the plan in the case of emergency.

❑ *Identify serious risks.* The planning committee should carry out a risk and business-impact analysis that includes a range of possible disasters, including natural, technical, and human threats. Each operational area of the organization should be analyzed to determine the potential consequence and impact associated with several disaster scenarios. The risk-assessment process should also evaluate the safety of critical documents and vital records. Traditionally, fire has posed the greatest threat to organizations. Intentional human tampering, however, should also be considered. The plan should provide for the "worst case" scenario: the destruction of the main building. It is important to assess the impacts and consequences resulting from the loss of information and services. The planning committee should also analyze the costs related with minimizing potential exposures.

❏ *Establish priorities.* Here you should determine what are the most important considerations for processing and operations and carefully evaluate the critical requirements of each department. Determine the maximum amount of time that the department and organization can operate without each critical system. Critical needs are defined as the necessary procedures and equipment required to continue operations should a department, computer center, main facility or a combination of these be destroyed or become inaccessible.

❏ *Determine recovery strategies.* Here, you should consider all aspects of your organization's information system, including the following:

- Facilities
- Hardware
- Software
- Communications
- Data files
- Customer services
- User operations
- End-user systems
- Other processing operations

❏ *Assign a disaster team.* Once this has been done, you should then develop disaster recognition and initial-reaction procedures. At a minimum, these must include the following:

- Initial reaction procedures to a disaster report
- Notification procedures for police, fire, medical care
- Notification procedures for management
- Procedures for mobilizing the disaster team
- Procedures for assessing the damage and registering critical-events logs for audit purposes

❑ *Take a complete inventory of all equipment and software.* This is an essential part of any recovery plan. At minimum, it should include the following:

- A listing of all equipment by type and model number. The list should include equipment such as mission-critical servers, mainframe computers, bridges, routers and gateways.
- Name, address and telephone number of the manufacturer/vendor.
- Date of purchase and original cost.
- Locations of third-party equipment suppliers.
- Associated software packages, including all software required for the operation of mission-critical equipment. The software inventory must include the following information: the purpose of the software; date of acquisition; license and version number; original cost; address and telephone number of the vendor; names, addresses, and phone numbers of service and technical-support centers, etc.

❑ *Develop recovery procedures.* You should take into consideration the following aspects:

- Procedures for ensuring and maintaining physical security
- Coordination of restoration for the original site
- Restoration of electronic equipment
- Reloading of software
- Restoration of power, UPS, common building systems
- Replacement of fire-suppression systems
- Rewiring of the building
- Restoring the LAN
- Restoring the WAN connections

❑ *Document the plan.* Try to make the plan easily understandable for any technical person or other co-workers who might be called upon to help execute the plan or support recovery efforts. Whenever possible, illustrate the plan with diagrams. A comprehensive recovery plan generally includes the following information:

- Emergency call lists for management and recovery teams
- Vendor call out and escalation lists
- Inventory and report forms
- Carrier call out and escalation lists
- Maintenance forms
- Hardware lists and serial numbers

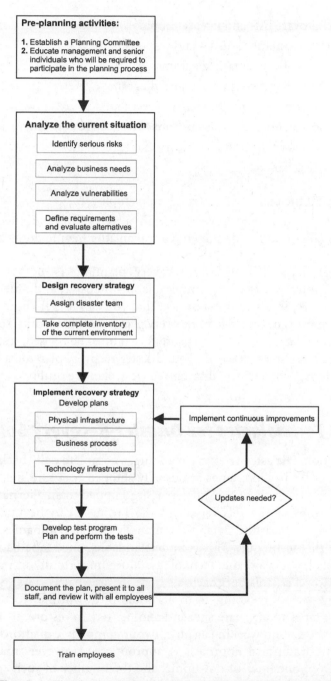

Fig. 2.1. The basic steps of a typical disaster recovery plan

- Software lists and license numbers
- Team-member duties and responsibilities
- Network schematic diagrams
- Equipment-room floor-grid diagrams
- Contract and maintenance agreements
- Special operating instructions for sensitive equipment
- Cellular telephone inventory and agreements
- Miscellaneous

☐ Present the plan to all staff and train employees.

☐ Test the plan and review it with all employees. If necessary, you should re-evaluate and re-document your plan after having done this.

Understand that disaster recovery planning is not a short-term project. On the contrary, it is a very complex, labor-intensive, and time-consuming process. Furthermore, it is also not a project that you can forget about after it has been set up and approved. An efficient recovery plan is one that works, so it must be kept current and updated. In order to ensure this, it must be revised, tested, and practised on a regular basis. In other words, your disaster-recovery plan must be a living plan! Basic steps of a typical disaster recovery plan are outlined in Fig. 2.1.

Emerging Technologies for Disaster-Recovery Solutions

In traditional disaster-recovery planning, a complete daily backup to tape is the key feature. After backup, tapes are usually shipped to a safe site. Theoretically, when a disaster strikes, these backup copies are shipped to an alternate site, where IT specialists perform the recovery, and the business can be up and running again. According to statistical data, more than 75% of all companies in the United States rely on this technique. This is understandable, since tape backup is a traditional, well-tested, and workable technology. More importantly, it involves relatively low costs. However, this approach also has its drawbacks. First, it carries a 24-hours recovery period, meaning 24 to 48 hours of downtime (for example, one day to ship the tapes to alternate site, and another day to restore, troubleshoot, and actually get the system working again). If your company can afford 48 hours downtime then this traditional approach is appropriate. However, many companies can't afford even one hour of downtime, and the number of such companies is growing constantly (e-businesses, for example).

To meet these needs, new technologies have been developed, such as electronic vaulting and mirroring. With electronic vaulting, data backup is performed over the network to a remote site. Some companies use vaulting because they find it to be a more convenient, reliable and automated way to do nightly backups. Some companies use the computer at the vaulting site (the "catcher") as a temporary replacement for the down server. In this case, performance might suffer, but service still won't be totally interrupted. However, electronic vaulting involves a minimum of twice the cost of a traditional tape backup and, furthermore, can't alone help you to achieve a recovery window of less than one hour. To achieve even shorter recovery times, it is necessary to mirror data to an identical system dedicated to performing the mirroring function. At the protected server, a probe is installed that continuously sends "OK" messages to the mirroring server. When the probe ceases to send these messages (or sends an emergency request), the mirroring machine steps in. Theoretically, this recovery scheme provides instantaneous recovery (even in the event of a large-scale emergency, where communication services or Internet services may be affected, it is possible to bring the mirroring system up within an hour). Banks, stock exchanges, or e-commerce companies often employ this scheme. Most other companies can't afford this technology, but current trends indicate that its use will grow significantly with the growth of e-commerce.

Disaster-Recovery Services Market

As has already been mentioned, disaster-recovery planning is very, very crucial and very, very complicated. Therefore, along with performing the basic steps in your disaster-recovery plan and making technical decisions, you have to decide whether you are going to implement the plan in-house or use the services of a specialized disaster-recovery firm. The main advantages of in-house disaster-recovery planning are obvious — better control and lower costs. However, despite these advantages, there are also drawbacks:

❑ Proper disaster-recovery planning is much easier said than done. It really is difficult and consumes a lot of employee time.

❑ Any money-saving techniques always involve certain compromises (such as performance degradation, for example).

Because of this, if you decide to implement the disaster-recovery plan in-house, it is recommended that you consider retaining a consulting firm to help you define your needs and develop proper procedures. After all, if you suffer a data loss as a result of disaster, you don't want any additional surprises.

In today's business environment, more and more organizations, especially large ones, are opting to utilize specialized companies providing disaster-recovery services. The largest and best-known of these service providers, accounting for a 90% share of the entire market, are the following:

❑ Comdisco Continuity Services (http://www.comdisco.com)
❑ SunGard Recovery Services (http://www.sungard.com)
❑ IBM Global Services Business Continuity and Recovery Services

If your company is a large one, it is clearly better to contact one of these three large service providers, since smaller disaster-recovery service providers are unlikely to fulfill your needs. In any case, a large disaster-recovery service provider is preferable for the simple reason that it has more resources at its disposal. For example, consider how many other companies may be experiencing a disaster situation simultaneously with you? Smaller disaster-recovery companies could be paralyzed with requests for help in such a situation.

But, over the long haul, the industry seems prepared to meet the needs of enterprises looking to beef up their disaster-recovery and storage options. One factor in this equation is the Storage Service Provider (SSP) market, which emerged based on a storage utility "pay-as-you-go" model. Recently, many SSPs have reinvented themselves, however, after anemic market uptake, and have begun to provide managed storage services for companies that are looking for someone to help them lasso their own runaway storage resources.

Some SSPs — such as StorageNetworks (www.storagenetworks.com) and StorageWay (www.storageway.com) — have entered into symbiotic relationships with telecommunication companies and other service providers (including Qwest, Yipes, and BellSouth, to name just a few). In some cases, they are using a service provider's infrastructure to deliver services to their own customers. This time around, the SSPs are primarily supplying the service providers with the software and know-how necessary to deliver managed storage, backup, and recovery services to their customers.

If you didn't have a Disaster Recovery Plan before now, the necessity to set one up should now be obvious. The lack of a disaster-recovery plan is, simply put, dangerous, so you can't afford to wait until the last minute to set one up. Always remember that surviving a disaster depends largely on comprehensive planning, selecting the appropriate products, documenting procedures, and constant updates to your disaster-recovery plan. These elements are essential for any IT firm or organization.

Data Backup as Part of Disaster-Recovery Plan

Surprisingly enough, most people only appreciate the importance of backup after a massive data loss occurs or important files get corrupted or accidentally deleted. Even among the most talented and qualified administrators, not all can say that they have a good set of backups at hand. The situation that must be avoided is that where a recent backup turns out to be unavailable at the moment when it is required.

Your backup plan must be an integral part of the disaster-recovery plan, and as such, it requires serious testing. General recommendations for creating a solid backup plan are as follows:

❑ Make sure that your backup hardware is adequate for the job and make certain to provide the proper backup capacity.

❑ Don't forget to consider how much time it requires to complete the backup procedure. If you have limited time, consider purchasing faster hardware or implementing a parallel backup scheme, which can significantly reduce the backup time, provided that it is properly configured.

❑ Be aware of open files. Although backup software supplied with Windows XP and Windows Server 2003 handle open files gracefully thanks to the new volume-snapshot technology first introduced with Windows XP, all of its predecessors simply skip open files during the backup process. Where necessary, purchase backup agents or modules to back up databases, mail servers and applications in which open files are continuously maintained. For example, it is strongly recommended to purchase such agents for Microsoft Exchange, SQL Server, and Oracle.

❑ Assign a person to be responsible for checking event logs to be certain that backup procedures are being carried out according to the plan.

❑ Keep your backup tapes as fresh as possible and store them properly. Also, be certain that tape devices remain clean and are in a clean environment. Since tapes are relatively fragile, test them periodically by doing a restore from each tape. Also, have multiple copies of tapes at hand and be certain that they are usable. It is also recommended to consider copying data to more stable media, such as MO diskettes or CD-RW.

❑ If your users prefer not to store their files on the server, make them responsible for backing up their own hard drives.

Note

In any case, a solid backup system must be considered a key component of any network, server, or even critical workstation. Do your best to avoid situations where the user, being asked to provide a backup copy, ends up answering: "What? A backup copy? What is a backup copy..."

For many organizations, particularly smaller ones, the concept of fault tolerance extends only as far as to doing a nightly tape backup. In many cases, the reason cited for using this measure alone is the lack of available funds to do more, but perhaps more common is a simple lack of appreciation of the impact a downed server can have. Tape backups provide an insurance policy against one thing — data loss. They do not, however, protect against downtime and, quite often, constitute the slowest link in the system-recovery process. Now, we come to the most interesting point — the role of registry backup and recovery in your plan for regular data backup. The saddest fact about this is that most users still don't realize how fast and easy the restoration process can be if, instead of reinstalling the OS and performing full system recovery, you simply restore the damaged configuration using one of the methods described in this chapter.

Preparing for Registry Editing

If you're a system administrator or technical-support specialist, you're certainly able to provide many examples of situations where users called for technical support when encountering registry problems. Sometimes (fortunately, this case isn't common), the user encounters registry-corruption problems before he or she can start Windows for the first time. Registry corruption is especially likely when inexperienced users modify the registry, because they often set incorrect values or even delete necessary keys. All these actions result in registry corruption.

Before proceeding any further, it is recommended that you study alternative methods of modifying the registry and various techniques for registry backup and recovery. There are several alternative methods of editing the Windows NT/2000, Windows XP, and Windows Server 2003 registry that you can use to solve the problem or configure the system parameters. Some of these methods were described in *Chapter 1*. Some Internet resources provide various tips on solving problems, using complicated registry-editing procedures. Users with a sound knowledge of the functionality provided by newer releases of Windows may find simpler and, at the same time, more elegant solutions, since most problems can be solved using Control Panel applets and other administrative utilities.

Caution

If you make an error while modifying the registry (for example, by setting incorrect values or deleting vital registry entries), you may prevent the system from booting. Whenever possible, modify the system configuration using Control Panel applets or other administrative utilities. Registry editor should be used only as a last resort. System administrators may wish to restrict user access to the registry in order to protect the system configuration. This topic will be discussed in detail in *Chapter 9*.

So, you need to open the registry and solve your problems by modifying it. This is a normal situation and you'll probably edit the registry directly. Some methods of configuring and troubleshooting the system, discussed later in this book, do require direct editing of the registry.

However, before you go any further, you need to back up the registry. Registry backup is the first thing that should be done before you begin editing the registry. Never start editing the registry without backing it up. Everyone makes mistakes, and registry editor (which will be discussed in the next chapter) doesn't have the **Undo** command that is present in most programs. Don't create unnecessary problems for yourself (unless this is the type of thing you enjoy doing). There is a ready solution, and the solution is registry backup.

Windows XP and products of the Windows Server 2003 family provide various methods for registry backup and recovery, along with reliability enhancements. Some of these features were inherited from Windows NT/2000, while others were first introduced with the newer versions of the operating system. This chapter provides detailed instructions on performing these procedures. Here, we will try to cover nearly all of the existing methods of registry backup.

Microsoft documentation and Microsoft Knowledge Base articles always contain standard warnings that inform the user about the potential danger of direct registry editing. Microsoft doesn't guarantee that problems caused by registry editing can always be solved. If the system registry is corrupted and you have no backup copy, it's possible that you'll need to reinstall the operating system.

Using the Microsoft Backup Program

Using the built-in Backup program is the officially recommended method of backing up Windows registry. The Backup version supplied with Windows NT 4.0 required a Windows NT-compatible tape device to be installed in the local system, which represented one of the most serious shortcomings of this utility. Furthermore, the list of supported tape devices that could be used with Windows NT Backup in Windows NT 4.0 is also quite limited. Moreover, this utility doesn't allow you to perform registry backup of remote systems, even if the user attempting to perform this operation has all the required access rights to the remote system.

The Backup version included with Windows 2000 has improved and extended functionality, including support for various types of backup media. This allows the user to back up information using any media supported by the operating system, including floppy disks, hard disks, floptical media, or other supported devices besides streamers. Windows XP and Windows Server 2003, in turn, provide several new technological improvements and enhancements.

▶ Note

Starting with Windows XP, Microsoft has introduced volume snapshots, a technology that provides a copy of the original volume at the instant a snapshot is taken. A snapshot of the volume is taken at the time a backup is initiated. Data are then backed up from the snapshot rather than from the original volume. The original volume continues to change as the process goes on, but the snapshot of the volume remains constant. This is helpful if users need access to files while a backup is taking place, since it significantly reduces the time required to accomplish the backup procedure. Additionally, the backup application can back up files that are kept open. In previous versions of Backup, including the one supplied with Windows 2000, files open at the time of the backup were skipped.

Besides working with the integrated Backup application, the Volume Shadow Copies function in Windows Server 2003 provides snapshots ("point in time copies") of files on network shares. To enable Volume Shadow Copies, right-click a drive or volume in **Windows Explorer** or **My Computer**, select the **Properties** command, and go to the **Shadow Copies** tab (Fig. 2.2). Select a volume from the **Select a volume** list, then click **Enable** and confirm your choice by clicking **Yes** in the **Enable Shadow Copies** window.

▶ Note

Volume Shadow Copies are enabled only in shared folders, since the feature is designed primarily for documents, which often happen to be accidentally deleted or overwritten with other versions. Besides this, it also provides you with version-checking capabilities while working with documents. However, the usage of this new feature also has some limitations:

- Client workstations that can benefit from this feature must run the Windows XP operating system. The client software for Volume Shadow Copies is located in the \\%*systemroot*%\system32\clients\twclient directory on the file server. After installing the twcli32.msi package, clients working with corporate documents will be provided with the Previous Versions functionality, allowing them to access shadow copies from their desktops. This software can be distributed to clients by a variety of means, including Group Policies, Microsoft Systems Management Server, or another third-party software management product.

- Shadow copies are read-only, and can be enabled on a per-volume basis. This means that you can't enable shadow copies on specific shares.

- Saving your work frequently is still the best way to ensure that your work is not lost. Furthermore, this feature isn't a replacement for regular backup.

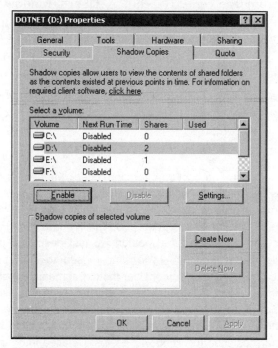

Fig. 2.2. The **Shadow Copies** tab of the disk properties window

Despite its convenience, the Volume Shadow Copies functionality is not a substitute for regular backups. To start the Backup utility in Windows XP and Windows Server 2003, select the **All Programs** | **Accessories** | **System Tools** | **Backup** commands from the **Start** menu. If you use this utility often (and you should do so), create a desktop shortcut for this program.

Note

Like in all Windows NT-based systems, in order to backup and restore files, the user must be assigned appropriate privileges. For example, members of local Administrators or

Backup Operators groups can back up and restore any files on a local computer. Users whose accounts don't belong to these groups must have at least read access permissions to the files that they need to back up. For computers participating in Windows 2000 or Windows Server 2003 domains, these abilities are greatly influenced by Group Policies. Detailed information on this topic will be provided in *Chapters 9* and *10*.

Besides the traditional method of starting the Backup utility, you can also start it using the right-click menu. Open the **Windows Explorer** or **My Computer** window, right-click on the disk that you need to back up, and select the **Properties** command from the context menu. A tabbed window will open. Navigate to the **Tools** tab, click the **Backup Now** button in the **Backup** group, and the **Backup or Restore Wizard** window will open (Fig. 2.3). The Backup utility can run in two modes: the wizard mode (in which it starts by default) and advanced mode, recommended for power users. If you want to change the default settings, clear the **Always start in wizard mode** checkbox and select the **Advanced Mode** option. The **Backup Utility** window will appear, opened at the **Welcome** tab (Fig. 2.4).

▶ *Note*

Before proceeding with a backup operation, check the file system of the disk you need to backup. This is important, because you need to have a usable backup copy. Remember that the backup software (including the Backup tool supplied with Windows 2000, Windows XP, and products of the Windows Server 2003 family) can't recognize errors and inconsistencies in user data. Note that the method we just described provides a convenient way of performing this operation — you simply need to click the **Check Now** button on the same tab. You also need to consider the defragmentation software used to defragment your hard drives. Microsoft recommends that everyone use the built-in defragmentation software supplied with the operating system. If you're planning to use a third-party defragmentation utility, make sure that this software is compatible with Windows Server 2003 and holds the "designed for Windows" status. Detailed information on software tested for compatibility with Windows 2000/XP or Windows Server 2003 can be downloaded from **http://www.microsoft.com**.

One of the most important goals of Windows XP and Windows Server 2003 development was to create an operating system, which would combine all the advantages of Windows 9*x*/ME with the traditional strong points of Windows NT/2000. Most of the attention was paid to tasks such as making the new operating system easy to use even for beginners, simplifying administrative tasks and making the system more reliable. Most tools and utilities were rewritten,

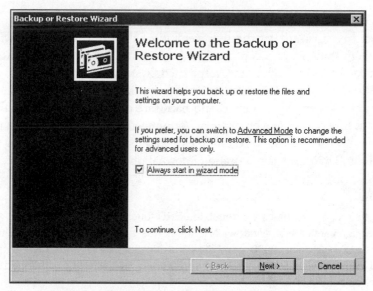

Fig. 2.3. The **Backup or Restore Wizard** window

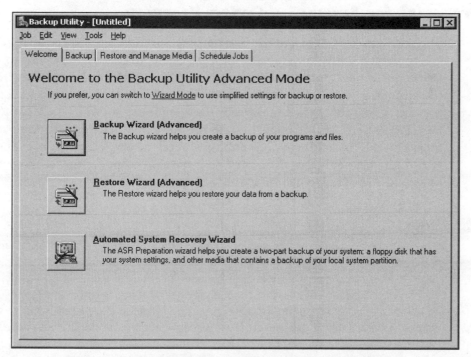

Fig. 2.4. The **Welcome** tab of the Backup Utility window

and the Backup tool is no exception. Besides the traditional functionality of backing up and restoring data, the new version of this utility supplied with Windows XP and Windows Server 2003 includes a function for preparing the Automated System Recovery (ASR). Although Automated System Recovery (ASR) actually debuted in Windows XP, it is new to Windows Server platform. ASR lets you backup operating system, system state, and hardware configuration so that they can be recovered in case of a system emergency. Automated System Recovery is a two-part recovery system that allows you to restore the operating system states by using files saved to tape media and hard disk configuration information saved to a floppy disk.

Note

Most experienced users will recall the ERD functionality that existed in Windows NT/2000. In earlier versions of Windows NT, there was a special Rdisk.exe utility used to perform this task. Windows 2000 combines the functionality of the Backup and Rdisk utilities, and in Windows XP/Windows Server 2003, as was already mentioned, ERD functionality was replaced by ASR.

Preparing for Automated System Recovery

The easiest method of using the Backup program is with the special wizards, which are similar to all other programs of this type. These wizards display dialogs prompting users to select options and provide instructions on selecting the options. Normally, these windows contain the following three buttons: **Back**, **Next**, and **Cancel**. When the user clicks the **Back** button, a window appears, allowing the user to correct the data entered after completing the previous step. To open the next window, the user needs to click the **Next** button. To cancel the whole operation, the user needs to click the **Cancel** button. This method is the easiest one for novice users who have little or no experience of working with the system.

Note

The materials provided in this section shouldn't be considered a complete description of the Backup program functionality, and in no circumstances should these materials be considered as a replacement for the user manual. This book is intended to describe the system registry. Because of this, this chapter provides only the most basic information related to using the Backup program for backing up and restoring the system registry. If you are interested in a detailed description of the Backup program or step-by-step instructions on performing typical tasks, you can find this information in the Backup Help system. Any user who intends to edit the registry should read this information very carefully.

To prepare for Automated System Recovery, proceed as follows:

1. If your computer is equipped with a tape device, prepare the backup media. If this is not the case, you will have to perform the backup operation on the hard disk. Therefore, make sure that you have sufficient disk space. In any case, you'll also need a blank formatted diskette.

2. Click the **Automated System Recovery Wizard** button at the **Welcome** tab of the **Backup Utility** window or, alternatively, select the **ASR wizard** command from the **Tools** menu. Click the **Next** button in the first window of the ASR wizard.

3. In the next window, you need to select the backup-media type and specify the backup destination (Fig. 2.5). If your computer is equipped with a tape backup device, select this device from the **Backup media or file name** list. Notice that if there is no tape backup device in your system, the **File** option will be set by default in the **Backup media type** field. Enter the path to the backup media or file into the **Backup media or file name** field (backup files always have a default BKF filename extension) or click the **Browse** button to navigate through the file system.

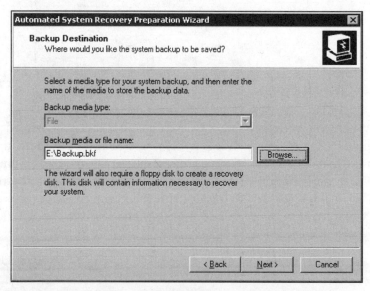

Fig. 2.5. The ASR preparation wizard prompts you to specify the backup-media type and select the backup media or file name

4. In the last window of the ASR preparation wizard, click the **Finish** button to start the backup process.

5. The Backup utility will scan your system and list files to save for an ASR backup. Next, it prompts you to provide backup media. Insert backup media when prompted by Backup and follow the directions on-screen. The wizard will display a series of messages such as: Mounting the media and Preparing to backup using a shadow copy. Then the **Backup Progress** window will appear (Fig. 2.6), reflecting the ASR backup progress.

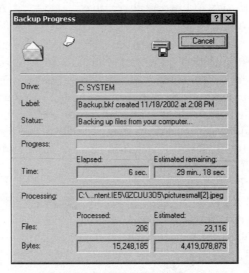

Fig. 2.6. The **Backup Progress** window

6. When the backup operation is completed, the ASR wizard prompts you to insert a blank floppy disk (Fig. 2.7), to which it saves hard disk configuration information, such as disk signatures, the partition table, volume data, the hardware configuration of your system and the list of files to be restored. No user data will be recorded to this diskette. If you run the ASR restore operation later, ASR Restore will configure disks using data saved to the ASR floppy disk.

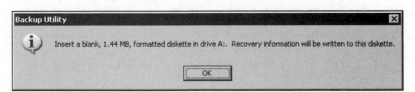

Fig. 2.7. As the final step of the ASR backup procedure, the wizard prompts you to provide a blank formatted diskette to store the recovery information

7. When the ASR backup wizard finishes creating the ASR diskette, it displays a message box with a message recommending you to label the diskette as the ASR recovery disk and store it in safe place. Click **OK** to close this message box. If you want to view a report on the results of the backup operation, click the **Report** button in the **Backup progress** window (Fig. 2.8).

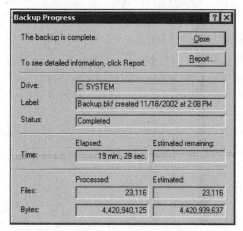

Fig. 2.8. The **Backup Progress** window informs you about completion of the backup operation and allows you to view the report

Performing the Automated System Recovery

The process of restoring a damaged system using the ASR procedure relies on the Windows XP/Windows Server 2003 Setup program; therefore, besides your backup media and the most recent ASR floppy disk, you will also need the distribution CD. In fact, this process is very similar to an unattended setup of the operating system, since ASR will restore your disk configuration using the data saved to the ASR floppy, reformat your %*Systemdrive*% partition (the one where the Windows XP or Windows Server 2003 copy to be recovered is installed), and then reinstall Windows XP or Windows Server 2003 on that partition and restore the system files using the backup media.

▶ *Note*

ASR is not a replacement for regular backup procedures, since it doesn't eliminate the danger of data loss. Remember that ASR doesn't back up application files and user data. As has already been mentioned, it only formats the %*Systemdrive*% partition as part of the recovery process and doesn't restore personal data or application files that may reside on that drive. Therefore, if you store user-data files or install applications on the system partition, these data will be lost. Because of this, always consider other recovery options, such as Recovery Console, before using ASR. More detailed information about Recovery Console will be provided later in this chapter.

To recover your system using ASR, proceed as follows:

1. Prepare everything that you'll need during the ASR restore process, including:
   - The most recent ASR floppy disk
   - The Windows XP or Windows Server 2003 distribution CD
   - The most recent ASR backup media set, typically removable media such as data-tape cartridges
2. Start the Setup program. Insert the distribution CD into your CD-ROM drive and reboot the computer.
3. Press any key to answer the `Press any key to boot from the CD…` prompt.
4. The Setup program will start. When you see the `Press F2 to run Automated System Recovery (ASR)` prompt, press the <F2> key to start the ASR restore process.
5. Insert an ASR floppy disk when prompted.
6. The Setup program will display the following message:

   ```
   Preparing to ASR, press <ESC> to cancel
   ```

   Note that at this stage you still have a chance to cancel the ASR by pressing the <ESC> key when prompted. This is important since, if you decide to continue, your %*Systemdrive*% partition will be formatted as a next step.
7. If you don't react to the message prompting you to cancel the ASR restore process, Setup will display a series of messages:

   ```
   Setup is starting the ASR…
   Setup is loading files
   Setup is starting Windows
   ```

   After that, the ASR process will reformat your %*Systemdrive*% partition and check other partitions that it may determine as requiring repair.

▶ *Note*

Besides formatting the %*Systemdrive*% partition, ASR might also initialize volumes that it determines to require repair. As has already been mentioned, it only restores operating-system files. Therefore, there is also a risk to user files stored on these volumes.

8. When formatting and disk checks are completed, ASR will build a list of files to be copied and prompt you to insert your ASR backup media (typically one or more removable media, such as data-tape cartridges). If you saved the ASR backup to a file, you will not be prompted to insert the media.

▶ *Note*

You must use locally attached devices, because restoring from network shares is not an ASR option. Examples of locally attached devices include tape backup drives, removable disks, or other hard disks. Concerning other hard disks, bear in mind that ASR supports FAT16 volumes up to 2.1 GB (32K maximum cluster size) and does not support 4 GB FAT16 partitions (64K maximum cluster size). If you start the ASR using a 4 GB FAT16 partition, the process will stop at this point. If this is the case, first convert that partition from FAT16 to NTFS before using ASR. Furthermore, if you are using local hard disks to store ASR backup sets, never save ASR backup on the System or Boot partitions. The reason is very simple — remember that, at the first stage of the ASR-restore process, the disk will be repartitioned and the %*Systemdrive*% partition will be reformatted. Thus, your BKF file will be destroyed and, when it comes to the actual restore process, the ASR-restoration procedure will fail.

Backing up and Restoring the System State Data

Besides other extended capabilities, the built-in Backup utility supplied with Windows XP and Windows Server 2003 allows the user to complete the procedure of backing up the whole set of system-configuration files — the so-called System State Data. As has already been mentioned, the registry is one of the most important system components, vital even at the early stages of the boot sequence. Because of this, the registry has to be included in this essential set of system files. However, there are some other files besides the registry that are included in the System State Data set. Let's take a look at these files.

The concept of System State Data was first introduced with Windows 2000. As you probably remember, in Windows NT 4.0 and earlier, built-in Backup programs can selectively back up and restore operating-system files, allowing for incremental backup and restore operations of most operating system files. Windows 2000/XP and the products belonging to Windows Server 2003 family, however, don't allow incremental backup and restoration of vitally important operating-system files, which must be backed up and restored as a single entity. This is the first, and the most important, thing that you should know about System State Data.

The second interesting thing related to the System State Data is the fact that this set differs slightly for different platforms. The System State Data set defined for client workstations running Windows 2000 Professional and Windows XP Professional operating systems and for servers (running Windows 2000 Server or Window Server 2003) that are not joined to a domain includes the following files:

❑ The registry
❑ COM+ classes registration database
❑ Boot files, which are necessary to boot the system

The System State Data set for server platforms joined to a domain contains the same components included in the System State Data set for Windows 2000/XP Professional, plus the following data:

❑ The Certificate Services database, if the server is a certificate server.
❑ The Active Directory database and the \SYSVOL directory, if the server is a domain controller.
❑ All information required to restore the cluster, if the server runs the cluster service. This information includes the registry checkpoints and quorum resource log, containing information on the cluster database.

Since the registry is included in the System State Data set, the procedures of backing up and restoring the system-state data can be considered a method of backing up and restoring the system registry.

Backing up the System State Data

It is recommended that you perform the procedures of backing up the System State Data on a regular basis. The simplest method of performing this operation is using the Backup Wizard. There are two methods of starting the Backup Wizard: you can click the **Backup Wizard** button on the **Welcome** tab of the Backup program main window, or you can select the **Backup Wizard** command from the **Tools** menu. To back up the System State Data, select the **Only back up the System State data** option displayed in the second dialog (Fig. 2.9), then click Next, and follow the instructions provided by the wizard.

The same procedure can also be carried out manually. To perform manual backup of the System State Data, start the Backup program, go to the **Backup** tab, and select the **System State** option (Fig. 2.10). When the user selects the **System State** option, the right pane of the **Backup** window will display the list of files to be included in the backup. As was mentioned previously, the System State Data set will be different for workstations and server platforms. As has also already been mentioned, the Backup utility doesn't allow the user to select options from this list to perform a selective backup — the checkboxes beside all the right pane options are grayed. Microsoft provides an explanation for this by stating that all the components included in the System State Data set are interrelated.

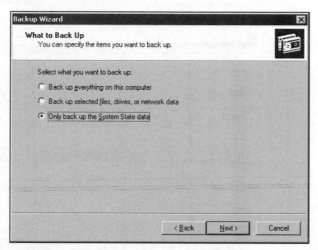

Fig. 2.9. To backup the System State Data, set the **Only back up the System State data** in the second dialog displayed by the Backup Wizard

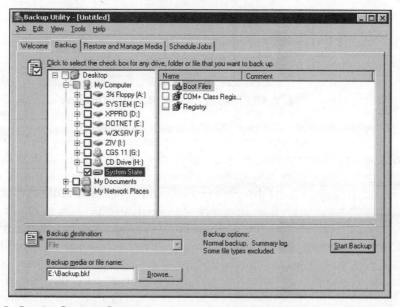

Fig. 2.10. Set the **System State** checkbox to include the System State data in the backup

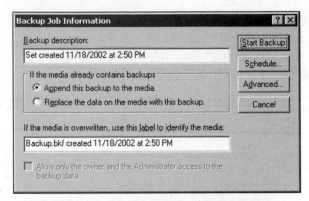

Fig. 2.11. The **Backup Job Information** window

Fig. 2.12. The **Advanced Backup Options** window

If you need to perform a backup operation, and your computer is equipped with a tape backup device, select this device from the **Backup destination** list. Otherwise, select the **File** option from this list. If your computer isn't equipped with a tape device, the **File** option will always be set by default.

If you need to back up data to a file, specify the file path in the **Backup media or file name** field, or click the **Browse** button to specify the path to the backup file. If you perform the backup to tape, select the tape to which you need to backup your data. To specify additional backup options, select the **Options** command from the **Tools** menu. To start the backup procedure, click the **Start Backup** button. The **Backup Job Information** window (Fig. 2.11) will open. Although you cannot perform a selective backup of the System State Data, you are still able to specify advanced backup options. To do so, click the **Advanced** button in the **Backup Job Information** window to open the **Advanced Backup Options** dialog (Fig. 2.12).

The advanced-backup options, along with their brief descriptions, are listed below:

❑ **Back up migrated Remote Storage data.** If you select this option, the Backup utility will back up data that has been designated for Remote Storage.

▶ *Note*

You can restore Remote Storage data only to an NTFS volume that is used with Windows 2000, Windows XP, or any product of the Windows Server 2003 family. Also note that Remote Storage is available only on Server-based computers.

❑ **Verify data after backup.** This option verifies that the backed up data are exactly the same as the original data. To ensure that you have a correct and usable backup copy, it is strongly recommended that you select this checkbox, despite the fact that this can substantially increase the time required to complete the backup procedure.

❑ **Use hardware compression, if available.** This option is useful if you need to save more data on a tape. Hardware compression is only available for tape devices. Therefore, if it is grayed, you do not have a tape drive on your computer or your tape drive cannot compress data.

❑ **Automatically backup System Protected Files with the System State.** Although you cannot change the components of the System State that are backed up, you can choose to include all system-protected files in the backup copy or to exclude them from the backup operation. By default, this option is enabled, but you can disable it by clearing this checkbox.

▶ *Note*

The system-protected files only change if you install a service pack or application, or upgrade your operating system. Typically, system-protected files represent a very large portion of System State data — the size of the default, including the protected files, is about 180 MB. Include these system-protected files only if new programs have been installed, otherwise a restore operation causes the new application to fail.

❑ **Disable volume shadow copy.** This allows you to disable volume-snapshot technology. As mentioned earlier in this chapter, the volume-snapshot technology introduced with Windows XP allows the Backup application to run together with other applications and services. By default, Windows XP and Windows Server 2003 use free disk space on any NTFS volume to store the snapshot data until the backup is completed. The amount of disk space temporarily consumed depends on how much file data on the volume has changed during backup. Windows XP and Windows Server 2003 products use volume-snapshot technology by default, but you can disable it if you only want to back up a few files or directories.

Note

If there is not sufficient disk space in your system for temporary storage of the snapshot data, Windows XP and Windows Server 2003 are unable to complete a volume snapshot, and Backup skips open files. Thus, you must provide sufficient disk space to create a snapshot of open files. Also note that you can't disable volume snapshot when backing up System State Data.

The following information should also be noted when backing up the System State Data:

❑ To back up the System State Data, you need to login to the system as a user with administrative rights (Administrator or member of the Administrators group) or backup operator (member of the Backup operators user group).

❑ The Backup utility will allow you to perform the System State Data backup only for a local system. You can't perform System State Data backup for remote systems.

❑ To ensure that the system starts properly, it is strongly recommended that you also back up the Boot and System volumes.

Restoring the System State Data

The System State data backup will be very helpful if you need to reinstall the operating system if it didn't boot.

To restore the System State Data, call up the Backup utility, go to the **Restore and Manage Media** tab, and select the **System State** option from the list of available media items (Fig. 2.13). The **Restore files to** combobox allows you to select one of the following options:

❑ **Original location** — the files will be restored to their original location.

❑ **Alternate location** — the files from the backup copy will be restored to a specified alternative folder. This option allows you to preserve the original folder structure.

❏ **Single folder** — the files from the backup copy will be restored to the specified alternative folder without preserving the original folder structure.

Click the **Start Restore** button, and the Backup utility will restore the System State Data using the options you have specified.

The Help system supplied with the Backup utility provides more detailed information on the System State Data, as well as step-by-step instructions on performing the backup and restore operations. All the limitations of the System State Data backup procedure are also applicable when performing the restore operation. These limitations are as follows:

❏ To perform this operation, you need to have administrator or backup operator authorization for the local system.

❏ Since all of the components of the System State Data set are interrelated, you can back up or restore this data only as a whole set.

❏ You can restore the System State Data only in the local system.

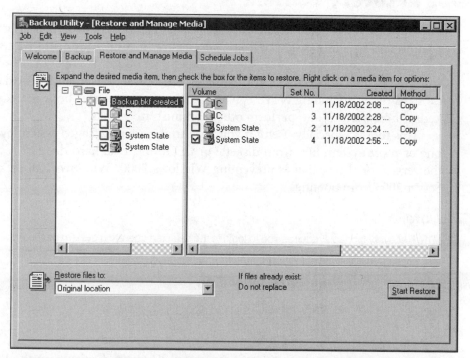

Fig. 2.13. The **Restore and Manage Media** tab of the **Backup** window

Note

If you don't specify an alternative folder when restoring the System State Data, the Backup utility will replace the current System State Data with the files restored from the backup copy. Note that, because all the components included in the System State Data set are inter-dependent, the Backup utility only allows backing up and restoring this data as a whole set.

However, it is possible to restore the System State Data to an alternative folder. In this case, Backup will restore only the registry files, the files stored in the \SYSVOL directory, cluster database files, and boot files. Active Directory database, the certificate sever database, and COM+ information will not be restored.

The following fact is important from a registry-backup point of view: when performing the System State Data backup, the system saves current copies of the registry files in the *%SystemRoot%*\repair folder. If the registry hives become corrupted, you can use these copies to restore the system without performing the procedure of restoring the System State Data. However, only advanced users should use this method.

Using Recovery Console

The Recovery Console, first introduced with Windows 2000, is a console with a command-line interface, providing administrators and administrative users with the necessary tools for repairing a system that won't boot. Recovery Console allows you to start and stop services, format disks, retrieve data from and write data to local hard disks (including NTFS drives), repair corrupt master boot records (MBR) and/or boot sectors, and perform other administrative tasks.

This tool is especially useful if you need to restore a damaged system by copying one or more system files from diskette or CD to the local hard drive or reconfigure the service or driver that is preventing Windows 2000, Windows XP, or Windows Server 2003 from booting.

Note

The Recovery Console requires you to login to the selected operating system as the Administrator.

Methods of Starting Recovery Console

There are several methods of starting Recovery Console:

☐ Start Recovery Console from Windows Setup program

☐ As an alternative method, you can install Recovery Console on the local hard drive and include it as an option in the boot menu

Starting Recovery Console Using the Setup Program

As already mentioned, you can start Recovery Console from the Windows 2000/XP or Windows Server 2003 Setup program. The easiest way of doing so is to boot your computer from the distribution CD (if your computer is equipped with a bootable CD-ROM device).

If you can't boot from the CD but have another operating system installed on your computer, you can use that operating system to start the Setup program. However, it is often the case that there is no other operating system on the computer that can be used to start the Setup program (or the alternative operating system is also unbootable). In Windows 2000, you can start the Setup program using four setup diskettes. In Windows XP, to perform the same task, you need five setup diskettes (or even more, if you are working with localized versions). In Windows Server 2003, unfortunately, there is no such option. However, to start the Setup program, you can proceed as follows:

❑ Create a Windows 98/ME Emergency Boot Disk. In addition to the files automatically copied to this diskette when it is created, copy the Smartdrv.exe file to this diskette (this file is needed to make the Setup procedure run faster).
❑ Reboot the system from this diskette and select the option of booting the system with CD-ROM support.
❑ Run SmartDrive from the command prompt, then start the Winnt.exe program located in the /I386 directory on the distribution CD. The Setup program will then start.

In either case, you'll need to wait until the system completes initial file copying. After this is completed, Setup prompts you to select one of the following options: you may install a new copy of Windows Server 2003, restore a damaged Windows Server 2003 installation, or exit Setup (Fig. 2.14). When this screen appears, press the <R> key.

Setup will then search your hard drives for existing Windows Server 2003 installations and prompt you to select the one that needs to be restored. Recovery Console provides a powerful set of tools, including the following capabilities:

❑ Formatting partitions
❑ Starting and stopping services
❑ Reading and writing files
❑ Repairing damaged boot sectors and master boot records (MBR)

After you select the **Recovery Console** option, Setup will prompt you to select the Windows Server 2003 installation to be repaired (if you have installed multiple copies of Windows Server 2003). Next, Setup will ask you to enter the Administrator's password for the installation selected.

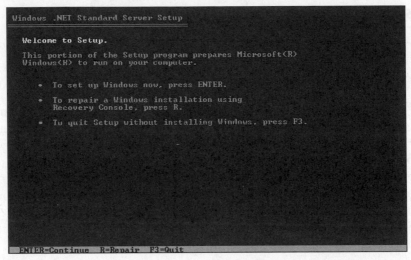

Fig. 2.14. The **Welcome to Setup** screen, prompting the user to select between installing Windows Server 2003 anew, repairing a damaged Windows Server 2003 installation, or exiting Setup

Including Recovery Console into the Boot Menu

If you need to include Recovery Console in the boot menu as an option, do the following:

1. Login to the local Windows 2000/XP or Windows Server 2003 system as the Administrator or a member of the Administrators group.
2. Insert the Windows 2000/XP or Windows Server 2003 distribution CD into the CD-ROM drive.
3. If you receive a prompt to upgrade your current operating system, click **No**.
4. Go to the distribution CD and, from the command line, execute the following command:

```
\i386\winnt32.exe /cmdcons
```

5. Follow the instructions that appear on the screen.

Deleting Recovery Console from the Boot Menu

If you need to delete Recovery Console from the boot menu, proceed as follows:

1. Go to the root directory of the system partition. Delete the \Cmdcons folder and Cmldr file.

Note

Both the \Cmdcons folder and Cmldr file have the Hidden and System attributes. This means that they are considered as operating-system protected files, which by default aren't displayed by Windows Explorer. To delete these files using Windows Explorer or My Computer, configure the file and folder display options (**Folder Options** Control Panel applet) to display the operating-system protected files.

2. Open the Boot.ini file for editing (notice that Windows XP and products from the Windows Server 2003 family allow you to do this from the System applet). Find the string corresponding to the Recovery Console option and delete this command string. An example of the syntax of this command is shown below:

```
C:\cmdcons\bootsect.dat="Microsoft Windows .NET Server Recovery Console"
   /cmdcons
```

Note

If you are working with Windows 2000, the instructions provided above are also applicable. The only difference is that you will need to clear the Read-Only attribute from the Boot.ini file and then open the file for editing using any text editor (Notepad, for example). Don't forget to restore the Read-Only attribute after saving the Boot.ini file.

Using Recovery Console

The Recovery Console provides a full-screen command-line interface similar to that existing in MS-DOS. You can easily get acquainted with the Recovery Console interface using the `help` command. This displays a complete list of all available Recovery Console commands. In Windows 2000/XP, as well as in Windows Server 2003, online-help system also provides a list of Recovery Console commands (search using the keywords *Recovery Console*).

Backing up and Restoring Windows NT/2000/XP/ Server 2003 Registries Manually

If the boot partition of Windows NT/2000/XP/Server 2003 is formatted using the FAT file system, you can easily back up the system registry manually by booting the computer under an alternative operating system (for example, MS DOS or Windows 9x/ME) or even using the boot diskette. When this is done, you will be able to copy registry-hive files to the backup media using any method of copying (for example, you may use both Windows Explorer and the command line).

If the Windows NT/2000/XP or Windows Server 2003 boot partition uses NTFS, you may have some difficulties using this method of backing up the registry (however, contrary to information provided in some sources, this isn't always the case). You may sometimes need to format the Windows NT/2000/XP/Server 2003 boot partition using NTFS (this may be required by the security rules adopted by your company or by certain software products, which need to be installed on NTFS partitions). However, you may wish to continue using a manual method of backing up the registry. The simplest method of avoiding any possible problems is a parallel installation of the operating system. Microsoft officially recommends this method of improving system reliability. This tip can be found in both the Resource Kit documentation and in Microsoft Knowledge Base articles. If you follow this recommendation, though, you'll need to consider the compatibility aspects of NTFS 4 and NTFS 5. You can also use shareware or freeware NTFS drivers, which can be downloaded from the Internet).

To back up Windows NT/2000/XP/Server 2003 registry manually, copy the files contained in the *%SystemRoot%*\System32\Config folder to the backup media. Note that you need to use backup media of sufficient capacity, since the contents of this folder almost certainly won't fit on a 1.44 MB diskette.

Selection of removable storage media for transporting your files (for system administrators and technical-support personnel these, most probably, will include recovery tools, drivers, system updates, diagnostic utilities and, certainly, backup files, such as registry backups) is very important. Till recently, ZIP disks and CD-Rs were used for this purpose. Over the past few years, however, newer and better media have become more and more popular. If you need a portable toolkit for emergency situations, such things as external USB card readers, Flash Memory cards, and, above all, USB Flash drives, will be invaluable. Such devices can hold up to 1 GB of data, are very portable, extremely light weight, and compatible with any PC equipped with a USB port. Just stick the flash drive into the USB port of your PC running Windows 2000/XP or Windows Server 2003 and Windows Plug and Play will immediately see it as an additional drive (more information on this topic will be provided in *Chapter 5*). Then copy the files you need to take with you, unplug the device from the PC, and you're ready to go. Flash drives hold more data than a floppy disk, are more portable than ZIP drives and other remote-storage devices, and are more convenient (and less fragile) than CD-RW disks. In short, USB Flash Drives may just be the perfect removable storage medium.

▶ Note

Unfortunately, the small size and large storage capacity of such devices, apart from the advantages that they bring, can also make them dangerous. In order to install such a device in Windows 2000/XP or Windows Server 2003, it isn't necessary for the user to belong to the Administrators group. For example, during the installation of portable USB drives the user can bypass entirely administrative safeguards against worms and viruses, unauthorized software such as shareware programs, software pranks, MP3 files, video clips, spyware or keystroke loggers that can enable users to capture passwords or other sensitive information. Another threat created by such devices is that of theft or loss of software and confidential data. Unless you disable all of the USB ports in your environment, they are impossible to defend against. Protective measures that you can take to safeguard your corporate network against these threats will be considered in *Chapter 9*.

The files that need to be copied from the *%SystemRoot%*\System32\Config folder are listed below:

Appevent.evt	Secevent.evt	Sysevent.evt
Default	Security	System
Default.log	Security.log	System.alt*
Default.sav	Software	System.log
Sam	Software.log	System.sav
Sam.log	Software.sav	Userdiff

* This file was eliminated in Windows XP and Windows Server 2003. It is only present in earlier versions of Windows NT/2000.

► **Note**

When backing up the registry manually, don't forget to create backup copies of user profiles, which are stored under *%Systemdrive%*\Documents and Settings*<Username>* folders. To create backup copies of user profiles for each user quickly, log in as the Administrator and copy the Ntuser.dat files for each existing user profile (more detailed information on user profiles will be provided in *Chapter 10*.

Restoring the registry from a backup copy that was created using this method requires booting the computer under an alternate operating system. After rebooting, you simply need to copy the registry files from the backup media back to the *%SystemRoot%*\System32\Config folder.

Registry Export and Import

Registry editor (Regedit.exe), which will be discussed in detail in *Chapter 3*, allows you to export the whole registry or individual keys. You may export the registry to any device installed in the local system.

▶ *Tip*

Export registry files to a folder specially created for this purpose. This folder may be located on the network drive and contain individual subfolders for each user. If you add this folder to the list of folders to be included in the regular backup procedure, you and all other users will benefit from the improvement in reliability.

To export the registry, proceed as follows:

1. Start Regedit.exe and select **My Computer** (to export the whole registry) or any individual key (to export that key only).
2. Select the **Export...** command from the **File** menu.
3. The **Export Registry File** dialog will open (Fig 2.15). Select the target folder and specify the file name for the file that will contain exported registry information.

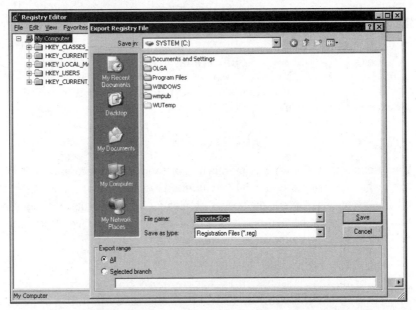

Fig. 2.15. The **Export Registry File** dialog. The whole process of exporting the registry file is very similar to the process of saving files

The exported registry file has an ASCII text format. You may open this file for editing using any text editor.

Exporting the whole registry or individual registry keys is the simplest method of backing up the registry before proceeding with any operations that modify registry content. To discard an incorrect modification introduced in the registry, simply import the previously exported registry file.

To restore registry keys using Regedit, select the **Import Registry File** command from the **File** menu. The **Import Registry File** dialog will open (Fig. 2.16). You need to select the file to be imported.

Note

After getting acquainted with the registry, you will be able to experiment with it and even solve problems by editing the exported registry file and importing it back to the system. However, before you proceed with editing the exported registry file, make a backup copy of this file to safeguard against possible errors.

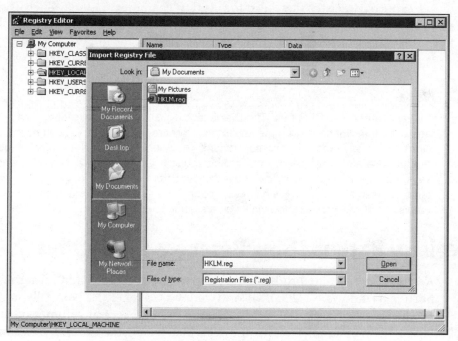

Fig. 2.16. Importing the registry file

Some tips concerning working with registry import and export functions are shown below.

☐ If you use the import/export function for backing up and restoring the registry, don't forget to copy the exported registry files to removable media or to the network drive.

☐ Before completing the export operation, make sure that the key range you are going to export is the particular one that you need. If the **All** option is set, the operation will export the whole registry. If you set the **Selected branch** option, the export operation will export the key specified in the field below.

❑ Be very careful when working with exported registry files. Don't attempt to import incompatible registry files (i.e., don't import registry files exported from Windows NT v. 4.0 or v. 3.51 to a Windows 2000/XP or Windows Server 2003 registry, and vice versa; never try to import Windows 9*x*/ME registry files to a registry of a Windows NT-based system). If you import incompatible registry files, the import process will fail but, if it saves incorrect registry data before the error occurs (which will probably happen), you will have problems that can manifest themselves immediately or the next time you reboot the system.

❑ Don't double-click on exported registry files of unknown origin. By default, all exported registry files bear the REG filename extension, which is associated with the Regedit.exe program. If you double-click on an incompatible registry file exported from a different operating system, the import procedure will begin before you can understand what's happened. The result can be devastating.

◤ *Note*

Be very careful with REG files! The Distribution disks of some applications include these files and use them when installing the application to set registry values needed by the application. Don't ignore any precautionary measures! If you double-click on a REG file, Regedit.exe will read this file and insert its contents into the registry. If the registry already contains the same keys, they will be replaced by new keys retrieved from the REG file. Before entering the contents of these files in the registry, always open REG files using a text editor (Notepad, for example). That way you will know what you are going to enter in the registry.

Registry Backup Using Resource Kit Utilities

Resource Kit software products can simplify the process of administering and supporting Windows NT/2000/XP or Windows Server 2003. Normally, any software product of this type includes a distribution CD and several volumes of supplementary documentation. Despite the fact that Microsoft doesn't officially support Resource Kit products and doesn't provide any warranties, Resource Kit utilities are valuable tools for the experienced system administrator. Furthermore, Microsoft warns customers that they use these tools at their own risk. Resource Kit utilities aren't subject to localization; they were only tested with the U.S. versions of Windows NT/2000, Windows XP, or Windows Server 2003, and their usage with localized versions may lead to unforeseeable results.

Despite of all the concerns mentioned above, Resource Kit software is very popular among system administrators, support specialists, and programmers. Most Resource Kit utilities were developed for internal use, and they significantly extend existing OS functionality. It's not surprising, then, that Resource Kits also contain registry tools.

Caution

Resource Kit utilities intended for working with the system registry are command-line tools. Use these tools with caution. Note that registry editors, which at least have a graphic user interface, are much easier to use. When using the Resource Kit command-line utilities for modifying the registry, you need to have a proper understanding of the changes you're going to make in the local or remote registry.

The REG Command-Line Utility

The REG Resource Kit utility allows you to add, modify, delete, and search registry keys and values, and to perform registry backup and restore and other administrative operations. This command-line utility can also be used in the batch files. It can operate over both local and remote registries.

The REG utility implements the functionality of the following registry tools from the Resource Kit versions, earlier than Windows 2000 Resource Kit: Regchg.exe, Regdel.exe, Regdir.exe, Regread.exe, Regsec.exe, Restkey.exe, Rregchg.exe, and Savekey.exe. In Windows 2000, it replaces all of these utilities. Starting with Windows XP, Reg.exe tool is built into the OS. Detailed information on the Reg.exe command-line syntax will be provided in *Chapter 15*.

To backup and restore the registry using Reg.exe command-line tool, use the following commands:

☐ REG SAVE and REG BACKUP

Saves the indicated registry values, keys, or hives to the specified file. This command is particularly useful for backing up the registry before introducing any changes. The REG SAVE and REG BACKUP commands are identical.

☐ REG RESTORE

Restores the specified value, key, or hive from the file created using the REG SAVE or REG BACKUP commands.

The REG SAVE and REG BACKUP commands use the following syntax:

```
REG SAVE RegistryPath FileName [\\Machine]
REG BACKUP RegistryPath FileName [\\Machine]
```

The *RegistryPath* argument specifies the registry path to the registry key or value in the following format: *[ROOTKEY\]Key*.

The *ROOTKEY* parameter specifies the registry root key containing the key to be backed up (the default value of this parameter is HKEY_LOCAL_MACHINE).

The root key may be specified using one of the following abbreviations:

```
HKEY_LOCAL_MACHINE — HKLM
HKEY_CURRENT_USER — HKCU
HKEY_CLASSES_ROOT — HKCR
HKEY_CURRENT_CONFIGURATION — HKCC
```

Key — this parameter specifies the complete path to the registry key contained within the root key specified by the *ROOTKEY* parameter.

FileName — this parameter specifies the file name (without an extension) where the registry data will be saved. (On a local computer, this file will be stored in the current directory. When working with remote systems, this file will be saved in the Windows installation directory.)

Machine — this parameter specifies the name of the remote computer (by default, the local system is used). Use a UNC notation when specifying computer names. For example: \\STATION1.

▶ *Note*

Only HKLM and HKU keys are available when working with remote systems.

The REG RESTORE command supports the following syntax:

```
REG RESTORE FileName KeyName [\\Machine]
```

where:

FileName — name of the file to be restored (without the filename extension). This parameter should specify a file previously created using REG SAVE or REG BACKUP.

KeyName — name of the registry key, in the following format: [*ROOTKEY*]*Key*.

Key — complete path to the registry key contained within the root key specified by the *ROOTKEY* parameter.

Machine — name of the remote system in UNC format (by default, the local computer will be used).

Summary

Any time you open the registry to modify it, the situation can arise where you cannot boot the system because of registry corruption. It is for just such occasions that you should always have a usable backup copy of the registry. Always test the usability of the backup copies you create. The material provided in this chapter contains detailed instructions on backing up Windows 2000, Windows XP, and Windows Server 2003 registries. It also provides tips on carrying out the emergency recovery of a damaged system.

CHAPTER 3

Using Registry Editor

*The user does have to take responsibility
for the computer and what happens on it.*

Lou Grinzo
"Zen of Windows 95 Programming"

If you call Microsoft for technical support and ask about editing the registry, they will answer that end users should not edit the registry. Microsoft documents are full of these notices, warning you that improper editing could make your system unbootable.

At the same time, registry tools are present in all Microsoft operating systems (what's more, they're installed by default). Why, then, does Microsoft provide these utilities to the end user? The answer is simple: these utilities are necessary because, in some cases, they are the only way to solve the problem. Try to imagine how the user community would react if the Windows operating systems did not include these utilities. Of course, some users wouldn't notice the lack of tools, but others... To understand this, take some time to read *"Zen of Windows 95 Programming"* by Lou Grinzo. Besides an alternative point of view on the Windows registry, you'll find lots of other interesting facts and ideas presented in Gringo's book. The author also states that he is one of the users who would protest if Microsoft tried to force him to write registry-editing applications himself.

He would surely find many supporters for this point of view. All contemporary Windows operating systems, including Windows 9x/ME, Windows NT/2000, Windows XP, and products of the Windows Server 2003 family, contain special utilities for viewing and editing the registry, which are called Registry Editors. Windows NT 4.0 and Windows 2000 actually contain two registry editors. Regedt32.exe is the traditional Windows NT registry-editing program inherited from previous Windows NT versions. It allows you to edit the registry using methods that aren't supported in Windows 9x/ME. Regedit.exe is a newer application that was initially written for Windows 95. This application offers many of the capabilities of Regedt32.exe and has a Windows Explorer user interface (UI). The Windows 2000/XP version of Regedit.exe is similar to applications included in Windows 9x/ME and Windows NT 4.0.

Note

In comparison to Windows NT/2000, Windows XP and Windows Server 2003 provide an improvement in this area. For the moment, all tasks related to registry administration and editing can be performed with a single utility — Regedit.exe, which now integrates its traditional strong points with the functionality that was earlier available only in Regedt32.exe. Beside this, Regedit.exe now supports extended import and export capabilities. However, Regedit.exe lacks one of the most useful Regedt32.exe functions, namely, read-only mode.

All versions of registry editors supplied with all versions of the Windows operating system are automatically installed during the OS installation. However, neither of these registry tools is included in the **Start** menu, and Setup doesn't create desktop shortcuts for them. To start these programs, use the **Run** command from the **Start** menu.

You can use registry editors for viewing, adding, deleting, and modifying registry elements. This chapter will probably seem boring to those of you with knowledge of earlier versions of Windows NT. However, but few books on Windows NT/2000/XP or Windows Server 2003 in general, and Windows registry in particular, omit a chapter dedicated to this topic. It's also almost impossible to find a book on this topic that doesn't warn that the Registry editor isn't a toy. It is also important to note that neither of the registry editors can be considered as a "program that will simplify your life" (despite the fact that developers have actually made some advances in this direction). On the contrary, most users (especially beginners) will create a number of problems for themselves and make their lives much more complicated. This warning is not here with the purpose of scaring off beginners, since this entire chapter is intended specifically for them.

Using Regedit

As mentioned earlier, Regedit.exe version included with Windows XP and Windows Server 2003 is very much like the application included in Windows 9*x*/ME and Windows NT/2000. However, the version included in newer products has many improvements and, starting with Windows XP, integrates the functionality that had earlier been available only in Regedt32.exe.

Like other utilities, this one is installed by default. However, the Setup program doesn't create a shortcut for this program and doesn't include it in the **Start** menu. The next section of this chapter contains a brief description of the Regedit.exe user interface, which can be used as a reference for all of the functions of this registry editor.

Note

Regedit.exe, especially the newer version supplied with Windows XP and Windows Server 2003, is easy to use. The difficult task is making sure that any registry modifications to the system configuration are correct. Because of this, it is recommended that you don't make any registry modifications without first reading this chapter. This chapter provides detailed instructions on registry editing and also some useful tips. Incorrect modifications made to the registry can result in software failures or even render your system unbootable. You should make a backup copy of the system registry, using any of the techniques shown in *Chapter 2*, before you proceed any further. Specifically, prepare the Automated System Recovery (ASR) and make a backup copy of the System State data. For workstations running Windows XP, don't neglect the System Restore tool. The boot diskette may also be helpful when eliminating possible problems.

Starting Regedit

By default, Regedit.exe is copied to the *%SystemRoot%* (for example, D:\WINNT) during the installation of the operating system. To start Regedit.exe, find the file and double-click it, or use the **Run** command from the **Start** menu.

Like most of the other viewing tools now available for Windows operating systems, Registry Editor has a user interface similar to that of Windows Explorer. Note that Regedit is simply a tool for registry visualization, and all of the magic is hidden behind the scenes rather than in the UI.

In practice, the similarity between Regedit and Explorer goes further than simple analogy. For example, the same menu commands for keyboard shortcuts are used for creating new registry elements. Regedit.exe uses context (right-click) menus similar to Explorer. Despite interface improvements, however, Regedit.exe doesn't provide any warnings to the user, nor does it recognize errors. What's more, it doesn't have an **Undo** command, meaning that most operations are irreversible.

Examining the Regedit User Interface

This section can be used as a brief reference when working with Regedit. It provides a description of all the functions of the registry editor. The following sections contain instructions and tips on using Regedit, as well as directions for modifying the registry.

The **Registry Editor** window contains four main regions (Fig. 3.1):

☐ *The menu bar.* The menu bar contains the following menu items: **Registry**, **Edit**, **View**, **Favorites** (this menu item was first introduced with Windows 2000), and **Help**.

☐ *Left pane.* The left pane displays the registry hierarchy organized in keys and subkeys.

☐ *Right pane.* The right pane displays value entries contained within a selected registry key. Each value entry is identified by its name, which is displayed in the **Name** column; data type, which is displayed in the **Type** column (a small icon to the left of the name helps to identify the data type); and the value, which is displayed in the **Data** column.

☐ *Status bar.* The status bar indicates the path to the selected registry entry. It is helpful when you need to view the full path to the registry key containing the selected registry entry.

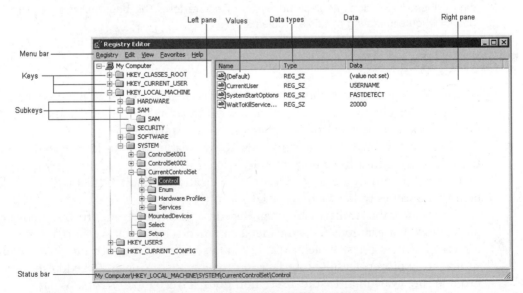

Fig. 3.1. The **Registry Editor** window

When you start Regedit, the **Registry Editor** window displays only the top-level registry keys below the **My Computer** icon. These are the root keys described in *Chapter 1*.

If you click [+] to the left of the folder, this will expand the respective registry key displaying its subkey hierarchical structure. This operation expands the key tree to the next nesting level and resembles similar methods of opening folders in Windows Explorer.

If the subkeys contain other nested keys, they'll also have the [+] sign to the left of the folder. The subkeys, in turn, can also be expanded to view the next level of the registry hierarchy. This method of organizing the registry information is known as nesting. Any number of nesting levels is possible. This hierarchical organization is the main difference between the registry and the initialization files. It provides a significant advantage over the methods for storing the initialization information used in Windows 3.*x*.

When you reach the lowest level of nesting, the [–] sign will appear to the left of the folder icon. This means that the key can't be expanded further and you can only go back up the hierarchical tree.

If neither the [+] nor [–] icons are present, this means that the key doesn't contain any subkeys.

Table 3.1 provides a list of keyboard shortcuts used for viewing and navigating the registry using Regedit.exe.

Table 3.1. Keyboard Shortcuts Used in Regedit.exe

Key	Description
<+>	Expands the selected registry key by one level to show its subkeys
<–>	Collapses the selected registry key by one level
<↑>	Moves you up to the next key
<↓>	Moves you down to the next key
<→>	Expands the selected key by one level to show subkeys; if there are no subkeys, moves you down to the next key
<←>	Collapses the selected key if it was open; otherwise, moves you up to the next key
<Tab>	Moves you to the next pane of the **Registry Editor** window

Registry value entries are displayed in the right pane of the **Registry Editor** window. Each value entry contains three parts: name, data type, and value data.

Like any parameter, each registry value entry has a name. Many value entries provided by Microsoft use a "Default" name (as you'll see later when you begin intense work with Regedit). All of the names of the value entries are displayed in the **Name** column in the right pane of the **Registry Editor** window. These names are assigned to the value entries by the software and hardware developers.

Data types that describe the registry value entries are displayed in the **Type** column.

Definitions of all of the registry data types defined and used in Windows NT/2000/XP as well as in Windows Server 2003 are provided in *Chapter 1*.

For the sake of convenience, the Regedit.exe utility uses special icons, which are displayed to the left of the value names. These icons allow the user to quickly distinguish between binary and text data. A brief description of the icons displayed in the **Registry Editor** window is provided in Table 3.2.

Table 3.2. Icons Used for Designating Registry Data Types in Regedit.exe

Data type	Description
	Designates binary data (including `REG_BINARY`, `REG_DWORD`, `REG_RESOURCE_LIST`, `REG_FULL_RESOURCE_DESCRIPTOR`, and `REG_RESOURCE_REQUIREMENTS_LIST`)
	Designates text data and readable characters. For example: "On The Microsoft Network" (string data types, such as `REG_EXPAND_SZ`, `REG_MULTI_SZ`, and `REG_SZ`)

The **Data** column contains text or binary data that correspond to the value of the selected registry entry. You can edit, create, or delete this data to optimize software functionality or troubleshoot.

A brief description of the Registry Editor menu items is shown below.

The File Menu Commands

The **File** menu contains the following commands:

☐ **Import** ...
☐ **Export**...
☐ **Load Hive**...

❑ **Unload Hive...**
❑ **Connect Network Registry...**
❑ **Disconnect Network Registry...**
❑ **Print...**
❑ **Exit**

The **Import...** command allows you to import previously exported registry files in ASCII or REG format.

The **Export...** command exports either the whole registry, or only a part of it, as a REG file or an ASCII file.

To export the registry branch, proceed as follows:

1. Select the registry branch you wish to export. Then select the **Export...** command from the **File** menu.

2. The **Export Registry File** window (Fig. 3.2) will open. Enter the file name in the **File name** field. By default, this file will be given the REG filename extension.

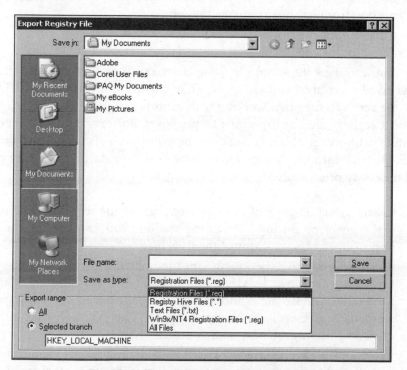

Fig. 3.2. The **Export Registry File** window

If you need to save the exported file in another format, select the option you need from the **Save as type** list below the **File name** field. Despite all of the apparent similarities between the Regedit.exe versions supplied with Windows 9*x*, Windows NT 4.0/Windows 2000, Windows XP, and Windows Server 2003, these are different versions of the same application. The Regedit.exe version included in Windows XP and Windows Server 2003 allows you to save exported registry files in various formats, including both the newer format used in Windows 2000/XP and Windows Server 2003 (use the **Registration files (*.reg)** option for this purpose) and the registry file format used by Windows 9*x* and Windows NT 4.0 (use the **Win9x/NT 4 Registration files (*.reg)** option for this purpose). Furthermore, now you can save the exported registry file as a hive (select the **Registry Hive Files** option) and in text format (use the **Text Files (*.txt)** option)

3. If you need to export only the branch that you have selected previously, set the **Selected branch** radio button in the **Export** range option group. However, if you frequently modify the system registry, exporting the whole registry would be better. Exported registry files will provide you with additional options if you need to troubleshoot a damaged system.

4. Click the **Save** button.

You can view the saved file using any text editor to make sure that everything was saved correctly. Exported registry files contain unformatted ASCII text.

Be very careful when working with exported registry files, especially when you export registry files for experimental purposes. For example, experienced administrators can solve problems by editing the exported registry file, and then importing this file back into the system. However, before you start introducing changes, take all necessary precautions:

1. Create a backup copy of the exported registry file that you need to edit. If you make an error during the editing session, you can correct the problem by importing the backup copy of the REG file.

2. If you're going to experiment with the registries of various operating systems (including Windows 9*x*/ME, Windows NT/2000, Windows XP and Windows Server 2003), store the exported registry files for each operating system in folders dedicated specifically to this purpose. This will help you avoid problems caused by importing incompatible registry files.

3. By default, REG files are associated with the Regedit.exe application (Fig. 3.3). The Regedit.exe application merges these files into the registry (**Merge** is

the operation performed by default). In contrast to its predecessors, Regedit.exe versions supplied with Windows XP and Windows Server 2003 prompt you to confirm if you really want to add the contents of an exported file to the registry (Fig. 3.4). Be very careful at this stage, in order to avoid accidentally importing incompatible or incorrect registry settings.

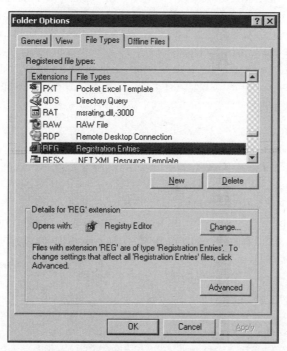

Fig. 3.3. By default, REG files are associated with the Regedit.exe application

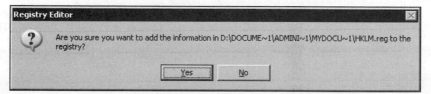

Fig. 3.4. Registry Editor prompts you to confirm that you really want to add the contents of the exported REG file to the registry

The **Load Hive...** and **Unload Hive...** commands were first introduced to Regedit.exe with the release of Windows XP and are also present in Regedit.exe version included with the products of the Windows Server 2003 family. We saw above that these represent the same functionality that was provided by the similarly named commands present in the older application, Regedt32.exe. These commands allow you to load registry files previously exported from the registry and saved in the registry hive format, or unload registry hives, respectively. Note that only those registry keys that actually represent physical hives can be saved in the registry hive format (a complete list of registry hives was provided in *Chapter 1*). Furthermore, the **Load Hive...** and **Unload Hive...** commands are only applicable to the HKEY_USERS and HKEY_LOCAL_MACHINE keys. Therefore, these commands will be available only if one of these registry keys is selected. In all other cases, the commands will be grayed and unavailable. The hive that you have loaded in the registry becomes one of the subkeys under the root keys mentioned above.

To load a registry hive, proceed as follows:

1. Select the HKEY_USERS or HKEY_LOCAL_MACHINE registry key to activate the appropriate menu command.
2. Select the **Load Hive...** command from the **File** menu. The **Load Hive** window will open, allowing you to select the previously exported registry hive. Select the required hive file and click **Open**.
3. Enter the name that will be used for the newly loaded hive (Fig. 3.5). This name will be used for the new subkey that will appear in the registry after you load the hive (Fig. 3.6). Now you are able to edit the loaded registry hive to carry out the required modifications.

▶ *Note*

In order to be allowed to carry out this procedure, you need to log on to the local system as the Administrator or a user belonging to the Administrators group. If your computer is part of a network, network security policy will also influence your ability to perform this operation.

4. Having finished the editing of the loaded registry hive, you can unload it by selecting it, and then choosing the **Unload Hive...** command from the file menu. You need to save any changes to the hive that you're going to unload, in order to restore them later.

▶ *Note*

The **Load Hive...** and **Unload Hive...** commands can be particularly useful for troubleshooting unbootable Windows installations. If you have a parallel OS installation that is bootable, you can boot into that system, load the hive from the damaged system, and edit it appropriately in order to eliminate the problem. More detailed information and step-by-step instructions for this process will be provided in *Chapters 6*, *12*, and *13*.

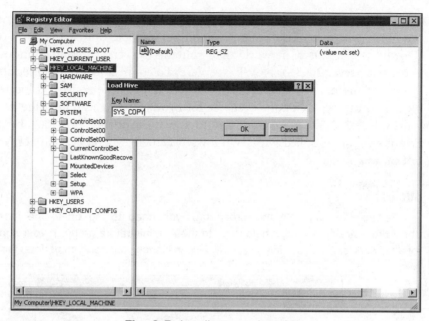

Fig. 3.5. Loading a registry hive

Fig. 3.6. The newly loaded copy of the SYSTEM hive (SYS_COPY) now appears as a nested subkey under HKEY_LOCAL_MACHINE root key

The **Connect Network Registry...** command allows you to edit the registry of a remote computer. This command will be available only if the computer running Regedit is part of a network that contains servers running Windows NT/2000, Windows Server 2003, or Novell NetWare. To connect to a remote registry, you need to specify the name of the computer where the remote registry is located (Fig. 3.7). Note that the set of options available for browsing and searching the network is significantly extended in comparison to the functionality provided by the Registry Editor version supplied with Windows NT/2000, where, actually, only the **Browse** option was available.

Note

To be able to carry out this procedure, you need to log on to the local system as the Administrator or a user belonging to the Administrators group. If your computer is part of a network, network security policy will also influence your ability to perform this operation.

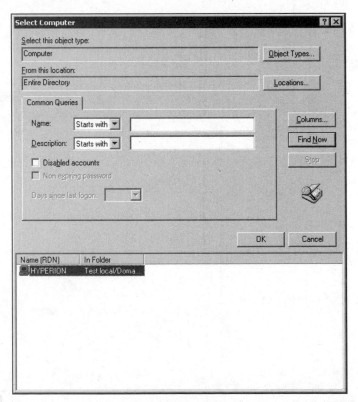

Fig. 3.7. The **Select Computer** window now provides extended browsing and searching functionality

To disconnect the remote registry, use the **Disconnect Network Registry…** command. If you are not currently part of a network, this command will be unavailable.

You can use the **Print…** command from the **File** menu to print the whole registry or only a part it. The ability to print a selected branch of the registry is a convenient alternative.

Use the **Exit** command to close the **Registry Editor** window and terminate the registry-editing session.

The Edit Menu Commands

The **Edit** menu contains commands that allow you to find and modify registry entries:

- ❐ **Modify**
- ❐ **Modify Binary Data**
- ❐ **New**
- ❐ **Permissions**
- ❐ **Delete**
- ❐ **Rename**
- ❐ **Copy Key Name**
- ❐ **Find**
- ❐ **Find Next**

The **Modify** command is used for editing data contained in the registry entries. This option will be available only if you select one of the entries displayed in the right pane of the **Registry Editor** window. **Modify Binary Data** allows you to edit any data (including other data types) in the binary-editor window. As with the previous command, this will also become available only after you select one of the registry values listed in the right pane of the registry-editor window.

The **New** command allows you to add new keys and value entries. Note that, in comparison to the Regedit.exe version supplied with Windows NT/2000, which allowed you to add only string data, binary data, and DWORD data, the newer version of Regedit.exe supplied with Windows XP and Windows Server 2003 provides an extended set of options. It also allows you to add multi-string and expandable-string data (Fig. 3.8). These options become available after selecting the **New** option. The same options will be available in the right-click menu.

▶ Note

As you certainly have noticed, even this extended functionality is rather limited, because an actual list of existing registry data types (which was provided in *Chapter 1*) is much longer.

For example, built-in registry editors don't allow you to manually create the data such as, for example, REG_QWORD, REG_RESOURCE_LIST, and so on. However, there are freeware utilities that provide such functions (for example, the REGLN tool available for downloading from **http://www.ntinternals.net** allows to create registry values of the REG_LINK data type). Of course, if you decide to use any of the tools of this type, you must do so at your own risk, because they are even more dangerous than registry editors.

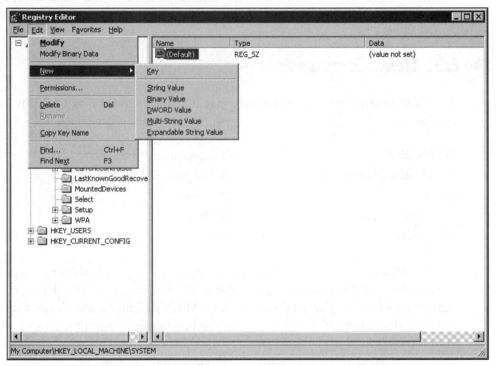

Fig. 3.8. The **New** command allows you to add new keys, string, binary, DWORD, multi-string, and expandable string values

Other options of the **Edit** menu, such as **Rename** and **Delete,** allow you to delete and rename the value entry. You can also delete the value entry by selecting it and clicking the <Del> key. To rename the value entry, right-click it, select the **Rename** command, and enter the new name.

▶ *Note*

Deletion of registry keys and value entries using the Regedit.exe utility is irreversible. Regedit.exe has no **Undo** command. Because of this, you should be very careful when deleting keys and value entries. Windows will display a warning message prompting you to confirm your intention to delete the registry entry. After you confirm it, it will be impossible to cancel the operation.

The **Copy Key Name** command allows you to copy the selected key name to the clipboard. Later, you can paste the copied key name using the **Paste** command present in any text editor. Remember that the registry is a hierarchical database and the path to the registry entry you need may be very long and difficult to memorize. Because of this, many users appreciate this feature. The **Copy Key Name** command is easy to use in combination with other commands such as **Find** and **Find Next;** you may use it for various purposes, including registry editing and inserting key names into the text.

Commands such as **Find/Find Next** are used for searching registry keys and value entries. When you select the **Find** command from the **Edit** menu, the **Find** dialog opens, allowing you to describe the key, value entry, or its data (Fig. 3.9). You can search for keys, value entries or data in any combination. The values to search for can be both text and numeric.

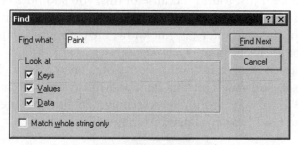

Fig. 3.9. The **Find** dialog

To find the registry entry you need, enter the value to be searched into the **Find what** field. You can also restrict the search range by selecting one of the following options listed in the **Look at** group:

❏ **Keys.** The function will only search for registry keys. Both root and nested keys will be found.

❏ **Values.** The function will only search for value names that are displayed in the right pane of the Registry Editor window (in the **Nam**e column).

❏ **Data.** The function will only search for data.

The **Find** dialog contains the **Match whole string only** option. When this option is set, Registry Editor will only find whole strings, excluding partial hits from the search range.

For example, if you've installed a number of applications with names including the "Paint" string (for example, Microsoft Paint, PaintShop Pro, etc.), Regedit.exe will find them all. However, if you only need to find entries related to Microsoft Paint, then use the **Match whole string only** option. If you need to find all the entries that contain the "Paint" string, clear the checkbox if it's set. This feature is useful if you don't remember the exact spelling of the string you're searching for, and need to find all possible variations.

Using the **Match whole string only** option increases the time required to perform the search. The amount of time can be significant if the registry is large.

To start the search procedure, fill in all the required fields in the **Find** dialog and click the **Find Next** button.

When Regedit.exe finds the matching item, it highlights it, thus helping to determine the key or subkey where the matching item resides. If Regedit.exe finds the data or value names, it will open the associated registry keys in the left pane and highlight the value name. However, it still may be difficult to determine the registry path to the item just found. Because of this, you should use the status bar, since it displays the path to the highlighted registry entry, including all parent keys and the name of the computer (as you know, the computer name won't necessarily be the name of the local system).

Now you have finally found the registry entry. But is it the entry you really need? If it is, you may edit this item and finish the search procedure; otherwise, ignore the result and continue searching. To find the next match, press <F3> or select the **Find Next** command from the **Edit** menu.

Note

When searching the registry, remember that the names of the keys and value entries may not be unique. The same name may be encountered many times. Because of this, the more information you provide for the search function, the more correct your result will be. For example, the "inbox" string is encountered about 10 times. Also, if you want to automate registry searches, consider using the Dureg.exe Resource Kit utility, which, besides estimation of the size of the whole registry or specific registry key, also provides searching capabilities. Command-line Resource Kit tools are especially useful for administrative scripting.

Finally, the **Permissions** command, allowing you to manage registry key permissions and audit the actions related to the registry keys, deserves special mention.

Once again, it is necessary to emphasize the fact that, in Windows NT/2000, this functionality was available only in Regedt32.exe, where there was the **Security** menu command. In Windows XP and Windows Server 2003, this functionality was integrated into a single version of the registry editor — the Regedit.exe utility. Registry-key permissions can be assigned independently from the file system type on the system partition.

Modifying Keys and Value Entries

Now, since we have provided a brief overview of the **Edit** menu commands, let us proceed with a more detailed discussion of their use for adding, modifying, or deleting registry keys and value entries, and for setting registry-key permissions.

Adding New Keys

To add a new key to any registry hive, select the **New | Key** commands from the **Edit** menu. The procedure is straightforward and very similar to that of creating new folders in Windows Explorer. The new key will be created without prompting the user to provide a name, but you will be able to rename the new key after it has been created.

Adding New Value Entries

To add new registry value entries, select the **New** command from the **Edit** menu, then select the appropriate command, depending on the data type of the value entry to be created. Using Windows XP or Windows Server 2003 version of Regedit.exe, you can create string-value types (REG_SZ, REG_MULTI_SZ, and REG_EXPAND_SZ) and binary values (REG_DWORD or REG_BINARY). The new value entry will be created without prompting the user to provide a name, but you'll be able to rename and edit the value after it has been created.

Using the Binary Editor

When you select the binary value (REG_BINARY data type) and then select the **Modify** command from the **Edit** menu, Regedit.exe opens the **Edit Binary Value** window (Fig. 3.10). Note that you can use the binary editor to edit a value of any type by selecting the **Modify Binary Data** command. Enter the data into the **Value data** field of the **Edit Binary Value** window.

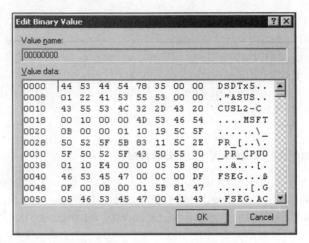

Fig. 3.10. The **Edit Binary Value** window

Editing String Values

Select the REG_SZ value in the right pane of the Registry Editor window. Then select the **Modify** command from the **Edit** menu to start the String Editor. The **Edit String** window (Fig. 3.11) allows you to edit string values.

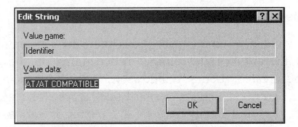

Fig. 3.11. The **Edit String** window

Editing DWORD Values

When you double-click a REG_DWORD registry value entry or highlight an entry of this type and select the **Modify** command from the **Edit** menu, the DWORD editor starts (Fig. 3.12). By default, all REG_DWORD data are displayed in hex format. However, you can also display data using decimal format by selecting the appropriate radio button from the **Base** group at the bottom of the window.

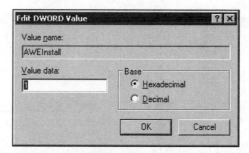

Fig. 3.12. The **Edit DWORD Value** window

Editing Multi-String Values

The **Edit Multi-String** window (Fig. 3.13) opens when you double-click the multi-string value or select a multi-string value and then choose the **Modify** command from the **Edit** menu. This window allows you to edit multi-string values.

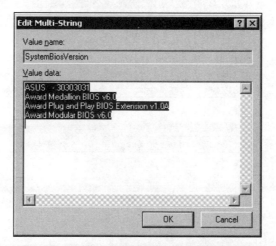

Fig. 3.13. The **Edit Multi-String** window

Viewing Resource Lists

As was already mentioned in *Chapter 1*, the system registry stores all information on the hardware installed on the computer. The registry even has special data types for this purpose, namely, REG_RESOURCE_LIST, REG_FULL_RESOURCE_DESCRIPTOR, and REG_RESOURCE_REQUIREMENTS_LIST. These data types are only used in the HKEY_LOCAL_MACHINE\HARDWARE registry key. The value entries of these types are viewed in the **Resource Lists** (Fig. 3.14) and **Resources** windows (Fig 3.15).

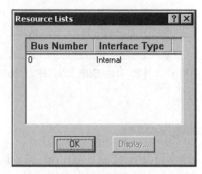

Fig. 3.14. The **Resource Lists** window

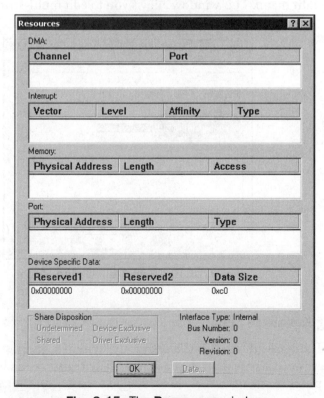

Fig. 3.15. The **Resources** window

Deleting Registry Keys and Value Entries

To delete a registry key or value entry, select the object that you wish to delete and then select the **Delete** command from the **Edit** menu. The system will prompt you to confirm your intention to delete the selected key or value entry (Fig. 3.16).

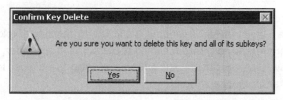

Fig. 3.16. The system prompts you to confirm your intention to delete
a registry key or value entry

 ### *Note*

Don't forget to back up the registry hives where you'll be deleting keys or value entries. Registry editors don't provide the capability to undo this operation. After having confirmed the deletion, you will have no other means of restoring the information other than the use of backup copies. As shown in Fig. 3.14, the warning message displayed by the system doesn't specify the name of the key you are about to delete. Before proceeding further, check the name of the selected key and make sure that you know what you're doing.

If you delete something from the `HKEY_LOCAL_MACHINE\System\CurrentControlSet`, you can restore this key using the **Last Known Good** configuration (see *Chapter 6*).

The View *Menu Commands*

The **View** menu contains commands that allow you to select the method of displaying the registry. It contains the following commands:

- ❑ **Status Bar**
- ❑ **Split**
- ❑ **Display Binary Data**
- ❑ **Refresh**

The **Status Bar** command in the **View** menu allows the user to hide the status bar. The status bar is useful because it helps you to navigate the registry. For this reason, I recommend that users (at least beginners) don't hide it.

The **Split** option moves the mouse cursor to the divider separating the left and right panes of the **Registry Editor** window. All you have to do is to move the mouse right or left to find a new position for the divider. After that, the only thing you need to do is to click the left (or right) mouse button.

Tip

Resizing the Registry Editor window is similar to resizing Explorer or My Computer windows. You just need to move the mouse cursor to the divider, wait until it changes to a double arrow, click the left mouse button and drag the divider left or right. When you are done, release the mouse button.

The **Display Binary Data** command from the **View** menu, which was introduced with Windows XP and is present in all products of the Windows Server 2003 family, becomes available only after you select one of the value entries listed in the right pane of the **Registry Editor** window. This command allows you to view the selected data item using one of three formats: **Byte**, **Word,** or **Dword**. Notice that it doesn't allow you to edit the data (if you need to, select the value entry and choose the **Modify Binary Data** from the **Edit** menu).

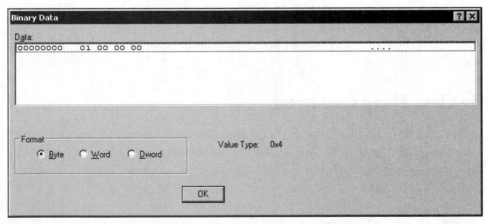

Fig. 3.17. The **Binary Data** window

Another option on the **View** menu is the **Refresh** command. Note that when you enter changes into the registry, not all of them will immediately be displayed in the **Registry Editor** window. To refresh the **Registry Editor** window, select the **Refresh** command or press <F5>.

Note

Normally, in earlier versions of Windows NT, including Windows NT 4.0, all changes introduced into the system (including the changes to the system registry) come into force only after rebooting the system. Starting with Windows 2000, full-featured Plug and Play support was integrated into the system, resulting in fewer reboots. Windows 2000, Windows XP, and products of the Windows Server 2003 family require fewer reboots than previous versions of Windows NT. However, there are certain modifications that can come into force only after rebooting the system.

The *Favorites* Menu

As has already been mentioned, each newer version of Regedit.exe comes with new, enhanced functionality. One of the most useful functions, which was first introduced with Windows 2000 and is also present in Windows XP and Windows Server 2003, is the **Favorites** menu (Fig. 3.18).

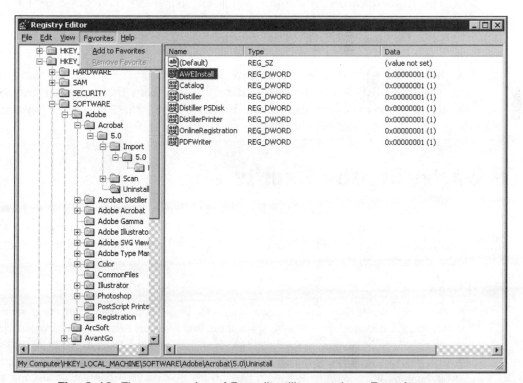

Fig. 3.18. The new version of Regedit utility contains a **Favorites** menu

Anyone who frequently searches and edits the registry will appreciate this convenient feature. Using the **Favorites** menu, you can create a list of the registry keys you edit most frequently and, thus, avoid time-consuming search procedures.

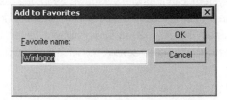

Fig. 3.19. The **Add to Favorites** dialog

To add a registry key to the **Favorites** list, proceed as follows:

1. Select the registry key that you want to add to the **Favorites** list.
2. From the **Favorites** menu, select the **Add to Favorites** command.
3. The **Add to Favorites** window will open (Fig. 3.19). You can accept the key name proposed by default, or enter a new name into the **Favorite name** field. Click **OK** to add the key to the **Favorites** list.

Now you will be able to navigate to this key by selecting its name from the **Favorites** list. If you need to delete the key from the **Favorites** list, select the **Remove Favorite** command from the **Favorites** menu. Select the key you need to delete from this list and click **OK**.

Managing Registry Security

To manage registry security, the Regedit.exe version supplied with Windows XP and products of the Windows Server 2003 family includes the **Permissions** command. Using this command, you can edit registry-key permissions and set the rules for auditing registry-key access.

Note

It should be noted that, in Windows NT/2000, these capabilities were only available in Regedt32.exe. As you remember, Regedt32.exe had a special **Security** menu, which allowed you to specify registry-key permissions and establish auditing rules. Beginning with Windows XP, this functionality was delegated to Regedit.exe. Note that registry key permissions can be set independently from the file-system type on the disk partition containing the operating-system files.

This chapter provides only a brief overview of these functions and general instructions for performing operations needed to protect the registry.

More detailed information on these topics will be provided in *Chapter 9*, which is dedicated to registry protection.

As in previous Windows NT/2000 versions, Windows XP and products of the Windows Server 2003 family possess the following capabilities for protecting the system and managing security:

❑ All access to system resources can be controlled.

❑ All operations that access system objects can be registered in the security log.

❑ A password is required for accessing the system, and all access operations can be logged.

Setting Registry-Key Permissions

The **Permissions** command opens the **Permissions for the** <*Keyname*> window intended for viewing and setting registry-key permissions. The capability to set registry key permissions doesn't depend on the file system used to format the partition that contains the operating-system files.

Note

Changing registry-key permissions can lead to serious consequences. For example, if you set the **No Access** permission for the key required for configuring network settings using the Control Panel applet, this applet won't work. **Full Control** permissions for the registry should be assigned to the members of the Administrators group and the operating system itself. This setting provides the system administrator with the ability to restore the registry key after rebooting the system.

Since setting registry-key permissions can lead to serious consequences, reserve this measure for the keys added in order to optimize software, or other examples of customizing the system.

Note

If you change permissions for the registry key, it is best also to audit the key access (or, at least, to audit the failed attempts at accessing this key). A brief overview of registry auditing will be provided later in this chapter.

The **Permissions** command follows the principles used by the Explorer commands to set file and folder permissions on NTFS partitions. To set registry-key permissions, proceed as follows:

1. Before modifying registry-key permissions, back up the registry keys you are going to modify.
2. Select the key for which you are going to set permissions, and then select the **Permissions** command.

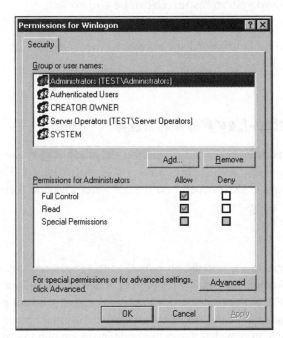

Fig. 3.20. The **Permissions for <*Keyname*>** window allows you to specify registry-key permissions

3. The **Permissions for <*Keyname*>** window, allowing you to specify registry-key permissions (Fig. 3.20) will open. Windows XP and Windows Server 2003 provide many enhancements, including security enhancements. However, the main types of access permissions and basic principles for setting these permissions are similar to the ones found in previous versions of Windows NT/2000. Select the name of the user or group from the list at the top of this window, and then set the required access level by selecting the option you need from the **Permissions for <*Username*>** list provided below. Brief

descriptions of the available access types (**Read, Full Control,** and **Special Permissions**) are listed in Table 3.3. To set permissions for a selected registry key, proceed as follows:

- From the list at the top of this window, select the user or group for which you need to set registry-key permissions. If the user or group should have read capabilities, but not those to modify the key, set the **Allow** checkbox next to the **Read** option.

- If the user or group should be able to open the selected registry key for editing ownership, set the **Allow** checkbox next to the **Full Control** option.

- To assign the user or group a special combination of permissions (special permissions), click the **Advanced** button.

Table 3.3. Registry-Key Permission Types

Permission type	Description
Read	Users who have permission to access this key can view its contents, but can't save any changes.
Full Control	Users who have permission to access this key can open the key to edit its contents, save the changes, and modify access levels for the key.
Special Permissions	Users who have permission to access this key have individual combinations of access rights for the selected key. A detailed description of all these types and their combinations will be provided later in this chapter.

4. Set the system audit for registry access (more detailed information on this topic will be provided later in this chapter). Audit the system carefully over a period of time to make sure that new access rights have no negative influence on the applications installed in your system.

Specifying Advanced Security Settings

To set special access types for a registry key, click the **Advanced** button in the registry-key permissions dialog (see Fig. 3.20). The **Advanced Security Settings for** *<Keyname>* window will open (Fig. 3.21).

If you are setting permissions for the registry subkey and want this subkey to inherit permissions from its parent key, set the **Allow inheritable permissions from parent to propagate to this object and all child objects...** checkbox.

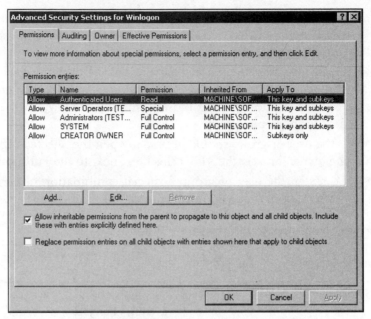

Fig. 3.21. The **Permissions** tab in the **Advanced Security Settings for <Keyname>** window

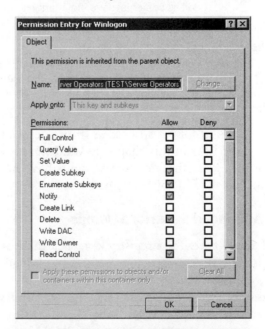

Fig. 3.22. The **Permission Entry** window

If you are setting permissions for the parent key and want all of its subkeys to inherit the permission from the selected key, set the **Replace permission entries on all child objects...** checkbox.

Double-click the name of the user or group for which you need to set special access (or select the name and click the **Edit** button). The dialog shown in Fig. 3.22 will appear. In the **Permissions** list, select **Allow** or **Deny** checkboxes next to the type of access that you need to allow or deny for the selected user or group. The list of special-access options is provided in Table 3.4. Note that the list doesn't differ from the similar list in Windows NT 4.0 and Windows 2000.

Table 3.4. The Special Access Options

Checkbox	Description
Query Value	Allows the user to read values within the selected registry key
Set Value	Allows the user to set values within the selected registry key
Create Subkey	Allows the user to create subkeys within the selected registry key
Enumerate Subkeys	Allows the user to identify the subkeys within the selected registry key
Notify	Allows the user to audit this key
Create Link	Allows the user to create symbolic links in the selected registry key
Delete	Allows the user to delete the selected registry key
Write DAC	Allows the user to access the key and create or modify its Access Control List (ACL)
Write Owner	Allows the user to take ownership of this registry key
Read Control	Allows the user to view the security parameters set for the selected registry key

Taking Registry Key Ownership

As a system administrator, you may take ownership of any registry key and restrict access to this key. Anyone who has logged in to the local system as a member of the Administrators group may take ownership of any registry key. However, if you have owner rights without full control access type, you won't be able to return this key to its initial owner at a later time and the appropriate message will appear in the security log.

To take ownership of the registry key in Windows XP or any product of the Windows Server 2003 family, proceed as follows:

1. Select the registry key for which you wish to take ownership.
2. Select the **Permissions** command from the **Edit** menu.
3. Click the **Advanced** button. The **Advanced Security Settings for** <*Keyname*> window will open. Go to the **Owner** tab (Fig. 3.23).
4. Select the new owner from the **Change owner to** list and click **OK**.

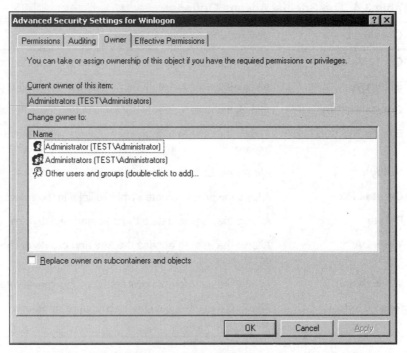

Fig. 3.23. The **Owner** tab of the **Advanced Security Settings for** <*Keyname*> window

 Note

If you need to change the owner for all nested objects of this key as well, set the **Replace owner on subcontainers and objects** checkbox. You can change the registry-key owner only if you log in as an Administrator (or a member of the Administrators group), or if the previous owner has explicitly assigned you owner rights for this key.

Registry Auditing

Auditing is the process used by Windows NT-based operating systems, including Windows 2000/XP and products of the Windows Server 2003 family, for detecting and logging security-related events. For example, any attempt to create or delete system objects or any attempt to access these objects are security-related events. Note that, in object-oriented operating systems, anything is considered an object, including files, folders, and registry keys. All security-related events are registered in the security-log file. Auditing is not activated in the system by default. So, if you need to audit security-related events, you will need to activate the audit. After the system audit has been activated, the operating system starts logging security-related events. You can view information registered in the security log using Event Viewer. When initiating auditing, you can specify the types of events to be registered in the security log, and the operating system will create a record each time the specified event type occurs in the system. The record written to the security log contains an event description, the name of the user who performed the action corresponding to the event, and the event date/time information. You can audit successful and failed attempts, and the security log will display both the names of the users who performed successful attempts and the names of the users whose attempts failed.

Detailed information on this topic and tips on auditing registry access are provided in *Chapter 9*, which is dedicated to registry protection.

To establish registry auditing, proceed as follows:

1. Activate the audit and set the audit policy for each event that requires auditing.
2. Specify users and groups whose access to the specified registry keys you wish to be audited.
3. Use the Event Viewer for viewing the audit results in the Security log.

To perform any of the actions mentioned above, you need to log in to the local system as a member of the Administrators group. The audit policy is specified individually for each computer. Before you can set the registry-auditing policy, you need to activate the audit in the system. Regedit.exe will display an error message if you attempt to set registry auditing without activating the audit in the system.

To set the auditing options for the registry, proceed as follows:

1. Select the key that you wish to audit.
2. Select the **Permissions** command from the **Edit** menu, and then click the **Advanced** button. The **Advanced Security Settings for** *<Keyname>* window will open. Go to the **Auditing** tab (Fig. 3.24).

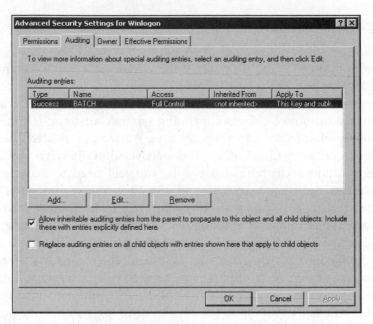

Fig. 3.24. The **Auditing** tab of the **Advanced Security Settings for <*Keyname*>** window

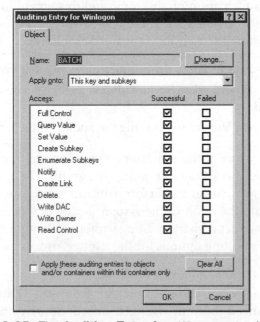

Fig. 3.25. The **Auditing Entry for <*Keyname*>** window

3. If you are setting the auditing options for this key for the first time, the **Auditing Entries** list will be blank. Click the **Add** button below this list, select the users and groups whose activity you need to audit, and add them to the list.

4. To audit the activity of a certain user or group, select the name of this user/group from the **Auditing Entries** list, and click the **Edit** button. The dialog shown in Fig. 3.25 will appear. In the **Access** list, set the **Successful** and/or **Failed** checkboxes for the access types that require auditing.

The auditing options available to you are described in Table 3.5. Note that the set of options hasn't changed from that in Windows NT/2000.

Table 3.5. Auditing Option Types for Registry Keys

Auditing option	Description
Query Value	Accessing the key with the right to query the value.
Set Value	Opening the key with the right to set the value.
Create Subkey	Opening the key with the right to create subkeys.
Enumerate Subkeys	Opening the key with the right to enumerate its subkeys. This option controls events that open the keys and attempts to get a list of the subkeys contained within the key being opened.
Notify	Accessing the key with the right to notify.
Create Link	Opening the key with the right of creating symbolic links within this key.
Delete	Deleting the key.
Write DAC	Attempts to modify the list of users who have access to this key.
Read Control	Reading owner-related information on this key.

Note

To set registry-key auditing, you need to log in to the local system as an Administrator or a member of the Administrators group. If the local computer is connected to the network, then network-security policy may prevent you from auditing the registry keys.

To view the auditing results, select the **Programs | Administrative Tools | Computer Management** commands from the **Start** menu. Expand the console tree in the left pane of the MMC window by selecting the **System Tools | Event Viewer | Security Log** options. The right pane will display a list of security-related events.

Viewing this list is similar to viewing the security log in Windows NT 4.0 and Windows 2000.

Options included in other menus, such as **Window** and **Help**, are standard for most Windows applications.

Summary

This chapter concentrated on the new version of the registry editor supplied with Windows XP and products of the Windows Server 2003 family and its use in modifying, viewing, importing, exporting, and printing the registry. Basic knowledge of this material allows you to simplify the troubleshooting process. However, always remember that improper use of registry-editing tools can lead to the introduction of errors directly into the registry. Use these tools carefully and at your own risk. If you are going to introduce any changes, remember the initial values. This will save you time later on if you need to restore the damaged system.

CHAPTER 4

Customizing the System with the Registry

Can the Ethiopian change his skin
or the Leopard his spots?

R. Kipling
How the Leopard Got His Spots

Now and then, you will hear the question: "Can a Leopard change his spots?" This epigraph, taken from the story by Rudyard Kipling, describes how one Leopard and an Ethiopian once managed to do just this very thing. This is a fable, of course, and all the events described in the tale took place "In the beginning of years, when the world was so new". Many things didn't even have their proper names yet, so in order to point something out, you needed to put a finger on it.

Windows NT/2000/XP and products of the Windows Server 2003 family are also very new, especially in comparison to the characters in Kipling's fable. Immediately after their final release, though, the entire user community began discussing the problems associated with optimizing and customizing these operating systems. Some methods of customization were obvious, but others weren't immediately evident (not to say, of course, that they aren't possible). Both the Internet and in many books available today, you can find a large number of tips on how to customize

Windows by editing the registry. However, before launching directly into editing the registry, it is always best to try to use the Control Panel applets and administrative tools first (in most cases, this approach is much safer and easier than registry editing). In any event, my goal is to point this out and even "put my finger on it".

As was mentioned above, most tasks related to configuring Windows NT/2000/XP and products of the Windows Server 2003 family can be carried out using Control Panel applets and administrative tools. However, some such tasks can only be completed by editing the system registry directly. This chapter describes various methods of customizing, fine-tuning, and troubleshooting Windows NT/2000/XP and Windows Server 2003. At the same time, this chapter should not be considered to be an exhaustive reference tool for Windows customization. Many other methods of modifying the registry will be discussed later in this book, in chapters dedicated to specific aspects of customization and troubleshooting the system.

Preparing to Edit the Registry

Even though this book is dedicated to the topic of registry editing, remember that an incorrect modification or the accidental deletion of an element of the registry element can result in rendering your system unbootable. Before you start editing the registry, pay close heed to the following recommendations:

❑ Microsoft doesn't provide any official support for users who want to solve their own problems by editing the registry. However, you can get additional information, and even some advice, by subscribing to Microsoft technical-support services.

❑ Modify the registry only when you know that all of the information related to the registry keys, values, and the restrictions for devices and applications that you intend to troubleshoot is correct.

❑ Start editing the registry only once all attempts to set or modify a certain function using the Control Panel applets or administrative utilities have failed. Note that using the Device Manager is the best way to modify hardware settings, since this tool won't let you delete any of the required registry keys or make other critical errors. Registry editors don't safeguard you against this type of mistake.

❑ When you start the registry editors, remember that these tools are incapable of undoing or redoing your actions. Any changes that you make will be saved automatically (and almost immediately). If you make an error, the only method of quickly undoing a change is to import the previously created registry file before rebooting the system.

> ► *Tip*
>
> Never introduce a large number of changes at once. Always try to introduce only one modification per registry-editing session and reboot the system when you're done. This will allow you to test the changes you've made. If you have made a number of changes during a single registry-editing session and, as a result, your system becomes unbootable, it will be difficult to identify which of the modifications is causing the problem. When you are sure that the modification to the registry is appropriate, you may then proceed with further changes. Don't forget to back up the registry on a regular basis. The frequency of the backup depends on the frequency of registry modifications (and on the tool used to edit the registry). Generally speaking, you should back up your registry at least once a week. If you edit the registry every day, create a backup copy at the end of each working day. It is also recommended to maintain the most recent backup copies of the files containing group policies, INF files, and system-policy templates.

More detailed information on registry backup and recovery procedures is provided in *Chapter 2*.

Before going any further, read *Chapter 2* carefully and make sure that you haven't skipped anything.

> ► *Tip*
>
> Before you edit the registry to make any of the changes described in this chapter, read the appropriate section carefully. You will to decide whether or not you (or the user whose computer you're going to configure) really need this customization and, if so, just how much you (or the other user) need it. The customizations described in this chapter will change the default settings of the operating system. Note that these default settings are satisfactory for most users. Before going any further, export the registry keys that you're going to modify. This will allow you restore the keys if you make an unnecessary change accidentally, or if you are unhappy with the effect of the modifications.

Customizing the Boot Sequence and System-Behavior Parameters

Most Windows operating systems automatically configure the default boot sequence. However, there are many users who may need to modify this. For example, if you have a multi-boot system, you may need to change the default operating system. Sometimes you may need to increase the default interval when the boot menu is displayed, add custom logo files and so forth. Here, we'll discuss some methods for customizing the boot sequence. These methods aren't complicated, and any system administrator, support specialist, or advanced user should be familiar with them.

A detailed description of all of the processes that take place when Windows NT-based systems, including Windows 2000/XP and products of the Windows Server 2003 family are booting, is provided in *Chapter 6*. You will also find information on the role of the system registry in the boot process there.

To customize the boot sequence of any Windows NT-based system, you simply need to edit a single INI file: Boot.ini. This file, which is necessary for the OS to boot, resides in the root directory of the system partition. Because of this, it has the Hidden, System, and Read-only attributes set. This means that Windows Explorer does not display this file by default.

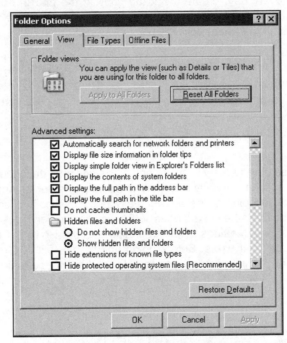

Fig. 4.1. The **View** tab of the **Folder Options** window

To be able to view this and other protected files protected files using Windows Explorer, log in to the local system as an Administrator. Start the Folder Options applet in Control Panel or select the **Folder Options** command from the **Tools** menu in Windows Explorer or My Computer. The dialog shown in Fig. 4.1 will open. Go to the **View** tab, and then go the **Advanced Settings** field. Select the **Show hidden files and folders** option and clear the **Hide protected operating system files (Recommended)** checkbox.

Modifying the Boot Sequence and System Behavior via the User Interface

If you are an experienced Windows NT/2000 administrator, you are already accustomed to the Boot.ini file format and can edit it manually using any text editor. More detailed information on the Boot.ini file format will be provided later in this chapter. For an advanced user, manual editing of this file won't be difficult. However, for a beginner, the easiest method of editing this file is to use the **System** applet located in **Control Panel**. This option allows you to specify the time interval for which the boot loader will display the boot menu, thus allowing you to select the operating system (for multi-boot systems). This option also allows you to specify the default operating system that will be loaded when this interval expires and you haven't selected an option from the boot menu. To configure these options in Windows NT 4.0, start the System applet from Control Panel, go to the **Startup/Shutdown** tab, and set the options you need using the **System Startup** option group.

 Note

Starting with Windows 2000, this capability has undergone significant changes. Windows XP and Windows Server 2003 introduce further enhancements. Let us consider these new features in more detail.

Configuring the Error Reporting Service

To modify system behavior and the boot sequence, open the **Control Panel** window and double-click on the **System** icon. The **System Properties** window will open. Go to the **Advanced** tab (Fig. 4.2).

A careful look at the **Advanced** tab of the **System Properties** window in Windows XP/Windows Server 2003 reveals a particular enhancement that was first introduced with Windows XP — the so-called *Error Reporting Options* (notice the **Error Reporting** button located directly below the **Startup and Recovery** option group). The error reporting function was designed by Microsoft in order to encourage users to help developers improve future versions of the operating system. Any time an error occurs, Windows XP/Windows Server 2003 displays a dialog prompting the user to let the OS automatically generate an error report and send it to Microsoft (Fig. 4.3).

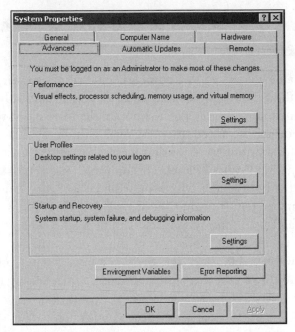

Fig. 4.2. The **Advanced** tab of the **System Properties** window

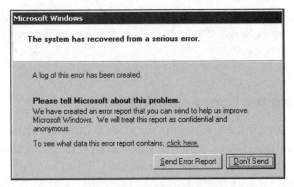

Fig. 4.3. A dialog prompting the user to create an error report
and send it to Microsoft

This option is enabled by default, but if you want to customize its settings or disable the feature entirely, click the **Error Reporting** button. The **Error Reporting** window will appear (Fig. 4.4). In this window, you can specify the following options:

❑ Totally disable the Error Reporting service by selecting the **Disable error reporting** radio button. Notice that, even if you disable the Error Reporting service altogether, you can still enable an option that allows the service to inform you of serious errors (such as STOP errors, also known as Blue Screens of Death). To do this, select the **But notify me when critical errors occur** checkbox directly below the **Disable error reporting** radio button.

❑ Enable the Error Reporting service by selecting the **Enable error reporting** option. In this case, you can configure the service by specifying the types of errors about which the service must inform you. For example, if the **Windows operating system** checkbox is set, the service will report any problems with the Windows components running in kernel mode. To enable the reporting of errors for add-on programs, select the **Programs** checkbox. To further customize the program list, click the **Choose Programs** button to open the **Choose Programs** window (Fig. 4.5). In this window, you can change the default reporting mode by creating a custom lists of programs to be included in or excluded from error reporting.

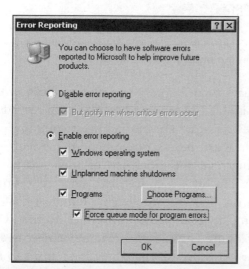

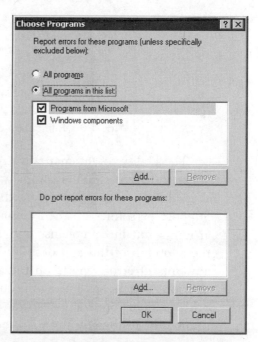

Fig. 4.4. The **Error Reporting** window (Windows Server 2003)

Fig. 4.5. The **Choose Programs** window

 Note

In comparison to Windows XP, the Error Reporting service in Windows Server 2003 has been enhanced further and provided with additional capabilities. For example, you can now report unplanned server shutdowns by selecting the **Unplanned machine shutdowns** option (see Figs. 4.4 and 4.6). Note also the **Force queue mode for program errors** checkbox, which was also newly introduced with Windows Server 2003. When this option is selected, the Error Reporting service will queue error messages. This option is particularly useful when multiple persistent application errors occur. In this instance, the service will display a notification of the 10 most recent errors when a user with administrative rights logs on to the system. Each error notification will be displayed in a separate window, thus providing the administrator with the opportunity to choose the appropriate steps to be taken.

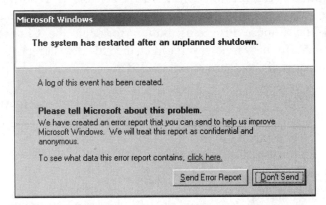

Fig. 4.6. Notification on the unplanned system shutdown

The ability to automatically create reports on system and application errors is particularly useful. If a company is able to keep and organize such records, it is then able to focus its efforts on the areas that are causing most common errors. Support personnel are then be able make necessary corrections, develop workarounds for the problems, and improve the efficiency of their work. Thus, the adoption of this approach by Microsoft is well justified, since collecting vast amounts of error reports on the areas that are problematic for most customers provides a database allowing the company to improve its products further. On the other hand, if your company is developing software or providing services to a large number of customers, it can also benefit from this by redirecting reports to a specially dedicated shared folder in your corporate network. Furthermore, as real-world experience has shown, not every organization is willing to support extra communication between their client systems and the outside world. Thus, the most effective approach for a corporate IT department is to use the error reporting feature to their advantage by redirecting automatically generated error reports to a corporate file share.

There are two ways of accomplish this: by configuring Group Policy and by editing the registry. To redirect error reports to a corporate share using Group Policy, proceed as follows:

1. On systems participating in workgroups, open the **Control Panel** window, double-click on the **Administrative Tools** icon, then open the Local Security Policy snap-in. To control systems attached to domains, start the Default Domain Security Policy MMC snap-in for the same purpose.

▶ *Note*

Remember that when a Group Policy setting conflicts with a local setting, Group Policy overrides local settings. Furthermore, in all cases, settings established using the MMC snap-in override Control Panel settings. The settings made in Control Panel apply only if no Group Policy is configured. Besides this, many additional settings are available when configuring error reporting via Group Policy. More detailed information on Group Policy will be provided in *Chapters 10* and *11*.

2. After opening Group Policy object, expand the console tree as shown in Fig. 4.7 (**Computer Configuration | Administrative Templates | System | Error Reporting**). Three items will be available to you: **Report Errors, Display Error Notification**, and a folder – **Advanced Error Reporting Settings**.

3. Double-click on the **Report Errors** item and select the **Enabled** radio button in the **Report Errors Properties** window. After you do this, several additional options will become available, among which is the one that you need to configure – namely, the **Corporate upload file path** text field. To change the error-report destination, specify a path to the new location using the UNC format, for example: \\myserver\myshare\my_dir. Note that the settings specified using Group Policy will be stored in the registry under the HKEY_CURRENT_USER\Software\Microsoft\ Windows\CurrentVersion\Group Policy Objects\Test.local{6AC1786C-016F- 11D2-945F-00C04fB984F9}Machine\Software\Policies\Microsoft\PCHealth\ ErrorReporting\DW key (Fig. 4.8).

To perform the same task by editing the system registry and, at the same time, enforce these settings for all users who log on in the local system, do the following:

1. Start Regedit.exe and expand the HKEY_LOCAL_MACHINE\SOFTWARE\Microsoft\PCHealth\ ErrorReporting key (Fig. 4.9). If this key doesn't contain the nested DW key, create it.

2. Create a REG_DWORD value named DWNoSecondLevelCollection, and set it to 0. Then create a string value named DWFileTreeRoot. To change the error-report destination, specify a path to the new location. For example, \\myserver\myshare\my_dir.

3. Click **OK** and close the Registry Editor.

4. To restore the original configuration and send reports directly to Microsoft, delete the DWFileTreeRoot entry.

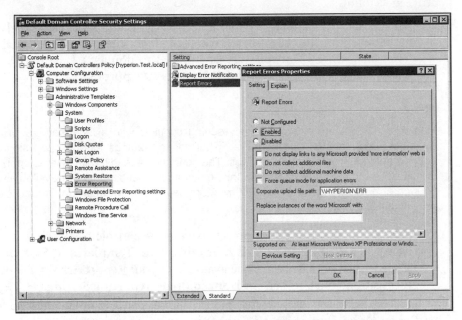

Fig. 4.7. Redirecting error reports using Group Policy

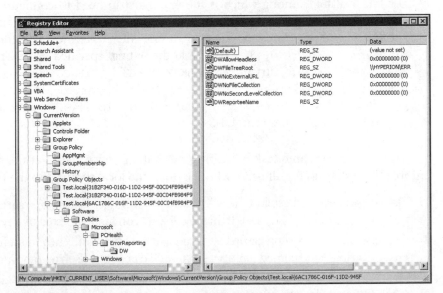

Fig. 4.8. Settings specified using Group Policy are saved in the registry

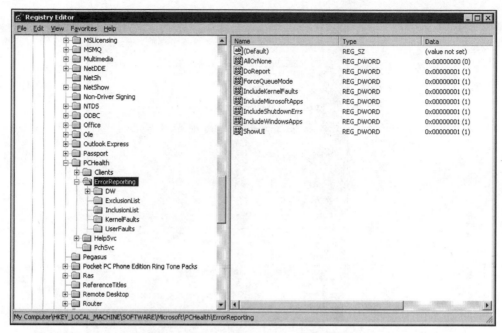

Fig. 4.9. The contents of the HKEY_LOCAL_MACHINE\SOFTWARE\Microsoft\ PCHealth\ErrorReporting registry key

Modifying the Boot Sequence

To set the boot and system behavior parameters, click the **Settings** button in the **Startup and Recovery** option group at the **Advanced** tab of the **System Properties** window. The **Startup and Recovery** window will open (Fig. 4.10).

At the top of this window is the **System startup** option group, which allows you to specify the default operating system and set the time interval during which the system will display the boot menu.

Note

In Windows 2000, the **System startup** options are the same as those in Windows NT 4.0, but Windows XP and Windows Server 2003 provide a very convenient enhancement — the **System startup** group now provides the option to edit the Boot.ini file manually. To do so, simply click the **Edit** button (Fig. 4.10). Besides this, Windows XP and Windows Server 2003 include the new Bootcfg.exe command-line utility that allows to manipulate the Boot.ini file from the command line.

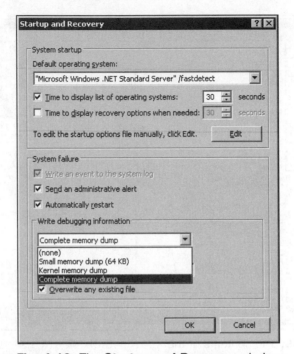

Fig. 4.10. The **Startup and Recovery** window

The most interesting option group is **System Failure**, which allows you to specify system behavior in case a STOP error occurs (these errors are also known as kernel errors or "blue screens"). Let's look at these options in more detail.

If you need to identify a problem and discover its cause, you shouldn't overlook the system log. Because of this, it is recommended that you select the **Write an event to the system log** checkbox. If this option is enabled, the system will register an event in the system log any time a STOP error occurs. An example of what this record will look like is shown below:

```
Event ID: 1001 Source: Save Dump Description: The computer has
rebooted from a bugcheck. The bugcheck was : 0xc000021a (0xe1270188,
0x00000001, 0x00000000, 0x00000000). Microsoft Windows NT (v15.1381).
A dump was saved in: C:\WINNT\MEMORY.DMP.
```

If you select the **Send an administrative alert** checkbox, the system will send an administrative alert to the network administrator's workstation any time a STOP error occurs.

Finally, if you need to get the computer up and running as soon as possible, you can configure it to reboot automatically whenever a STOP error occurs. To enable this option, select the **Automatically restart** checkbox.

Note

The following tip explains how to edit the Windows NT/2000/XP and Windows Server 2003 registry to make the system reboot automatically when a STOP error occurs. Open the system registry using Regedit.exe, expand the `HKEY_LOCAL_MACHINE\SYSTEM\CurrentControlSet\Control\CrashControl\` key, and set the `Autoreboot` value to 1. Theoretically, this tip is accurate, but there is a much easier way to do this. Just select the **Automatically reboot** checkbox in the **Startup and Recovery** window.

If STOP errors persist, you need to find out what's causing them. The best way to do this is to analyze the memory dump. To instruct the system to create a memory dump when a STOP error occurs, use the **Write Debugging Information** option. To specify the name of the file in which to store the debugging information, fill in the **Dump File** field. If you need to overwrite the contents of this file when the memory dump is created, select the **Overwrite any existing file** checkbox. Note that these options haven't changed since the release of Windows NT 4.0.

Starting with Windows 2000, Microsoft introduced an extended function for saving the memory dump. If you are an experienced Windows NT user, you will remember that Windows NT 4.0 dumps the entire contents of the physical memory. The size of the memory-dump file generated by this system is slightly larger than the amount of physical memory that is present on the computer. Since STOP errors initiate in the system kernel, the kernel data (for example, the state of a system at the time of a crash, including what applications were active, what device drivers were loaded, and what code was being executed) are of interest to the support specialists analyzing the dump. User-mode data aren't useful for determining the cause of a crash. They just contribute to the size of a crash dump file.

Because of this, starting with Windows 2000, the developers introduced a new option in the **Startup and Recovery** window. This option provides you with some control over the size of the crash dump. The first combobox from the **Write Debugging Information** option group allows you to select the mode used for saving the crash dump. Beside the ability to save the complete dump (this option is similar to the one existing in Windows NT 4.0), Windows 2000/XP and Windows Server 2003 provide a **Kernel Memory Dump** option that allows you to exclude application (user-mode) data. Only kernel information will be stored in the crash dump. All crash-analysis tools compatible with newer Windows versions, including Dumpexam and WinDbg, will interpret this file correctly. This option allows you to save disk space (the amount will be different for each system; it will also depend on the type of crash). My own experience has shown that, on computers with 128 MB of RAM, a complete crash dump will consume about 128 MB (actually, a little more); while a kernel dump will only consume about 40 MB.

Note

Starting with Windows XP, this function was enhanced even further by providing an additional option — namely, the **Small Memory Dump**, which allows you to limit the dump to 64 KB (see Fig. 4.10). Note that when a STOP error occurs, Windows XP and Windows Server 2003 always create a small memory dump. Thus, the Error Reporting service considered above is always capable of creating a report on the problem on the basis of this dump file, even if you have configured the system in such a way as to create kernel, or even a complete memory dump.

Editing the Boot.ini File Manually

As has already been mentioned, Windows XP and Windows Server 2003 provide a very convenient way of editing the Boot.ini file. However, if you are working with Windows NT/2000 or you still want to use a text editor of your choice to open the Boot.ini file for editing, clear the Read-Only attribute. This is necessary to save your changes.

To do this, run the following command from the command line:

```
attrib -r boot.ini
```

Boot.ini File Format

The Boot.ini file is created automatically by the Setup program during the installation of the operating system. This file is located in the root directory of the system partition and is needed by the boot loader in order to display the boot menu (the screen that allows the user to select the operating system).

A typical example of the Boot.ini file is shown below:

```
[Boot Loader]
Timeout=5
Default=multi(0)disk(0)rdisk(0)partition(2)\WINXP
[Operating Systems]
multi(0)disk(0)rdisk(0)partition(2)\WINXP="Microsoft Windows XP
Professional" /fastdetect
multi(0)disk(0)rdisk(0)partition(3)\WINNT="Microsoft Windows 2000
Professional" /fastdetect /noguiboot
multi(0)disk(0)rdisk(0)partition(7)\XPRC1="Microsoft Windows XP
Professional" /fastdetect
multi(0)disk(0)rdisk(0)partition(9)\WINDOWS="Microsoft Windows
2002 Server (Tchek)" /fastdetect
multi(0)disk(0)rdisk(0)partition(8)\WINDOWS="Microsoft Windows XP
Home Edition (RC2 Tchek)" /fastdetect
```

```
multi(0)disk(0)rdisk(0)partition(1)\WINDOWS="Microsoft Windows
Whistler Professional" /fastdetect /sos
C:\CMDCONS\BOOTSECT.DAT="Microsoft Windows Recovery Console"
/cmdcons
C:\="Microsoft Windows" C:\="Microsoft Windows"
```

The Boot.ini file contains two sections: `[boot loader]` and `[operating systems]`. Both of these sections are described below.

The *[boot loader]* Section

The parameters contained in this section are described in Table 4.1.

Table 4.1. [boot loader] Section Parameters

Parameter	Description
Timeout	The number of seconds the boot loader provides for the user to select an operating system from the boot menu displayed on the screen. If the time interval expires and the user hasn't yet chosen an operating system, Ntldr will start loading the default operating system. If this value is set to 0, the boot loader starts loading the default operating system immediately without displaying the boot loader screen, which prevents the user from making a choice. If this value is set to −1, the boot loader will wait until the user selects an operating system. Note that you must edit the Boot.ini file to set this value, since the **System** option in the **Control Panel** interprets it as invalid.
Default	The path to the default operating system.

Note

The startup menu does not appear if Windows XP or Windows Server 2003 is the only system installed on your computer. In this case, Ntldr ignores the time-out value and starts Windows immediately.

The *[operating systems]* Section

This section contains the list of available operating systems. Each record contained in this section specifies the path to the boot partition of the operating system, the string displayed in the boot loader screen, and optional parameters.

The Boot.ini file supports the capability of loading multiple Windows NT/2000/XP or Windows Server 2003 installations, as well as starting other operating systems, including Windows 9*x*, MS-DOS, OS/2, LINUX, and UNIX.

The entries contained in the `[operating systems]` section of the Boot.ini file support several optional switches, which are described in Table 4.2. Note that these switches aren't case-sensitive. Switches that were introduced with Windows 2000 (Win2K) are marked with an asterisk (*).

Table 4.2. Boot.ini Switches

Switch	Description
/BASEVIDEO	This switch causes Windows to load using a standard VGA driver. If you have installed a new video driver that isn't working correctly, this switch will allow you to start the computer so that you can change the video driver.
/BAUDRATE	This switch enables kernel-mode debugging (it also sets the /DEBUG parameter) and specifies the baud rate to be used for this purpose. If you don't set the baud rate, a default value will be used. If a modem is attached, the default baud rate is 9,600 (for a null-modem cable, the default baud rate is 19,200).
/BOOTLOG*	If this switch is specified, Windows will write the boot-process log into the *%SystemRoot%*\NTBTLOG.TXT file. This log will enable you to find out which drivers were loaded successfully and which weren't.
/CRASHDEBUG	If you include this switch, the kernel debugger is loaded when the system boots, but remains inactive unless a crash occurs. This allows the specified COM port (or COM1 by default) to remain available for other uses while the system is running. This switch is especially useful if your system is subject to random STOP errors.
/DEBUG	Enables kernel-mode debugging. The debugger is loaded when the system boots and can be activated at any time by a host debugger that is connected to the computer. This mode is recommended when STOP errors are persistent and reproducible.
/DEBUGPORT=comx	Enables kernel-mode debugging and specifies an override for the default serial port (COM1) to which the remote debugger is connected. For example: /DEBUGPORT=COM2.
/FASTDETECT*	This switch is new in Windows 2000. When you dual boot NT 4.0 and Windows 2000 or later, the newer version of NTDETECT.COM is used during the boot process. In Windows 2000/XP and Windows Server 2003, the detection of parallel and serial devices is carried out by plug-and-play device drivers. Windows NT 4.0, however, expects NTDETECT to carry out the detection. Specifying FASTDETECT causes NTDETECT to skip parallel and serial device enumeration for a boot into Windows 2000/XP or Windows Server 2003, while omitting the switch directs NTDETECT to perform enumeration for a boot into Windows NT 4.0. Windows Setup program automatically recognizes dual-boot configurations and sets this switch for BOOT.INI lines that specify a boot or a newer Windows version.

continues

Table 4.2 Continued

Switch	Description
/MAXMEM	This option will limit Windows to using only the amount of memory that you specify. The number value represents the number of MBs. For example: /MAXMEM=16 would limit NT to using 16MB of the system's memory. This option is useful if you suspect that a memory chip is bad.
/NODEBUG	Prevents kernel-mode debugging from being initialized. Overrides the specification of any of the three debug-related switches, /DEBUG, /DEBUGPORT, and /BAUDRATE.
/NOGUIBOOT*	This switch is new in Windows 2000. When this option is selected, the VGA video driver that is responsible for presenting bitmapped graphics during Win2K's boot process isn't initialized. The driver is used to display boot-progress information, as well as to print the Blue Screen crash screen. Disabling it will disable Win2K's ability to do those things as well.
/NOSERIALMICE= [COMx,y,z,...]	Disables serial mouse detection of the specified COM port(s). Use this switch if you have a component other than a mouse attached to a serial port during the startup sequence. If you use /NOSERIALMICE without specifying a COM port, serial mouse detection is disabled on all COM ports.
/SAFEBOOT*	This option is new in Windows 2000. You should never have to specify this option manually, since NTLDR does it for you when you use the F8 menu to perform a safe boot. Following the colon in the option, you need to specify one of three additional switches: MINIMAL, NETWORK, or DSREPAIR. The MINIMAL and NETWORK flags correspond to a safe boot with no network and a safe boot with network support, respectively.
	A safe boot is a boot where OS loads only drivers and services that are specified by name or group in the Minimal or Network registry keys under HKLM\System\CurrentControlSet\ Control\SafeBoot. The DSREPAIR (Directory Services Repair) switch causes Windows 2000 Server or Windows Server 2003 to boot into a mode where it restores the Active Directory from a backup media that you present.
	An additional option you can use is "(ALTERNATESHELL)". This tells Windows to use the program specified by HKLM\System\CurrentControlSet\SafeBoot\ AlternateShell as the graphic shell, rather than the default, which is Explorer.
/SOS	This switch causes Windows NT/2000/XP or Windows Server 2003 to print information about which drivers are being loaded as the system boots. This is useful when Windows NT/2000/XP or Windows Server 2003 won't start and you suspect that a device driver is missing.

The list of Boot.ini switches shown above should not be considered as exhaustive, since it includes only the most frequently used switches. The most complete and up-to-date list of Boot.ini switches can be downloaded from **http://www.sysinternals.com/bootini.htm**.

Customizing the Login Process

The standard login process can be customized by editing the registry. The procedures described in this section are also applicable for Windows NT 4.0, Windows 2000, Windows XP and Windows Server 2003.

Specifying the Custom Logo Displayed at Login Time

This tip is useful for each of Windows NT/2000, Windows XP and Windows Server 2003. You can change the screen logo used as a background for the login dialog. Any BMP file can be used for this purpose (for example, a custom logo or any graphic file). To introduce this modification, you need to do the following:

1. Start the registry editor and expand the `HKEY_USERS\.DEFAULT\ Control Panel\Desktop` registry key.
2. Find the `Wallpaper` value entry, and specify the path to the BMP file that you want to use as a background for the login dialog (Fig. 4.11).

▶ *Note*

This tip will also work for Windows XP, but only if you disable the Welcome screen, which by default, is enabled. To disable the Windows XP Welcome screen, open the **Control Panel** window, start the User Accounts applet, click the **Change the way users log on or off** option, and clear the **Use Welcome screen** checkbox. Note that you can customize the Windows XP Welcome screen itself by adding or removing user accounts to it. To do so, simply expand the `HKEY_LOCAL_MACHINE\SOFTWARE\Microsoft\Windows NT\ CurrentVersion\Windologon\SpecialAccounts\UserList` registry key. Add the value `REG_DWORD` data type, name it as required, and set the value to `0`. This account will be hidden from the Welcome screen. If you want to make the account visible again set the value to 1, and it will appear on the Welcome screen. For example, if you want the Administrator account (which is hidden by default) to appear on the Welcome screen, create the `REG_DWORD` value, name it `Administrator`, and set it to `1`.

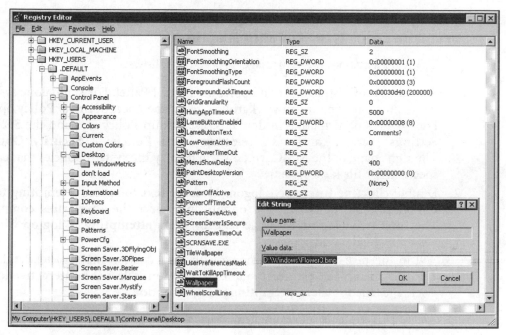

Fig. 4.11. To specify the custom logo displayed at login time, edit the `Wallpaper` value under `HKEY_USERS\.DEFAULT\Control Panel\Desktop`

Adding a Custom Message to Be Displayed at Login Time

You can also add custom messages to be displayed for all users at login. If you make this change, a small message box containing the custom message text and an **OK** button will appear when the user logs on to the system. The boot process will continue as usual after the user clicks the **OK** button. You can find tips on this both in Internet forums and in other books. However, there's a much easier and safer method of performing this customization. In Windows NT 4.0, you can use the System Policy Editor tool that is supplied with Windows NT 4.0 Server. In Windows 2000, Windows XP and Windows Server 2003, you can use either the Local Security Policy snap-in (for systems participating in workgroups) or the Group Policy snap-in (for systems joined to domains). In this section, we'll cover different ways of adding a custom message, both by using administrative tools and by editing the system registry directly.

Adding a Custom Login Message
Using the Local Security Policy Snap-in

To create a custom login message, proceed as follows:

1. Start the Administrative Tools applet in Control Panel. For standalone systems or systems participating in workgroups, select the **Local Security Policy** option. For systems participating in domains, use Group Policy. Expand the **Security Settings** hierarchical list by selecting **Local Policies | Security Options**. The right pane of the MMC window will display the system policies that can be specified for the local system.

2. Double-click the **Interactive logon: Message text for users attempting to log on** option, or right-click this option and select the **Properties** command. The **Interactive logon: Message text for users attempting to log on** window will appear (Fig. 4.12).

3. Fill in the text field in this window with your custom message text and click **OK**. To specify the text for the title bar caption, select **the Interactive logon: Message title for users attempting to log on** option.

Chapter 10 contains more detailed information on using system policies.

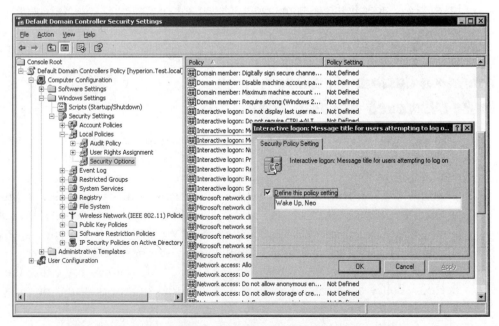

Fig. 4.12. Using MMC for specifying a custom login message
(Windows Server 2003 domain controller)

Adding a Custom Logon Banner by Editing the Registry Directly

To specify a custom logon banner by direct registry editing, proceed as follows:

1. Open the `HKEY_LOCAL_MACHINE\SOFTWARE\Microsoft\WindowsNT\CurrentVersion\WinLogon` key.
2. Find the `LegalNoticeCaption` value entry. Edit its value to specify the phrase that will be displayed as the caption in the custom-message box.
3. Next, open the `LegalNoticeText` value entry and edit its value to specify the text of your custom message.

► ***Note***

In Windows XP and Windows Server 2003, the `LegalNoticeCaption` and `LegalNoticeText` values were moved to the following registry key: `HKEY_LOCAL_MACHINE\SOFTWARE\Microsoft\Windows\CurrentVersion\policies\system`. These are the registry values that are set when you use Local Security Policy or Default Domain Controller Security Settings snap-ins. Values with the same names also exist under `HKEY_LOCAL_MACHINE\SOFTWARE\Microsoft\WindowsNT\CurrentVersion\WinLogon`. However, the `LegalNoticeCaption` and `LegalNoticeText` values under `HKEY_LOCAL_MACHINE\SOFTWARE\Microsoft\Windows\CurrentVersion\policies\system` have priority, and if they are set, the values under the `Winlogon` registry key will have no effect.

Automating the Logon Process

In contrast to Windows 9*x*/ME, the logon procedure used in all Windows NT-based operating systems is an integral part of the security subsystem. However, there may be times when you want to automate this procedure so that other users can start your computer and use the account you establish for automatic logon.

► ***Note***

Note that enabling the Autologon feature, however convenient it may seem, also involves a security risk. Setting a computer for Autologon means that anyone who can physically obtain access to the computer can gain access to all of the computer's contents, including any network or networks to which it is connected. Any users who have logged on remotely can view and read it. Therefore, this option is not available in the UI for server platforms (for example, you can't configure Windows 2000 Server or Windows Server 2003 to use Autologon). The automatic logon feature is also unsupported when you log on to a domain and, therefore, you must join a workgroup to use this feature. However, if your computer belongs to a Windows 2000 or Windows Server 2003 domain, you can still enable automatic logon by editing the registry (in this case, however, doing so is highly risky and undesirable).

To add logon information using Regedit.exe

1. Start Regedit.exe and locate the following Registry subkey:

   `HKEY_LOCAL_MACHINE\SOFTWARE\Microsoft\WindowsNT\`
   `CurrentVersion\Winlogon`

2. Locate the `DefaultUserName` entry, and set its value to the user name that you want to be logged on automatically.

3. If the `DefaultPassword` value does not exist, create a new value entry of the `REG_SZ` data type, rename it to `DefaultPassword`, and specify the default password as its value.

4. If the `AutoAdminLogon` value entry doesn't exist, create a new value of the `REG_SZ` data type, rename it `AutoAdminLogon`, and set its value to 1.

5. Save your changes, and then exit Regedit.

6. Shut down and restart your computer.

When you restart the computer, the default user will be logged on automatically.

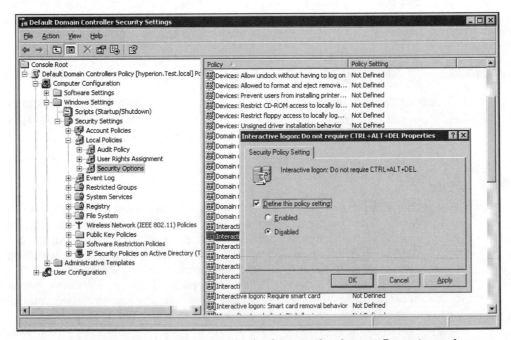

Fig. 4.13. To enable automatic logon, the **Interactive logon: Do not require CTRL+ALT+DEL** local security setting must be disabled

Note

Note that the `AutoAdminLogon` is a `REG_SZ` type value entry, not a `REG_DWORD` registry value entry. Also note that, in order to enable automatic logon, you need to disable the **Interactive logon: Do not require CTRL+ALT+DEL** Local Security Setting (Fig. 4.13).

Hiding the Last User Name Logged On

In the previous section, we discussed a setting that weakens your security system and exposes it to risk. Now we are going to discuss a method that will allow you to strengthen security. When the standard Windows NT/2000/XP or Windows Server 2003 configuration is used, the system displays the name of the user who last successfully logged. If you hide this name, the security rules will become more restrictive, since guessing both the user name and password is more difficult. This customization is one of the most frequently made. As you can guess, it also requires that you to add a new value to the registry. To hide the user name from the last log on, proceed as follows:

1. Run Regedit.exe and open the following key: `HKEY_LOCAL_MACHINE\SOFTWARE\Microsoft\Windows\CurrentVersion\policies\system`.
2. Add the `DontDisplayLastUserName` value and specify the `REG_DWORD` data type for it.
3. Set this entry to 1. When you next log on to the system, the name of the user who logged on last won't be displayed. If you need to disable this feature later, set this value to 0.

 Note

You can carry out the same task using MMC snap-ins to edit the **Interactive Logon: Do not display last logged on user name** local security setting. Note that the same effect can be produced by setting a value with the same name under `HKEY_LOCAL_MACHINE\SOFTWARE\Microsoft\WindowsNT\CurrentVersion\WinLogon`. However, the settings under `HKEY_LOCAL_MACHINE\SOFTWARE\Microsoft\Windows\CurrentVersion\policies\system` have priority, and if they are set, the same value under the `Winlogon` key has no effect.

Configuring Shutdown Event Tracker

Shutdown Event Tracker is a new feature provided with Windows Server 2003 that allows you to track the reason why users restart or shut down their computers. This feature is enabled by default on all Windows Server 2003 operating systems —

any time you need to shut down or restart Windows Server 2003, the **Shut Down Windows** dialog prompts you to specify the reason for shutdown or restart. Note that Shutdown Event Tracker doesn't allow you to complete the action until you have specified a reason (Fig. 4.14).

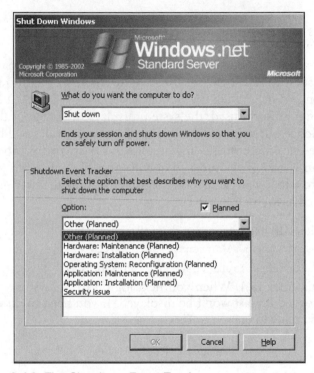

Fig. 4.14. The Shutdown Event Tracker prompts you to specify the reason for shutdown or restart

Note

The Shutdown Event Tracker documents only startup and shutdown events and doesn't gather information related to the reason users might choose other options, such as **Log off** or **Hibernate**.

When Shutdown Event Tracker feature is enabled, Windows Server 2003 provides you with the options for entering descriptive comments, for selecting from a list of predefined shutdown reasons, or for adding custom shutdown reasons, including:

❑ **Other (Unplanned)**
❑ **Other (Planned)**
❑ **Hardware: Maintenance (Unplanned)**

❑ Hardware: Maintenance (Planned)

❑ Hardware: Installation (Unplanned)

❑ Hardware: Installation (Planned)

❑ Operating System: Upgrade (Unplanned)

❑ Operating System: Upgrade (Planned)

❑ Operating System: Configuration (Unplanned)

❑ Operating System: Configuration (Planned)

❑ Application: Maintenance (Unplanned)

❑ Application: Maintenance (Planned)

❑ Application: Hung (Unplanned)

❑ Application: Unstable (Unplanned)

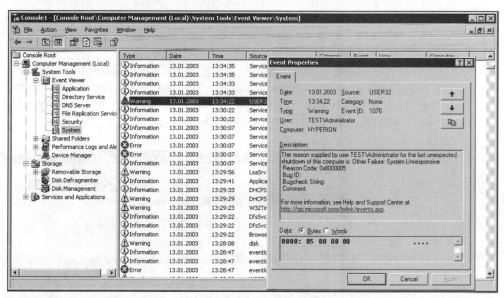

Fig. 4.15. The restart and shutdown reasons collected by Shutdown Event Tracker are recorded in the System event log

The restart and shutdown reasons gathered by Shutdown Event Tracker are recorded in the System Event Log in order to help the administrator to create a comprehensive picture of the organization's system environment (Fig. 4.15). To view Shutdown Event Tracker information:

1. Start Event Viewer from the **Start** menu by clicking **Run** and typing eventvwr.msc in the **Open** field.

2. Under **Event Viewer (local)**, click **System.**

3. Search for an entry that contains **USER32** in the **Source** column and **1075**, **1075** or **1076** in the **Event** column by clicking **Find** on the **View** menu.

4. Double-click the entry and view the information found under **Description**.

As was mentioned earlier, Shutdown Event Tracker is enabled by default on all Windows Server 2003 operating systems. However, if this feature seems boring to you (for example, you simply don't like to have to supply a reason any time you need to shutdown or reboot your server), you can disable this feature using Group Policy. To do so, proceed as follows:

1. To disable the feature on your local computer, start the Local Computer Policy MMC snap-in. To do so, select **Run** from the **Start** menu and enter mmc in the **Open** field. Select **Add/Remove Snap-in** from the **File** menu. Then click **Add** and select the **Group Policy Object Editor** from the list of available standalone snap-ins.

2. Expand the console tree as shown in Fig. 4.16 (**Local Computer Policy | Computer Configuration | Administrative Templates | System**) and double-click on the **Display Shutdown Event Tracker** policy. On the **Setting** tab, select the **Disabled** option, click **Apply**, and click **OK**.

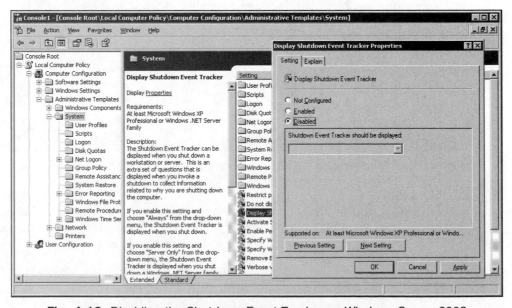

Fig. 4.16. Disabling the Shutdown Event Tracker on Windows Server 2003

Note

To configure Shutdown Event Tracker on a domain or Organizational Unit, use Active Directory Users and Computers, expand the console tree, select the required domain or organizational unit, right-click it and select the **Properties** command. After that, go to the **Group Policy** tab (Fig. 4.17) and click **Edit**.

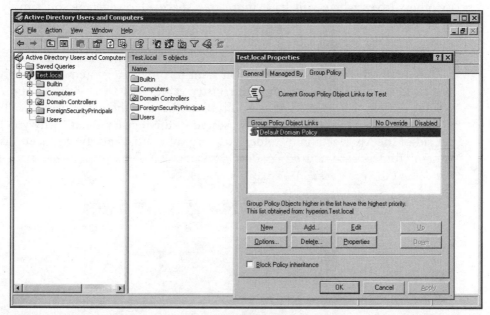

Fig. 4.17. Configuring Shutdown Event Tracker on a domain or Organizational Unit

Using Group Policy is the best method for configuring Shutdown Event Tracker on servers running any OS of the Windows Server 2003 family. However, this situation is different for Windows XP clients. As was already mentioned, Shutdown Event Tracker is disabled by default on Windows XP Professional. Sometimes, however, you might want to enable this feature on a standalone Windows XP workstation. The best way of achieving this is direct registry editing.

1. Start Regedit.exe and find the following key: HKEY_LOCAL_MACHINE\SOFTWARE\ Microsoft\Windows\CurrentVersion\Reliability.
2. Edit or create the REG_DWORD value named ShutdownReasonUI. To enable the tracking feature for shutdown events, assign a value of 1 to this registry entry. Click **OK** and close the Registry Editor.

After you have done this, Windows XP Professional will implement the Shutdown Event Tracker function similar to the one found on Windows Server 2003.

Configuring System Folders

If you've had previous experience with Windows (including both Windows 9*x*/ME and Windows NT 4.0/Windows 2000/Windows XP), you know there will be times when you want to move your system folders to different locations (for example, to other drives where you have more free space). However, if you simply move these folders, what you end up with will be a new copy for each of these folders in the previous locations. Why is this the case?

This is because all operating systems of the Windows family store the system folders paths in the registry. So, if you want to move the system folders properly, you need to modify the appropriate registry values that specify the location of the system folders. Microsoft Office applications behave the same way — all of the paths to the standard folders are also stored in the registry. That's why you cannot get rid of the My Documents folder. Registry values that specify the locations of the system folders are stored under `HKEY_CURRENT_USER\SOFTWARE\Microsoft\Windows\CurrentVersion\Explorer\Shell Folders`.

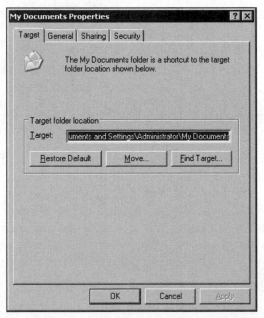

Fig. 4.18. Windows XP and Windows Server 2003 provide you with
the capability of moving the My Documents folder

Notice that, even in Windows 2000, the user interface provided you with the ability to move the My Documents folder to the location you wished.

In Windows XP and Windows Server 2003 this function was further enhanced. Right-click the My Documents folder to open the **My Documents Properties** window (Fig. 4.18) and click on the **Move** button. In the next window, you will be prompted to select a new location for the My Documents folder, either by selecting an existing folder or by creating a new folder. There is now, therefore, no need to edit the registry directly.

Other Popular Customization Methods

There are many other customizations that allow you to modify the standard behavior of Windows NT/2000/XP or Windows Server 2003 operating systems. This section describes some helpful customizations that are safe from a system-stability point of view.

Changing the Color that Windows Explorer Uses to Display Compressed and Encrypted Objects

If your drives are NTFS-formatted, you can use Folder Options to display compressed or encrypted files and folders in color (by default, compressed-file system objects are displayed in blue, while encrypted ones are displayed in green). These default options are the only ones that UI provides you. If you want to display these objects using alternate colors, you can do it by means of editing the registry.

To change the default color for compressed-file system objects, proceed as follows:

1. Start Regedit.exe, and open the HKEY_CURRENT_USER\Software\Microsoft\ Windows\CurrentVersion\Explorer registry key. If you want the new settings to apply to each user, open the HKEY_USER\.DEFAULT\Software\Microsoft\ Windows\CurrentVersion\Explorer registry key.

2. Create the new REG_BINARY value entry and name it AltColor. Set the value for the new entry to the RGB (Red, Green, Blue) equivalent of the desirable color in the following format: "AltColor"=hex:rr,gg,bb,00 where rr is the **Red** component, gg is the **Green** component, and bb is the **Blue** component. The patterns for the most common colors are provided in Table 4.3.

3. Close the Registry Editor and reboot the system to review the effect. If you don't like it, simply delete the AltColor entry.

Table 4.3. RGB Patterns for the Most Common Colors

Color	Red	Green	Blue
red	ff	00	00
yellow	ff	ff	00
green	00	ff	00
cyan	00	ff	ff
blue	00	00	ff
magenta	ff	00	ff
brown	a5	2a	2a
black	00	00	00

Proceeding in a similar way, you can also change the default color used to display encrypted files. This time, you will need to open the HKEY_CURRENT_USER\SOFTWARE\Microsoft\Windows\CurrentVersion\Explorer registry key and create there a new REG_BINARY value named AltEncryptionColor. Assign this new entry the value corresponding to the color of your choice, using the same format: "AltColor"=hex:rr,gg,bb,00 where rr is the **Red** component, gg is the **Green** component, and bb is the **Blue** component. The patterns are the same as in the previous example (see Table 4.3).

Configuring the AutoRun Function

The AutoRun function is a useful add-on included with Windows 95/98 and Windows NT 4.0, Windows 2000, Windows XP, and Windows Server 2003. It is particularly useful when you start programs from CDs or install new software. However, if you only need to copy one or two files from the CD, waiting for the AutoRun function to finish can be annoying.

▶ **Note**

If you use a portable PC (like a Notebook), it is recommended to you disable the AutoRun function — especially if your Notebook runs on batteries. The AutoRun function will significantly decrease the time you can work without recharging the batteries, while bringing no advantages.

Experienced users will recall that Windows NT/2000 required you to edit the registry directly in order to disable the `AutoRun` function. One of the most common tips found on Internet sources recommended that you open the registry using one of the registry editors, find the `HKEY_LOCAL_MACHINE\System\CurrentControlSet\Services\Cdrom` key, set the `AutoRun` value to 0, and reboot the system.

▶ *Note*

The tip above, of course, worked. Officially, however, Microsoft recommends that you not use the `HKEY_LOCAL_MACHINE\System\CurrentControlSet\Services\Cdrom\Autorun` registry value entry to turn off the `AutoPlay` feature in Windows 2000, Windows XP, and Windows Server 2003, since the real function of this registry element is different — its purpose is to turn on or off the media-change notification (MCN). There is a better way to disable the `AutoRun` feature for CDs. The real registry entry that disables the `AutoRun` function for CDs is as follows: `HKEY_CURRENT_USER\SOFTWARE\Microsoft\Windows\CurrentVersion\Policies\Explorer\NoDriveTypeAutoRun`. Setting this value to `0xb5` switches off the `AutoRun` function for CDs efficiently, without affecting other features that you probably do not want to disable.

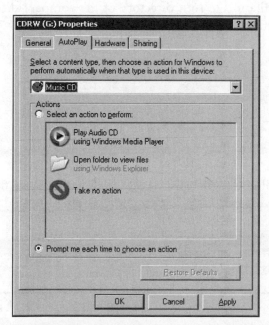

Fig. 4.19. Windows XP and Windows Server 2003 provide
a rich set of options for configuring the `AutoPlay` function

After a brief investigation of Windows XP and Windows Server 2003, you will notice a new enhancement— the `AutoPlay` capability (Fig. 4.19). `AutoPlay` is a new feature that detects content such as pictures, music, or video files on removable media and removable devices, and then automatically starts applications required to display or reproduce the appropriate content. This simplifies the use of specialized peripheral devices such as MP3 players and digital photo readers. It also makes it easier for users who are unfamiliar with the software needed to access various content types. If you are an experienced Windows user, you may remember that Windows Millennium Edition (Windows ME) also performed a similar function for photographic content on imaging devices, automatically running the Windows Image Acquisition user interface (Scanner and Camera Wizard) when a camera or scanner was plugged in. Windows XP and Windows Server 2002 extend this function by making it universally available for all hot-plug removable-storage devices that appear in **My Computer**. `AutoPlay` is extensible so that other devices and media can benefit from this architecture, even the legacy ones.

Note, however, that `AutoPlay` should not be confused with `AutoRun`. The `AutoRun` function, introduced in Windows 95, enables a compact disc to automatically launch a function (such as an application installer or game play) when the user inserts the CD into the CD-ROM drive. This is carried out by an Autorun.inf file in the root directory of the compact disc. If you want to disable the `AutoRun` function in Windows XP or Windows Server 2003, proceed as follows:

1. Find the `NoDriveTypeAutoRun` value entry under one of the following registry keys:
   - `HKEY_CURRENT_USER\Software\Microsoft\Windows\CurrentVersion\Policies\Explorer`
   - `HKEY_USERS\.DEFAULT\Software\Microsoft\Windows\CurrentVersion\Policies\Explorer`
   - `HKEY_LOCAL_MACHINE\SOFTWARE\Microsoft\Windows\CurrentVersion\Policies\Explorer`
2. If this value doesn't exist, create it (it must be of the `REG_DWORD` data type). Set the value for this new element according to the desired function (valid entries are listed in Table 4.4).

Table 4.4. Effects of the `NoDriveTypeAutoRun` Value

Value	Meaning
0x1	Disables `AutoPlay` on drives of unknown types.
0x4	Disables `AutoPlay` on removable drives.

continues

Table 4.4 Continued

Value	Meaning
0x8	Disables `AutoPlay` on fixed drives.
0x10	Disables `AutoPlay` on network drives.
0x20	Disables `AutoPlay` on CD-ROM drives.
0x40	Disables `AutoPlay` on RAM disks.
0x80	Disables `AutoPlay` on drives of unknown type.
0xFF	Disables `AutoPlay` on all types of drives.

A data value of `0x95` is the default, which disables Autoplay on drives of unknown type, floppy drives, and network drives.

If `Autorun` is set to `0`, Autoplay is disabled on all drives. If `Autorun` is set to `1`, you can hold down the shift key as you change media to prevent Media Change Notification (MCN). Appropriate settings in `NoDriveAutoRun` also disable `Autoplay`.

When `Autoplay` is enabled, it begins as soon as you insert media, so setup programs and music start immediately.

 Note

If `NoDriveAutoRun` or `NoDriveTypeAutoRun` are set in the `HKEY_LOCAL_MACHINE` root key, then these settings in `HKEY_USERS` and `HKEY_CURRENT_USER` are ignored. If you set the `NoDriveTypeAutoRun` value via the **Disable Autoplay** Group Policy, you can add the CD-ROM drive type or disable `Autoplay` on all drive types. Any other settings must be created via the registry.

When you change the media in a CD-ROM drive, a MCN message is sent to trigger media features, such as `AutoPlay`. You can suppress the MCN message for specific vendor/products by configuring the `AutoRunAlwaysDisable` value name, a `REG_MULTI_SZ` data type, at `HKEY_LOCAL_MACHINE\SYSTEM\CurrentControlSet\Services\Cdrom`.

Typically, `AutoRunAlwaysDisable` contains a list of devices that do *not* support `AutoPlay`, such as a changer, because they must load the media to verify that the device is a CD-ROM.

The entries in `AutoRunAlwaysDisable` suppress the MCN message for all devices that match the character string you enter, starting at the beginning. You can, for example, disable all CD-ROMs manufactured by ABC Company, by setting one line to ABC.

If a device is identified in `AutoRunAlwaysDisable`, `AutoPlay` does *not* operate on the device, regardless of the value of `Autorun`, `NoDriveAutoRun`, or `NoDriveTypeAutoRun`.

Use `AutoRunAlwaysDisable` as a last resort for disabling Autoplay.

Summary

The tips found in this chapter are just some of the most common and frequently used, but I hope they will help you in customizing system behavior and user interface in Windows 200, Windows XP, and Windows Server 2003 systems.

CHAPTER 5

How the Registry Stores Hardware Information

We all are prisoners in the dungeon of our devices...
Plug and Pray!

IT folklore

Many tasks related to configuring and fine-tuning the different operating systems in the Windows family (be it Windows 9x/ME, Windows NT/2000/XP, or Windows Server 2003) can be carried out using Control Panel applets. These applets are closely related to the registry. When you are viewing configuration information using Control Panel applets, this information is retrieved from the registry. On the other hand, all configuration changes introduced using Control Panel applets are saved in the registry. This is the main reason why Windows NT 4.0 and earlier versions of Windows NT required you to restart the computer after performing certain configuration changes. This is because the changes that you have introduced don't come into force until they have been read from the registry while the system is booting.

▶ *Note*

The entire boot process is dependent on the registry. To identify the boot stage where the registry is initialized, it is necessary to understand the processes that take place when Windows starts loading. These topics will be covered in detail in the next chapter.

Limited hardware support and frequent reboots were the most serious drawbacks of Windows NT. In Windows 2000 and newer releases, including Windows XP and products of the Windows Server 2003 family, these disadvantages have been eliminated by the introduction of Plug and Play support. In this chapter, we will consider Plug and Play (PnP) concepts in more detail and cover the following topics:

❏ How the registry stores hardware information.

❏ Plug and Play specification, its evolution, and PnP support present in Windows NT 4.0, Windows 2000, Windows XP, and Windows Server 2003. We will pay special attention to PnP-support enhancements that were introduced with Windows XP and products of the Windows Server 2003 family.

❏ Plug and Play specification and the registry, Plug and Play device detection, installation, and management.

❏ Advanced power-management capabilities in Windows 2000, Windows XP, and Windows Server 2003.

Registry and Plug and Play Subsystem

At the end of *Chapter 1*, there was a simple example providing a general understanding of the process used by the system to install new devices and resolve hardware conflicts. However, this example was overly simplistic and, more importantly, covered the process of hardware installation only from the user's point of view. But what actually happens when the system installs new hardware? What components are required to accomplish this task? How should we configure hardware and resolve hardware conflicts? These are clearly topics of great interest to anyone who is initiating full-scale support for Windows XP and Windows Server 2003. With the release of Windows 95, Microsoft introduced a new concept for simplifying PC usage: Plug and Play (or PnP). What is Plug and Play? A standard, a specification, or a concept? Actually, Plug and Play is a combination of the general approach to designing PCs and a set of specifications describing the hardware architecture. Strictly speaking, it is a combination of the system BIOS, hardware devices, system resources, device drivers, and the operating-system software.

All Plug and Play components have the same purpose: to facilitate the automatic functioning of the PC, peripheral devices, and their drivers, with a minimum of intervention from the user. Users working with systems that meet all Plug and Play requirements don't have to spend time wondering if a newly installed device will create hardware conflicts with another device. The registry provides the basis for developing such a system.

The HKEY_LOCAL_MACHINE\HARDWARE registry key contains a description of the system hardware and the relationship between hardware devices and their drivers. Before we go any further, you should note that this key is volatile and that all of the information it contains is re-created every time the operating system is booted.

The hardware recognizer (Ntdetect.com) collects information related to system hardware, and the OS kernel stores the information under the HKEY_LOCAL_MACHINE\HARDWARE\DESCRIPTION registry key. As the drivers are loading, they pass their information on to the system so that it can associate the hardware devices and their appropriate drivers. The operating system saves this information under the HKLM\HARDWARE\DEVICEMAP registry key. Finally, all the necessary information related to resources for the hardware devices (including ports, DMA addresses, IRQs) is stored under HKLM\HARDWARE\RESOURCEMAP.

With the arrival of Windows 2000, two new Executive subsystems were introduced: Plug and Play Manager and Power Manager. Plug and Play Manager is integrated with the I/O Manager and doesn't participate in the initialization process. However, the drivers are initialized in such a way that Plug and Play drivers recognize some hardware devices. Windows NT 4.0, on the other hand, uses only Ntdetect.com to recognize hardware devices, because of its limited Plug and Play support.

Though Windows XP and Windows Server 2003 are based on the Windows NT/2000 kernel, the Plug and Play support provided by these newer operating systems has been further enhanced, improved, and optimized. The general idea of this design was to combine the respective advantages of the two lines of Windows products — Windows NT/2000 and Windows Millennium Edition (Windows ME). The approach has been a success, providing greater stability in the OS and delivering better device compatibility.

For the moment, Windows XP and Windows Server 2003 include Plug and Play support for hundreds of devices not recognized by Windows 2000, including scanners, cameras, audio devices, storage devices, and media (CDs and DVDs). At the same time, these systems also provide better support for Universal Serial Bus (USB), IEEE 1394, Peripheral Component Interconnects (PCI), and other buses. Improvements introduced in the Plug and Play subsystem have lead to better stability and performance. This is especially true with regard to the device-installation process, which has been streamlined and automated, as shown in the example in *Chapter 1*. Beside this, power-management support has also been improved, which is of benefit to both desktop and mobile computer users.

Plug and Play Historical Overview

Plug and Play is a technology that allows the automatic configuration of the PC and all of the devices installed on the system. It allows you to start using newly installed hardware (for example, a sound card or modem) immediately after installation, and without having to configure the device manually. Plug and Play operates at the hardware level, the operating-system level and in the device drivers and BIOS.

The introduction of Plug and Play was the result of cooperation between software and hardware vendors, who created an industrial committee in order to unite their efforts. This committee was founded in May of 1993, and initially included three corporations: Microsoft, Intel, and Compaq. By the end of 1995, a number of vendors were already producing hundreds of hardware devices complying with this standard.

Microsoft® Windows® 95 was the first operating system that implemented Plug and Play support. However, since then, PnP standards have undergone a significant evolution, mainly as a result of the efforts of the members of the OnNow industry initiative. OnNow is aimed at identifying a standardized approach to controlling both the operating system and hardware-device configuration. The main achievement of OnNow has been the *Advanced Configuration and Power Interface* (ACPI) *Version 1.0* specification, which defines the basic interface between the motherboard and the system BIOS. This interface expands Plug and Play capabilities, allowing the operating system to control power and provide other extended configuration capabilities.

Windows 2000, Windows XP and Windows Server 2003 all provide extended Plug and Play functionality. Windows 2000 was the first operating system from the Windows NT family that provided full-featured support for Plug and Play and power management. However, those of you who want all of the advantages of Plug and Play and power-management support need to ensure that both the system BIOS and the computer system as a whole meet ACPI specification requirements. More detailed information concerning this topic will be provided later in this chapter.

At present, Plug and Play technologies are defined for USB, IEEE 1394, PCI, ISA, SCSI, ATA, LPT, COM, and Card/CardBus. Each Plug and Play device must have the following capabilities:

❐ Be uniquely identifiable
❐ Be able to provide a list of services that it supports and resources it requires
❐ Be able to identify the driver that supports it
❐ Be able to provide the software capabilities for its configuration

Plug and Play Implementation
in Windows 2000, Windows XP, and Windows Server 2003

Plug and Play systems require interaction between the PC BIOS, hardware components, device drivers, and operating-system software. In contrast to all the previous versions of Windows NT, Windows 2000/XP and Windows Server 2003 provide improved reliability and decreased downtime. These improvements are the result of an extended range of supported hardware and full-featured Plug and Play support. The introduction of all of the new capabilities is part of the Microsoft Zero Administration initiative, which is aimed at minimizing Windows downtime. For example, Plug and Play devices can often be plugged in or removed while Windows is running, and the system detects the change automatically. Devices that can be removed while the system is running include any USB device and a number of IEEE 1394.

Decreasing the frequency of required reboots is one of the most significant advantages here, as it simplifies the procedure of installing both the operating system and hardware components. In most cases, new devices can be added dynamically; that is, without rebooting the system. The Hardware Compatibility List has also been extended significantly. Now, the HCL includes hundreds of new printers, modems, tape devices, floptical drives, and other devices. All of this is possible thanks to full-featured Plug and Play support and Power Management features.

Removing a device from a computer without prior notifying the operating system is known as a *surprise removal*. Typically, Windows XP and Windows Server 2003 can handle this situation effectively, since device drivers developed according to the *Windows XP/Windows Server 2003 Logo Requirements* specification must notify the operating system when the device is removed. For such devices, the removal of the device does not affect the system. However, surprise removal is not always recommended. Particularly, the surprise removal of some storage devices, modems, and network adapters causes the operating system to display an **Unsafe Removal of Device** screen (Fig. 5.1), which tells the user to use the Safe Removal application when unplugging the device the next time. The user can manually disable the message for devices that can withstand surprise removal. The Safe Removal application is used to notify the operating system that a device is going to be unplugged, and can be found in the notification area (Fig. 5.2), if such a device is installed on the system.

▶ Note

Some devices must be installed or removed only when the system is turned off. When the device requires internal installation on the computer, this is the case. Also, if data transfers are in progress while certain devices are removed or if the operating system tries to access particular types of devices that have been removed, data loss, data corruption, or even a system failure might result. For example, surprise removal of a PC Card, a CardBus, or parallel or COM-port devices while the device driver is attempting to write to its ports can freeze the system or cause a STOP error, which requires you to reboot the system.

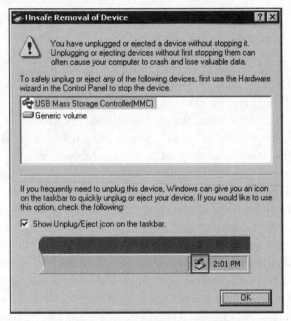

Fig. 5.1. The **Unsafe Removal of Device** window

Fig. 5.2. To remove a hardware device safely, it is necessary to notify the OS that a device is going to be unplugged using the Safe Removal application, which can be found in the notification area

In contrast to Windows 95, Plug and Play implementation in Windows 2000, Windows XP, and products of the Windows Server 2003 family isn't based on Advanced Power Management (APM) BIOS or Plug and Play BIOS. These two legacy Plug and Play functions are supported for backward compatibility only. Actual Plug and Play support in Windows 2000, Windows XP and Windows Server 2003 is based on the ACPI interface.

Some ACPI-compliant types of system BIOS may cause STOP errors in Windows 2000, Windows XP and Windows Server 2003. To minimize this possibility,

Microsoft developers have included a special function with a text-based phase of the OS installation procedure. This capability allows for the disabling or activating of ACPI mode support based on the following lists:

☐ *Good BIOS list.* This list is used for activating ACPI mode for some types of BIOS' dated earlier than 01/01/1999. If the system BIOS ACPI tables match any entries in the Good BIOS List, ACPI mode will be enabled. Microsoft isn't adding any new entries to the "Good BIOS List".

☐ *Incompatible BIOS list.* This list is used to disable the ACPI mode for certain BIOSs dated 01/01/1999 or later. If the system BIOS ACPI tables match any entries in the "Windows Non-Compliant ACPI List", the ACPI mode will be disabled. BIOSs are added to this list if they have been found by the Microsoft test teams or the BIOS developers to cause system-stability problems. If a system doesn't pass the ACPI Hardware Compatibility Test (HCT), fails to boot, or doesn't provide minimal functionality operating on Windows 2000, then Microsoft will place the machine's BIOS on the "Windows Non-Compliant ACPI List". The ACPI HCT is available on the Web at **http://www.microsoft.com/ hwdev/acpihct.htm.**

If a system's BIOS isn't on either of these lists, the ACPI mode will be enabled if the BIOS presents itself as an ACPI BIOS that is dated later than 01/01/1999. The date that's used by the operating system is the standard PC-AT date, which is found at F000:FFF5.

▶ *Note*

If the ACPI BIOS is detected as non-compliant in the Windows 2000, Windows XP or Windows Server 2003 pre-setup system check, then the BIOS must be updated to ensure complete Plug and Play and power-management functionality. Complete information on this topic is available at **http://www.Hardware-Update.com**.

For *x*86-based systems, there is a significant difference in the way the system BIOS interacts with the Plug and Play devices. For some systems, the BIOS Setup program contains the **Enable Plug and Play operating system** option, which affects this interaction. Strictly speaking, this option specifies whether the system BIOS or the operating system controls the hardware. If you have a non-compliant ACPI system or a non-ACPI system, it is recommended that you set this option to **No/Disabled**. Microsoft also recommends that you disable this option if you dual-boot Windows XP or Windows Server 2003 and Windows 9*x*/ME, especially if the system check for Plug and Play on a Windows 98/ME ACPI system passes but the system check for Plug and Play on Windows XP/Windows Server 2003 fails. If you have a fully compliant ACPI system (which means that ACPI BIOS is present and ACPI HAL installed), the device resources are assigned by Windows XP/ Windows Server 2003, rather than by BIOS settings. BIOS settings are ignored, including the **Enable Plug and Play operating system** option. Because of this, this BIOS setting can be left as it is. However, Microsoft still suggests the **No/Disabled** setting as the preferable option.

The main idea of Plug and Play implementation is the simplification of PC operation for end users. The presence of Plug and Play in Windows 2000, Windows XP and Windows Server 2003 also carries out the following tasks:

❑ Extending the existing Windows NT I/O infrastructure in such a way as to support Plug and Play and power management while providing backward compatibility for existing Plug and Play hardware.

❑ Developing common driver interfaces that support Plug and Play and power management for multiple device classes under Windows 2000/Windows XP/ Windows Server 2003 and Windows 98/ME.

❑ Optimizing Plug and Play support for various types of computers, including portables, desktops, and servers equipped with ACPI-compliant motherboards. Additionally, support for Plug and Play drivers is provided by Microsoft Win32® Driver Model, WDM, which also supports power management and other new and extended functions that can be configured and managed by the operating system.

ACPI Specification

The Plug and Play system requires the interaction of the system BIOS, its hardware components, device drivers, and the operating system. The ACPI specification identifies all the necessary requirements for the motherboard and system BIOS to support Plug and Play in Windows 2000, Windows XP and Windows Server 2003. Both Windows 98/ME and Windows 2000/XP/Windows Server 2003 use this specification as a basis for Plug and Play architecture, according to the requirements of the OnNow initiative.

The ACPI specification defines the new interface between the operating system and the hardware components that provide power management and Plug and Play support. Notice that all of the methods defined in ACPI are independent of both the operating system and the processor type. ACPI defines the interface on the registers level for basic Plug and Play and power management functions. It also defines a descriptive interface for additional hardware functionality. This allows developers to implement a whole range of Plug and Play and power management functions for multiple hardware platforms while using the same driver. ACPI also provides a general mechanism for managing system events for Plug and Play and power management.

Besides ACPI, there are other industrial standards. For example, Universal Serial Bus, Version 1.0, PCI Local Bus Specification, Revision 2.1, and PCMCIA.

Support Levels for Devices and Drivers

The Plug and Play support level that is provided by a device depends both on the hardware support for Plug and Play and on the Plug and Play support provided by the device driver. This concept is illustrated by the data presented in Table 5.1.

Table 5.1. Plug and Play Support Levels for Devices and Drivers

Device type	Plug and Play driver	Non-Plug and Play driver
Plug and Play device	Full-featured Plug and Play support	No Plug and Play support
Non-Plug and Play device	Partial support for Plug and Play	No Plug and Play support

As shown in this table, the appropriate driver is necessary for providing complete PnP support. A brief description of all possible configurations is given below.

❑ *Full-featured support — both the device and its driver support Plug and Play.* To provide optimum Plug and Play support, the hardware component has to meet the OnNow initiative requirements, including ACPI specification. Plug and Play support introduced in Windows 2000, Windows XP and Windows Server 2003 is oriented towards ACPI systems only.

❑ *Plug and Play device/legacy driver — no Plug and Play support.* If the device driver doesn't support Plug and Play, then the Plug and Play device will behave as a legacy device. Notice that this may limit Plug and Play functionality for the whole system.

❑ *Legacy device/Plug and Play driver — this combination may provide partial Plug and Play support.* If you have a legacy device that doesn't support Plug and Play at the hardware level, it may provide limited PnP support if the appropriate Plug and Play driver has been loaded. Although this system won't be able to automatically and dynamically detect hardware and load the appropriate drivers, it will be capable of managing hardware resources. This system will also provide the interface for the driver to interact with the Plug and Play subsystem and register device-notification events. If your hardware device has a Plug and Play driver, it will be displayed by the Device Manager. The tabs that allow you to configure device properties are available in the Device Manager window.

☐ *Neither the device nor its driver support Plug and Play: no Plug and Play support.* Legacy drivers will function as usual, but they won't support Plug and Play functions. All newly developed drivers should support Plug and Play.

As you can see, Plug and Play support depends on both the hardware device and the device driver. For example, if you have a manually installed legacy device, you can still gain functionality and provide partial Plug and Play support by installing a Plug and Play driver.

▶ *Note*

Windows XP and Windows Server 2003 support Plug and Play for monitors only if the monitor, the display adapter, and the display driver are Plug and Play. Otherwise, the monitor is identified by the system as a default monitor.

Plug and Play Architecture in Windows 2000, Windows XP, and Windows Server 2003

The Windows 2000/XP/Windows Server 2003 kernel provides Plug and Play support during booting. It provides interfaces to interact with various operating-system components, such as the Hardware Abstraction Layer (HAL), the Executive subsystem, and device drivers. User-mode functions interact with kernel-mode functions, thus providing the capability for dynamic configuration and interface with all other components supporting Plug and Play, such as Setup program and Control Panel applets. A schematic representation of PnP architecture in Windows 2000, Windows XP, and Windows Server 2003 is shown in Fig. 5.3.

Kernel-Mode Plug and Play Manager

The Kernel-mode Plug and Play Manager supports functions for centralized management and manages bus drivers during enumeration. It also supports device drivers, which include adding or starting a new device.

For example, Plug and Play Manager queries if the device can be unplugged or removed, and allows the driver of this device to synchronize pending I/O requests with the newly received one. The kernel-mode Plug and Play Manager interacts with the user-mode Plug and Play Manager when identifying devices available for these operations.

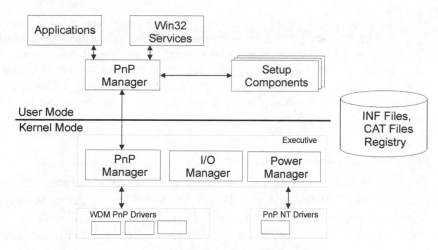

Fig. 5.3. Plug and Play architecture in Windows 2000, Windows XP, and Windows Server 2003

Power Manager and Policy Manager

Power Manager is the kernel-mode component that works together with Policy Manager to process API calls, coordinate events, and generate I/O Request Packets (IRP). For example, if devices send unplugging requests, Power Manager collects these requests, identifies which of them should be serialized, and generates the appropriate IRPs.

Policy Manager monitors system activity and collects integrated status information on the users, applications, and device drivers. Under certain conditions (or by direct request), Policy Manager generates IRPs for changing device-driver status.

Input/Output Manager

Input/Output Manager provides basic services for device drivers. Input/Output Manager is the kernel-mode component that translates user-mode read and write commands into the appropriate IRPs. I/O Manager also manages all of the other basic operating system IRPs. These interfaces function the same way as those in Windows NT 4.0.

Note

Windows XP and Windows Server 2003 enhance the I/O subsystem by adding new APIs that will be available to drivers developed according to the Windows XP/Windows Server 2003 Logo requirements. Device drivers written specially for Windows XP or Windows Server 2003 will take advantage of the new functions, including System Restore (Windows XP systems only) and Volume Snapshot Service. At the same time, Windows XP and Windows Server 2003 provide full backward compatibility with drivers developed for Windows 2000. Notice that, despite the fact that all existing Windows 2000 drivers will work with Windows XP and Windows Server 2003, it is strongly recommended that you check if Windows XP/Windows Server 2003 drivers are available. To obtain an updated driver, contact the device vendor or visit the Windows Update site.

WDM Interface for Plug and Play

The Input/Output system provides leveled driver architecture. This section discusses types of WDM (Win32 Driver Model) drivers, driver levels, and device objects. If you are interested in this topic and intend to develop device drivers, you can find all of the necessary information in the documentation supplied with the latest version of Windows DDK.

Driver Types

From the Plug and Play system point of view, there are the following types of drivers:

❐ *Bus driver* — serves the bus controller, adapter, bridge, or any other device that has child devices. Bus drivers are required drivers and are normally supplied by Microsoft. Each type of the bus present in the system has its own bus driver.

❐ *Function driver* — this is the main device driver, which provides the operational interface for the device. This is a required driver unless the device is used raw (an implementation in which I/O is done by the bus driver and any bus filter drivers). The function driver for a device is typically set up as a driver/minidriver pair. In these driver pairs, a *class driver* (usually written by Microsoft) provides the functions required by all devices of that type and a *minidriver* (usually written by the device vendor) provides device-specific functions. The Plug and Play Manager loads one function driver for each device.

❐ *Filter driver* — sorts I/O requests for a bus, a device, or a class of devices. Filter drivers are optional, and any number of them can exist placed above or below a function driver and above a bus driver. Usually, system original-equipment manufacturers (OEMs) or independent hardware vendors (IHVs) supply filter drivers.

In most cases, lower-level filter drivers modify the behavior of the device hardware. For example, a lower-level class filter driver for mouse devices can provide acceleration, performing a non-linear conversion of mouse movement data.

Upper-level filter drivers usually provide value-added features for a device. For example, an upper-level device filter driver for a keyboard can enforce additional security checks.

Driver Layers

For any given device, there are two or more driver layers: a bus driver for the underlying I/O bus (or the Plug and Play Manager for root-enumerated devices) and a function driver for the device. Optionally, one or more filter drivers can be provided for the bus or device.

Device Objects

A driver creates a *device object* for each device it controls. The device object represents the device to the driver. From the Plug and Play perspective, there are three kinds of device objects: physical device objects (PDOs), functional device objects (FDOs), and filter device objects. PDOs represent a device on the bus. Every Plug and Play API that refers to a device refers to the PDO. FDOs represent the functionality of a device to a function driver. Filter device objects represent a filter driver as a hook to add value. These three kinds of device objects are all of the DEVICE_ OBJECT type, but are used differently and can have different device extensions.

Additional Interfaces

Plug and Play drivers in Windows 2000/XP and in Windows Server 2003 aren't limited to using only the WDM interfaces. Drivers can call on other interfaces to support legacy Windows NT drivers, detection, or other Windows NT-specific capabilities that aren't provided under WDM. Notice that if a driver is intended for work in both Windows 98/ME and Windows 2000 or later, only WDM interfaces can be used.

WDM Bus Drivers

Bus power management and Plug and Play are controlled by WDM bus drivers, which are standard WDM drivers that expose bus capabilities. Notice that, in this context, any device from which other devices are enumerated is referred to as a *bus*. A bus driver responds to new Plug and Play and power management I/O request packets (IRPs), and can be extended using filter drivers.

The bus driver is mainly responsible for the following tasks:

❐ Enumerating the devices on its bus
❐ Reporting dynamic events on its bus to the operating system

❐ Responding to Plug and Play and power management IRPs
❐ Multiplexing access to the bus (for some buses)
❐ Generically administering the devices on its bus

During enumeration, a bus driver identifies the devices on its bus and creates device objects for them. The method a bus driver uses to identify connected devices depends on the particular bus.

A bus driver performs certain operations on behalf of the devices on its bus, but usually doesn't handle reads and writes to the devices. (A device's function driver handles reads and writes to it.) A bus driver acts as a function driver for its controller, adapter, bridge, or other device.

Microsoft provides bus drivers for most common buses, including PCI, Plug and Play ISA, SCSI, and USB. Other bus drivers can be provided by IHVs or OEMs. A bus driver can be implemented as a driver/minidriver pair, in the way a SCSI port/miniport pair drives a SCSI host adapter. In these driver pairs, one driver is linked to the second driver, and the second driver is a DLL.

The ACPI driver plays the role of both bus driver and function driver. ACPI allows the system to learn about devices that either don't have a standard way of enumerating themselves (that is, legacy devices) or are newly defined ACPI devices to be enumerated by ACPI (for example, the embedded controller device). ACPI also installs upper-level filter drivers for devices that have functions beyond the standard for their bus. For example, if a PCI bus driver installs a graphics controller with power controls not supported by the PCI bus, the device can access its added functions if the ACPI driver loads an upper-level filter driver for it.

WDM Device Drivers

WDM device drivers are usually the function driver/minidriver pair and filter drivers. In addition to providing the operational interface for thier devices, function drivers play an important role in a power-managed system, contributing information about power management capabilities as the policy owner for the device and carrying out actions related to transitions between sleeping and active power states.

User-Mode Plug and Play Components

The user-mode APIs for managing and configuring Plug and Play devices are 32-bit extended versions based on the Configuration Manager API for Windows 95. Windows 95 Configuration Manager is a virtual device driver (VxD) that exposes these routines as services to both ring 0 and ring 3 components.

In Windows 2000, Windows XP, and Windows Server 2003, these procedures extend the user-mode Plug and Play Manager functions. Actually, they are exclusively user-mode APIs. Windows NT/2000/XP/Server 2003 Setup program performs driver installation. The Setup program uses 32-bit device installation APIs, which represent a superset of the Windows 95 installation procedures.

Windows 2000, Windows XP, and Windows Server 2003 provide APIs that can be used by applications for customized-hardware event management and creating new hardware events.

Plug and Play Device Tree

Plug and Play Manager supports the device tree that can be viewed using Device Manager (Fig. 5.4). This device tree keeps track of the active devices in the system and information about those devices. The Plug and Play Manager updates the device tree as devices are added and removed or as resources are re-allocated. The device tree is hierarchical, with devices on a bus represented as children of the bus adapter or controller. The registry is the central repository for static hardware information. Plug and Play system components and drivers build, maintain, and access new and existing subtrees in the registry.

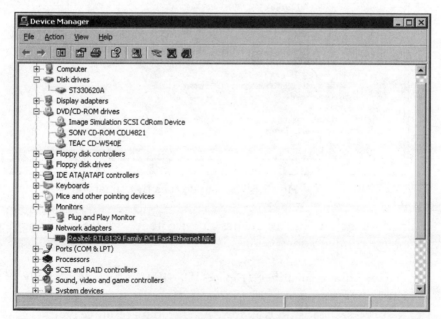

Fig. 5.4. The device tree displayed by the Device Manager is supported by the Plug and Play Manager

During enumeration, data for each device is stored under a new `HKEY_LOCAL_`
`MACHINE\System\CurrentControlSet\Enum` key in the registry (this is the `enum` tree).
Plug and Play makes decisions about which device drivers are loaded
based on the results of enumeration. Thus, there is an important connection between the `enum` tree and the list of services under `HKEY_LOCAL_MACHINE\System\`
`CurrentControlSet\Services`.

Note that Device Manager allows you to view devices both by type and by connection. To view devices by connection, simply select the **Devices by connection**
command from the **View** menu. The device tree displaying devices by connection is
shown in Fig. 5.5.

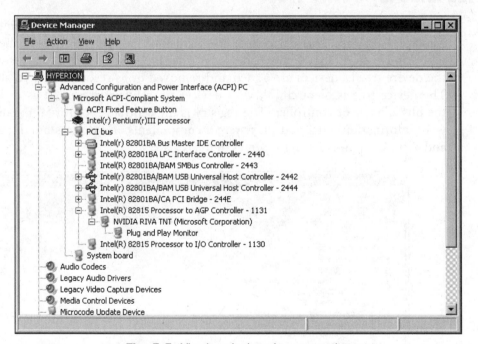

Fig. 5.5. Viewing devices by connection

Each branch in the tree defines a device node with the following requirements
for system configuration:

❑ Device-unique identifier (Device ID, DID), which is typically identified by
a friendly name
❑ Resources, such as IRQs and DMAs, including resource type
❑ Allocated resources

❏ Indicates whether the device node is a bus, if applicable (each bus device has additional device nodes under it in the tree)

Specific icons indicate the device type and any device conflict on the computer. Problem codes and icons for troubleshooting devices are also displayed.

Device Manager does not display all devices by default. Legacy devices, devices that are no longer attached to the computer, and some other devices are hidden. To view such hidden devices, select the **Show hidden devices** command from the **View** menu.

▶ *Note*

You can set Device Manager to show a list of non-present devices. In Control Panel, double-click **System**, click the **Advanced** tab, and then in the **Environment Variables** dialog box (Fig. 5.6), create the variable DEVMGR_SHOW_NONPRESENT_DEVICES=1.

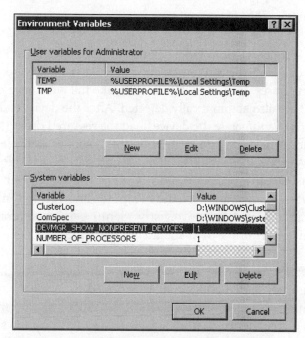

Fig. 5.6. The **Environment Variables** window

You can use Device Manager to enable, disable or troubleshoot devices, update drivers, use driver rollback, and change resources assigned to devices. In order to scan for hardware changes, update the driver for the device, disable or uninstall the device, troubleshoot the device or view its properties, right-click the appropriate device node in the device tree, and then select the appropriate command from the popup menu.

Plug and Play Device Detection

The inclusion of Plug and Play in Windows XP and Windows Server 2003 provides the following advantages:

- ❏ Detects and enumerates devices
- ❏ Allocates resources during detection
- ❏ Dynamically loads, initializes, and unloads drivers
- ❏ Notifies other drivers and applications when a new device is available
- ❏ Works with power management to insert and remove devices
- ❏ Supports a range of device types

After Windows XP/Windows Server 2003 detects a Plug and Play device, the device driver can be configured and loaded dynamically, requiring little or no user input. Some buses, such as PCI and USB, take full advantage of Plug and Play capabilities and are also automatically detected. After the device is detected, PnP Manager and Bus driver enumerate the device, load the required driver(s), and start the device. If the device is new (no information on this device is available in the registry), Windows XP/Windows Server 2003 will install and start driver(s) for this device.

As was already noted, Windows XP/Windows Server 2003 Setup inspects the hardware configuration of the computer and records information on the devices it had detected in the registry. Setup gets configuration information for system devices from the INF file associated with each device and, with Plug and Play devices, from the device itself.

On a PnP system, a device undergoes transitions through various PnP states as it is configured, started and, possibly, stopped to rebalance resources or removed. The transitions between various states of the PnP device are shown in Fig. 5.7.

When a new device is installed, Windows XP/Windows Server 2003 uses the device ID to search INF files for an entry for that device. Windows uses this information to create an entry for the device under the HKEY_LOCAL_MACHINE branch in the registry and copies the drivers needed. The registry entries are then copied from the INF file to the driver's registry entry.

Windows XP and Windows Server 2003 use driver-ranking schemes to determine which driver to load when multiple drivers are available for a device. Drivers are ranked based on whether they carry a digital signature and how closely they match the device's hardware ID (HW ID). If there are multiple drivers for a device, the driver with the highest ranking is selected for installation. The list of driver-ranking schemes from the highest to the lowest rank is as follows:

❑ Signed driver with a perfect four-part HW ID match to the driver
❑ Signed driver with a two-part HW ID match to the driver
❑ Unsigned driver with a perfect four-part HW ID match to the driver
❑ Unsigned driver with a two-part HW ID match to the driver

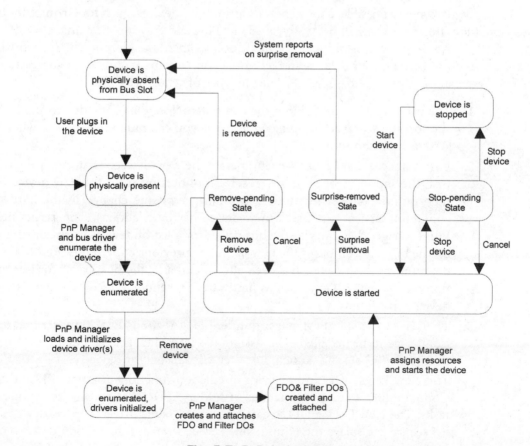

Fig. 5.7. PnP device states

When you need to install a new device, rely first on Windows XP/Windows Server 2003 to detect and configure it. How you do it depends on what type of device you have, as the following list explains:

- [ ] For Plug and Play-compliant devices, plug the device in.
- [ ] For PCI and ISA Plug and Play cards, turn the computer off, and then install the device. When you restart the computer, Windows XP or Windows Server 2003 detects the device and starts the Plug and Play installation procedures automatically.
- [ ] For legacy devices, run the Add Hardware wizard and let Windows detect the device. This requires administrator privileges.

Devices are installed after the user logs on to the computer.

Whenever possible, choose new Plug and Play devices, even for a computer that does not have an ACPI BIOS, to gain some Plug and Play functionality.

An example illustrating all of the processes that take place in the system when the user installs new devices and all of the components required for successful installation is provided in Fig. 5.8. The sequence of action is as follows:

1. The user plugs the device into the computer. Note that if the device and its bus support the so-called *hot-plug notification,* you can plug the device in when the system is up and running.

2. PnP Manager and bus driver enumerate the new device. First, the bus driver, with the support from the bus, receives notification from the new device, and then notifies the kernel-mode PnP Manager on the change in the hardware configuration (in our case, a new device has been added). The kernel-mode PnP Manager then queries the bus driver for a list of devices physically present on the bus and compares the new list to the previous copy. Thus, PnP Manager determines which device has been added, and asks the bus driver for information on the new device (such as hardware ID, vendor ID, compatible IDs, and device capabilities).

3. The kernel-mode PnP Manager notifies the user-mode PnP Manager that there is a device to be installed. The user-mode PnP Manager creates a new process using *rundll32.exe* and launches *newdev.dll* to install the device.

4. The New Device DLL calls device installation functions (Setup API) and PnP Configuration Manager functions (CfgMgr API) to carry out its installation tasks. The New Device DLL creates a list of possible drivers for the device and, if necessary, displays the Found New Device wizard. Information on driver selection was provided earlier in this chapter.

5. The class installer and co-installers, if there are any, can participate in device installation.

6. Setup transfers control to kernel mode to load drivers and start the device. Once Setup has selected the best driver for the device, copied the appropriate driver files, registered any device-specific co-installers, registered any device interfaces, and so on, it transfers control to kernel mode to load the drivers and start the device. The appropriate CfgMgr function sends a request to the user-mode PnP Manager, which passes it to the kernel-mode PnP Manager.

7. The PnP Manager loads the appropriate function driver and any optional filter drivers for the device.

8. Installers can supply wizard pages to change device settings.

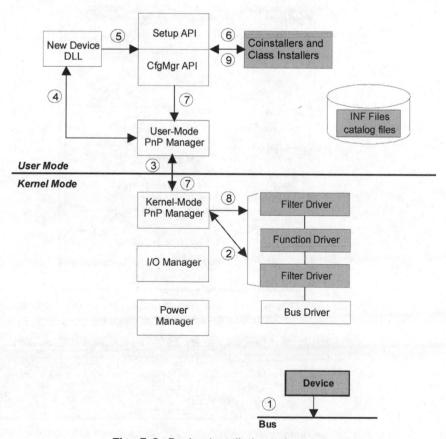

Fig. 5.8. Device Installation scheme

Driver Rollback

This new feature, first introduced with Windows XP and also present in all products of the Windows Server 2003 family, provides a useful reliability enhancement. Problems, such as hardware conflicts, persistent STOP errors or system instabilities, occur after you install an incompatible driver. Needless to say, in such a situation, it is a big plus to be able to replace the driver causing the problems without needing to reinstall the operating system. Now, Windows XP and Windows Server 2003 provide this capability.

Driver Rollback is an indispensable troubleshooting tool when you need to restore a damaged system. It is also very useful when debugging beta-versions of drivers. For example, if, after updating the driver version, your system displays a STOP message during boot up, you can try to boot the system in safe mode and perform rollback of the faulty driver.

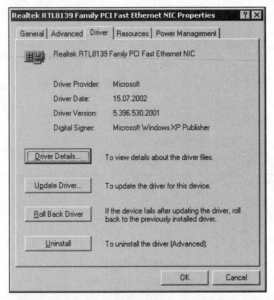

Fig. 5.9. The **Driver** tab of the device properties window now allows you to perform driver rollback

Fig. 5.10. The driver can't be rolled back, since there are no driver files backed up for the device

To use Driver Rollback, proceed as follows:

1. Start the System applet in Control Panel, go to the **Hardware** tab, and click the **Device Manager** button.
2. Right-click the device whose updated driver is causing the problem, and select the **Properties** command from the context menu.
3. Go to the **Driver** tab (Fig. 5. 9). Click **Roll Back Driver**.
4. The Device Manager will prompt you to confirm driver rollback. Click **Yes**. If a previous version of the driver is unavailable, Driver Rollback will display an error message (Fig. 5.10), and then prompt you to use other troubleshooting tools.

Hardware Profiles

Windows 2000, Windows XP and Windows Server 2003 allow you to store multiple hardware configurations in the registry. For example, you can create hardware profiles for docking stations, which is an important function for those of you with portable computers. You can also create hardware profiles for removable devices. A hardware profile is a set of instructions that informs the operating system which devices to start, which drivers to load, and which settings to use for each device when you start your computer. To create a new hardware profile in Windows 2000, Windows XP, or Windows Server 2003, start the System applet, go to the **Hardware** tab, and click the **Hardware Profiles** button. The **Hardware Profiles** window will appear (Fig. 5.11).

During OS installation, the Setup program creates the default hardware profile, which includes all hardware detected on the computer during the installation.

To change the hardware profile's properties, select its name from the **Available hardware profiles** list and click the **Properties** button. You can also create a new hardware profile based on existing ones. To do so, select the hardware profile, click **Copy**, and enter the name for the new profile in the **Copy Profile** dialog. To delete the existing hardware profile, select it and click the **Delete** button.

Finally, the **Hardware Profiles** dialog allows you to specify the system's behavior as related to the hardware-profile selection. The bottom part of this dialog contains the **Hardware profiles selection** option group, containing two radio buttons. If you set the **Wait until I select a hardware profile** option, Windows will display a list of existing hardware profiles during startup. The system will wait until the user selects one of the displayed hardware profiles. If you set the second radio button, navigate to the field directly below this radio button and specify a time interval (in seconds). This instructs Windows 2000, Windows XP, or Windows Server 2003 how long to wait before the default hardware profile is loaded automatically.

Hardware profiles are stored in the registry under HKEY_LOCAL_MACHINE\System\ CurrentControlSet\Hardware Profiles (Fig. 5.12).

Fig. 5.11. The **Hardware Profiles** window

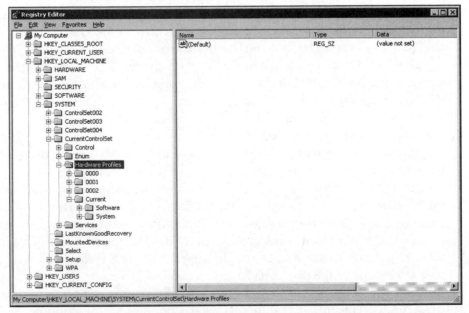

Fig. 5.12. Hardware profiles are stored in the system registry under
HKEY_LOCAL_MACHINE\SYSTEM\CurrentControlSet\Hardware Profiles

Power Management

The power-management system in Windows 2000, Windows XP, and Windows Server 2003 is an integrated approach to power management within the whole computer system (for both hardware and software). This means that the computer system supporting power management must include both hardware and software support for the following functions:

- Minimum time expenses for startup and shutdown. This means that the system may stay in a hibernation state as long as necessary. It may "wake up" from this mode very quickly (this doesn't require rebooting).
- Efficient and economic power consumption, meaning an increase in the working life of the hardware. Devices consume power only when they process a system request or perform operations requested by the user. Devices that aren't in use during a specified time period are switched to a "sleeping" state, and subsequently "wake-up" as needed.
- Silent operation.

Requirements for power-aware hardware and software are defined by the OnNow initiative. Windows XP and Windows Server 2003 provide this support and both the PC as a whole and each individual device consume the minimum amount of power (if the hardware meets the OnNow requirements). Notice that power management and PnP are interrelated and depend on each other.

This approach provides the following advantages:

- Intelligent behavior by the system. The operating system and applications work together to operate the PC, delivering effective power management in accordance with your current needs. For example, applications won't inadvertently keep the PC busy when they aren't necessary, they proactively participate in shutting down the PC to conserve energy and reduce noise.
- Improved robustness and reliability.
- Higher level of integration.

By using the Power Options applet in the Control Panel, it is possible to decrease energy consumption by any device installed in the system. However, this is only the case if you have an ACPI-compliant computer system.

The Power Schemes *Tab*

To start the Power Options applet, proceed as follows:

1. From the **Start** menu, select **Settings | Control Panel**. Double-click **Power Management**.

2. The **Power Options Properties** window will appear (Fig. 5.13).

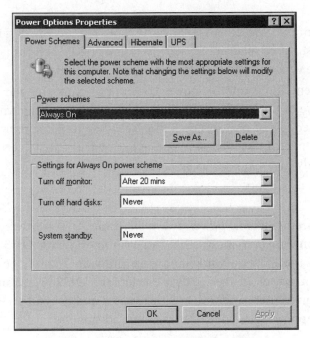

Fig. 5.13. The **Power Schemes** tab of the **Power Options Properties** window

3. To reduce the power consumption of your computer devices — or of your entire system — choose a *power scheme*, which is a collection of settings that manage the power usage of your computer. You can select one of the existing power schemes or create a user-defined power scheme. For example, depending on your hardware, you can do the following:

   - Specify the conditions where the system will automatically turn off your monitor and hard disks to save power.

   - Put the computer on standby if it is idle for a long period of time. While on standby, your entire computer switches to a low power state, where devices such as the monitor and hard disks turn off and your computer uses less power. When you want to use the computer again, it comes out of standby quickly, and your desktop is restored exactly as you left it. Standby is particularly useful for conserving battery power in portable computers.

- Put your computer in hibernation. The hibernate feature saves everything in memory on disk, turns off your monitor and hard disk, and then turns off your computer. When you restart your computer, your desktop is restored exactly as you left it. It takes longer to bring your computer out of hibernation than out of standby.

Table 5.2 lists the registry keys that you can modify using the **Power Schemes** tab of the **Power Management Properties** window.

Table 5.2. Registry Keys Modified Using the Power Schemes Tab Controls

Power Schemes option	Registry key
Power schemes	HKCU\Control Panel\PowerCfg\CurrentPowerPolicy
Standby detection threshold values (for the system, monitor, hard disk — **System hibernates**, **Turn off monitor**, **Turn off hard disks** fields, respectively)	Binary-encoded parameters HKCU\Control Panel\ PowerCfg\PowerPolicies\n\Policies
Deleting the power scheme (the **Delete** button)	Deletes the following key HKCU\Control Panel\PowerCfg\ PowerPolicies\n\Policies Decreases the following index counter: HKLM\SOFTWARE\Microsoft\Windows \CurrentVersion\Controls Folder\PowerCfg\LastID
Adding new power scheme (the **Save As** button)	Adds new subkey under the following key: HKCU\Control Panel\PowerCfg\ PowerPolicies\n\Policies Increases the following index counter: HKLM\SOFTWARE\Microsoft\Windows \CurrentVersion\Controls Folder\PowerCfg\LastID

Generally, you need to turn off your monitor or hard disk for a short period of time to conserve power. The most convenient mode for this is the standby mode, which puts your entire system in a low-energy state.

The Hibernate *Tab*

Beside the standby mode, the Power Options applet allows you to put your system into hibernation mode. As already mentioned, the hibernate feature saves everything in memory on disk, turns off your monitor and hard disk, and then turns off your computer. After rebooting the system, your desktop is restored exactly as you left it. It takes longer to bring your computer out of hibernation than out of standby.

If you are planning to be away from your computer for any length of time, it is recommended to put the system into hibernation. To activate hibernation support, proceed as follows:

1. Open the **Power Options Properties** window and go to the **Hibernate** tab (Fig. 5.14). If your system doesn't support this option, the tab will be unavailable.
2. Set the **Enable hibernate support** checkbox. Please note that when your computer is set to hibernation, everything in the physical memory is saved to the hard disk. Because of this, you need to have sufficient disk space on the hard disk (the file storing memory dump will be as large as your RAM).

Fig. 5.14. The **Hibernate** tab of the **Power Options Properties** window

Fig. 5.15. When you enable hibernation support, the **Shut Down Windows** window
will display a new option — **Hibernate**, allowing you to put
the system to hibernation manually

After hibernation support is activated, the **What do you want the computer
to do?** list in the **Shut Down Windows** dialog will contain a new option —
Hibernate, which allows you to put the computer into hibernation manually
(Fig. 5.15).

The Advanced Tab

The **Advanced** tab of the **Power Options Properties** window (Fig. 5.16) allows you
to do the following:

☐ Enable and disable the power options indicator on the taskbar (Fig. 5.17). This
   indicator is a small icon that provides quick access to the Power Options applet.

☐ Enable and disable password protection for the standby mode.

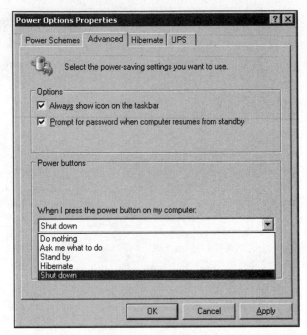

Fig. 5.16. The **Advanced** tab of the **Power Options Properties** window

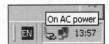

Fig. 5.17. The taskbar indicator provides quick access
to the Power Options applet

Registry keys that correspond to the parameters set using this tab are listed in Table 5.3.

Table 5.3. Registry Keys Modified by Setting Parameters of the Advanced Tab

Advanced tab option	Registry key
Always show icon on the taskbar checkbox	HKCU\Control Panel\PowerCfg \GlobalPowerPolicy\Policies
Display a prompt for a password when the computer goes off standby checkbox	HKCU\Control Panel\PowerCfg \GlobalPowerPolicy\Policies

The UPS Tab

If Uninterruptible Power Supply (UPS) is present in your system, it can also be managed via Power Options. To configure and manage the UPS service, start the Power Options applet in Control Panel, and go to the **UPS** tab (Fig. 5.18). This tab displays the current power status, details on your UPS equipment and the current status of the UPS service.

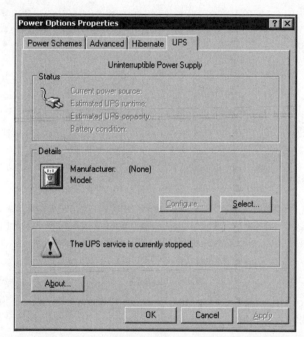

Fig. 5.18. The **UPS** tab of the **Power Options Properties** window

Power Management Tools in Windows 2000, Windows XP, and Windows Server 2003

Having already discussed the power-management tools provided by Windows 2000, Windows XP, and Windows Server 2003, let's now discuss the basic concepts that allow these tools to be implemented.

The topics covered here include:

❑ Power-management policies and power schemes
❑ Parameters included in the power scheme

❏ How power-management settings specified by the Power Options Control Panel applet are stored in the registry

Power Schemes

Power management configuration in Windows 2000, Windows XP, and Windows Server 2003 is based on the concept of power schemes. A power scheme is a group of preset power options that are passed to the Power Policy Manager component of the operating system to control the machine's power-management behavior.

Each power scheme consists of a global power-policy structure and a power-policy structure.

❏ Global power-policy structures contain preset power options that are global across all power schemes.

❏ Non-global power-policy structures contain power options that are unique to a particular power scheme.

These power-policy structures are further divided into machine structures and user structures.

❏ Values in machine structures are stored in the HKEY_LOCAL_MACHINE registry key, and none of these values are exposed in the user interface. For example, you can't set any of these values using the Power Options applet in the Control Panel.

❏ Values in user structures are stored in the HKEY_CURRENT_USER registry key and some of these values are displayed in the user interface. Some of these parameters can be set using the Power Options applet in Control Panel.

The data structures defining power management policy are listed below:

❏ GLOBAL_POWER_POLICY — used to manage global power policies. This structure contains the data common to all power schemes. This structure is a container for a GLOBAL_USER_POWER_POLICY structure and a GLOBAL_MACHINE_POWER_POLICY structure, which contains elements that are read from and written to the registry.

❏ GLOBAL_MACHINE_POWER_POLICY — this structure is a part of the GLOBAL_POWER_POLICY structure. It contains the data common to all power schemes and users. The elements in this structure are read from and written to the HKLM key in the registry.

❏ GLOBAL_USER_POWER_POLICY — this structure is a part of the GLOBAL_POWER_POLICY structure. It contains the data common to all power schemes for the user. The elements in this structure are read from and written to the HKCU key in the registry.

❑ POWER_POLICY — used to manage non-global power policies. This structure contains the data unique for all power schemes. This structure is a container for the USER_POWER_POLICY and MACHINE_POWER_POLICY structures that contain the elements to be read from and written to the registry. There is one POWER_POLICY structure for each power scheme on a machine.

❑ MACHINE_POWER_POLICY — this structure is a part of the POWER_POLICY structure. It contains the data unique to each power scheme, but common to all users. The elements in this structure are read from and written to the HKLM key in the registry.

❑ USER_POWER_POLICY — this structure is a part of the POWER_POLICY structure. It contains the data unique to each user and power scheme. The elements in this structure are read from and written to the HKCU key in the registry.

Registry Keys Intended for Power Management

In this section, we'll discuss the registry keys that are used for power management. You may edit any of them using one of the registry editors.

▶ **Note**

Changing registry entries responsible for power management won't have an immediate effect. Windows only reads settings from the registry when you log on, when you click **OK** in Control Panel, or when a Powerprof.dll function is called on to read the registry.

The registry keys used for power management are listed below.

❑ HKCU\AppEvents\EventLabels\LowBatteryAlarm — descriptive name of a low battery-power-alarm event

❑ HKCU\AppEvents\EventLabels\CriticalBatteryAlarm — descriptive name of a critical battery- power-alarm event

❑ HKCU\AppEvents\Schemes\Apps\PowerCfg\LowBatteryAlarm\.Current,
HKCU\AppEvents\Schemes\Apps\PowerCfg\LowBatteryAlarm\.Default,
HKCU\AppEvents\Schemes\Apps\PowerCfg\CriticalBatteryAlarm\.Current,
HKCU\AppEvents\Schemes\Apps\PowerCfg\CriticalBatteryAlarm\.Default — filenames of the WAV files that will play as a low and critical power-alarm events

❏ `HKCU\Control Panel\PowerCfg\CurrentPowerPolicy` — index of current user and machine power policy

❏ `HKCU\Control Panel\PowerCfg\GlobalPowerPolicy\Policies` — the user global power policy (binary encoded data)

❏ `HKCU\Control Panel\PowerCfg\PowerPolicies\n\Name` — name of power scheme n, where $n = 0, 1, 2$, etc.

❏ `HKCU\Control Panel\PowerCfg\PowerPolicies\n\Description` — descriptive string for power scheme n, where $n = 0, 1, 2$, etc.

❏ `HKCU\Control Panel\PowerCfg\PowerPolicies\n\Policies` — user power policy n, where $n = 0, 1, 2$, etc. (binary encoded data)

❏ `HKLM\SOFTWARE\Microsoft\Windows\CurrentVersion\Controls Folder\PowerCfg\LastID` — index of the last power policy in the lists of user and machine power policies (for example, if there are six user power policies and six machine power policies in the registry, the value of this key is 5)

❏ `HKLM\SOFTWARE\Microsoft\Windows\CurrentVersion\Controls Folder\PowerCfg\DiskSpinDownMax` — the maximum disk spin-down time that Control Panel will allow the user to set

❏ `HKLM\SOFTWARE\Microsoft\Windows\CurrentVersion\Controls Folder\PowerCfg\DiskSpinDownMin` — the minimum disk spin-down time that Control Panel will allow the user to set

❏ `HKLM\SOFTWARE\Microsoft\Windows\CurrentVersion\Controls Folder\PowerCfg\GlobalPowerPolicy\Policies` — the machine global power policy (binary encoded data)

❏ `HKLM\SOFTWARE\Microsoft\Windows\CurrentVersion\Controls Folder\PowerCfg\PowerPolicies\n\Policies` — machine power policy n, where $n = 0, 1, 2$, etc. (binary encoded data)

Summary

In this chapter, we briefly discussed the role of Plug and Play architecture in Windows 2000, Windows XP and Windows Server 2003. You also learned how hardware information is stored in the system registry and what happens to this information when you configure hardware using Device Manager or add/remove devices. Next, we discussed the OnNow initiative, ACPI specification, power management, and registry keys responsible for power management on the computer. If your system is ACPI-compliant, there shouldn't be any hardware conflicts when you install new devices in the system.

CHAPTER 6

Registry and the System Boot Process

As mentioned in *Chapter 1*, the Windows Server 2003 registry plays an extremely important role, because it actually manages the whole configuration of your system. As in Windows NT/2000/XP, the registry information also manages the Windows boot process. A proper understanding of the registry data's influence on the system's startup will allow you to solve most startup problems, such as the inability to boot or incorrect operation on start up.

Note

As we will see in this chapter, the Windows Server 2003 boot process closely resembles the Windows NT/2000/XP boot process. This is not surprising, since both Windows XP and Windows Server 2003 are built on the basis of the Windows NT/2000 kernel. However, there are several improvements in this area that will be emphasized later in this chapter. These include a logical prefetcher for faster booting, boot-loader improvements and operating-system-boot improvements.

The role played by the system registry should never be underestimated, since it is required even in the early phases of the boot process (in actuality, as soon as the operating-system loader starts executing). For example, if the loader can't find the \System hive necessary for loading the drivers (or the hive happens to be corrupt), you'll see an error message like the one shown at the beginning of *Chapter 1*:

```
Windows could not start because the following file is missing
 or corrupt:
\WINDOWS\SYSTEM32\CONFIG\SYSTEM
You can attempt to repair this file by Starting Windows .NET Standard
Server Setup using
the original Setup floppy disk of CD-ROM.

   Select 'r' at the first screen to repair.
```

When Windows XP or Windows Server 2003 is up and running, the \System registry hive is visible under HKEY_LOCAL_MACHINE. This hive defines the loading order for all drivers installed in the system. Both the operating system loader (Ntldr) and I/O Manager access this hive.

Each driver installed in the system has its own key under HKEY_LOCAL_MACHINE\ System\CurrentControlSet\Services. Each of the driver keys, in turn, contains a Start value entry. The value assigned to this entry defines the phase during the system boot process during which the driver is loaded and initialized. We'll talk about the Start value in more detail later in the chapter.

What Happens When You Start Your Computer

As stated earlier in this chapter, the Windows XP/Windows Server 2003 boot sequence closely resembles that of Windows NT/2000. Listed below are the processes that take place when Windows NT-based operating system successfully starts on an *x*86-based computer:

❑ Power On Self Test (POST)
❑ Initial startup process

❏ Boot loader process

❏ Operating-system selection (if you have a multi-boot system)

❏ Hardware detection

❏ Hardware-profile selection

❏ Kernel-loading process

❏ Kernel-initialization process

❏ User-logon process

► ***Note***

The startup sequence quoted above applies to systems started or restarted after a normal shutdown. The startup processes begin when you do one of the following:

• Turn on the computer

• Reboot the system

However, this startup sequence does not apply when resuming from hibernate or standby modes.

When you log on, the process of loading Windows NT/2000, Windows XP, or Windows Server 2003 is completed, as well as are most of the initialization procedures. However, the startup can only really be considered as successfully completed after you log on to the system.

The following requirements need to be met to successfully begin the Windows NT/2000/XP/Windows Server 2003 startup:

❏ Correct initialization of all the hardware.

❏ Presence of all required files for starting the OS. If any of these files aren't present in the correct folder or are corrupt, the startup will fail.

Power on Self Test

When you turn on or restart your computer, it undergoes the Power On Self Test (POST) procedure. The POST routine is a set of tests performed by the CPU, which, as soon as power is switched on, starts to perform the code contained in the motherboard system firmware. Firmware, known as the basic input output system (BIOS) on *x*86-based systems and internal adapters, contains the code necessary to start the computer.

The POST routine performs the following two tasks:

❏ Runs the POST diagnostic routine, which, depending on the firmware, might run some rudimentary hardware checks, such as determining the amount of memory present. The POST diagnostic routine also verifies that all hardware devices needed to start an operating system (such as a hard disk) are present and have been correctly initialized.

❏ After completing the diagnostic routine, POST retrieves the system-configuration settings from the Complementary Metal Oxide Semiconductor (CMOS) memory, located on the motherboard. After the motherboard POST completes, each add-on adapter with built-in firmware (for example, video and hard-drive controllers) runs a device-specific POST routine.

If there are problems related to the computer hardware or BIOS settings, POST will emit a series of beeps. POSTs are controlled by your computer's BIOS and may differ from machine to machine. Because of this, it is recommend to always have on hand the documentation supplied with your computer.

The topic of troubleshooting hardware problems goes beyond the range of problems discussed in this book. As a matter of fact, it deserves a separate comprehensive volume. However, you should be aware of some helpful resources on the topic that will certainly help you to make sense of BIOS error codes:

❏ BIOS Survival Guide, available at **http://burks.bton.ac.uk/burks/pcinfo/ hardware/bios_sg/bios_sg.htm**

❏ Definitions and Solutions for BIOS Error Beeps and Messages/Codes, available at **www.earthweb.com**

Files Required to Start up Windows NT-Based Operating Systems

If the POST routine has been completed successfully, then your computer's hardware has also been initialized successfully. It is now time to start the operating system. This process requires the presence of all of the files necessary to boot the system. The Startup procedure will fail if any of these files are missing or corrupt.

The files required to start Windows NT, Windows 2000, Windows XP or Windows Server 2003 (for *x*86 platforms) are listed in Table 6.1.

Table 6.1. Files Required to Start Up Windows NT/2000/XP Server 2003 (x86 Platforms)

File	Location
Ntldr	Root directory of the startup disk
Boot.ini	Root directory of the startup disk
Bootsect.dos*	Root directory of the startup disk
Ntdetect.com	Root directory of the startup disk
Ntbootdd.sys (for SCSI only)	Root directory of the startup disk
Ntoskrnl.exe	%SystemRoot%%\System32
Hal.dll	%SystemRoot%\System32
The \SYSTEM registry hive	%SystemRoot%\System32\Config
Device drivers	%SystemRoot%\System32\Drivers

* This file is required only in multi-boot systems, where MS-DOS, Windows 3.1x, or Windows 9x are used as alternative operating systems. You can also use the NT loader to boot UNIX or Linux. Copy the first sector of your native root Linux or FreeBSD partition into a file in the NT/2000 partition and name the file, for example, C:\Bootsect.inx or C:\Bootsect.bsd (by analogy to C:\Bootsect.dos). Then edit the [operating systems] section of the Boot.ini file by adding strings such as:

```
C:\BOOTSECT.LNX="Linux"
C:\BOOTSECT.BSD="FreeBSD"
```

 Note

Windows NT, Windows 2000, Windows XP and Windows Server 2003 define the "system" and "boot" partitions differently from other operating systems. These are the most important things that you should know. The system partition contains the files necessary to start Windows NT/2000/XP/Windows Server 2003. The boot partition, which contains the %SystemRoot% and %SystemRoot%\System32 directories, can be another partition on the same or on a different physical disk. The term %SystemRoot% is an environment variable.

Initial Startup Process

When the POST routine has been successfully completed, the system BIOS tries to locate the startup disk. The search order for locating the startup disk is specified by the system BIOS. In addition to floppy disks and hard disks attached to SCSI or ATA controllers, firmware might support the starting of an operating system from other devices, such as CD-ROM, network adapters, or Zip or LS-120 disks.

The system BIOS allows you to reconfigure the search order (also known as the boot sequence). You can find detailed information concerning boot-sequence editing in the documentation supplied with your computer. If drive A: is the first item in the boot-sequence list, and there is a disk present in this drive, the system BIOS will try booting from the disk. If there is no disk in drive A:, the system BIOS will check the first hard drive that is powered up and initialized. The first sector on the hard disk, which contains the Master Boot Record (MBR) and partition table, is the most critical data structure to the startup process.

The system BIOS reads the Master Boot Record, loads it into memory, and then transfers execution to the Master Boot Record. The code scans the partition table to find the system partition. When has been found, MBR loads sector 0 of the system partition and executes it. Sector 0 on the system partition is the partition boot sector, containing the startup code for the operating system. This code uses a method defined by the operating system.

Note

If the startup disk is a floppy disk, the first sector of this disk is the Windows NT/2000/XP/Windows Server 2003 partition boot sector. For a successful startup, this disk must contain all of the boot files required for starting Windows NT/2000/XP/Windows Server 2003.

If the first hard disk has no system partition, MBR will display one of the following error messages:

- ❏ `Invalid partition table`
- ❏ `Error loading operating system`
- ❏ `Missing operating system`

Generally, the form of MBR doesn't depend on the operating system. For example, on *x*86 computers the same MBR is used to start Windows NT/2000/XP/Windows Server 2003, Windows 9*x*, MS-DOS, and Windows 3.1*x*. On the other hand, the partition boot sector depends on both the operating system and the file system. On an *x*86 platform, the Windows NT/2000/XP/Windows Server 2003 partition boot sector is responsible for the following actions:

- ❏ Detecting the file system used to find the operating-system boot loader (Ntldr) in the root directory of the system partition. On FAT volumes, the partition boot sector is 1 sector long. On FAT32 volumes, this data structure takes up 2 physical sectors, because the startup code requires more than 512 bytes. On NTFS volumes, the partition boot sector data structure can consume up to 16 sectors, with the extra sectors containing the file-system code required to find Ntldr.

❏   Loading Ntldr into memory.

❏   Executing the boot loader.

On *x*86 computers, the system partition must be located on the first physical hard disk. Don't confuse the system partition and the boot partition. The boot partition contains Windows NT/2000/XP/Windows Server 2003 system files and can be the same as the system partition. It can also be located on a different partition or even on a different hard disk.

If the first hard disk has no system partition that is used to start the computer, you need to power down this disk. This will allow the system BIOS to access another hard disk, which will be used to start the operating system.

If there is a disk in drive A:, the system BIOS will try loading the first sector of this disk into the memory. If the disk is bootable, its first sector is the partition boot sector. If the disk isn't bootable, the system will display errors such as:

```
Non-System disk or disk error
Replace and press any key when ready
```

(if the disk is DOS-formatted) or

```
Ntldr is missing
Replace and press any key when ready
```

(if the disk is formatted under Windows NT/2000/XP/Windows Server 2003).

If you need to boot the system from a bootable CD (for example, to install Windows XP or Windows Server 2003 from the distribution CD or use the CD-based Recovery Console), you must set the CD-ROM as the primary boot device — the first item listed in the boot order. When you start your system using the bootable CD, Setup checks the hard disk for existing Windows installations. If Setup finds an existing installation, it provides you with the option of bypassing CD-ROM startup by not responding to the "Press any key to boot from CD-ROM" prompt. If you do not press a key within three seconds, Setup does not run and the computer passes control from the CD-ROM to the hard disk.

Note

If you don't want to start Windows XP/Windows Server 2003 Setup to install this operating system or repair the damaged OS installation, remove the CD from your CD drive. This will allow you to minimize the time required to start Windows XP or Windows Server 2003. Also note that the presence of a non-bootable CD in the CD-ROM drive can significantly increase the time required to start Windows XP/Windows Server 2003.

Boot Loader Process

The boot loader allows you to select the operating system to be started and loads the operating system files from the boot partition. The tasks performed at this phase include installing a 32-bit memory model with flat memory space, detecting hardware configuration data, generating its configuration in the memory, and transferring the handle of this description to the loader. Ntldr then loads the kernel image, the HAL, the device drivers, and the file-system drivers for the volume, from which the operating system will start. Beside other tasks at this phase, the system loads the drivers for which the Start registry value is set to 0. The Start registry entry for device drivers is located in the registry under the following key:

```
HKEY_LOCAL_MACHINE\SYSTEM\CurrentControlSet\Services\ServiceName
```

The *ServiceName* here is the name of the service. For example:

```
HKEY_LOCAL_MACHINE\SYSTEM\CurrentControlSet\Services\atapi
```

Ntldr Functions

Ntldr controls the process of selecting the operating system to be loaded and detecting hardware prior to initializing the Windows NT/2000/XP/Windows Server 2003 kernel. Ntldr must be located in the root folder of the system partition. Beside the operating-system loader, the partition must contain all the files listed in Table 6.1.

When Ntldr starts executing, it clears the screen and performs the following actions:

❏ Switches the processor to 32-bit flat memory mode. All *x*86-based computers first start in real mode, similar to an 8088 and 8086 start mode. Because Ntldr is a 32-bit program, it must switch the CPU to a 32-bit flat memory mode before it can perform any actions.

❑ Starts an appropriate minifile system. The code intended for accessing files on FAT and NTFS partitions is built into NTFS. This code enables Ntldr to access the files.

❑ Reads the Boot.ini file located in the root directory of the system partition and displays the boot menu. This screen is also known as a boot-loader screen. If your computer is configured for starting multiple operating systems and you select an alternative operating system (other than Windows NT/2000, Windows XP, or Windows Server 2003), Ntldr will load the Bootsect.dos file and transfer all control to the code contained in this file. The alternative operating system will start normally, because the Bootsect.dos file contains an exact copy of the partition boot sector necessary to start the operating system.

❑ If you select one of the Windows NT/2000/XP/Windows Server 2003 installations, Ntldr finds and executes Ntdetect.com to collect information on the hardware currently installed.

❑ Ntldr loads and starts the operating system kernel (Ntoskrnl.exe). After starting the kernel, Ntldr passes on the hardware information collected by Ntdetect.com.

▶ Note

One of the most significant improvements introduced with Windows XP and Windows Server 2003 is the so-called Fast Boot feature, which was introduced by increasing the boot loader performance. The Ntldr version included with Windows XP and Windows Server 2003 is optimized for fast disk reading. When the system is loaded for the first time, all information on the disk configuration, including file-system metadata, is cached. The Logical Prefetcher, which is new in Windows XP/Windows Server 2003, brings much of this data into the system cache with efficient asynchronous disk I/Os that minimize seeks. During the boot, the logical prefetcher finishes most of the disk I/Os that need to be carried out for starting the system parallel to device initialization, providing faster boot and logon performance. Furthermore, during the boot, each system file is now read only once, within a single operation. As a result, Windows XP/Windows Server 2003 boot loader is 4 to 5 times faster than Windows 2000 boot loader.

As you can probably guess, the prefetcher settings are also stored in the registry. You can find them under the following key (Fig. 6.1):

```
HKEY_LOCAL_MACHINE\SYSTEM\CurrentControlSet\Control\Session Manager\
Memory Management\PrefetchParameters
```

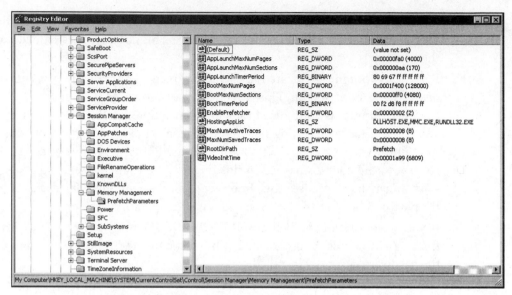

Fig. 6.1. Logical Prefetcher settings in the registry

The values that interest us the most are the RootDirPath (data type REG_SZ, the default value is Prefetch) and EnablePrefetcher (data type REG_DWORD). The EnablePrefetcher setting can take the following values:

❏ 0x00000001 — application launch prefetching
❏ 0x00000002 — boot prefetching

If both options are enabled, the setting will be 0x00000003. The setting takes effect immediately. Note that, in the Server product line, only the boot prefetch is enabled by default. Application prefetch can be enabled by the registry setting cited here. The system boot prefetch file is in the *%SystemRoot%\Prefetch* directory (and the path to it is specified by the RootDirPath parameter mentioned above). Although these prefetch-readable files can be opened using Notepad, they contain binary data that will not be recognized. If you are going to view these files, make them read-only or copy them to a different location before opening.

Selecting the Operating System to Start

Ntldr displays a menu where you can select the operating system to be started. What is shown on this screen depends on the information contained in the Boot.ini file, which was described in *Chapter 4*. An example of the screen is shown below:

```
Please select the operating system to start:
    Windows XP Professional
    Windows 2000 Professional
    Windows NT Server Version 4.0
    Windows NT Server Version 4.0(VGA mode)
Use ↑ and ↓ keys to move the highlight to your choice.
Press Enter to choose.
Seconds until highlighted choice will be started automatically: 29
For troubleshooting and advanced startup options for Windows, press F8
```

The process of selecting the operating system to start is similar to the process for earlier Windows NT versions (for example, Windows NT 3.51 and Windows NT 4.0). The operating system that appears first in the list is the default operating system. To select another operating system, use the arrow keys (↑ and ↓) to move the highlight to the string you need. Then press <Enter>.

If you don't select an item from the boot menu before the counter specified in the following string reaches zero, you'll see the following message:

```
Seconds until highlighted choice will be started automatically: 29
```

Ntldr will load the default operating system. Windows Setup specifies the most recently installed copy of the operating system as the default option. You can edit the Boot.ini file to change the default operating system. A detailed description of the Boot.ini file format was provided in *Chapter 4*.

▶ *Note*

The startup menu will not appear if you only have one copy of Windows XP or Windows Server 2003 installed on your computer. In this case, Windows XP/Windows Server 2003 ignores the time-out value in the Boot.ini file and starts immediately.

Windows Advanced Startup Options

Any experienced Windows NT user will notice that there is small, but very significant, difference between the boot loader screens in Windows 2000/XP/ Windows Server 2003 and Windows NT 4.0. This is the string placed at the bottom of the screen:

```
For troubleshooting and advanced startup options for Windows 2000, press F8
```

In Windows 9x/ME, there was a similar option. If you have any problems booting Windows 2000, Windows XP, or Windows Server 2003, try using the advanced startup options menu displayed when you press the <F8> key.

The menu looks like this:

```
Windows Advanced Options Menu

Please select an option:

Safe Mode

Safe Mode with Networking

Safe Mode with Command Prompt

Enable Boot Logging

Enable VGA Mode

Last Known Good Configuration (your most recent settings that worked)*

Directory Services Restore Mode (Windows domain controllers only)

Debugging Mode

Start Windows Normally**

Reboot**

Return to OS Choices Menu**
```

_ _ _ _ _ _ _ _ _ _ _ _

*This option is an improvement over Windows 2000.

**Options that are new in Windows XP and Windows Server 2003.

Note that this menu will remain on the screen until you select one of the available options.

When Windows 2000/XP or Windows Server 2003 boots in safe mode, it uses the standard settings (VGA driver, no network connections, default system services only). When the system starts in safe mode, only vitally important drivers necessary for starting Windows are loaded. The safe boot mode allows the system to boot even with an incompatible or corrupt service or driver. Thus, the safe mode increases the probability of successful booting because you load the system with the minimum set of services and drivers. For example, if your Windows 2000/XP/ Windows Server 2003 installation became unbootable after installing new software, it is likely that an attempt to boot the system in safe mode will be successful. After booting the system, you will be able to change the settings preventing Windows from booting correctly or delete the software that caused the problem.

The options on the Windows XP/Windows Server 2003 advanced startup menu are described below:

❏ **Safe Mode**

As already mentioned, this option is similar to the one that was introduced with Windows 2000. If the user selects this option, only the basic services and drivers will be loaded. These services and drivers are vitally important for the operating system (this set includes standard mouse, keyboard and mass-storage drivers, base video, and default system services). If you can't start Windows using this mode, you will probably need to restore the damaged system. More detailed information concerning this topic will be provided later in this chapter.

❏ **Safe Mode with Networking**

Similar to the option that existed in Windows 2000, Windows XP/Windows Server 2003 will start in safe mode (very much like the previous option) but, in addition, there will be an attempt to start networking services and restoring network connections.

❏ **Safe Mode with Command Prompt**

When you select this option, Windows 2000/XP/Windows Server 2003 will start using only the basic set of drivers and services (just the same as in safe mode, except that a command prompt will be started instead of the Windows GUI).

❏ **Last Known Good Configuration (your most recent settings that worked)**

In Windows NT 4.0/Windows 2000, there was a similar option. However, in Windows XP and Windows .NET Server, this option includes an improvement that deserves special mention. If you select this option in Windows 2000, the operating system starts using registry information saved immediately after successful startup (the system startup is considered to be successful if at least one user has successfully logged on to the system). It should be pointed out that, in Windows NT/2000, this option only allows you to correct configuration errors and does not always work successfully. Use this option only when you are absolutely sure that you have made an error while configuring the system. The problems caused by missing or corrupt system files or drivers will not be corrected. Also note that using this option will discard all modifications introduced into your registry since the last successful boot of Windows NT/2000.

In Windows XP/Windows Server 2003, this option has been enhanced by additional functions. In contrast to Windows NT/2000, Windows XP and Windows Server 2003 create backup copies of the drivers before updating the currently used set of drivers. In addition to restoring the most recent registry settings, the **Last Known Good Configuration** startup option also restores the last set of drivers used after the last successful user logon. This allows you to recover from system errors such as unstable or improperly installed applications and drivers that prevent you from starting Windows XP/Windows Server 2003.

❏ **Directory Services Restore Mode (Windows domain controllers only)**
This option shouldn't be used with clients running Windows 2000/XP Professional because it is intended for domain controllers running Windows 2000 Server or later versions. As the name of this option suggests, it is used for restoring directory services.

❏ **Debugging Mode**
This option starts Windows XP/Windows Server 2003 and establishes the debugging mode.

❏ **Start Windows Normally**
First introduced with the release of Windows XP, this option allows you to start Windows XP/Windows Server 2003 normally.

❏ **Reboot**
When the user selects this option, the boot process will restart from the beginning (actually, with the POST routine). Like the previous option, this was first introduced with Windows XP.

❏ **Return to OS Choices Menu**
New in Windows XP, this option returns you to the boot loader screen, allowing you to select the operating system.

As has been said, the last three options were first introduced with Windows XP. While these options do not provide anything completely new, being largely cosmetic improvements, they clearly make the Advanced Startup Options menu more convenient than that in Windows 2000.

You may be wondering where the system stores safe mode configurations used to start the system when you select one of advanced boot options. Like everything else in the system, these parameters are stored in the registry, under HKEY_LOCAL_MACHINE\SYSTEM\CurrentControlSet\Control\SafeBoot (Fig. 6.2). This key contains all configuration settings used to boot the system in safe mode. It contains two subkeys: Network and Minimal. The Network key contains the information necessary to boot the system using the **Safe Mode with Networking** option, while the Minimal key contains the same information without the networking settings. The SafeBoot key contains the AlternateShell value entry, which specifies the name of the program used instead of the Windows GUI. Ususally, this entry has the value of "cmd.exe" (Windows 2000/XP/Windows Server 2003 command processor), which corresponds to the **Safe Mode with Command Prompt** option.

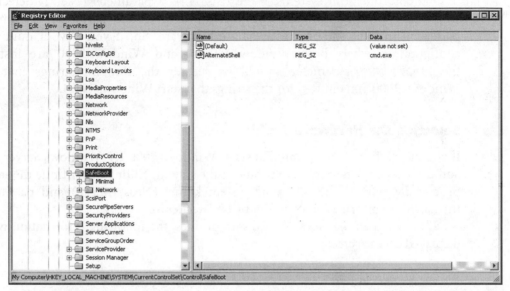

Fig. 6.2. The advanced startup menu options in Windows 2000/XP/.NET Server are specified by the HKEY_LOCAL_MACHINE\SYSTEM\CurrentControlSet\ Control\SafeBoot registry key

Hardware Detection

When you select one of the Windows NT/2000/XP or Windows Server 2003 installations from the boot menu (or the default operating system starts loading after the timer has expired), Ntldr calls on Ntdetect.com to collect information on the currently installed hardware. Ntdetect.com returns the collected information to Ntldr.

This phase of the initialization is different for Windows NT 4.0 and Windows 2000/XP/Windows Server 2003. As mentioned in *Chapter 5*, beginning with Windows 2000, the system includes two new Executive subsystems: Plug and Play Manager and Power Manager. Plug and Play Manager is integrated with I/O Manager and doesn't participate in the initialization process. However, because Windows 2000 and later versions support Plug and Play, PnP-aware drivers play a certain part in hardware detection in the operating system. The main difference from Windows NT 4.0 is that Windows 2000 performs hardware detection using Ntdetect.com only. Because of this, a new Boot.ini parameter was introduced in Windows 2000 — /FASTDETECT, which is used when Windows NT 4.0 and Windows 2000/XP/Windows Server 2003 coexist on the same computer. If you have this type of configuration, the Windows 2000 version of Ntdetect.com will be used to load both operating systems. If the /FASTDETECT parameter is set, Ntdetect.com won't try to recognize Plug and Play devices. If this parameter is omitted, Ntdetect.com will enumerate all of the hardware. So, if you have a multi-boot configuration where both Windows NT 4.0 and Windows 2000 are installed, the /FASTDETECT parameter should be set for the Boot.ini strings that start Windows 2000 and omitted for the strings that start Windows NT 4.0.

Selecting the Hardware Profile

If you have selected the option that starts Windows 2000/XP/Windows Server 2003, and there is only one hardware profile in the system, Ntldr will continue the startup process by starting the operating system kernel (Ntoskrnl.exe) and passing on the hardware information collected by Ntdetect.com.

If your system has several hardware profiles, the following information will be displayed on the screen:

```
Hardware Profile/Configuration Recovery Menu
This menu allows you to select a hardware profile
to be used when Windows is started.

If your system is not starting correctly, then you may switch to a
previous system configuration, which may overcome startup problems.

IMPORTANT: System configuration changes made since the last
successful startup will be discarded.


Profile 1
Profile 2
Profile 3


Use the up and down arrow keys to move the highlight
to the selection you want. Then press ENTER.
To switch to the Last Known Good Configuration, press 'L'.
To Exit this menu and restart your computer, press F3.
Seconds until highlighted choice will be started automatically: 5
```

After displaying this menu, the boot loader will allow you time to select from the available options. You can select one of the existing hardware profiles, switch to the **Last Known Good Configuration** option, or quit this menu and restart the computer.

The first hardware profile is highlighted. To select other hardware profiles, highlight the option you need and press <Enter>.

You can also choose between the default configuration and LastKnownGood Configuration. If you select the **Last Known Good Configuration** option, Windows will load the registry information that was saved immediately after the last successful boot. If you don't select this option, Windows will use the default configuration that was saved in the registry the last time you performed a system shutdown. The Last Known Good Configuration is stored in the registry under HKEY_LOCAL_MACHINE\SYSTEM\Select. More detailed information concerning this topic will be provided later in the chapter.

▶ *Note*

Windows XP and Windows Server 2003 create the default hardware profile for desktop computers. This default profile includes all of the hardware detected when you installed the system. For portable computers, Windows XP creates two default hardware profiles (Docked Profile and Undocked Profile), and selects the appropriate profile depending on the way you are presently using your computer (as a dock station or standalone). Note that, despite the fact that full-featured Plug and Play support has eliminated the necessity of manually configuring hardware profiles, they still can be very useful for troubleshooting hardware problems.

Loading the Kernel

When the boot loader has obtained information on the currently installed hardware and selected hardware profile, it starts the operating system kernel Ntoskrnl.exe and passes on the hardware information collected by Ntdetect.com.

Information on the currently selected hardware profile is passed to the loader when you press <Enter> in the **Hardware Profile/Configuration Recovery Menu** screen. The loader can also make this choice automatically (if the timer has expired or if there is only one hardware profile).

When the kernel starts loading, you will see several dots on the screen. These dots serve as a progress indicator displayed when the boot loader loads Ntoskrnl.exe and the hardware abstraction layer into the memory. At this phase, neither of these programs are initialized. Ntldr then scans the registry and retrieves information on the size of nonpaged pool and registry quota (for Windows NT/2000). Next, Ntldr loads the HKEY_LOCAL_MACHINE\SYSTEM registry hive from *%SystemRoot%*System32\Config\System.

At this point, the boot loader enables the registry API and creates a control set that will be used to initialize the computer. Both of these tasks are preliminary steps necessary for preparing the drivers for loading. The value specified in the HKEY_LOCAL_MACHINE\SYSTEM\Select registry key (Fig. 6.3) defines which control set in HKEY_LOCAL_MACHINE\SYSTEM should be used to load the system. By default, the loader will select the Default control set. If you select LastKnownGood configuration, the loader will use the LastKnownGood control set. Based on your selection and on the value of the Select key, the loader will determine which control set (ControlSet00x) will be enabled. The loader will then set the Current value of the Select key to the name of the control set it will be using.

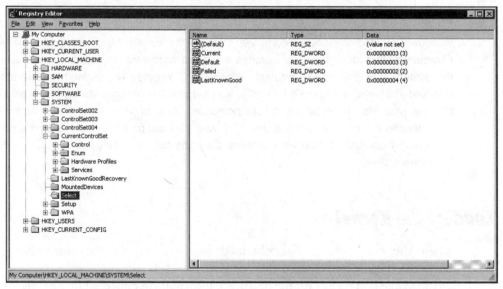

Fig. 6.3. The HKEY_LOCAL_MACHINE\SYSTEM\Select registry key

The loader then scans all of the services defined by the HKEY_LOCAL_MACHINE\SYSTEM\CurrentControlSet\Services registry key and searches device drivers with a Start value of 0x0 (this means that the drivers should be loaded, but not initialized). Normally, drivers with these values are low-level device drivers (for example, disk drivers). The Group value for each device driver defines its load order. The HKEY_LOCAL_MACHINE\SYSTEM\CurrentControlSet\ControlServiceGroupOrder registry key defines the loading order.

When this phase is completed, all of the basic drivers are loaded and active. If one of the critical drivers cannot be initialized, the system starts rebooting.

Initializing the Kernel

When the Windows NT 4.0 kernel begins initializing, the screen turns blue, and a text similar to the one presented below appears:

```
Microsoft ® Windows NT (TM) Version 4.0 (Build 1345)
1 System Processor (64 MB Memory)
```

If this message appears, it means that all of the previous stages of the boot sequence have been successfully completed. Obvious difference between Windows NT and Windows 2000 (or later) is the fact that all system messages that appear during the Windows NT 4.0 boot process are displayed in 80×50 text mode, while Windows 2000, Windows XP, and Windows Server 2003 display these messages in VGA mode. The Windows NT 4.0 Hardware Abstraction Layer (HAL) provides all of the support for this mode and is also responsible for displaying the messages. Windows 2000 and its successors have a special driver — Bootvid.sys — that performs these tasks. In Windows 2000/XP/Windows Server 2003, you will know that the kernel is initializing when the animated screen displaying the OS logo appears (Fig. 6.4). This cosmetic improvement doesn't change the basic principles of the loading process in comparison to previous versions of the Windows NT operating system.

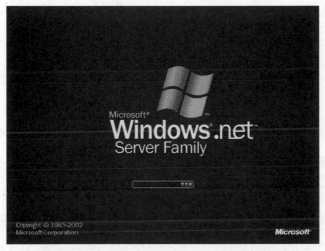

Fig. 6.4. The animated screen displaying the OS logo indicates that
the kernel is initializing

If you want to check things out for yourself, add the /sos option to the Boot.ini file string that starts Windows 2000/XP/Windows Server 2003, then save your changes and reboot the system. You will see the whole loading sequence for all of the drivers. The graphics logo will be used as a background and, in the foreground, you will see something very much like the following:

```
Microsoft ® Windows XP Professional (TM) (Build 2600)
1 System Processor (256 MB Memory)
```

The kernel creates the HKEY_LOCAL_MACHINE\HARDWARE registry key based on information obtained from the boot loader. The HKEY_LOCAL_MACHINE\HARDWARE key contains hardware data collected when the system starts. This data includes information on the hardware components and IRQs used by each hardware device.

The kernel then creates a Clone control set by making a copy of the control set indicated by the Current value.

▶ *Note*

In Windows NT 4.0, the Clone control set was visible but, after a successful boot, it became unavailable (the system displayed an error message any time an attempt was made to open this key). In Windows 2000/XP/Windows Server 2003, the registry editors simply don't display this key.

The Clone control set should never be modified, since it must be an identical copy of the data used for configuring the computer. It shouldn't contain any changes introduced in the course of system startup.

As the kernel initializes, it performs the following operations:

❑ Initializes low-level device drivers loaded at the previous stage
❑ Loads and initializes other device drivers
❑ Starts programs, such as Chkdsk, which should run before starting any services
❑ Loads and initializes system services
❑ Creates the paging file (Pagefile.sys)
❑ Starts all the subsystems necessary for Windows 2000/XP/Windows Server 2003

Loading and Initializing the Device Drivers

Now the kernel initializes the low-level device drivers that were loaded at the previous stage (kernel loading). If any of these drivers cannot be initialized, the system performs corrective action based on the data defined by the following registry entry:

```
HKEY_LOCAL_MACHINE\SYSTEM\CurrentControlSet\Services
\DriverName\ErrorControl
```

Ntoskrnl.exe then scans the registry, this time for device drivers that have an HKEY_LOCAL_MACHINE\SYSTEM\CurrentControlSet\Services*DriverName*\Start value of 0x01. The Group value for each device driver defines the order in which the drivers are loaded. The HKEY_LOCAL_MACHINE\SYSTEM\CurrentControlSet\Control\ServiceGroupOrder registry subkey defines the loading order.

In contrast to the kernel-loading phase, device drivers that have a Start value of 0x01 aren't loaded using BIOS calls. Instead, they use device drivers loaded and initialized in the kernel-loading phase. Error handling for device drivers belonging to this group is based on the ErrorControl value for each device driver.

▶ Note

Windows XP and Windows Server 2003 initialize device drivers simultaneously in order to improve boot time. Instead of waiting for each device to initialize separately, many can now be brought up concurrently. The slowest device has the greatest effect on boot time.

Loading Services

The Session Manager (Smss.exe) starts the higher-level subsystems and services of the operating system. All information used by the Session Manager is also stored in the registry under the following key: HKEY_LOCAL_MACHINE\SYSTEM\CurrentControlSet\Control\Session Manager. The Session Manager uses information stored under the following registry items:

- ❑ The BootExecute data entry
- ❑ The Memory Management key
- ❑ The DOS Devices key
- ❑ The SubSystems key

The *BootExecute* Data Entry

The BootExecute registry entry contains one or more commands that the Session Manager has to run before it starts loading services. The default value for this registry item is Autochk.exe, which is simply the Windows NT/2000/XP/Windows Server 2003 version of the Chkdsk.exe program. The example shown below shows the default setting for this registry item:

```
BootExecute: REG_MULTI_SZ: autochk autochk*
```

The Session Manager is capable of running more than one program. The example shown below shows how to start the Convert utility, which will convert the x volume to NTFS format next time the system starts:

```
BootExecute: REG_MULTI_SZ: autochk autochk* autoconv \DosDevices\x:
/FS:ntfs
```

When the Session Manager executes all of the commands specified, the kernel will load the other registry hives stored in the *%SystemRoot%*\System32\Config directory.

The Memory Management Key

In the next step, the Session Manager must initialize the information in the paging file, which is necessary for the Virtual Memory Manager. The configuration information is stored in the following data items:

```
PagedPoolSize: REG_DWORD 0
NonPagedPoosSize: REG_DWORD 0
PagingFiles: REG_MULTI_SZ: c:\pagefile.sys 32
```

In versions of Windows earlier than Windows XP, as device drivers, system services, and the user shell load, the required memory pages will not be in memory until loaded from the disk drive. Another key improvement in Windows XP and Windows Server 2003 is the overlap of prefetching these pages before loading the device drivers that require them.

The prefetcher in Windows XP and Windows Server 2003 has the following functions:

❑ Dynamically traces each boot to build a list of what to prefetch. Boot files are laid out together on disk during idle time, or when the Bootvis.exe tool is used to arm boot traces. The prefetcher needs at least two boots after installation to learn which files to lay out. The prefetcher monitors the previous eight boots on an ongoing basis.

❑ Enables fast asynchronous I/O during boot to load required files in highly efficient transfers.

As was already mentioned, the prefetcher settings are stored in the registry under KEY_LOCAL_MACHINE\SYSTEM\CurrentControlSet\Control\Session Manager\ Memory Management\PrefetchParameters key.

The *DOS Devices* Key

The Session Manager needs to create symbolic links that direct certain command classes to the appropriate file-system components. The configuration data resides in the following registry entries:

```
PRN: REG_SZ:\DosDevices\LPT1
AUX: REG_SZ:\DosDevices\COM1
NUL: REG_SZ:\Device\Null
UNC: REG_SZ:\Device\Mup
PIPE:\REG_SZ:\Device\NamedPipe
MAILSLOT:\REG_SZ\Device\MailSlot
```

The *SubSystems* Key

Since the architecture of all subsystems in Windows NT/2000, Windows XP, and Windows Server 2003 is message-based, it is necessary to start the Windows (Win32) subsystem that controls all input/output operations and video-display access. The process of this subsystem is called CSRSS. The Win32 subsystem starts the WinLogon process, which, in turn, starts other important subsystems.

Configuration information for subsystems is defined by the `Required` value under the following registry key: `HKEY_LOCAL_MACHINE\SYSTEM\CurrentControlSet\Control\SessionManager\SubSystems`.

Logging on

The Win32 subsystem starts the Winlogon.exe process, which, in turn, starts the Local Security Administration process (LSA) — Lsass.exe. When the kernel initializes successfully, it is necessary to log on to the system. The log-on procedure may be carried out automatically, based on the information stored in the registry, or it can be done manually. When you log on manually, the system displays the **Begin Logon** dialog or the Welcome screen (Windows XP-specific new feature). The Graphical Identification and Authentication (GINA) component collects your user name and password and passes this information securely to the LSA for authentication. If you have supplied the proper credentials, you are granted access using either Kerberos V5 (for network) or NTLM (local machine) authentication.

▶ *Note*

Windows NT/2000 may continue initializing network drivers, but you can now log on to the system. As for Windows XP and Windows Server 2003, if your computer isn't joined to a domain, network initialization will be carried out at the same time as the boot. However, PCs that are members of a domain will still wait.

At this stage, the Service Control Manager loads the services that start automatically. The `Start` value under `HKEY_LOCAL_MACHINE\SYSTEM\CurrentControlSet\Services\`*`DriverName`* is set to `0x2`. Now the services are loaded according to their dependencies, which are described by the values `DependOnGroup` and `DependOnService` under the `HKEY_LOCAL_MACHINE\SYSTEM\CurrentControlSet\Services\DriverName` registry key.

 ### *Note*

As with Windows NT/2000, Windows XP/Windows Server 2003 has not been successfully loaded until you have logged on to the system. After that, the `Clone` control set will be copied to the `LastKnownGood` configuration.

The services listed in the following registry keys start and run asynchronously with the **Welcome to Windows** and **Log On to Windows** dialog boxes:

☐ `HKEY_LOCAL_MACHINE\Software\Microsoft\Windows\CurrentVersion\` `RunServicesOnce`

☐ `HKEY_LOCAL_MACHINE\Software\Microsoft\Windows\CurrentVersion\RunServices`

The Plug and Play device detection process also runs asynchronously with the logon process and relies on system firmware, hardware, device drivers, and operating-system features to detect and enumerate new devices. When these components are properly coordinated, Plug and Play allows for device detection, system-resource allocation, driver installation, and device installation with minimal user intervention. Detailed information on the Plug and Play detection process was provided in *Chapter 5*.

After you log on, the following events occur:

☐ **Control sets are updated.** The control set referenced by the `LastKnownGood` entry is updated with the contents in `Clone`. `Clone`, a copy of the `CurrentControlSet` entry, is created each time you start your computer.

☐ **Group Policy settings take effect.** Group Policy settings that apply to the user and computer take effect. For more information about Group Policy, see *Chapter 10*.

☐ **Startup programs run.** Windows XP and Windows Server 2003 start logon scripts, startup programs, and services referenced in these registry and folder locations:

• `HKEY_LOCAL_MACHINE\Software\Microsoft\Windows\CurrentVersion\` `RunOnce`

- `HKEY_LOCAL_MACHINE\Software\Microsoft\Windows\CurrentVersion\`
  `Policies\Explorer\Run`
- `HKEY_LOCAL_MACHINE\SOFTWARE\Microsoft\Windows\`
  `CurrentVersion\Run`
- `HKEY_CURRENT_USER\SOFTWARE\Microsoft\Windows\`
  `CurrentVersion\Run`
- *%systemdrive%*\Documents and Settings\All Users\Start Menu\Programs\
  Startup
- *%systemdrive%*\Documents and Settings*%username%*\Start Menu\Programs\
  Startup
- *%windir%*\Profiles\All Users\Start Menu\Programs\Startup
- *%windir%*\Profiles*%username%*\Start Menu\Programs\Startup

▶ Note

The last two *%windir%* folders exist only on systems upgraded from Windows NT 4.0.

Loading Other Services and Drivers

As mentioned earlier, the system may continue loading and initializing certain services and drivers from the moment you log on. Future sections of this chapter concentrate on the following important topics:

❑ Control sets in the registry. Control sets contain information on the system configuration used during system startup. Proper understanding of control sets is necessary to use the `LastKnownGood` configuration effectively.

❑ How the registry data specifies the loading order of services and drivers. We will discuss the Start value that specifies the loading order of the service or driver. We will also discuss the `Error Control` value that defines the default behavior of the system in the event that the driver or service cannot be loaded or initialized correctly.

Control Sets in the Registry

The Control set contains system-configuration data, including information on the device drivers that need to be loaded and the services that need to be started. Control sets are stored in the registry under the `HKEY_LOCAL_MACHINE\SYSTEM` registry key. The system may have several control sets. Their number depends on how frequently you modify the system settings or how often problems arise. A typical installation of any Windows NT-based operating system contains the following control sets:

❏ Clone
❏ ControlSet001
❏ ControlSet002
❏ ControlSet003
❏ CurrentControlSet

The CurrentControlSet subkey points to one of the ControlSet00x subkeys. The Clone control set is an exact copy of the control set used for starting and initializing the system (Default or LastKnownGood). The kernel-initialization process creates this control set at each system startup. The Clone control set becomes inaccessible after the first successful logon.

The HKEY_LOCAL_MACHINE\SYSTEM\Select registry key contains the following entries:

❏ Current
❏ Default
❏ Failed
❏ LastKnownGood

These parameters contain REG_DWORD data that point to a specific control set. For example, if the Current value is set to 0x1, then the CurrentControlSet points to ControlSet001. Similarly, if the LastKnownGood value is set to 0x2, it points to the ControlSet002. Usually, the Default value is the same as the Current value. The Failed parameter indicates the control set specified by the Default parameter when the user last used the LastKnownGood control set.

Earlier in the chapter, we discussed the process of system initialization using the Default and LastKnownGood configurations. When the kernel uses the default configuration, it uses the Default value to identify the control set that should be used for initialization.

There are only two situations in which the kernel uses the LastKnownGood configuration.

❏ During system recovery after a critical failure (for example, if one of the critical-device drivers couldn't be loaded or initialized). We will discuss this topic in greater detail later in the chapter.

❏ When the user selects the LastKnownGood configuration from the **Hardware Profile/LastKnownGood** menu.

If you have either of the following problems, using the LastKnownGood control set may help you recover the damaged system:

❏ Problems caused by a device driver added to the system since the last successful startup
❏ Boot problems caused by invalid registry modifications

The LastKnownGood control set can help you recover from configuration errors.

 ### Note

If you suspect that changes made since the last successful user-logon process are causing problems, do not log on, since this causes the LastKnownGood control set to be overwritten. Instead, restart the computer, and press F8 when prompted. Select **Last Known Good Configuration** from the Advanced Options startup menu. If you select the **Last Known Good** option during startup, all modifications introduced since the last successful startup will be discarded.

After the first user logs on, all configuration changes introduced using Control Panel applets will be reflected only by the CurrentControlSet control set. Thus, if you need to modify the control set, the only control set worth editing is the CurrentControlSet.

If you have problems finding subkeys of the CurrentControlSet, use the **Find Key** command from the **View** menu of the registry editor (Regedit.exe).

The *Start* Value

Each of the HKEY_LOCAL_MACHINE\SYSTEM\<control set>\Services\ <DriverName> (where DriverName is the name of specific driver) keys contains the Start value that defines the loading order for the driver or service. The Start parameter can take one of the following values:

❏ 0x0 (*Boot*). The driver or service is loaded by the operating-system boot loader before the kernel initialization phase starts. Disk drivers, for example, belong to this group.
❏ 0x1 (*System*). The service or driver is loaded by the I/O subsystem during kernel initialization. This value type, for example, is used by mouse drivers.

❑ 0x2 (*Auto load*). The service or driver is loaded by the Service Control Manager. This type of loading order is generally used for services that start automatically under any conditions, regardless of the service type. This type of value is used, for example, by parallel port device drivers. An example of a service that uses this value is the Alerter service.

❑ 0x3 (*Load on Demand, Manual*). The Service Control Manager will load this service only after obtaining explicit instructions to do so. Services of this type are always available, but load only when the user starts them manually.

❑ 0x4 (*Disabled*). This service or driver will never be loaded. Windows disables services or drivers if they can't be loaded by the Service Control Manager (for example, if the appropriate hardware isn't installed). If the Start parameter is set to this value, the Service Control Manager never tries to load the service or driver. The only exception to this rule is the case of file-system drivers, which the system always tries to load, even when the Start entry for these drivers is set to 0x4.

The *ErrorControl* Value

The list shown below provides brief descriptions of all of the possible values of the ErrorControl registry entry located under HKEY_LOCAL_MACHINE\SYSTEM\ <control set>\Services\<DriverName>.

❑ *Ignore* (0x0). If an error occurs while loading or initializing the device driver, the startup procedure continues without displaying an error message.

❑ *Normal* (0x1). If an error occurs while loading or initializing the device driver, the startup procedure will continue after displaying an error message. The ErrorControl value entries for most device drivers are set to this value.

❑ *Severe* (0x2). If the kernel detects an error while loading or initializing the driver or service, it switches to the LastKnownGood control set. The startup process then restarts. If the LastKnownGood control set is already in use, the startup procedure continues, and the error is ignored.

❑ *Critical* (0x3). The procedure used in this case is similar to the one used for Severe errors. But there is one exception. If the system has already switched to the LastKnownGood control set and this didn't eliminate the error, the boot process stops and the system displays a failure message.

Preventing System Failures

Now it is time to discuss the measures that will help you prevent system failures. Naturally, all emergency planning should be done beforehand.

Performing maintenance procedures on a regular basis allows you to prevent possible problems or, at least, minimize their negative effect. The general procedures are listed below:

❏ Most of the time, system malfunctions, or even boot failures, are caused by overwritten system files or by incompatible drivers. This usually happens when you install incompatible third-party software. This problem exists not only in Windows 2000, Windows XP, and Windows Server 2003, but in all earlier versions of the Windows NT operating system as well. Windows 2000, Windows XP and Windows Server 2003 implement additional tools, though, which protect system files and drivers with a digital signature. The digital signature guarantees that the system file or driver is Windows-compatible. If you want to avoid any possible problems, it is recommended that you use these tools. This topic will be covered in greater detail later in the chapter.

❏ Back up the System State data and prepare for the Automated System Recovery process (ASR) on a regular basis. Don't forget to perform these operations before introducing significant modifications in the system configuration (including new hardware and software installations). A usable and up-to-date backup copy of all your important data will also be helpful.

❏ In Windows XP systems, don't disable System Restore. Although some users may think that this tool consumes too much free disk space, it can still be very useful if you need to restore a damaged system.

Detailed instructions on performing these operations were provided in *Chapter 2.*

❏ View system event logs on a daily basis (or, at the very least, view the system and application logs). Pay close attention to the messages generated by the FtDisk driver and hard-disk drivers, because they may report possible file-system errors. If you don't follow this rule, file-system errors may remain unnoticed until the Chkdsk utility detects them. Notice that, in this case, the damaged data may even be included in the backup copy, since most backup utilities (including the Backup program supplied with Windows 2000 and later versions) don't recognize errors in user data.

❏ Check your disks on a regular basis for early detection of possible file-system errors. It is also recommended that you defragment your disks regularly to eliminate any possible performance problems. Use only built-in tools or third-party disk utilities certified for Windows 2000/XP/Windows Server 2003. An official list of third-party software products tested for compatibility with Windows 2000/XP/Windows Server 2003 can be downloaded from **http://www.microsoft.com**.

❑ Install a parallel copy of the operating system to improve reliability.

If the POST procedure has been completed successfully, this means that the hardware has initialized correctly. If the boot process still fails, the boot problem may come from one of the following sources:

❑ Problems related to the hard disk containing the system partition.

❑ Corruption of the Master Boot Record (MBR) or partition boot sector.

❑ One of the boot files may be missing or corrupt. A list of the files necessary to boot Windows NT, Windows 2000, Windows XP, or Windows Server 2003 was provided earlier in this chapter.

Windows XP and Windows Server 2003 include several advanced tools that help restore the damaged system. These tools are briefly described in the list below.

❑ *Windows file protection with a digital signature.* Windows 2000, Windows XP, and Windows Server 2003 provide a set of tools that protect system files and device drivers from being overwritten during software-installation procedures. Previous versions of Windows NT didn't provide protection for system files (which also include dynamically loaded libraries (DLL) and executables (EXE)). If these files were accidentally overwritten by incompatible versions, the possible consequences range from performance degradation to catastrophic failures. Windows 2000 and its successors include the following system-file protection tools: System File Protection (SFP), System File Checker (SFC), and File Signature Verification (FSV).

❑ *Automatic Updates.* Automatic Updates automates the process of downloading updates from the Windows Update website. You can configure Automatic Updates to check for and download updates.

❑ *Safe mode.* This option closely resembles a similar boot option included in Windows 95/98. It is one of the most important and useful features introduced with Windows 2000 and further enhanced in Windows XP and Windows Server 2003. When the system boots in safe mode, it loads the minimum set of device drivers and services. Safe mode improves reliability and provides an easy way to recover a system damaged by incorrect software installation. Notice, however, that the safe-mode option isn't a universal tool that helps in all cases. For example, this option is almost useless if there's a problem with your hard disk or if any of the system files are missing or corrupt.

❑ *Automated System Recovery*. Automated System Recovery (ASR) is a two-part recovery system that allows you to restore a damaged Windows XP or Windows Server 2003 installation by using files saved to tape media, and hard-disk-configuration information saved to a floppy disk. It replaces the Emergency Repair Disk (ERD) function that was present in earlier Windows NT versions and, with some improvements, was also included with Windows 2000. Step-by-step descriptions required in order to prepare and perform the Automated System Recovery are provided in *Chapter 2*.

❑ *Driver Rollback*. This is probably one of the most useful recovery tools introduced with Windows XP and Windows Server 2003. Now, if you have installed an updated version of the driver after installing Windows XP or one of the products of the Windows Server 2003 family, and suspect that this operation has caused system instability or boot problems, you can replace a specific device driver with a previously installed version. Replacing a driver is the simplest way of restoring the system, provided, of course, that it is the driver that is causing the problem. The **Roll Back Driver** button in Device Manager enables you to revert to an older driver while you investigate issues with the new one. The procedures for performing Driver Rollback are described in *Chapter 5*. Note that, if you update several drivers during a single session, it might be more convenient to use the **Last Known Good Configuration** startup option.

❑ *Error Reporting*. Error Reporting, if enabled, monitors your system for problems that affect Windows XP or Windows Server 2003 components and applications. When a problem occurs, you can send a problem report to Microsoft and receive a response with more information.

❑ *Recovery Console*. Recovery Console provides a command-line interface to perform the recovery of a damaged system. Using Recovery Console, you can enable or disable services, restore damaged Master Boot Records and/or partition-boot sectors and replace damaged system files. This is a powerful recovery tool, available only for users with administrative rights in the local system. The syntax of the Recovery Console commands will be discussed later in this chapter.

System File Protection in Windows 2000, Windows XP and Windows Server 2003

All system files and device drivers in Windows 2000, Windows XP, and Windows Server 2003 are protected by a digital signature, which confirms that these system files and drivers are compatible with the operating system. A Microsoft digital signature verifies that the signed file was successfully tested for compatibility at Windows Hardware Quality Labs (WHQL), and wasn't modified or overwritten when installing add-on software.

According to the configuration settings, Windows 2000/XP and Windows Server 2003 might ignore drivers that aren't digitally signed, display a warning message when detecting these drivers (this option is set by default), or simply prohibit their installation. To configure system-file protection options in Windows 2000/XP/ Windows Server 2003, proceed as follows:

1. Open Control Panel and start the **System** applet. The **System Properties** window will open. Go to the **Hardware** tab (Fig. 6.5).

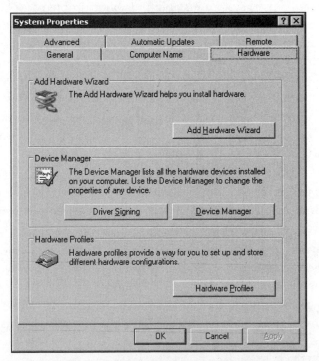

Fig. 6.5. The **Hardware** tab of the **System Properties** window

2. Click the **Driver Signing** button. The **Driver Signing Options** window will appear (Fig. 6.6). This window contains the **What action do you want Windows to take?** option group, which allows you to specify the following options:

   - If you select the **Ignore** radio button, the system will allow you to install any of the drivers. However, it won't check if the driver you are going to install has a digital signature. (If this option is installed, Windows 2000/XP or Windows Server 2003 behaves like Windows NT 4.0). As already mentioned, the presence of a digital signature confirms that the file has been officially tested for compatibility. If the system file or device driver doesn't have a digital signature, this means that the file isn't officially guaranteed to be compatible.

   - If you set the **Warn** radio button, the system will display warnings any time an attempt is made to install a system file or driver that isn't digitally signed (Fig. 6.7). Notice that, despite this warning, the system file or driver will be installed. Furthermore, you can encounter situations where Microsoft currently has no certification program for the device that you are attempting to install (Fig. 6.8). In particular, this is true for devices that have appeared on the market recently. Still, most of these devices (such as portable USB disk drives, infrared ports, digital cameras, Bluetooth devices, etc.) will install without problems and operate smoothly.

   - If you set the **Block** radio button, the system won't allow anyone to install drivers without a digital signature.

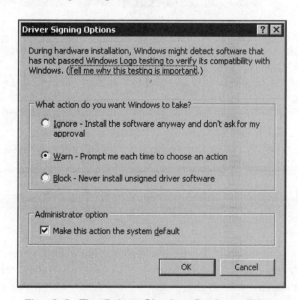

Fig. 6.6. The **Driver Signing Options** dialog

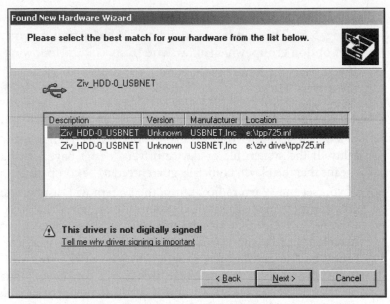

Fig. 6.7. Any time an attempt is made to install a system file or driver that isn't digitally signed, Windows 2000/XP and Windows Server 2003 operating systems display a warning

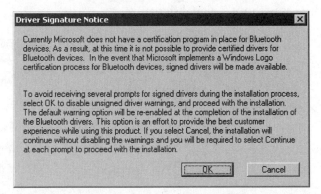

Fig. 6.8. For the moment of this writing, Microsoft had no certification program for Bluetooth devices

Note

Users with administrative rights (Administrator and members of the Administrators group) can specify the default option, which will be used by default for all users who log on to the computer. To establish this mode, set the **Apply setting as system default** checkbox in the **Administrator option** group.

Mechanism of Driver Protection by a Digital Signature

How do Windows 2000, Windows XP and products of the Windows Server 2003 family install drivers? There are two methods:

☐ Automatic driver installation by the PnP subsystem. This method, first introduced in Windows 2000, was further streamlined in Windows XP and Windows Server 2003 and is the recommended option. More detailed information on this topic was provided in *Chapter 5*. Here, you should remember that Windows 2000 and its successors only attempt driver installation after the Plug and Play subsystem (PnP subsystem) has discovered a new device. The User-Mode Plug and Play Manager (UMPNPMGR, which is the system DLL: *%SystemRoot%*\System32\Umpnpmgr.dll) waits until the kernel-mode PnP subsystem notifies it that a new device has been detected. When the notification arrives, UMPNPMGR searches the INF file for a device driver that contains the necessary installation information. All INF files for drivers included with Windows 2000, Windows XP or Windows Server 2003 are located in the *%SystemRoot%*\INF folder. If you are installing an OEM driver, the INF file will probably be located on the floppy disk or CD supplied by the vendor.

☐ There is also another method for installing device drivers — using the Hardware Installation Wizard located at *%SystemRoot%*\System32\Newdev.dll. The Hardware Installation Wizard performs the same operations as the user-mode PnP Manager. It also searches the INF file for the device driver to be installed.

Both UMPNPMGR and Hardware Installation Wizard use Setup API (SETUPAPI — *%SystemRoot%*\System32\Setupapi.dll) for reading the information contained in the INF file. Besides handling driver-installation instructions, Windows 2000/XP/Windows Server 2003 checks the Policy value under HKEY_LOCAL_MACHINE\SOFTWARE\Microsoft\Driver Signing (Fig. 6.9). If this entry is missing, Windows 2000 and Windows XP/Windows Server 2003 will check the Policy value under HKEY_CURRENT_USER\Software\Microsoft\Driver Signing. Note that you set these parameters using the **Driver Signing Options** dialog. If you have logged on to the system as an Administrator and you instruct the system to use this option by default, the system will follow the Policy setting under HKEY_LOCAL_MACHINE. Otherwise, it will follow the HKEY_CURRENT_USER parameter. When the system checks these settings, it turns first to the Policy setting under HKEY_LOCAL_MACHINE (if this value is set, it will have priority over the parameters set for individual users). If the Policy value is set to 0, the system will install

all of the drivers, including those with no digital signature. If this value is set to 1, the system will allow you to install drivers without a digital signature, but a warning message will be displayed. If this value is set to 2, all of the drivers that aren't digitally signed will be ignored.

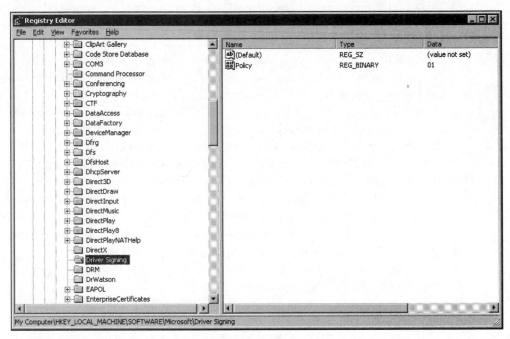

Fig. 6.9. The `HKEY_LOCAL_MACHINE\SOFTWARE\Microsoft\Driver Signing` registry key

If the policy on unsigned drivers makes it necessary to check the digital signature, Setupapi.dll calls on CryptoAPI services to decrypt the signature using the VeriSign open key.

But where does the system store the digital signatures that protect Windows 2000/XP/Windows Server 2003 device drivers and system files? Microsoft stores all the digital signatures protecting Windows distribution files in special catalog files that are located in the *%SystemRoot%*\System32\Catroot directory. OEM device drivers should be supplied along with their individual catalog files. Microsoft supplies these files to the device supplier after the device has been successfully tested and included in the Hardware Compatibility List (HCL). The \Catroot directory contains the master index of the device-driver catalog files (sysmast.cbd and sysmast.cbk) and the nested folder. The nested-folder name represents a long combination of digits and characters. When you open this folder, you will find catalog files for all of the operating system's built-in components. The Nt5.cat and Nt5inf.cat files deserve special attention, because they store the digital signatures for all of the Windows 2000/XP/Windows Server 2003 system files included in the distribution set.

If the result of decrypting the digital signature of a device driver or system file doesn't coincide with the digital signature contained in the driver-catalog file, or if the driver has no catalog file, you will either get a warning message or (if the option has been set) the driver installation will fail.

Other Tools for Protecting Windows 2000/XP/ Windows Server 2003 System Files

Windows 2000/XP/Windows Server 2003 also includes tools which allow you to protect the device drivers and system files. These tools guarantee that the device drivers and system files remain unchanged, and include the following:

❑ Windows File Protection
❑ System File Checker
❑ File Signature Verification

Windows File Protection

All earlier versions of Windows had one common drawback — when installing third-party add-on software, all shared files (including DLL and EXE files) could be changed or even overwritten by incorrect or incompatible versions. This, of course, could lead to unpredictable results. For example, the system performance could be affected, certain applications could behave incorrectly, or STOP errors could become persistent. In some cases, this could even render your system unbootable.

Windows 2000 is the first Windows operating system in which an attempt was made to correct this situation. This functionality is also present in Windows XP and all products of the Windows Server 2003 family. The Windows File Protection feature contains the following two components:

❑ Windows File Protection service
❑ The System File Checker command-line utility (Sfc.exe)

Windows File Protection service (WFP) is based on the principle of detecting the digital signatures of all protected system files (such as SYS, DLL, OCX, TTF,

FON, EXE files) and protecting these files from being modified or replaced accidentally. Windows File Protection services runs in background mode and protects all files installed by the Setup program during installation of the operating system.

WFP detects any attempts made by other programs to replace the protected system files. It performs this task by checking to make sure that the file intended to replace the protected version is digitally signed. The presence of a digital signature verifies that the version is compatible with the operating system. If the newer version is incorrect, Windows File Protection replaces this file with the one from the backup copy of the *%SystemRoot%*\System32\Dllcache folder or from the distribution CD. If the Windows File Protection function can't locate a correct version of the file, it prompts you to specify the path to a directory that stores this version. It also registers any attempt at system-file replacement in the system-event log. This function is enabled by default, which means that it will allow you to replace protected system files only when you are installing the following types of software:

❐   Service Packs (using the Update.exe program)

❐   Hotfix packs (using the Hotfix.exe program)

❐   Operating-system upgrades (using the Winnt32.exe program)

❐   Any Windows Update software

System File Checker

Windows 2000, Windows XP, and Windows Server 2003 include a special utility for checking system files (System File Checker, Sfc.exe). This is a command-line utility, which scans all installed system files and checks their versions when rebooting the system. If this utility detects replaced versions of any protected system file, it will find the correct version in the *%SystemRoot%*\System32\Dllcache directory and will replace the modified file with this version.

This utility uses the following syntax:

```
sfc [/scannow] [/scanonce] [/scanboot] [/cancel] [/quiet] [/enable]
    [/purgecache] [/cachesize=x]
```

where:

/scannow — if this parameter has been specified, SFC will perform the check immediately.

/scanonce — if you specify this parameter, SFC will scan all protected system files only once.

/scanboot — if you specify this parameter, a scan will take place each time you reboot the system.

/revert — returns scan to the default settings (Windows XP only).

/cancel — cancels all pending scans of protected system files (Windows 2000 only).

/quiet — replaces all incorrect file versions without prompting the user (Windows 2000 only).

/enable — enables WFP for standard operation (Windows 2000 only).

/purgecache — this switch clears the file cache of the System File Protection function and scans all protected system files immediately.

/cachesize=x — allows you to specify the size of the file cache of the System File Protection function (in MB).

Note

To use the Sfc.exe utility, you need to log on as an Administrator or member of the Administrators group.

If the contents of the *%SystemRoot%*\System32\Dllcache folder become corrupt, use Sfc /scanonce, Sfc /scannow or Sfc /scanboot commands to restore the contents of the \Dllcache folder.

Now, let's answer the following question: Where does the system store all of the settings that control SFC? Not surprisingly, they are stored in the registry. All registry settings that control SFC behavior are located under HKEY_LOCAL_MACHINE\SOFTWARE\Microsoft\Windows NT\CurrentVersion\Winlogon. These settings are listed below:

- SFCDisable — the first registry setting read by SFC. If this value isn't set to 0 and the system is running in debugging mode (WinDbg kernel debugger is active), SFC disables all of the functions for protecting system files and device drivers.
- SFCScan. If this value is set to 1, SFC will scan the system files immediately after system initialization. If the SFCScan value is set to 2, SFC will reset it to 0 immediately after performing the scan. The default value for this setting is 0 and the value instructs SFC to protect system files (however, without scanning immediately after system initialization).
- SfcDllCacheDir — specifies the path to the \Dllcache folder.
- SFCQuota — this value specifies the total size of the system files that need to be scanned and protected.

Note

None of the registry settings listed above are mandatory, nor are they present in the registry by default. If any of these settings are missing, SFC behaves as if the missing parameters are present and set to default values (the default value for SFCQuota is equal to -1; this value specifies an unlimited size of data to be checked).

File Signature Verification

As mentioned before, there are some cases where the system file is replaced by incorrect or incompatible versions during the installation procedures for third-party add-on software that isn't digitally signed. This replacement can make your system unstable (and be a potential source of persistent boot problem STOP errors).

To avoid this kind of problem, all of the system files installed during Windows 2000/XP/Windows Server 2003 Setup are protected by Microsoft digital signatures. This guarantees that the digitally signed files are compatible with the operating system. The digital signature also verifies that the signed file is either the original version developed by Microsoft or has been tested for compatibility. Verification of the files' digital signatures allows you to identify all of the files installed on the computer that aren't digitally signed. The File Signature Verification utility also displays the following information on the detected files:

❑ Name and fully qualified path to the file
❑ Date of modification to the file
❑ File type and version number

To start the verification procedure, click the **Start** button, select **Run,** and enter the following command: sigverif.

If you save the information collected by sigverif in the log file, this tool will prove to be very useful for troubleshooting problems related to incorrect versions of system files. To log this information, proceed as follows:

1. Start the sigverif program. The **File Signature Verification** window will open (Fig. 6.10). Click the **Advanced** button.
2. The **Advanced File Signature Verification Settings** window will open. Go to the **Logging** tab (Fig. 6.11) and set the **Save the file signature verification results to a log file** checkbox.

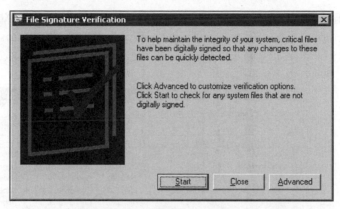

Fig. 6.10. The initial dialog of the File Signature Verification program

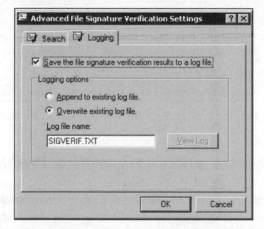

Fig. 6.11. The **Logging** tab of the **Advanced File Signature Verification Settings** window

3. Go to the **Logging options** group, which provides you with the following logging options:

   • **Append to existing log file**: if you select this radio button, the results of the new scanning operation will be added to the end of the existing log file.

   • **Overwrite existing log file**: if you select this option, the existing log file will be overwritten by the results of the new scan.

   • You can manually enter the log file name into the **Log file name** field.

4. Click **OK**. You'll return to the **File Signature Verification** window. To start scanning, click the **Start** button in this window. The **Scanning files...** progress indicator will show the scanning progress. To cancel scanning, click **Stop**.

When finished, the program will display the **Signature Verification Results** window (Fig. 6.12), containing a complete list of all the unsigned files the program has detected.

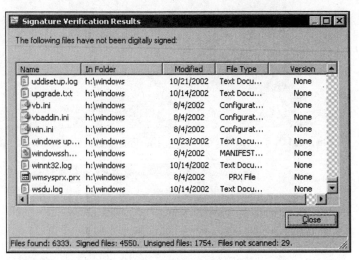

Fig. 6.12. The **Signature Verification Results** window

Starting the System with Configuration Problems

When the Windows NT 4.0, Windows 2000, or Windows XP/Windows Server 2003 operating system detects a severe error that it can't correct, it generates a system message known as a "blue screen". The Blue Screen of Death (BSOD) may also appear when Windows NT/2000/XP/Windows Server 2003 stops during the boot process to prevent further data corruption. A typical example of the "blue screen" as it appears in Windows 2000, Windows XP, and Windows Server 2003 is shown in Fig. 6.13.

In earlier Windows NT versions, the STOP consisted of 5 parts. The Windows 2000 STOP screen consists of only three parts: bugcheck information, recommended user action, and debug port information. Even so, the interpretation of STOP messages and the identification of the true source of problems still remains a difficult task. If the STOP message appears during the startup process, the following are the most probable sources of the problem:

❑ The user has installed add-on software that has destroyed one of the most important parts of the system registry — the HKEY_LOCAL_MACHINE root key. This usually happens when an application program attempts to install a new system service or device driver. As a result, the "blue screen" either informs you that the system could not load the registry, or one of the registry files, will be indicated.

❑ The user configured the system hardware incorrectly. As a result, critical system files were overwritten or were corrupted.

❑ The user tried to install a system service or device driver that is not compatible with the hardware installed on the computer. When the user tries to reboot the system, it will attempt to load the incorrect file. This will destroy the correct version of this system file that was loaded before the failure.

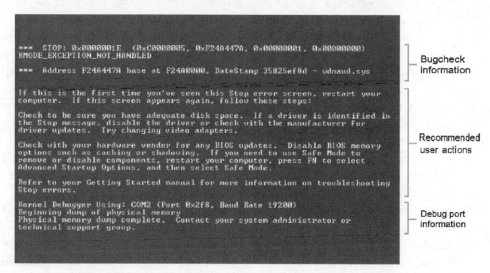

Fig. 6.13. Typical "blue screen of death" in Windows NT 4.0

▶ *Note*

Active use of the Windows 2000/XP/Windows Server 2003 system file-protection features described in the previous section is one of the most efficient and reliable methods of preventing boot-time STOP screens. If you really want to avoid startup problems, don't neglect these tools!

What can be done if a problem already exists? Sometimes the message displayed in the case of a boot failure may explicitly refer to the missing or corrupt registry file (the message that informs you of a missing or corrupt SYSTEM hive file, shown at the beginning of this chapter, is an example). In certain cases, STOP messages may also inform you of an instance of registry corruption that is preventing the system from booting. Unfortunately, this isn't always true. If you suspect that the boot problems are related to the registry, first try to restore the damaged system using the LastKnownGood configuration.

Ntldr displays a boot menu that allows you to select the operating system to be started. For *x*86-based computers, this menu depends on the contents of the Boot.ini file. To use the **LastKnownGood Configuration** in Windows NT 4.0, press the <Space> key when the boot menu appears. Then select the **LastKnownGood Configuration** option. To use the **LastKnownGood Configuration** in Windows 2000, Windows XP, and Windows Server 2003, press <F8> to display the Advanced startup menu, which was described earlier in this chapter.

If you are an experienced Windows NT 4.0 user, you will recall that most of the boot problems in the system were caused by incompatible or incorrect device drivers. Incompatible drivers can either result in a system crash immediately after installation or after a certain period of time, during which they seem to work correctly. The second situation, when the corrupt driver works for some time without causing any problems, has always been difficult to explain. Why did it work at all? What actually caused the problem? Sometimes it may even seem that there are no reasonable explanations. However, remember one variant of Murphy's Law: "If there are two or more ways to do something, and one of those ways can result in a catastrophe, then someone will do it".

Suppose that there is a bug in the driver (after all, "there is always one more bug") that didn't reveal itself right away. Both the hardware and software configuration of your computer may change with time, and these changes may wake the wretched thing up (because, if something can go wrong, it will). Remember, Windows 2000/XP/Windows Server 2003 can also be prevented from booting by an incompatible driver. However, Windows 2000 and, especially, Windows XP/ Windows Server 2003 are more reliable and robust than Windows NT 4.0 because booting the system in the safe mode (the concept borrowed from Windows 9*x*) presents a more convenient means for quick recovery after such errors.

If an incompatible driver causes a problem when you reboot the system for the first time after installing it, you are lucky. In this case, the **LastKnownGood Configuration** will be very helpful. When you select this option from the safe-boot menu, the system will use the HKEY_LOCAL_MACHINESYSTEM\CurrentControlSet registry key and restore all the configuration information stored since the last successful boot. If using the **LastKnownGood Configuration** option didn't help and you know for certain which driver has caused the problem (the sigverif utility discussed earlier in the chapter gives you a list of these drivers), you can try other methods of quick recovery. For example, try using safe-mode options, such as **Safe Mode, Safe Mode with Networking,** or **Safe Mode with Command Prompt.** After the system boots with the minimum set of services and drivers, you can try deleting the corrupt driver using administrative tools such as Hardware Wizard or Device Manager. If both system and boot partitions are formatted using the FAT file system, you can try booting from an MS-DOS system disk and manually delete or rename the driver that is causing the problems.

Note

The **LastKnownGood Configuration** option provides the quickest and easiest method of recovering a corrupt registry for both Windows NT 4.0 and Windows 2000/XP/Windows Server 2003 (if it works, of course). Unfortunately, this method has some limitations. For example, it restores only one part of the registry (namely, the `ControlSet00x` branch under `HKEY_LOCAL_MACHINE\SYSTEM`). As a result, it will only help you to recover the damaged system if the problem is limited to this registry branch and if you use this method immediately. Note that all configuration changes introduced in the system since the last successful boot will be lost if you use this method.

If the information provided above does not help you to solve the problem, then it is time to use one of the methods for restoring the corrupt registry discussed in *Chapter 2.*

Note

A disk partition other than the boot partition is a safe place for storing the backup copies of your registry (ideally, you should store registry backups on another physical disk). This will help you to safeguard the registry backups from hardware failures, which might make your backup copies unavailable.

Recovery Console

Windows 2000/XP/Windows Server 2003 Recovery Console provides a command-line interface, providing administrators and users with administrative privileges with the ability to recover a system that will not boot. Using the Recovery Console, you can start and stop system services, read and write data to the local hard drives (including NTFS drives), and repair damaged boot sectors and MBR.

This new function is especially useful when you need to copy one or more system files to the local hard drive in order to recover a damaged system. You can copy these files from a CD or disk. Recovery Console will also be very helpful if you need to reconfigure a service or driver that causes boot problems.

▶ *Note*

You need to log in as an Administrator to access the Recovery Console.

Methods of starting, installing, or deleting the Recovery Console were discussed in detail in *Chapter 2*. In this chapter, we will concentrate on using this tool for recovering a system that has configuration problems.

Using Recovery Console

Recovery Console provides an MS-DOS-like command-line interface. Like any other tool of this sort, Recovery Console has a `help` command that displays a list of available commands. You can also find a complete list of Recovery Console commands in the Windows 2000/XP/Windows Server 2003 online Help system (search using the keywords "Recovery Console").

A brief listing of Recovery Console commands is provided below:

- ❑ `Attrib` — changes file or folder attributes
- ❑ `Batch` — executes commands contained in the text file you specify
- ❑ `Bootcfg` — manipulates the Boot.ini file
- ❑ `ChDir (CD)` — changes to another directory
- ❑ `Chkdsk` — starts the Chkdsk program
- ❑ `Cls` — clears the screen
- ❑ `Copy` — copies a single file you've specified
- ❑ `Delete (DEL)` — deletes a single file
- ❑ `Dir` — lists the contents of the current directory
- ❑ `Disable` — disables the system service or driver
- ❑ `Diskpart` — manages partitions on your hard disk
- ❑ `Enable` — enables the service or driver
- ❑ `Exit` — exits Recovery Console and reboots the computer
- ❑ `Expand` — expands the compressed file
- ❑ `Fixboot` — repairs the corrupt boot sector on the system partition
- ❑ `Fixmbr` — repairs the corrupt Master Boot Record
- ❑ `Format` — formats the hard drive
- ❑ `Help` — displays a list of Recovery Console commands
- ❑ `Listsvc` — displays a list of all of the available services and drivers
- ❑ `Logon` — allows you to log on to the Windows 2000/XP system
- ❑ `Map` — displays a list of drive mappings
- ❑ `MkDir (MD)` — creates a new directory

- ❏ More — displays text files in screen-size portions
- ❏ Rename (REN) — renames the file
- ❏ RmDir (RD) — deletes the directory
- ❏ Set — displays and sets the Recovery Console environment variables
- ❏ SystemRoot — marks the current directory as *SystemRoot*
- ❏ Type — prints the text file on the screen

To display information concerning the use of a certain command, use the following syntax:

```
HELP command name
```

(for example, HELP FIXBOOT) or

```
command name /?
```

(for example, LISTSVC /?).

Note

There are certain limitations that restrict the usage of the Recovery Console. For example, in Win2K, you could copy the files from disks to the local hard disk, but any attempt at copying the files from the hard drive to disk failed. You can only create a new directory within the *%SystemRoot%* folder (\WINNT, for example), but this operation fails if you attempt to create a new directory at the root level (C:\). You can only copy files to the root folder or to the *%SystemRoot%* directory. Finally, the copy command doesn't support wildcard characters and, consequently, doesn't allow you to copy multiple files.

Summary

This chapter concentrated mainly on the role of the system registry in the startup process, methods of preventing boot failures, and the most common procedures for recovering a system with configuration problems related to a corrupt registry.

CHAPTER 7

Software Settings
in the Registry

Put up in a place
where it's easy to see
the cryptic admonishment
T.T.T.
When you feel how depressingly
slowly you climb,
it's well to remember that
Things Take Time.

Piet Hein
Grooks

Every day, system administrators have to engage in extremely difficult tasks; they need to manage all the hardware, operating systems, and applications installed on their organization's computers. They often need to administer the registry as well. A very short description of the root registry keys existing in Windows NT/2000, Windows XP, and Windows Server 2003 registries was provided in *Chapter 1*. This chapter considers the topic in more detail. Since it was written as a brief reference on the main registry keys existing in all Windows NT-based operating systems and emphasizes the new keys that have been added to Windows XP and products of the Windows Server 2003 family, system administrators can greatly benefit from it.

Note

Like many other system components, the registry is very similar to the Windows NT/2000 registry, due to the fact that Windows XP and Windows Server 2003 are based on the Windows NT/2000 kernel. However, because of new functionality and kernel enhancements, introduced with newer versions, new registry keys and value entries have appeared. This is not surprising, since all new features must be reflected in the registry.

The *HKEY_LOCAL_MACHINE* Key

HKEY_LOCAL_MACHINE is one of the most important and most interesting root keys of the registry. It contains configuration data for local computer. Information stored in this registry key is used by applications and device drivers and by the operating system itself for obtaining information on the local computer's configuration. Moreover, the information doesn't depend on the user who's logged in to the system.

The HKEY_LOCAL_MACHINE root key contains five subkeys, briefly described in Table 7.1. The rest of this section describes the subkeys in greater detail.

Note

You can read the information contained in any of these subkeys, but it only makes sense to edit the contents of the Software and System keys.

Table 7.1. Subkeys Contained within the HKEY_LOCAL_MACHINE Root Key

Subkey	Contents
HARDWARE	This subkey contains a database describing all the hardware devices installed on the computer, the method of interaction between device drivers and hardware devices, and the data that connects kernel-mode device drivers with user-mode code. All the data contained within this subkey are volatile. The system re-creates these data each time it starts.
	The Description subkey describes all the hardware physically present on the computer. The hardware recognizer collects this information at system startup and the kernel stores this information under the HKEY_LOCAL_MACHINE\HARDWARE\DESCRIPTION registry key.
	The DeviceMap subkey contains various data in formats defined by certain device driver classes. As device drivers are loading, they pass their information to the system so that it can associate specific hardware devices and their drivers.

continues

Table 7.1 Continued

Subkey	Contents
HARDWARE	The ResourceMap subkey contains information on the system resources allocated to each device (including ports, DMA addresses, IRQs). Notice that all Windows NT-based operating systems, including Windows 2000, Windows XP and Windows Server 2003 provide a much more convenient way to view the contents of this subkey. To view (and possibly change) this data, it is recommended that you use various administrative tools. For example, if you're using Windows NT 4.0, you can view the information using the Windows NT Diagnostics utility (Winmsdp.exe). In Windows 2000/XP and Windows Server 2003, you can use the MMC console or Device Manager for the same purpose.
SAM	This subkey contains the directory services database, which stores information on user and group accounts and security subsystems (SAM stands for the Security Account Manager). By default, you can't view this key using reglstry editors even if you're logged in as an Administrator. The data contained within the HKLM\SAM registry key isn't documented, and user passwords are encrypted.
	Note that for Windows NT domains the SAM database also stores a domain directory services database. In native-mode Windows 2000 or Windows Server 2003 domains, the directory services database is stored in the Ntds.dit file on domain controllers. However, the SAM database remains important, since it stores local accounts (required to log on locally). If your computer that is running Windows XP or Windows Server 2003 does not participate in a domain, SAM database is the main storage of the user and group accounts information.
SECURITY	This database contains the local security policy, including user rights and permissions. The key is only used by the security subsystem. For example, it contains information that defines whether or not an individual user can reboot the computer, start or stop device drivers, backup/recover files, or access the computer through the network. Information contained within this key is also encrypted. The HKLM\SAM key is the link to the HKLM\SECURITY\SAM key.
SOFTWARE	This database contains information on the software products installed on the local computer, along with various configuration data.
SYSTEM	This database contains information on controlling the system startup, the loading order of device drivers and system services, and on operating system behavior.

If the HKEY_CURRENT_USER registry key contains data similar to that contained under HKEY_LOCAL_MACHINE, then by default the HKEY_CURRENT_USER data takes priority.

Note

If you read the previous chapter carefully, you'll recall that the Policy setting under HKEY_LOCAL_MACHINE is given priority over the individual settings specified for each user. This is only true if you logged in to the system as an Administrator and specified the default value for the power policy, as described in *Chapter 5*.

However, the settings under this key may also extend the data under HKEY_LOCAL_MACHINE rather than replace them. Furthermore, there are certain settings (for example, those that manage the device driver loading order) that have no meaning outside the HKEY_LOCAL_MACHINE root key.

The HKEY_LOCAL_MACHINE\HARDWARE *Key*

The HKEY_LOCAL_MACHINE\HARDWARE registry key contains hardware data recreated during each system startup. This data includes information about the devices on the motherboard and the data on the IRQs used by individual device drivers.

The HARDWARE key contains important data sets subdivided between the following three subkeys: DESCRIPTION, DEVICEMAP, and RESOURCEMAP.

All the information contained under HKEY_LOCAL_MACHINE\HARDWARE is volatile. This means that the settings are computed and recreated each time the system starts up, and are lost when you shut the system down. All drivers and applications use this subtree for obtaining information on system components and for storing the data directly under the DEVICEMAP subkey and indirectly under the RESOURCEMAP subkey (Fig. 7.1).

Note

As was explained in *Chapter 5*, integrated support for Plug and Play and power management in Windows 2000, Windows XP, and Windows Server 2003 is only available on computers that have an Advanced Configuration and Power Interface (ACPI) BIOS. At boot time, the operating system loader checks whether such a BIOS is loaded. If so, ACPI is enabled in the operating system. If such a BIOS is not loaded, ACPI is disabled and the less reliable Advanced Power Management (APM) model is used instead. Microsoft supplies the ACPI driver as part of the operating system. On systems that have an ACPI BIOS, the HAL causes the ACPI driver to be loaded during system start-up at the base of the device tree, where it acts as the interface between the operating system and the BIOS. The ACPI driver is transparent to other drivers. If your system has ACPI BIOS, the HKEY_LOCAL_MACHINE\HARDWARE registry tree will contain the nested ACPI subkey (Fig. 7.1).

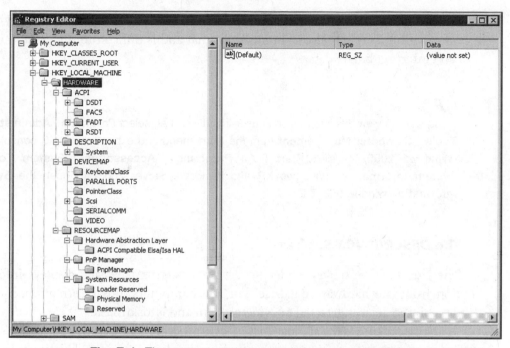

Fig. 7.1. The HKEY_LOCAL_MACHINE\HARDWARE registry key

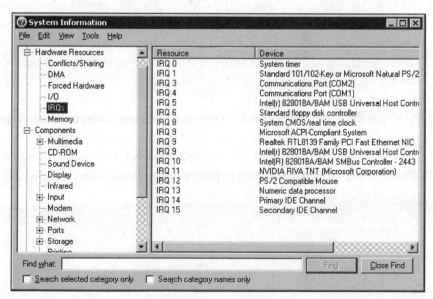

Fig. 7.2. The System Information utility allows you to view hardware information in user-friendly format

Don't try to edit the data under HKEY_LOCAL_MACHINE\HARDWARE directly. This information is usually stored in binary format and is difficult to understand if you can't interpret binary data.

► **Tips**

If you want to view this information in user-friendly format, select **Programs | Administrative Tools | Computer Management** from the **Start** menu and expand the MMC console tree (Windows 2000) or click **Start | All Programs | Accessories | System Tools | System Information** (Windows XP and Windows Server 2003) to open the **System Information** window (Fig. 7.2).

The *DESCRIPTION* Subkey

The DESCRIPTION subkey under HKEY_LOCAL_MACHINE\HARDWARE displays information from the hardware database. For *x*86 computers, this information contains data on the devices detected by Ntdetect.com and Ntoskrnl.exe.

Ntdetect.com is the standard DOS-style program that uses BIOS calls for selecting hardware information and configuring hardware devices. This includes date and time information stored in the CMOS chip; bus types (for example, ISA, PCI, EISA) and identifiers of the devices on these buses; data on the number, type, and capacity of the hard drives installed in the system; and the number and types of parallel ports. Based on this information, the system creates internal data structures that Ntoskrnl.exe stores under HKEY_LOCAL_MACHINE\HARDWARE\DESCRIPTION during system startup.

A specific feature of the Ntdetect.com version included with Windows 2000, Windows XP, and Windows Server 2003 is that PnP detection functions are delegated to PnP drivers. In contrast, the Windows NT 4.0 version of Ntdetect.com detects all installed hardware (due to limited PnP support in Windows NT 4.0).

Ntdetect.com detects the following hardware:

- Type of bus/adapter
- Keyboard
- SCSI adapters
- COM-ports
- Machine ID

- Video adapter
- Arithmetic coprocessor
- Mouse
- Floppy drives
- Parallel ports

Note

Network adapters aren't detected at this phase. The system detects network adapters either during OS installation, or when you install a new network adapter. More detailed information on this topic will be provided in *Chapter 8*.

There are more subkeys, each of them corresponding to a certain bus controller type. These subkeys are located under HKEY_LOCAL_MACHINE\Hardware\Description\ System\MultifunctionAdapter. Each of these keys describes a specific controller class (including hard disk controllers, display controllers, parallel port controllers, and SCSI controllers). The path to the subkey describes the component type. All physical devices are numbered, beginning from 0.

Each detected hardware component has Component Information and Configuration Data settings, which contain binary data on the version of a specific component and its configuration (Fig. 7.3). The Identifier setting contains the component name (if specified).

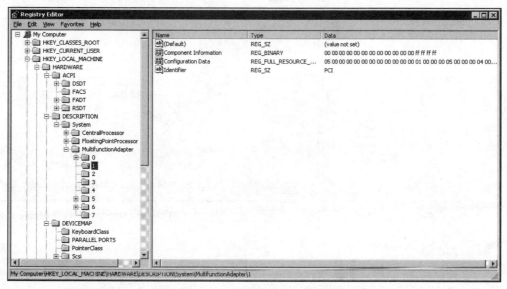

Fig. 7.3. The HKEY_LOCAL_MACHINE\HARDWARE\DESCRIPTION\System\ MultifunctionAdapter registry key

The *DEVICEMAP* Subkey

The HKEY_LOCAL_MACHINE\HARDWARE\DEVICEMAP registry key contains a set of subkeys equipped with one or more settings that specify the path to the drivers required by each device. Let's consider using this information for searching for device drivers. For example, how does the registry store information on the video drivers? Fig. 7.4 shows an example illustrating the contents of the VIDEO subkey under the DEVICEMAP key (the information you'll see when you open the registry key will differ from what's shown in this figure). However, the information will show you what you'll see in general.

The HKEY_LOCAL_MACHINE\HARDWARE\DEVICEMAP\VIDEO registry key contains settings that are actually links to currently active devices. These registry items use an ordinal-naming scheme (for example, in Fig. 7.4 it's \Device\Video*N*, where *N* is an ordinal number (0, 1, 2...)). The values of each of these registry settings are REG_SZ strings that reference particular device drivers.

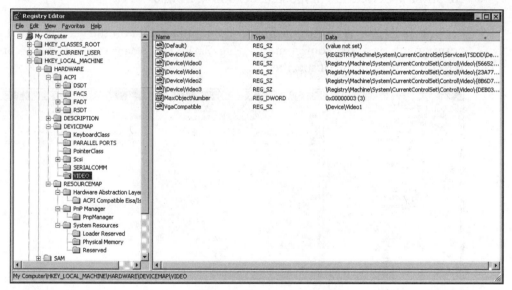

Fig. 7.4. The HKEY_LOCAL_MACHINE\HARDWARE\DEVICEMAP\VIDEO registry key

Note

Notice that these strings have a specific data format. For example, the Device\Video0 setting represented in Fig. 7.4 is set to \Registry\Machine\System\CurrentControlSet\ Control\Video\{56652C39-3E1C-4A83-AD68-1CF58F0EDEE9}\0000 value. This format is different from the one that's normally used (for example, HKEY_LOCAL_MACHINE, HKEY_CURRENT_USER). What does this mean?

All Windows NT-based operating systems, including Windows 2000, Windows XP, and Windows Server 2003, are object-oriented, which means that they manipulate several object types, including devices, ports, events, directories, and symbolic links. Registry keys are objects of special types. The registry root key is the object of the Key type named

REGISTRY. In the DDK (Device Driver Kit) documentation, the names of all the registry keys begin with the \REGISTRY string (for example, \REGISTRY\Machine\CurrentControlSet\ Services). Thus, the HKEY_LOCAL_MACHINE handle is the key named \REGISTRY\Machine, and the HKEY_USERS handle is the key named \REGISTRY\User.

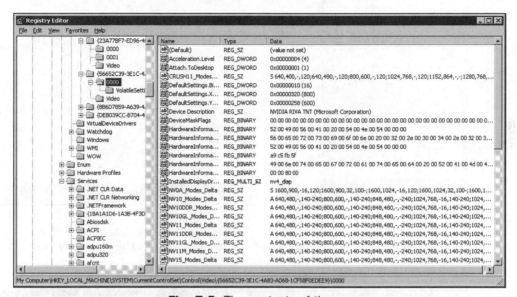

Fig. 7.5. The contents of the
HKEY_LOCAL_MACHINE\SYSTEM\CurrentControlSet\Control\Video\
{56652C39-3E1C-4A83-AD68-1CF58F0EDEE9}\0000 registry key

Now let's expand the HKEY_LOCAL_MACHINE\SYSTEM\CurrentControlSet\ Control\Video\{56652C39-3E1C-4A83-AD68-1CF58F0EDEE9}\0000 registry key (Fig. 7.5).

This key contains quite a lot of entries, mainly in binary format, among which is the Device Description value (data type REG_SZ) that contains the device description (NVIDIA RIVA TNT, in our example). Besides, it also possesses another value, InstalledDisplayDrivers, which references the driver for this device (nv4_disp in our example). The nested Video key contains the Service value entry referencing the nv service (Fig. 7.6). Information on this service can be found in the registry under HKEY_LOCAL_MACHINE\SYSTEM\CurrentControlSet\Services registry key (Fig. 7.7). It must exist for the device to function properly, and you'll certainly find it.

► *Tip*

Use Regedit.exe searching capabilities to find the key, since in our case this is the easiest way to locate the required key.

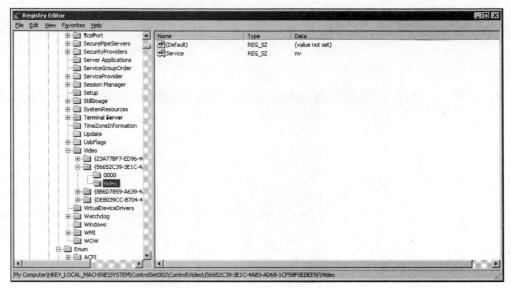

Fig. 7.6. The contents of the
HKEY_LOCAL_MACHINE\SYSTEM\CurrentControlSet\Control\Video\
{56652C39-3E1C-4A83-AD68-1CF58F0EDEE9}\Video **registry key**

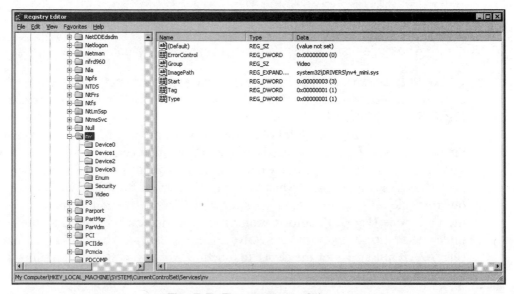

Fig. 7.7. The contents of the
HKEY_LOCAL_MACHINE\SYSTEM\CurrentControlSet\Services\nv **registry key**

The key that you are locating contains standard settings that specify the start mode for the driver: `Start`, `Tag`, `Type`, `ErrorControl`, and `Group`. Depending on the driver type, its key may contain several other settings, such as the `ImagePath` setting that specifies an actual path to the directory where the driver resides (`system32\DRIVERS\nv4_mini.sys`, in our example).

► *Note*

Notice how the image path has been specified. The loading order for the driver is specified by the `Start` setting (as we saw in the previous chapter). Sometimes the system doesn't assign drive mappings at the time the driver's loaded. Because of this, an error may result if you specify, for example, "C:\WINNT\System32\DRIVERS\<*YourDriver*>" as a value for `ImagePath`.

The `HKEY_LOCAL_MACHINE\SYSTEM\ControlSetnnn\Services\<Driver>` key may contain an optional `REG_SZ` setting named `DisplayName`. The value assigned to this parameter is a text string displayed by administrative utilities. If the `DisplayName` setting is omitted, then the actual name of the service or driver will be displayed in the list.

In addition to the settings listed above, the video driver key under `HKEY_LOCAL_MACHINE\SYSTEM\ControlSetnnn\Services` contains several subkeys. One of the most important subkeys within this key is `DeviceN` — in our example, this is the `Device0` subkey (Fig. 7.8).

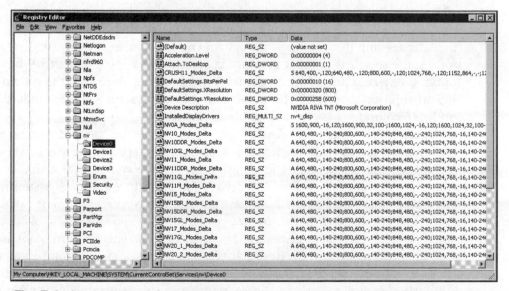

Fig. 7.8. An example of the contents of the `DeviceN` nested key for the device driver subkey under `HKEY_LOCAL_MACHINE\SYSTEM\ControlSetnnn\Services`

Depending on the video driver implementation, this key may contain a variety of parameters, including the VgaCompatible standard setting, which is set to FALSE for most modern drivers. If the parameter is set to FALSE, the driver is based on the MS VGA miniport driver.

The following REG_BINARY settings under the HKEY_LOCAL_MACHINE\ SYSTEM\CurrentControlSet\Control\Video\{56652C39-3E1C-4A83-AD68- 1CF58F0EDEE9}\0000:

HardwareInformation.AdapterString,

HardwareInformation.BiosString,

HardwareInformation.ChipType,

HardwareInformation.Crc32,

HardwareInformation.DacType

HardwareInformation.MemorySize

contain hardware information displayed by administrative utilities. Notice that similar settings are also present in Windows NT/ 2000 registries, but under different locations.

When Windows GUI starts, the system reads the video settings contained under the following registry key (Fig. 7.9):

HKEY_LOCAL_MACHINE\SYSTEM\CurrentControlSet\
Hardware Profiles\Current\System\CurrentControlSet\Control\VIDEO\
{56652C39-3E1C-4A83-AD68-1CF58F0EDEE9}\0000

After reading these settings, the system checks whether the display driver supporting the specified mode is present. As soon as the appropriate driver has been found, the startup procedure continues. What happens, though, if the system can't find an appropriate driver? The answer's simple: the system will use standard VGA mode (16 colors).

Thus, we have considered the usage of the HKEY_LOCAL_MACHINE\ HARDWARE\DEVICEMAP information for searching for specific device driver data. We've used the video adapter as an example, but the system uses a similar algorithm for locating the appropriate drivers for any other device. To summarize, let's note that the HKEY_LOCAL_MACHINE\HARDWARE\DEVICEMAP data describes either an actual port name or the path to the appropriate subkey under HKEY_LOCAL_MACHINE\System\ControlSet*nnn*\Services. This, in turn, contains the necessary information on the device driver. Sometimes, system administrators may need this information for troubleshooting purposes. It should be noted again that administrative utilities, such as Device Manager, display the same information presented in user-friendly format rather than raw binary data.

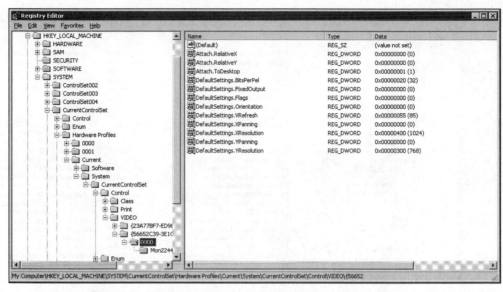

Fig. 7.9. Registry settings that specify the video mode

The *RESOURCEMAP* Subkey

The RESOURCEMAP subkey under HKEY_LOCAL_MACHINE\HARDWARE maps device drivers and hardware resources allocated to these drivers. Each setting stored within the RESOURCEMAP key contains the data reported by the device driver concerning memory addresses, IRQs, and DMA channels requested by respective drivers. All the data contained within this key is volatile. Windows NT/2000/XP and Windows Server 2003 recreate the key during every system startup.

Because Windows 2000/XP and Windows Server 2003 implement full-featured Plug and Play support and include a new kernel-mode component (Plug and Play Manager), the contents of the HKEY_LOCAL_MACHINE\HARDWARE\RESOURCEMAP registry key are different for Windows 2000/XP/Windows Server 2003 from what they are for Windows NT 4.0. In the Windows NT 4.0 registry, the RESOURCEMAP key contains multiple *<DeviceClass>* subkeys, which are used to store information on specific device driver classes. Each of these keys contains one or more *<DriverName>* subkeys that store information related to individual drivers.

The RESOURCEMAP key in Windows 2000/Windows XP/Windows Server 2003 registries looks somewhat different (Fig. 7.10). The kernel-mode Plug and Play Manager now controls all the hardware devices. Because of this, the data concerning system resources is stored under the following registry key: HKEY_LOCAL_ MACHINE\HARDWARE\RESOURCEMAP\PnP Manager\PnpManager.

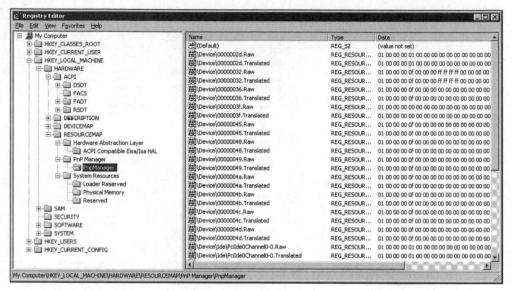

Fig. 7.10. The RESOURCEMAP key in Windows XP/Windows Server 2003

The HKEY_LOCAL_MACHINE\SAM *Key*

For computers that are not joined to a domain, the HKEY_LOCAL_MACHINE\SAM registry key contains information on local user and group accounts stored in the directory database (which was formerly known as the SAM database). For Windows 2000 Server and Windows Server 2003 computers joined to a domain, this key also contains security data for domain users and groups.

This key references the HKEY_LOCAL_MACHINE\Security\SAM key, and any modification introduced into one of these keys is immediately introduced into another one.

Note

Starting with Windows 2000, domain controllers both in Windows 2000 and Windows Server 2003 domains store security data in the Active Directory database file (Ntds.dit). However, SAM database is still preserved for storing local security information on servers that are not joined to a domain, as well as for backward compatibility with the existing Windows NT 4.0 domains. Besides this, it is used for restoring Active Directory information when the user selects the **Directory Services Restore Mode (Windows domain controllers only** option from the Windows Advanced Startup Options menu during system boot.

Default security settings both in Windows 2000 Server and in Windows Server 2003 prevent users (even those with administrative permissions) from viewing the contents of this registry key. More detailed information on this topic will be provided in *Chapter 9*.

The HKEY_LOCAL_MACHINE\SECURITY *Key*

The `HKEY_LOCAL_MACHINE\SECURITY` registry key contains information about the security subsystem on the local computer, including user rights and permissions, password policies, and local group membership. All of this information is specified using administrative utilities such as User Manager (Windows NT 4.0 Workstation), User Manager for Domains (Windows NT 4.0 Server), User Management MMC snap-in (Windows 2000 Professional and Windows XP) and Active Directory Users and Computers (Windows 2000 and Windows Server 2003 domain controllers).

The `HKEY_LOCAL_MACHINE\SECURITY\SAM` key references the `HKEY_LOCAL_MACHINE\SAM` key; because of this, any modification introduced into one of these keys will immediately appear within another one.

The HKEY_LOCAL_MACHINE\SOFTWARE *Key*

The `HKEY_LOCAL_MACHINE\SOFTWARE` registry key contains configuration data concerning the software installed on the local computer. Settings that reside under this key contain settings for the software installed on the local PC and are in force for any user who's logged on to the local system.

The `HKEY_LOCAL_MACHINE\SOFTWARE\Classes` key contains filename extension association data. It also stores registry data associated to COM objects. The data stored under the `Classes` key are also displayed under `HKEY_CLASSES_ROOT`. Fig. 7.11 shows the typical contents of the `HKEY_LOCAL_MACHINE\Software` registry key.

The `HKEY_LOCAL_MACHINE\SOFTWARE` subtree contains several nested keys, the most important being the `Classes`, `Program Groups`, and `Secure` subkeys. Later in this chapter, we'll discuss several `<Description>` subkeys that may appear in the registry.

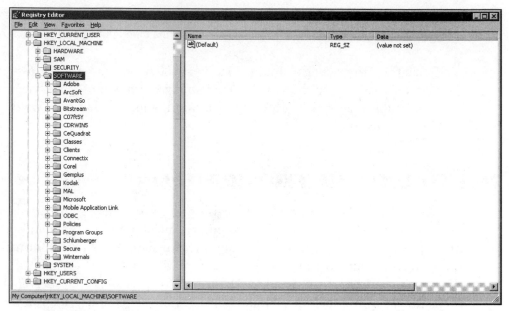

Fig. 7.11. Typical contents of the HKEY_LOCAL_MACHINE\SOFTWARE key

The *Classes* Subkey

The parameters contained under this key are the same as the parameters stored under HKEY_CLASSES_ROOT. Detailed information on the contents of this key is provided in the "OLE Programmer's Reference" document included with the Windows Platform Software Development Kit. The HKEY_LOCAL_MACHINE\SOFTWARE\ Classes key contains subkeys of the following types:

❑ Subkeys of the `<Filename-extension>` type associate applications installed on local computers with file types (identified by filename extensions). These subkeys contain data that you can add using the **File Types** tab of the **Folder Options** window, as well as information added by the Setup programs that install Windows applications.

❑ `<Class-definition>` subkeys. These subkeys contain information associated with COM objects. The data contained within these keys specify the shell and OLE (COM) properties for specific objects. If the application supports DDE (Dynamic Data Exchange), the shell subkey may, in turn, contain other subkeys such as Open and Print. The subkeys define DDE commands for opening and printing files. Notice that the information contained under these keys is very similar to that which is stored in the registry database of previous Windows versions, such as Windows 3.1x.

Note

The COM object information contained in the registry must be created by an application supporting COM. Direct registry editing can't be considered the easiest method of editing the information. If you need to perform this task in Windows NT 4.0, select the **Options** command from the **View** menu in Windows NT Explorer, then go to the **File Types** tab of the **Options** dialog. If you need to perform the same task in Windows 2000, Windows XP, or one of the Windows Server 2003 products, start the Folder Options applet from the Control Panel, or select the **Folder Options** command from the **Tools** menu in Windows Explorer; then go to the **File Types** tab in the **Folder Options** window.

The *Description* Subkeys

The HKEY_LOCAL_MACHINE\Software*Description* keys contain names and version numbers of the software installed on the local computer. (Configuration settings specified for individual users are stored under HKEY_CURRENT_USER.)

During installation, applications register this information in the following form:

HKEY_LOCAL_MACHINE\Software\Description*CompanyName**ProductName*\Version.

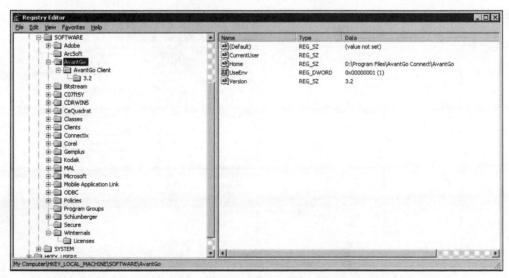

Fig. 7.12. An example of application registration information under
HKEY_LOCAL_MACHINE\Software registry key

Note

Version information for each application must be added to the registry by the appropriate application. Don't edit values under these keys except when the application vendor instructs you to do so.

An example illustrating how the registration information of an application (AvantGo in our case) is stored under the HKEY_LOCAL_MACHINE\SOFTWARE registry key is presented in Fig. 7.12.

The *Microsoft* Subkey

The HKEY_LOCAL_MACHINE\SOFTWARE\Microsoft subkey contains configuration settings for Microsoft software products installed on the local computer.

One of the most important subkeys under HKLM\SOFTWARE\Microsoft is the HKLM\SOFTWARE\Microsoft\Windows NT\CurrentVersion key. This key contains information on the software that supports Windows built-in services and the type and version number of the current OS installation (for example, the data specify whether the system has a multiprocessor kernel). Obviously, a single-processor kernel will work on a multi-processor computer, but it won't provide any advantages over the single-processor configuration. To identify the kernel type, view the following registry key: HKEY_LOCAL_MACHINE\SOFTWARE\Microsoft\Windows NT\CurrentVersion (Fig. 7.13).

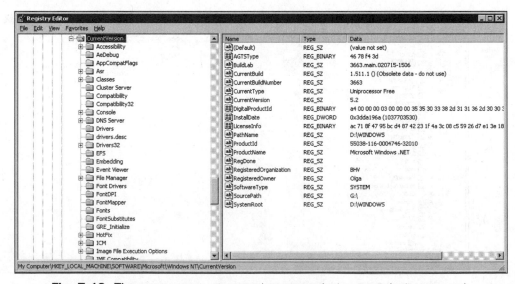

Fig. 7.13. The HKEY_LOCAL_MACHINE\SOFTWARE\Microsoft\Windows NT\CurrentVersion **registry key**

Note

When speaking about the `HKEY_LOCAL_MACHINE\SOFTWARE\Microsoft\Windows NT\` `CurrentVersion` registry key, it is simply impossible not to mention one of the most appreciated performance enhancements introduced with Windows XP and Windows Server 2003. These newer operating systems provide built-in user mode heap-leak detection. The problem is that poorly written or miscoded applications can "leak" heap memory. In versions released earlier than Windows XP, special tools were needed to help identify the cause of the memory leak when this situation arose. To enable leak detection, set the following registry key:

```
[HKEY_LOCAL_MACHINE\SOFTWARE\Microsoft\Windows NT\CurrentVersion\
Image File Execution Options\<ImageName>]

"ShutdownFlags"="3"
```

The *Program Groups* Subkey

The `Program Groups` subkey, residing under the `HKEY_LOCAL_MACHINE\Software` registry key, has undergone some changes in comparison to previous versions of Windows NT (Windows NT 3.51 and earlier). In Windows NT 4.0, this key was redefined. In earlier Windows NT versions, the key contained a list of program groups used by all users of the local computer. In Windows NT 4.0 and its successors, this key is only used to specify whether or not all the program groups that existed in the previous operating system (for upgraded systems) were converted to a new format.

The `Program Groups` key contains a single entry named `ConvertedToLinks`, which determines whether the program groups have been converted. If the `ConvertedToLinks` value is set to 1, the conversion has been completed successfully.

If you install a fresh copy of the operating system rather than upgrade an earlier version to Windows XP or Windows Server 2003, the `Program Groups` subkey won't contain any subkeys. If you've performed an upgrade, the `Program Groups` key will contain subkeys containing binary data defining general program groups.

The *Secure* Subkey

Applications can use the `Secure` subkey for storing configuration settings that can only be changed by the system administrator.

The *Windows 3.1 Migration Status* Subkey

The `Windows 3.1 Migration Status` subkey contains data only if the current operating system was installed as an upgrade from Windows 3.1. The parameters contained in this key specify if all INI files and the registry database (Reg.dat) were successfully converted to the Windows NT 4.0/Windows 2000 registry format.

If you delete this key, Windows will make another attempt to convert these files after rebooting.

Windows 3.1 Migration Status also exists under HKEY_CURRENT_USER. It specifies the conversion status of the program groups files (GRP files) to the Windows Explorer program group format.

The HKEY_LOCAL_MACHINE\System *Key*

All the data related to the startup process, which the system needs to read rather than calculate, are stored in the System hive. The System.alt file (existing in Windows 2000 and earlier) also contains complete copies of these data. The data stored under HKEY_LOCAL_MACHINE\System are organized into Control Sets, each containing a complete set of parameters for device drivers and system services. Now and then, the system administrator may need to edit the items stored under the CurrentControlSet subkey.

Chapter 6 contains detailed information on the contents of the CurrentControlSet subkey.

The *ControlSet* nnn, *Select,* and *CurrentControlSet* Subkeys

The registry, in particular the System hive, has the most important role at system startup. To guarantee that the system will start, Windows NT-based operating systems save the backup copy, allowing you to discard any configuration modifications that have led to unexpected results. In this section, we'll discuss the mechanism used for this purpose.

All data necessary to control the startup process are organized in subkeys called Control sets. Each control set contains the following four subkeys:

❑ The Control subkey that contains configuration settings used for system management, including the network name of the local computer and subsystems that should start.

❑ The Enum subkey contains hardware data, including data on the hardware devices and drivers to be loaded.

❑ The Hardware Profiles subkey contains hardware settings and driver configurations related to the individual hardware profile. You can create individual hardware profiles for each control set. The Hardware Profiles subkey will contain any data if only the data are different from the standard settings for device drivers and system services. The current hardware profile stored under CurrentControlSet is also stored under the HKEY_CURRENT_CONFIG root key.

❏ The `Services` subkey contains a list of drivers, file systems, and service programs that run in user mode, together with virtual hardware keys. The data contained in this key define the drivers to be loaded and specify their loading order. The data also define the methods used by the services to call each other.

Multiple control sets are stored as subkeys under the `HKEY_LOCAL_MACHINE\System` registry keys under the names from `ControlSet001` to `ControlSet003`. There can be as many as four control sets, but normally there are only two. This mechanism is similar to the one used to create the Config.sys backup copies for MS-DOS computers. Normally, there's one copy of Config.sys used to start the system, and the backup copy. In our case, however, the whole job of creating and maintaining the backup copies is performed automatically by the system.

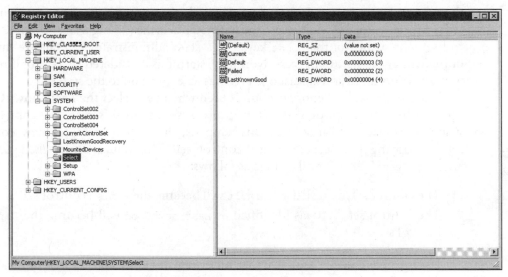

Fig. 7.14. The contents of the `HKEY_LOCAL_MACHINE\SYSTEM\Select` registry key

The `Select` subkey, shown in Fig. 7.14, contains four parameters, which describe the control set usage:

❏ The `Default` setting identifies the number of the control set (for example, `001=ControlSet001`) that the system should use next time it starts up. This may happen when a system error prevents the system from booting or when you manually select the **LastKnownGood** option.

❏ The `Current` setting specifies the ordinal number of the control set that's actually been used to start the computer.

❏ The LastKnownGood setting specifies the ordinal number of the control set that was used the last time you successfully started up the system.

❏ The Failed setting specifies the control set that was replaced by the LastKnownGood control set (if it was used to start up the system). You can also examine this control set to identify the source of the problem, which you have to do in order to replace the current control set with the last known good one.

The CurrentControlSet key is actually a symbolic link to the control set specified by the Current setting under HKEY_LOCAL_MACHINE\SYSTEM\Select. This is necessary so that constant paths can be used to refer to subkeys in the currently used control set, even though its name may change.

Any time you start the system, the control set used to start up the system is stored under HKEY_LOCAL_MACHINE\System\Clone. If the system started successfully, this control set is considered "good", and the system discards the existing LastKnownGood control set. Actually, the system replaces the existing LastKnownGood control set with a copy of the Clone key. The system administrator can change this requirement at the startup process. Normally, startup is considered successful if no severe errors occurred and at least one user was able to log on to the system.

The LastKnownGood configuration is used when you select the **LastKnownGood** option during startup, or if the startup process fails (in this case, the control set won't be considered "good"). If this happens, the system creates a new control set by copying the LastKnownGood control set. The values under HKEY_LOCAL_MACHINE\System\Select will change as follows:

❏ The control set identified as Default will became the Failed control set.

❏ The control set that was identified as LastKnownGood will become the Default control set.

User profile data are stored under other registry keys, and these modifications won't be reflected in user profiles.

▶ *Tip*

If you need to identify the control set used to start up your system, view the Select subkey.

Using administrative utilities and Control Panel applets is the easiest method of modifying the data stored under the keys previously discussed.

It's the CurrentControlSet subkey that you need to edit when modifying the configuration settings using one of the registry editors.

Control Subkeys for Controls Sets

Each control set contains a `Control` subkey. This subkey stores the startup parameters, including information on the subsystems to be loaded, environment variables, and the size and location of the paging file. The most important subkeys located under the `Control` key present in the control set are listed in Table 7.2.

Table 7.2. Typical subkeys of the `Control` Key for All Control Sets

Subkey	Description
BackupRestore	This key contains nested keys that specify parameters for the Ntbackup program, including subkeys such as `FilesNotToBackup` and `KeysNotToRestore` (Fig. 7.15), which contain exclusion lists for files and registry keys not to be involved into backup or restore processes. The contents of the `BackupRestore` subkey can be used for customizing the built-in Microsoft Backup utility. Also notice the `AsrKeysNotToRestore` nested key, which is new In Windows XP and Windows Server 2003. This key relates to the Automated System Recovery process, which in newer releases has replaced the Emergency Repair Disk functionality included with Windows NT and Windows 2000. By default, it contains a single value entry named `Plug & Play` (data type `REG_MULTI_SZ`, value `CurrentControlSet\Control\CriticalDeviceDatabase\`). This information will not be restored during the ASR process, which is not surprising, since such information must be re-created by the Setup program when it inspects the hardware configuration of your system.
BootVerificationProgram	This value can be used to specify a non-standard mechanism of declaring the system startup as successful ("good"). If an additional verification mechanism hasn't been specified, this subkey won't contain any settings.
ComputerName	Default computer names and active computer names are stored under `ComputerName` and `ActiveComputerName` subkeys. To set the computer name, use the Network option in the Control Panel (Windows NT 4.0), the **Network Identification** tab in the **System Properties** window (Windows 2000) or the **Computer Name** tab of the **System Properties** window (Windows XP and Windows Server 2003).
CrashControl	This key contains value entries that manage system behavior in case of a system crash, including options for creating a memory dump file. Notice the `MinidumpDir` string value, which is new to Windows XP and Windows Server 2003. As its name implies, this setting specifies the path to the directory where the small dumps, mainly used by the Error Reporting service, are stored. You can specify these settings in the **Startup and Recovery** window.

continues

Table 7.2 Continued

Subkey	Description
GroupOrderList	Specifies the order in which the system should load the services for all groups that have one. This option is used in combination with the Tags option. The ServiceGroupOrder setting specifies the loading order for the groups.
ServiceGroupOrder	Specifies the order in which to load various groups of services. The services loading order within a group is defined using the Tags and GroupOrderList settings.
HiveList	This setting specifies the location of the registry hive files (the contents of this key are shown in Fig. 7.16).
	The value is maintained by the system because the settings under this key show the exact location of the registry hive files (if these files can't be loaded, the startup process will fail). Pay attention to the format used to represent the names of these settings (Fig. 7.16). Note that they are represented as follows: \REGISTRY\MACHINE\<hivename>, where the <hivename> is the name of the appropriate registry hive. Also note the following scheme: \Device\HarddiskVolumeN\ %SystemRoot%\System32\Config\<hive>, which is adopted because when an appropriate registry file needs to be loaded, the system has not yet created drive mappings for logical disks.
KeyboardLayout	DLL for the keyboard layout, the default language used as a default, plus a subkey named DosKeybCodes, which lists all other available keyboard layouts.
LSA	The authentication packages for the Local Security Authority (LSA). This value is maintained by the system. If you make an error editing this value, it may prevent everyone from logging in to the local system.
NetworkProvider	This key can contain subkeys that specify network providers and the order in which to load them. You can manage the settings for network providers using the Network option in the Control Panel (Windows NT 4.0), the Network and Dial-up Connections option (Windows 2000) or Network Connections option (Windows XP and Windows Server 2003).
NLS	This subkey contains information on national language support (NLS). You can manage the national language support using the following Control Panel applets: Regional Settings (Windows NT 4.0), Regional Options (Windows 2000) or Regional and Language Options (Windows XP and Windows Server 2003).
Print	This subkey contains information on the currently installed printers and printing environment. It has the following important subkeys:
	Environments — this subkey contains other subkeys that define drivers and print processors for various system environments.

continues

Table 7.2 Continued

Subkey	Description
Print	`Monitors` — this subkey contains other subkeys that store data for specific network printing monitors.
	`Printers` — this subkey contains other subkeys that describe the settings for each installed printer.
	`Providers` — this key can contain subkeys describing print services' DLLs.
	To modify the printer settings, click the **Start** button, then select **Settings	Printers**.
PriorityControl	This subkey specifies the priority separation in Win32. You should only set this value using the System option in Control Panel.
ProductOptions	This subkey defines the software product type (Windows NT, for example). These values are maintained by the system. Notice one especially interesting fact: the `ProductType` value in Windows 2000 registry is set to "WinNT".
SessionManager	This subkey specifies global variables used by Session Manager. This key can, in turn, contain the following subkeys:
	`DOS Devices` — the subkey that identifies various DOS devices such as `AUX`, `MAILSLOT`, `NUL`, `PIPE`, `PRN`, and `UNC`.
	`Environment` — this key identifies environment variables such as `ComSpec`, `Path`, `Os2LibPath`, and `WinDir`. These variables are set using the System option in Control Panel (this is the same for both Windows NT 4.0 and Windows 2000 and its successors).
	`FileRenameOperations` — this key is used during the startup process. It allows you to rename certain files in order to replace them. These values should be maintained only by the operating system.
	`KnownDLLs` — this key defines the directories and filenames for Session Manager DLLs. Again, all these values are maintained by the operating system.
	`MemoryManagement` — this key defines the paging options. Normally, you specify the paging file parameters using the System applet in the Control Panel. Notice that in Windows NT/2000 this key contains the `RegistrySizeLimit` setting mentioned in *Chapter 1*. Also notice that in Windows XP and Windows Server 2003 this setting has become obsolete.
	`SubSystems` — this key defines information intended for Windows NT/2000, Windows XP, and Windows Server 2003 subsystems. The values under this key are maintained by the system.

continues

Table 7.2 Continued

Subkey	Description
Setup	This key specifies hardware setup options. Once again, all the values under this key are maintained by the operating system. If you need to modify these settings, the easiest way is to start the Windows Setup program.
TimeZoneInformation	This key contains the values that define time zone information. Normally, you set these values using the Date/Time option in the Control Panel.
VirtualDeviceDrivers	This subkey contains virtual device drivers. These values must be maintained by the system.
Windows	This subkey specifies the paths to the Windows directory and system directory.
WOW	The settings stored under this key define options for 16-bit Windows applications. Once again, these settings should be maintained by the system.

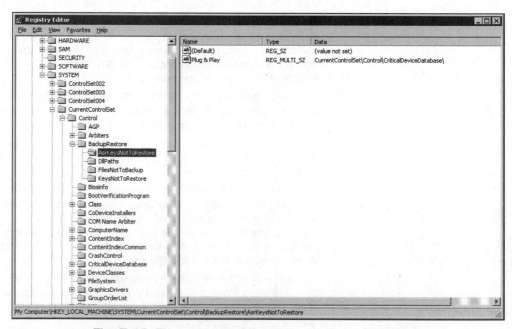

Fig. 7.15. The contents of the BackupRestore nested key

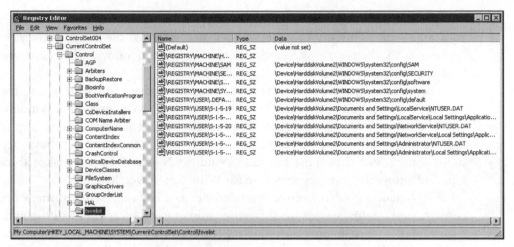

Fig. 7.16. The `hivelist` subkey

The *Enum* Subkey for All Control Sets

The Enum subkey contains configuration data for all hardware devices, independent of the drivers these devices use.

This subkey was first introduced in Windows NT 4.0. It was added to enable Windows NT to access devices and their drivers and manage them using methods similar to those used in Windows 95. (Notice that these methods are similar, but not the same, because Windows NT architecture is different from that of Windows 95.)

These changes were intended to lay the groundwork for providing support for new Plug and Play devices in future versions of Windows NT. As we saw in *Chapter 5*, full-featured PnP support was first implemented in Windows 2000, and further enhanced in Windows XP and Windows Server 2003.

▶ *Note*

Don't use registry editors to modify this key. If you make an error, neither Windows NT/2000 nor Windows XP/Windows Server 2003 will be able to detect hardware devices.

Normally, the Enum key contains configuration data for hardware devices. The subkeys under the Enum key form a hierarchical structure known as the hardware device tree. The hardware tree starts at the tree root and ends at the lowest branch containing configuration data for a specific instance of the device (for example, the keyboard on the local computer).

The Enum key itself can be considered to be a container that isn't associated with any value. This key contains at least two subkeys: the Htree subkey, which represents the hardware tree; and one or more enumerators, which are used by Windows to get information about specific devices.

The Htree\Root\0 key is a reserved registry space representing the root of the hardware tree (this is the same for Windows NT 4.0, Windows 2000, Windows XP, and Windows Server 2003). Since Windows 2000 and newer releases implement full-featured Plug and Play support, the contents of the Enum key have become more complicated than those found in Windows NT 4.0. The screenshot shown in Fig. 7.17 shows the Enum key structure for Windows Server 2003.

The remaining subkeys directly under the Enum key represent enumerators and contain subkeys for devices on the same enumerator. According to Plug and Play requirements, each enumerator has its respective device bus (for example, PCI or ISAPNP). The default enumerator (Root) is used for non-PnP (legacy) devices.

Each subkey of the enumerator contains multiple subkeys that represent various device types and models. The subkeys representing device types, in turn, contain their own subkeys that identify specific instances of the devices of this type. The name of each device type subkey identifies the device as a legacy device or as a Plug and Play device.

For most non-Plug and Play devices, Windows NT-based OS creates a device-type ID in the LEGACY_<DriverName> format. This subkey contains data for all the devices managed by this driver.

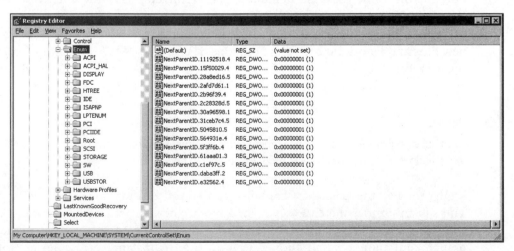

Fig. 7.17. The HKEY_LOCAL_MACHINE\SYSTEM\CurrentControlSet\Enum
key structure

The subkeys below the device type keys are keys representing specific device instances. They contain the setting, which specifies device configuration.

The settings and subkeys directly below the device instance keys may be different, and vary depending on the devices and their drivers.

The *Services* Subkey for All Control Sets

Each control set contains a `Services` subkey that lists the device drivers, file system drivers, and Win32 service drivers. All the drivers listed under this key may be loaded by the operating system boot loader (Ntldr), I/O Manager, or Service Control Manager.

As I already mentioned earlier in this chapter while discussing the `HKEY_LOCAL_MACHINE\HARDWARE\DEVICEMAP` registry key, all the subkeys under this key contain the settings that reference the entries under the `Services` key within the control set. For example, in Windows NT/2000, the following entry may be present in the `DeviceMap\PointerPort` subkey for the parallel port mouse:

```
\Device\PointerPort0:
```

```
\REGISTRY\Machine\System\ControlSet001\Services\Sermouse
```

The `Services` key must contain the key corresponding to this link, which is named `Sermouse`. This subkey identifies the mouse driver settings. This mechanism is called device mapping, which explains why the registry key is called `DEVICEMAP`.

► *Note* (

In Windows XP and Windows Server 2003, to facilitate device installation, devices are set up and configured using device setup class grouping. The device setup class defines the class installer and class co-installer components that are involved in installing the device.

Therefore, the following entry for the parallel port mouse under `HKEY_LOCAL_MACHINE\HARDWARE\DEVICEMAP\PointerClass` will result (Fig. 7.18). Notice that the key name is `PointerClass` and not `PointerPort`, as it was in Windows NT/2000:

```
\Device\PointerClass0:
```
```
\REGISTRY\MACHINE\SYSTEM\ControlSet001\Services\Mouclass
```

Like in Windows NT/2000, the `Services` key contains the key corresponding to this link, which is named `Mouclass`. This subkey identifies the mouse driver settings (Fig. 7.19). At the beginning of the chapter, we discussed this mechanism in the example on video drivers.

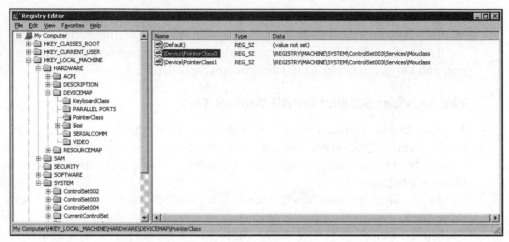

Fig. 7.18. An example of the contents of the
`HKEY_LOCAL_MACHINE\HARDWARE\DEVICEMAP\PointerClass` registry key
in Windows XP

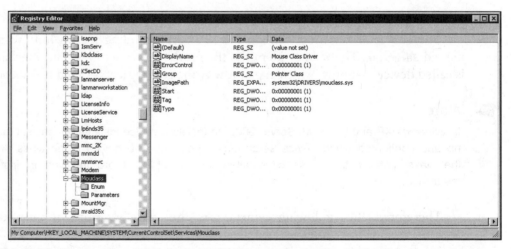

Fig. 7.19. The `Services` key contains the key corresponding to the link provided under
`DEVICEMAP` registry key

Microsoft defines setup classes for most devices. IHVs and OEMs can define new device setup classes, but only if none of the existing classes apply. For example, a camera vendor doesn't need to define a new setup class because cameras fall under the `Image` setup class. Similarly, uninterruptible power supply (UPS) devices fall under the `Battery` class.

The class installer defines the class of the component to be installed by the `ClassGuid` value. There is a GUID associated with each device setup class. The `ClassGuid` value is the Globally Unique Identifier (GUID) for the class. You can generate GUID values using the Uuidgen.exe utility. More detailed information about this utility is provided in Platform SDK supplementary documents.

The device setup class GUID defines the `...\CurrentControlSet\Control\Class\ClassGUID` registry key under which to create a new subkey for any particular device of a standard setup class.

Each subkey under the `Services` key may contain several optional settings. For example, the content of the `Alerter` key specifies the Alerter service parameters.

Settings such as `ErrorControl`, `Group`, `DependOnGroup`, `DependOnService`, `ImagePath`, `ObjectName`, `Start`, `Tag`, and `Type` manage service behavior.

The loading order for services and drivers is specified by the `\Control\ServiceGroupOrder` key under the control set key.

The *Hardware Profiles* Key for All Control Sets

The `Hardware Profiles` subkey is present in any control set. These subkeys contain configuration data for all hardware profiles created in Windows NT/2000, Windows XP, or Windows Server 2003. This key was first introduced in Windows NT 4.0.

As you already know, the hardware profile is a set of modifications introduced to facilitate standard device and service configuration (including Win32 services and drivers) loaded at system startup.

Windows NT-based operating system creates a default hardware profile based on the original configuration detected during OS installation. You can create multiple hardware profiles and select existing profiles at boot time.

Fig. 7.20 shows a typical structure of the `HKEY_LOCAL_MACHINE\SYSTEM\CurrentControlSet\Hardware Profiles` registry key.

Each subkey under the `Hardware Profiles` key contains configuration data for its respective hardware profile. If the system has more than one hardware profile, it identifies the hardware profile as current when you select it at boot time. The `HKEY_LOCAL_MACHINE\SYSTEM\CurrentControlSet\Hardware Profiles\Current` registry key represents a symbolic link to one of the keys named `0000`, `0001`, ...

The `HKEY_CURRENT_CONFIG` tree is an alias that references the `Hardware Profiles\Current` key under the `CurrentControlSet`. The contents of the `Current` key also appear under the `HKEY_CURRENT_CONFIG` tree.

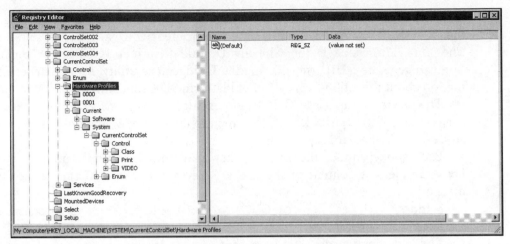

Fig. 7.20. The contents of a typical
HKEY_LOCAL_MACHINE\SYSTEM\CurrentControlSet\Hardware Profiles key

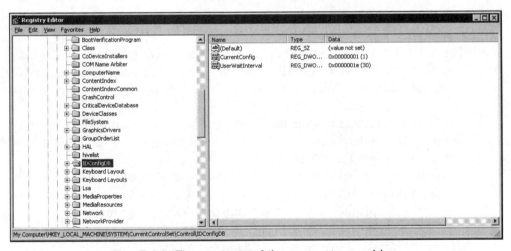

Fig. 7.21. The contents of the IDConfigDB subkey

Tip

To define which of the 0000, 0001, ..., 000*n* keys under the Hardware Profiles keys is selected as the current one, view the HKEY_LOCAL_MACHINE\System\CurrentControlSet\
Control\IDConfigDB key. This key contains the CurrentConfig setting (Fig. 7.21),
whose value specifies the number corresponding to the key that contains the current hardware profile.

The settings contained within each hardware profile subkey represent individual modifications of the standard configuration of the system services and device drivers. These modifications correspond to the goals of each hardware profile. Notice that these keys only store data different from the standard configuration, which is defined by the data stored under the Software and System subkeys under HKEY_LOCAL_MACHINE. Consequently, the hardware profile structure is modeled based on the structure of the HKEY_LOCAL_MACHINE registry key. Strictly speaking, it can be considered to be a limited, or compressed, version of this key.

If the hardware profile contains a changed version of a value entry under the Software or System keys of HKEY_LOCAL_MACHINE, then the original value isn't changed. Rather, the changed version of this value is stored within a similar key of the Hardware Profiles\<Number> subtree.

For example, let's look at a situation when you create a new hardware profile that excludes the Iomega Parallel Port Legacy Filter Driver (ppa3). The HKEY_LOCAL_MACHINE\System\CurrentControlSet\Enum\Root\LEGACY_PPA3 key won't be changed in Windows NT 4.0, Windows 2000, Windows XP, or Windows Server 2003. On the contrary, this modification will be stored under the following key:

HKEY_LOCAL_MACHINE\System\CurrentControlSet\Hardware Profiles

\<Number>\System\CurrentControlSet\Enum\Root\LEGACY_PPA3.

The *Setup* Subkey

The Setup subkey under the HKEY_LOCAL_MACHINE\System tree is intended for internal use by the Setup program. You need not (and should not) change the value entries under this key, because they are to be maintained by the operating system.

The *Disk* Subkey

The HKEY_LOCAL_MACHINE\SYSTEM\Disk subkey has undergone significant changes since its appearance in Windows NT 4.0. In the Windows NT 4.0 registry, this key contained all the information needed to manage the volumes. This key is created by the Disk Administrator built-in Windows NT utility and contains the Information setting (data type is REG_BINARY). This setting contains all configuration information, including the data on the hard disk partitions that were recognized by Windows, drive mappings, and the data concerning fault-tolerant disk configurations (mirror sets, stripe sets with or without parity), if you've created the fault-tolerant disk configurations. Detailed information concerning fault-tolerant disk configurations is provided in the documentation supplied with the Windows NT 4.0 Workstation Resource Kit software.

The `HKEY_LOCAL_MACHINE\System\Disk` key is created in the Windows NT 4.0 registry when you start the Disk Administrator utility for the first time. This utility creates both the key and the `Information` binary setting, which stores all the data on the hard disks present in the system. As you create or delete hard disk partitions using the Disk Administrator utility, or configure fault-tolerant volumes, the program stores all configuration changes in the `Information` setting.

If you explicitly establish drive mapping for the CD-ROM drive (for example, you need to map this drive as "H:"), the `Disk` key will contain another setting named `\device\CdRom0`. This string setting will have a value that corresponds to the drive mapping that you've specified. Besides the Disk Administrator utility, there are other drivers and subsystems that access the `Disk` key information. For example, this information is available to the fault-tolerant file system driver (Ftdisk.sys) and to the Win32 subsystem. The Ftdisk.sys driver identifies whether or not there are fault tolerant disk configurations in the system, such as mirror or stripe sets. The driver does this by reading the `Information` setting. The Win32 subsystem needs the `Information` setting data for establishing drive mappings.

▶ Note

The `Information` setting is a variable-length setting, because the number of logical disks and fault tolerant volumes in each individual Windows NT 4.0 system are also variable.

With the release of Windows 2000, the disk management subsystem has undergone significant changes (for example, a new type of volume was introduced — dynamic volume). The `HKEY_LOCAL_MACHINE\SYSTEM\Disk\Information` setting is present in the registry (in order to provide backward compatibility), but it no longer stores information on fault-tolerant volumes.

Windows 2000, Windows XP, and Windows Server 2003 store the information on fault-tolerant volumes directly on the hard disk. There's a noticeable difference, though. The Ftdisk.sys driver in Windows 2000/XP and Windows Server 2003 manages all disk partitions, including the fault-tolerant volumes and all other partitions that exist on the hard disks. So, even if you don't configure the fault-tolerant volumes on your computer running Windows 2000, Windows XP, or any product of the Windows Server 2003 family, Ftdisk.sys loads anyway and detects all requests to the hard disks.

The *HKEY_CLASSES_ROOT* Key

The HKEY_CLASSES_ROOT root key contains information on all existing filename associations and data associated with COM objects. However, in Windows 2000 and later versions, including Windows XP and products of the Windows Server 2003 family, the contents of this root key became more complex. Similar to Windows NT 4.0, the data under this key references the Classes subkey of the HKEY_LOCAL_MACHINE\ Software hive, but, besides this, it also joins the contents of the HKEY_CURRENT_ USER\Software\Classes key. The latter key is actually a link to the HKEY_USERS\ <*SID*>_Classes keys, where *SID* stands for security identifier of the current user.

▶ *Note*

As was already mentioned, the HKEY_LOCAL_MACHINE registry key contains global settings applicable to all users who log on to the local system. The HKEY_CURRENT_USER root key, on the other hand, contains settings that are specific to the user who is currently logged on to the system. With a small number of exceptions, user settings have the priority above general computer settings. Therefore, if the file type or COM class is specified both under HKEY_LOCAL_MACHINE and HKEY_CURRENT_USER, the OS will use the setting existing under HKEY_CURRENT_USER.

The HKEY_CLASSES_ROOT key contains the data that associates file types (by filename extensions) with specific applications supporting formats of these files.

The *HKEY_CURRENT_CONFIG* Key

The HKEY_CURRENT_CONFIG registry root key was first introduced with the release of the Windows NT 4.0 operating system. This key contains configuration data for the currently used hardware profile. Actually, this key is an alias that references the HKEY_LOCAL_MACHINE\System\CurrentControlSet\ Hardware Profiles\Current registry key.

The HKEY_CURRENT_CONFIG registry key was introduced with the release of Windows NT 4.0 in order to provide backward compatibility with the HKEY_ CURRENT_CONFIG root key present in Windows 95. Now that the HKEY_CURRENT_ CONFIG tree is present both in Windows 9*x* and Windows NT/2000/XP/Windows Server 2003 registries, all applications designed for Windows 95 will also work under Windows NT-based operating systems.

Fig. 7.22 illustrates the `HKEY_CURRENT_CONFIG` registry key structure. This screenshot demonstrates that the `HKEY_CURRENT_CONFIG` key simply represents a symbolic link to the `HKEY_LOCAL_MACHINE\System\CurrentControlSet\` `Hardware Profiles\Current` registry key.

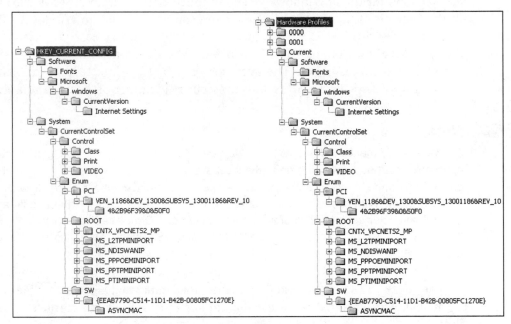

Fig. 7.22. The `HKEY_CURRENT_CONFIG` and
`HKEY_LOCAL_MACHINE\System\CurrentControlSet\Hardware Profiles\Current`
registry keys

The `HKEY_CURRENT_CONFIG` key contains data describing the current hardware profile.

The *HKEY_CURRENT_USER* Key

The `HKEY_CURRENT_USER` registry key contains the data describing the user profile for the user currently logged on to the local system. The user profile contains information defining individual settings for the desktop, network connections, and environment variables. Provided that the user profile for the user exists and is available on the local computer or in the same domain, Windows will look and behave the same way at any workstation where the user logs on to the network.

The HKEY_CURRENT_USER registry key contains all the information necessary for setting up the working environment for that particular user. It includes the settings and individual preferences for various applications, screen colors, and other user preferences. The user profile also includes security settings for the user. Many settings existing in HKEY_CURRENT_USER are similar to those that existed in the Win.ini for earlier Windows versions.

Standard subkeys of the HKEY_CURRENT_USER are listed in Table 7.3.

Table 7.3. Standard Subkeys of the HKEY_CURRENT_USER Registry Key

Subkey	Description
AppEvents	Subkeys defining application events, including sound scheme events, the set of relationships between user actions, and the sounds produced by your computer as a reaction.
Console	The Console subkey contains nested subkeys that define console window size and other settings for console applications. A console represents the interface between user-mode and character-mode applications. This key also includes settings for the command prompt sessions. In Windows 2000 and later, you set command prompt default options — such as window color, cursor size, and font size and style — directly in the command prompt window. You can also specify whether the options you set are used for every session or for the current session only.
Control Panel	The subkeys under the Control Panel subkey correspond to the parameters that can be changed using Control Panel applets. These data also include the information that was stored in the Win.ini file in earlier Windows versions.
Environment	These settings correspond to the environment variable settings specified for the individual user who's currently logged on to the system. The value entries contain information, which under earlier Windows versions was stored in the Autoexec.bat file. Normally, you can set these values using Control Panel applets.
Keyboard Layout	The subkeys under this key specify the national language used for the current keyboard layout.
Printers	The subkeys under this key describe currently installed printers that are available for the user currently logged on to the system. To change these settings, click the **Start** button, then select **Settings	Printers**.

continues

Table 7.3 Continued

Subkey	Description
Software	This key contains subkeys that describe configuration settings for the software installed on the local computer and available to the user who's currently logged on to the system. This information has the same structure as the HKEY_LOCAL_MACHINE\Software registry key. The information also includes application-specific data that was previously stored in the Win.ini file or in application-specific INI files.
UNICODE Program Groups	This key is provided for backward compatibility. It wasn't used in Windows NT 4.0. If your system was upgraded from earlier versions of the Windows NT operating system (for example, from Windows NT 3.51 to Windows NT 4.0), this key may contain some subkeys inherited from the previous versions and store binary data. However, neither this key nor its subkeys contain any data needed by Windows NT 4.0/Windows 2000 or Windows XP/ Windows Server 2003.
Windows 3.1 Migrations Status	This key will contain data only if you've upgraded your operating system from an earlier Windows version (for example, from Windows 3.x to Windows NT 4.0). The subkeys present within this key specify whether the process of upgrading program group files (GRP files) and initialization files (INI files) has completed successfully. If you delete this key, Windows will attempt the conversion next time you reboot the system. Note that the Windows 3.1 Migration Status subkey also exists within the HKEY_LOCAL_MACHINE \Software key.

As I mentioned earlier in the section dedicated to the HKEY_LOCAL_MACHINE root key, the HKEY_CURRENT_USER data normally has priority over similar data existing under HKEY_LOCAL_MACHINE. For example, let's look at how this convention works for environment variables. The environment variable settings defined for the currently logged on user have priority over the system environment variables (use the System applet in Control Panel to set environment variables).

The HKEY_CURRENT_USER key references the HKEY_USERS\<SID_#> registry key, where the <SID_#> is a string containing the security identifier (SID) of the user who's currently logged on to the system. The logon process creates the user profile environment based on the data found under the HKEY_USERS\<SID_#>. If this data is unavailable, the HKEY_CURRENT_USER is built based on the data contained in the *%SystemRoot%*\Profiles\Default User\Ntuser.dat file (Windows NT 4.0) or in the *%SystemRoot%*\Documents and Settings\Default User\Ntuser.dat file (Windows 2000 and later versions).

▶ *Note*

To find the file supporting the registry hive, view the HiveList subkey under the HKEY_LOCAL_MACHINE\System\CurrentControlSet\Control key. To find the user profile hive (whether or not this user is currently logged on), view the ProfileList subkey under the HKEY_LOCAL_MACHINE\Software\Microsoft\Windows NT\CurrentVersion key.

The *HKEY_USERS* Key

The HKEY_USERS key contains all actively loaded user profiles. In this case, the key contains the following subkeys: the .DEFAULT subkey, *<Security ID>* subkeys for all user accounts currently logged on to the system, and *<SID>*_Classes subkeys that contain file associations and COM classes for specific SIDs (Fig. 7.23).

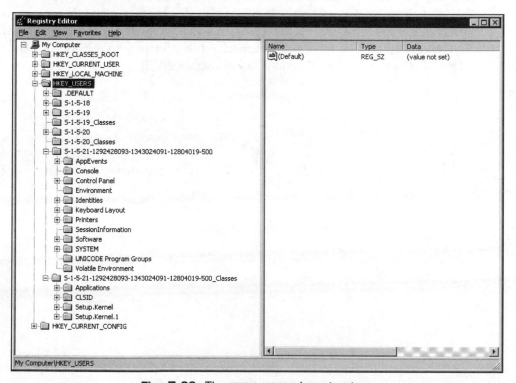

Fig. 7.23. The HKEY_USERS key structure

Note

More detailed information on the contents of the HKEY_USERS registry key will be provided in *Chapter 10*.

The data from the .DEFAULT subkey is used if no one is currently logged on to the system. The .DEFAULT subkey contains the same subkeys as the HKEY_CURRENT_USER key. These keys were listed in Table. 7.3.

Summary

In this chapter, we discussed the most important keys that exist in the registries of Windows NT-based operating systems, including Windows NT 4.0, Windows 2000, Windows XP and products of the Windows Server 2003 family. The description provided here is more detailed than that provided in *Chapter 1* and was mainly intended as a brief overview. Unfortunately, it would be impossible to create a complete reference on all the registry keys and make it fit into a single chapter (or else this chapter would become a book in itself). However, the information presented here is a "must" for any system administrator or support specialist who intends to use and support Windows NT/2000, Windows XP and Windows Server 2003.

CHAPTER 8

Network Settings in the Registry

A new system creates new problems.
Technological Murphy's Law

A bit beyond perception's reach
I sometimes believe I see
that Life is two locked boxes, each
containing the other's key.

Piet Hein
Grooks. The Paradox of Life

Windows XP and Windows Server 2003 networking is mainly based on similar functionality provided by Windows 2000, including local networking, dial-up, and remote connectivity. Like Windows NT 4.0/2000, the basic network settings in Windows XP and Windows Server 2003 registry are normally set during system setup. Most installation problems, caused by network adapters installed on the computer, occur at this time. Many Windows NT 4.0/2000 drawbacks have been eliminated in Windows XP and Windows Server 2003. One remaining problem, though, is the incorrect detection of network adapters during installation. This hasn't been completely eliminated, and can still occur. Unfortunately, the Setup program doesn't provide any other options for installing network adapters, except for automatic detection.

There's a solution though: simply install the operating system without the network adapter (you should physically remove it from the computer). When the installation procedure has been successfully completed, you add the network adapter using the Add Hardware applet on the Control Panel, and then install the network components.

Installing Network Components Using Control Panel Applets

When you install network components and configure network settings, new entries are added into the system registry. Before we open the registry editor and start exploring these entries, let's discuss an easy method of installing network components and specifying their settings.

In Windows NT 4.0, you use the Network applet on the Control Panel.

In Windows 2000, by combining their functionality, the Network and Dial-up Connections Control Panel applet has replaced two independent Windows NT 4.0 administrative tools: the Network applet and the Dial-up Connections applet. In Windows XP and Windows Server 2003, this situation has not changed significantly. To start configuring network connections, start the Network Connections applet on the Control Panel to open the **Network Connections** window. Provided that you have installed the network adapter, and the system has correctly detected it, the **Network Connections** window will look as shown in Fig. 8.1.

 Note

Certain conditions, such as a malfunctioning network adapter card, can keep your LAN connection from appearing in the Network Connections folder.

Notice that the appearance of the **Local Area Connection** icon in this window changes according to the status of the connection. By design, if your computer doesn't detect a network adapter, a local area connection icon does not appear in the Network Connections folder. Possible states of your LAN connections and their respective icons are summarized in Table 8.1.

Table 8.1. Local Area Connection Icons

Icon	Description
Local Area Connection	Network adapter has been correctly installed and detected by your computer. You are connected to the LAN (the LAN connection is active).
Local Area Connection	Network adapter is physically present, but the cable is unplugged from your computer.
	The cable is unplugged from your computer, or from the hub. This icon appears at the taskbar at the same time as the previous one.
Local Area Connection	Network adapter is present, but the driver is disabled.
None	The network adapter was not detected.

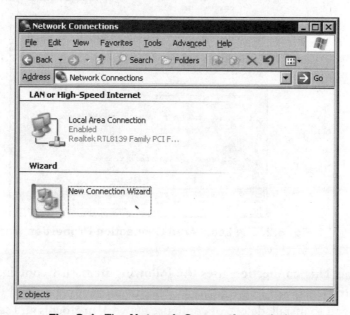

Fig. 8.1. The **Network Connections** window

To view or modify network settings, right-click the **Local Area Connection** and select **Properties**. The **Local Area Connection Properties** will open (Fig. 8.2).

The **Connect using** field at the top of the window specifies the network adapter used for local area connections. You can configure network adapters by clicking the **Configure** button below the field. Notice that this method only configures network adapters that you've already installed. If you need to install a new network adapter, use Add Hardware on the Control Panel. The dialog that appears when you click the **Configure** button is the same as the network adapter properties window that opens when you use the Device Manager (Fig. 8.3). This window only allows you to configure network adapter properties (if the driver has already been installed).

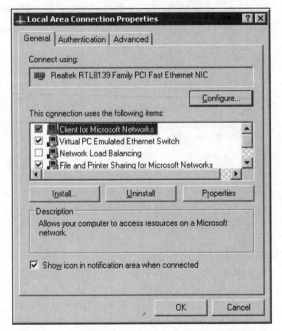

Fig. 8.2. The **Local Area Connection Properties** window

The **This connection uses the following items** list contains network services and protocols used by the adapter. The **Install**, **Uninstall**, and **Properties** buttons allow you to install, delete, or configure network protocols and services.

The **Show icon in taskbar when connected** checkbox at the bottom of the **Local Area Connection Properties** window (Fig. 8.2) allows you to specify a mode in which you can view the local area connection status using the taskbar indicator (Fig. 8.4).

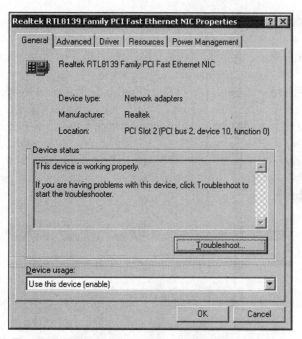

Fig. 8.3. The network adapter properties window

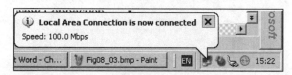

Fig. 8.4. The taskbar indicator displays the local area connection status

As I already mentioned, the Network and Dial-up Connections applet (Windows 2000) and Network Connections applet (Windows XP and Windows Server 2003) combine the functionality of two Windows NT 4.0 Control Panel applets. This change reflects the fact that certain components of the network subsystem, such as Remote Access Service (RAS) and Dial-Up Networking (DUN) have undergone modifications. The improvements are listed below.

❑ The Remote Access Service (RAS) is now closely integrated with other components of the network subsystem. Thus, this service is easier to use. In contrast to the method used in Windows NT 4.0 where RAS management involved using a separate utility, both local and remote network connections in Windows 2000, Windows XP, and Windows Server 2003 are managed using the same utility (Network and Dial-up Connections in Windows 2000, Network

Connections in Windows XP/Windows Server 2003). This enhancement simplifies the tasks for both system administrators and end users.

❑ The procedure for establishing and managing network connections is now much easier. Windows 2000 has introduced a special wizard for this purpose. Windows XP and Windows Server 2003 continue this tradition. This program contains a large list of configuration options displaying a series of dialogs that show available options and step-by-step instructions for configuring connections. The New Connection Wizard is capable of establishing and configuring various types of network connections (Fig. 8.5), including VPN (Virtual Private Network) connections, Internet connections, corporate network connections, and connections with the RAS server.

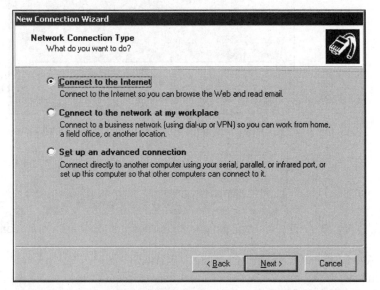

Fig. 8.5. The **Network Connection Wizard** is capable of establishing various connections

❑ New networking functions implemented in Windows 2000, Windows XP, and Windows Server 2003 include network connection sharing. A user can now establish a remote connection (for example, an Internet connection), and then allow other users to connect to the Internet using this connection. This is convenient for small networks (especially home networks). Although this functionality allows you to share a connection with any remote network, it's most frequently used for sharing Internet connections.

❑ Windows 2000/XP and Windows Server 2003 provide support for Virtual Private Networks (VPN). In addition to the PPTP protocol for accessing virtual private networks (also supported in Windows NT 4.0), Windows 2000/XP and Windows Server 2003 support various new VPN technologies, including Layer 2 Tunneling Protocol (L2TP) and IP Security (IPSec). IPSec is an open standard using Level 3 encryption technology.

❑ Stability of RRAS (Routing and Remote Access) is increased. Windows 2000, Windows XP and Windows Server 2003 also combine RAS and RRAS features.

❑ In comparison to Windows NT 4.0, Windows 2000, Windows XP, and Windows Server 2003 provide an extended set of functions for customizing dial-up connections.

As compared to Windows 2000, Windows XP and Windows Server 2003 also introduce several improvements and new features, among which the most important are:

❑ *Institute of Electrical and Electronics Engineers (IEEE) 802.1D Transparent Bridge* — this feature enables you to add multiple network segments (usually, of different media types) and have a single IP subnet.

❑ *DNS resolver* — provides name resolution for the local network.

❑ *Discovery and Control* — allows network clients to find the Internet Connection Sharing host, know its status, and control its Internet connection.

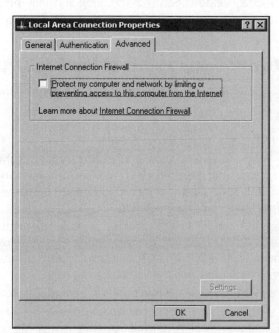

Fig. 8.6. Enabling Internet Connection Firewall

❏ *Personal Firewall* — provides basic Internet security for the computer, or when used in conjunction with ICS, for home or small office networks. To enable or disable Internet Connection Firewall for a specific connection, open the **Network Connections** window (see Fig. 8.1), right-click the connection that you want to protect, select the **Properties** command from the right-click menu, and go to the **Advanced** tab (Fig. 8.6). Set the **Protect my computer and network by limiting or preventing access to this computer from the Internet** checkbox. To configure the Internet Connection Firewall, click the **Settings** button at the bottom of this window.

Network Parameters in the Registry

Networking features in Windows 2000, Windows XP, and Windows Server 2003 include several improvements. These improvements have also influenced the method of storing network data in the registry. The main improvements introduced into the networking are: support for NDIS 5.0 (Windows 2000) and NDIS 5.1 (Windows XP and Windows Server 2003), Plug and Play support, power management, and the new INF file format used for installing network components.

Installing Network Components in the Registry

To install networking components in Windows 2000, Windows XP and Windows Server 2003, the operating system requires the following:

❏ *Class installer and optional co-installer*
Class installer is a dynamically loaded library (DLL) that installs, configures, or deletes devices of a specified class. Networking components in Windows 2000, Windows XP, and Windows Server 2003 must be installed by a network class or by a vendor-supplied class installer.
If the standard class installer doesn't provide all of the necessary functionality for an individual device, the device vendor may develop an optional coinstaller. This coinstaller is a Win32 DLL that implements all the necessary functions for the individual device.
A list of existing network components is provided below:
- Net — this class defines network adapters.
- NetTrans — this class defines network protocols (such as TCP/IP and IPX) and connection-oriented network clients.

- `NetClient` — this class specifies network clients, such as Microsoft Client for Networks or NetWare Client. The `NetClient` component is considered a network provider. It can also be used to provide print services (in this case, it's also the print provider).

- `NetService` — this class specifies network services, such as a file or print service.

The network class installer defines the class of the network component to be installed by the `ClassGuid` value. The `ClassGuid` value is the Globally Unique Identifier (GUID) for the class. You can generate GUID values using the Uuidgen.exe utility. More detailed information about this utility is provided in Platform SDK supplementary documents.

All standard network component classes and their respective `ClassGuid` values are listed in Table 8.2.

Table 8.2. Network Component Classes and Their Respective ClassGuid Values

Network component class	ClassGuid value
Net	{4D36E972-E325-11CE-BFC1-08002BE10318}
NetTrans	{4D36E973-E325-11CE-BFC1-08002BE10318}
NetClient	{4D36E974-E325-11CE-BFC1-08002BE10318}
NetService	{4D36E975-E325-11CE-BFC1-08002BE10318}

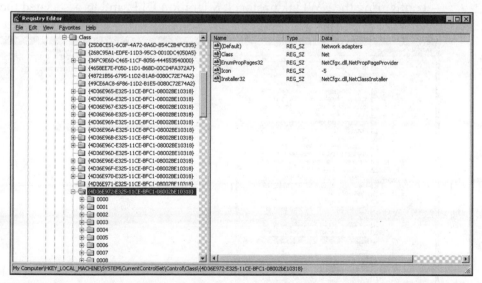

Fig. 8.7. The contents of the `HKEY_LOCAL_MACHINE\SYSTEM\CurrentControlSet\ Control\Class\{4D36E972-E325-11CE-BFC1-08002BE10318}` registry key defines the settings of the class installer for the network adapter class

Class installer information is stored in the registry under `HKEY_LOCAL_MACHINE\` `SYSTEM\CurrentControlSet\Control\Class`. For each class installer, this key contains a subkey named... No, it won't have the name you're expecting it to have. And it won't be something like "Net" either. Rather, it will be the `ClassGuid` value (Fig. 8.7). Compare this name to the `ClassGuid` values listed in Table 8.2.

❑ *One or more INF files*

INF files contain the necessary information for the class installer of the network component to install this component. A detailed description of the INF file format is provided in the documents supplied with Windows Driver Development Kit (DDK).

❑ *Optional notify object*

Network software components, such as network protocols, services, or network clients, may have to notify objects that allow you to display the user interface for manual configuring of the network components. For example, the UI provides capabilities for manual control over the binding process. Notice that hardware components, such as network adapters, may also provide both UI and software control over the binding process. However, all these tasks are performed by the INF file or coinstaller, rather than by notify objects. Fig. 8.8 shows information on the notify object that provides the capability of manually configuring the NWLink protocol, Migration DLL, and its associated files.

Fig. 8.8. Information on the notify object that configures the NWLink protocol

If the device driver isn't included with the standard Windows 2000, Windows XP, and Windows Server 2003 distribution package, then the device vendor should provide the necessary support.

In addition to the files listed above, the following files are needed to install network components.

❐ *One or more device drivers.* Normally, each driver contains a driver image (the SYS file) and a driver library (DLL).

❐ *The driver catalog file* is optional, but highly desirable. We discussed catalog files in *Chapter 6.* Here, we'll only note that if the device vendor needs to include a device into the Hardware Compatibility List (HCL), it's necessary to test both the device and its driver in the Windows Hardware Quality Lab (WHQL). If the test results are satisfactory, WHQL includes the device into the HCL and provides the catalog file (CAT file) for the driver. The CAT file contains the digital signature.

❐ *The optional Txtsetup.oem file.* This file contains the data needed by the Setup program that installs Windows 2000, Windows XP, and Windows Server 2003 to install the device driver during the earliest phases of the setup process (the text-mode setup).

Network Adapter Registration Information

Like Windows NT 4.0, Windows 2000, Windows XP, and Windows Server 2003 also have software registration subkeys for all of the installed network adapter cards. These keys are stored under `HKEY_LOCAL_MACHINE\SOFTWARE\Microsoft\`
`Windows NT\CurrentVersion\NetworkCards\`*Netcard*# (Fig. 8.9).

▶ *Note*

Notice that network adapters are numbered beginning from 1, rather than from 0 as is usual.

The `HKEY_LOCAL_MACHINE` root key also contains two more subkeys containing data on the network adapter:

`HKEY_LOCAL_MACHINE\SYSTEM\CurrentControlSet\Enum`. Here, Plug and Play enumerators store the data concerning individual devices, such as device identifiers (device ID) and identifiers of compatible devices (if they exist). Fig. 8.10 provides information about the Realtek RTL8139 Family PCI Fast Ethernet NIC stored under `HKEY_LOCAL_MACHINE\SYSTEM\CurrentControlSet\Enum`. Notice that some of this information (including the device description and its type) is displayed by the Network Connections applet in Control Panel (see Fig. 8. 3).

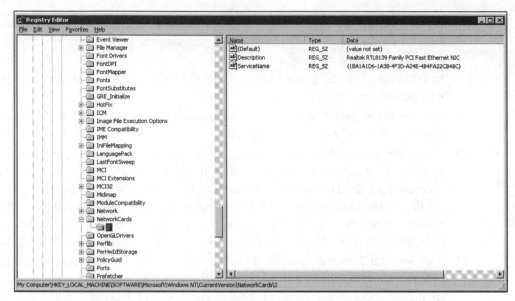

Fig. 8.9. The `HKEY_LOCAL_MACHINE\SOFTWARE\Microsoft\Windows NT\`
`CurrentVersion\NetworkCards\2` registry key in the registry

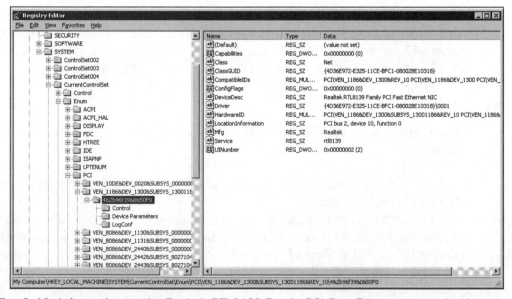

Fig. 8.10. Information on the Realtek RTL8139 Family PCI Fast Ethernet network adapter
under `HKEY_LOCAL_MACHINE\SYSTEM\CurrentControlSet\Enum`

`HKEY_LOCAL_MACHINE\SYSTEM\CurrentControlSet\Class\<`*`ClassGUID`*`>`.   Here, device installers store data on each individual class of devices, its respective class installer, and coinstallers (if present). For each installed driver, there's a subkey under the key, named "0000", "0001", ... These subkeys contain information on individual drivers, including a description string, the path to the driver's INF file, and vendor information. Fig. 8.11 shows the contents of the registry key storing data on the driver we're discussing — the network driver for Realtek RTL8139 Family PCI Fast Ethernet adapter.

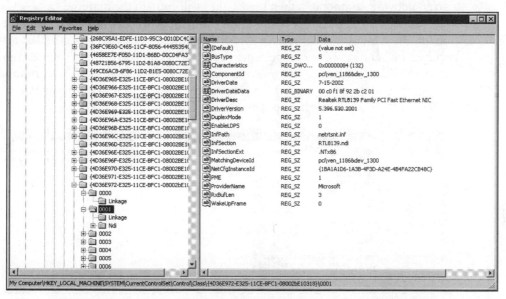

Fig. 8.11. Network adapter settings in Windows Server 2003 registry

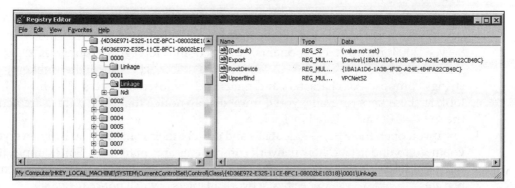

Fig. 8.12. Typical contents of the `Linkage` key for the network adapter driver

Each of the driver keys also contains a set of required subkeys: `Linkage` and `Ndi`. The typical contents of the `Linkage` subkey for the network adapter driver are shown in Fig. 8.12. As you can see, this subkey contains the following standard settings: `Export`, specifying the list of created objects; `RootDevice` (the setting that specifies the root device); and `UpperBind` (the setting that specifies protocol binding).

The `Ndi` key contains subkeys and settings that depend on the type of installed network component. If the network component has an associated service or device driver, then the `Ndi` key will contain a `Service` setting. This setting specifies the name of the appropriate service or driver (Fig. 8.13). If there are several services associated with a given network component, then the `Ndi` key will contain the required `CoServices` setting (`REG_MULTI_SZ` data type). This setting will list all services associated with the component, including the main service specified by the `Service` setting. The last setting is required for all `NetTrans` components (transport protocols), `NetClient` components (network clients), and `NetService` components (network services). The components of the `Net` type (network adapters) have no such setting (Fig. 8.14). As you can see, only the RTL8139 device driver has been associated with the network adapter.

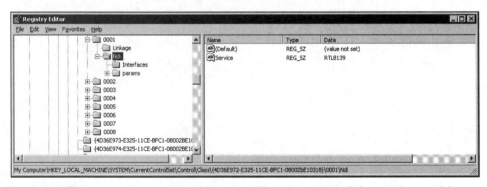

Fig. 8.13. The `..\Ndi\Service` setting specifies the name of the service or driver associated with the network component

All further configuration information on Windows 2000/XP and Windows Server 2003 network components is stored in the registry under `HKEY_LOCAL_MACHINE\SYSTEM\CurrentControlSet\Control\Network`. Notice the subkeys, long strings composed of characters and digits and enclosed in braces (Fig. 8.14). If you look at these keys carefully, you'll immediately notice that their names are actually the `ClassGuid` values listed in Table 8.2.

If you open these keys sequentially and explore their contents, you'll find everything you need to understand how network components are configured. For example, if you open the subkey named `{4D36E972-E325-11CE-BFC1-08002BE10318}` (if you remember, this `ClassGuid` value specifies network adapters), you'll notice the `Connection` key at the lower level of the hierarchy (Fig. 8.15). It's not difficult to see that this key specifies the LAN connection properties. First, the Name string setting specifies the "Local Area Connection" string that you see in the **Network and Dial-up Connections** window. Next, the string setting named PnPInstanceID is the link to the subkey under the Enum key, which contains the data concerning the network adapter. Finally, the binary setting named ShowIcon specifies if the toolbar indicator is enabled. The relationship between registry settings and Control Panel applets is illustrated by Fig. 8.16.

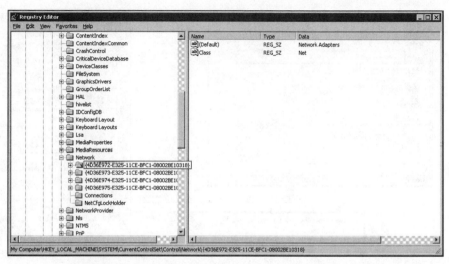

Fig. 8.14. The contents of the HKEY_LOCAL_MACHINE\SYSTEM\ CurrentControlSet\Control\Network **registry key**

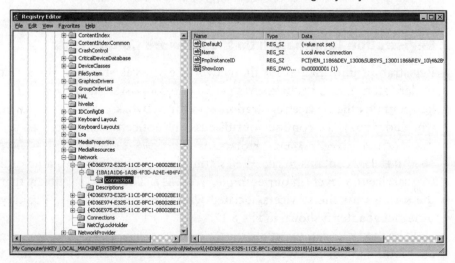

Fig. 8.15. Local Area Connection properties in the system registry

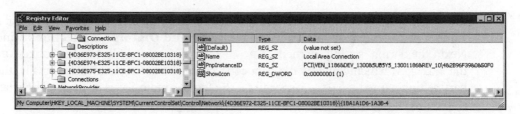

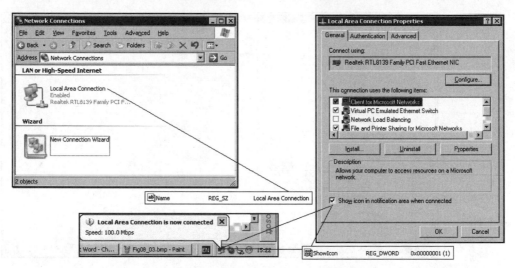

Fig. 8.16. Relationship between registry information and the Network
Connections applet in Control Panel

Registration Information on the Network Components

Registration information for the network services is stored in the system registry
under `HKEY_LOCAL_MACHINE\SYSTEM\CurrentControlSet\Services`. This registry
key contains the service registration keys for network components (including network adapters). To continue our discussion, notice that the `HKEY_LOCAL_MACHINE\`
`SYSTEM\CurrentControlSet\Control\Class\{4D36E972-E325-11CE-BFC1-08002BE10318}\`
`0000\Ndi` key contains the `Service` setting, which specifies the name of the respective service or driver (in our example, `RTL8139`). The `RTL8139` subkey that describes
the settings for the service associated with the Realtek RTL8139 Family PCI Fast
Ethernet adapter is shown in Fig. 8.17.

The `HKEY_LOCAL_MACHINE\SYSTEM\CurrentControlSet\Services` registry key
also contains subkeys that describe each network component installed in the system
(Fig. 8.18).

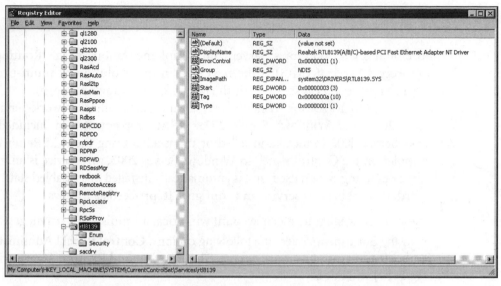

Fig. 8.17. The `HKEY_LOCAL_MACHINE\SYSTEM\CurrentControlSet\`
`Services\RTL8139` key contains configuration data for
a `Realtek RTL8139` network adapter

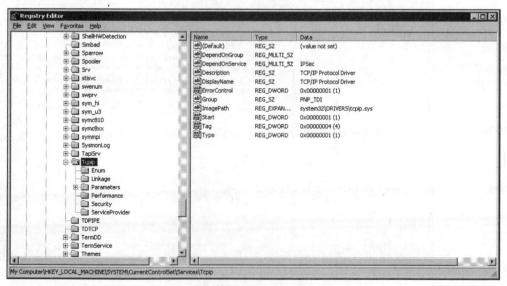

Fig. 8.18. The `HKEY_LOCAL_MACHINE\SYSTEM\CurrentControlSet\`
`Services` registry key contains subkeys for all
installed network components

Remote Access

As aforementioned, Windows Server 2003 implementation of the Routing and Remote Access Server (RRAS) is the next step in the evolution of multi-protocol routing and remote access services for the Microsoft Windows platform.

In contrast to RRAS for Windows NT 4.0 and most other network services of Windows 2000 and Windows Server 2003, RRAS implementation included with Windows Server 2003 cannot be installed or uninstalled using the Add/Remove Programs applet on the Control Panel. In Windows Server 2003, this service is an integral part of the operating system itself, and is automatically installed in a disabled state.

In order to enable this service and configure it, proceed as follows:

1. Logon to the system using an account with local administrator privileges.

2. From the **Start** menu, select the following options: **Control Panel** | **Administrative Tools** | **Routing and Remote Access**. The **Routing and Remote Access** window (Fig. 8.19) will open.

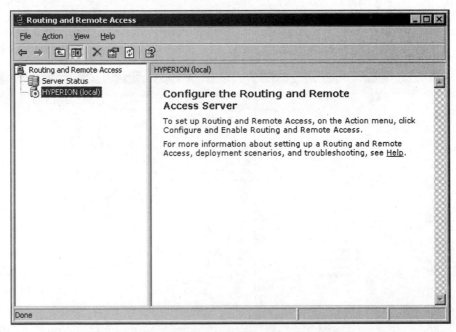

Fig. 8.19. The Routing and Remote Access MMC snap-in

3. For a local computer, right-click the server icon and select the **Configure and Enable Routing and Remote Access** command from the context menu. For a remote

computer, right-click the **Server Status** icon and click **Add Server**. In the **Add Server** dialog boxes, select the server you want to add. Then, right-click the remote server icon and select **Configure and Enable Routing and Remote Access**.

4. The Routing and Remote Access Server Setup Wizard will start, enabling you to select the required options (Fig. 8.20).

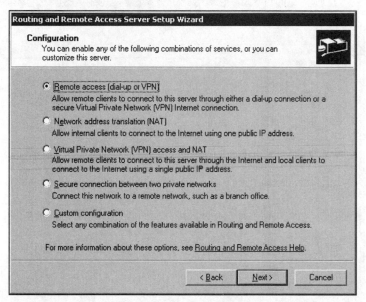

Fig. 8.20. The Routing and Remote Access Server Setup Wizard enables the user to select the required configuration options

Once the wizard has finished, the remote access router is enabled and configured based on your selections in the wizard. For further configuration, use the Routing and Remote Access snap-in (Fig. 8.21).

When the Routing and Remote Access service is enabled, it creates and maintains its settings in the system registry. For performance reasons, most of the Routing and Remote Access service configuration information is stored in binary in large configuration blocks, not as separate registry entries that can easily be viewed and changed. All configuration of the Routing and Remote Access service should be done through the Routing and Remote Access snap-in or through the Netsh command-line utility.

The most important registry settings for RRAS in Windows Server 2003 reside in the registry under the following keys:

❑ HKEY_LOCAL_MACHINE\System\CurrentControlSet\Services\RemoteAccess — Routing and Remote Access service and router interface configuration information

❑ HKEY_LOCAL_MACHINE\Software\Microsoft\Router — Router component configuration information

❑ HKEY_LOCAL_MACHINE\Software\Microsoft\RouterPhonebook — Router phone book settings

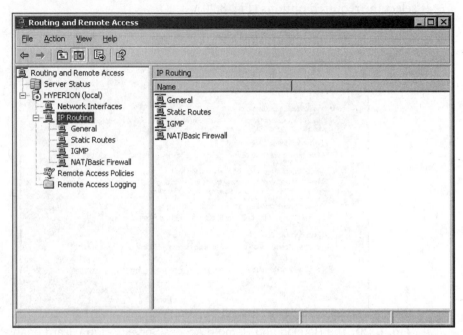

Fig. 8.21. The Routing and Remote Access MMC snap-in provides a set of options for configuring the Routing and Remote Access Service

Terminal Services

Since its introduction in the early 1990s, Windows Terminal Services was developed in parallel with the evolution of the Windows platform itself. Similar to UNIX and X Windows, Windows Terminal Services provide a server-centric computing model, but ensure much greater flexibility for accessing Win32 applications. The main benefit of Windows Terminal Services deployment is the fact that it enables you to provide access to specific Win32 applications without the necessity of installing those applications on every workstation within your Windows environment. Windows Terminal Services have been popular since 1995, when Citrix introduced its WinFrame product that provided full access to Windows NT 3.51 for the users of Windows terminals — so-called thin-client devices specially designed to provide users with access to Windows Terminal Services.

Note

Windows terminals or thin-client devices are solid-state devices that have their OS burned into ROM (i.e., they have no moving parts). Such devices are exclusively used for communicating with terminal servers, UNIX servers, or mainframes. Typically, they run Windows CE or embedded Linux.

Unfortunately, up to now many administrators have considered Terminal Services to be rather difficult to deploy and limited in functionality and application support. This is mainly due to the fact that Windows NT 4.0 Terminal Server Edition (WTS) represented a separate operating system rather than a Windows NT 4.0 Server add-on. However, with the release of Windows 2000, Terminal Services became an integral part of the OS itself, including Windows 2000 Server, Windows 2000 Advanced Server and Windows 2000 Datacenter Server. Products of the Windows Server 2003 family, in turn, offer several enhancements to Terminal Services, which will be covered later in this chapter. Furthermore, most contemporary programs that comply with the Windows Logo requirements can run in a terminal server environment with little or no modifications. Therefore, in today's computing environment Terminal Services can be successfully utilized for achieving the following administrative goals:

☐ *Desktop replacement.* Windows 2000/Windows Server 2003 Terminal Services can allow you to completely eliminate standard PCs and replace them with thin-client devices. When considering this approach, one must carefully weigh its benefits (such as the elimination of end-node support, reduced power consumption, increased security, and rapid application deployment) against its potential drawbacks (for example, increased initial deployment costs for purchasing thin-client devices and robust servers, reduction of end-user personalization, limited sound and multimedia capabilities).

☐ *Remote Access and Remote Administration.* Remote access can be rather beneficial for large corporations having a large number of remote or migrating users, such as telecommuters, travelling executives, and so on.

Currently, there are many changes being introduced into Terminal Services technology. One of the most obvious ones, introduced with Windows Server 2003, is the fact that now it is not necessary to install Terminal Server for remote administration of your server. Remote Desktop for Administration is installed by default. To use Remote Desktop for Administration, you must first enable remote connections. To enable or disable remote connections to your server, proceed as follows:

1. Start the System applet on the Control Panel, and go to the **Remote** tab (Fig. 8.22).

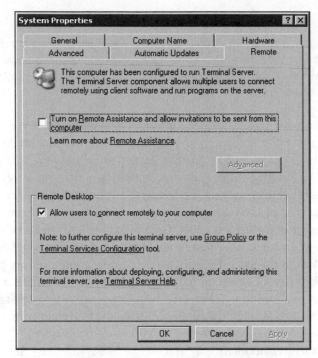

Fig. 8.22. The **Remote** tab of the **System Properties** window

2. In the **Remote Desktop** option group, set the **Allow users to connect remotely to your computer** check box, and then click **OK**.

Note

You must be logged on as a member of the Administrators group to enable or disable Remote Desktop for Administration.

Among the most significant changes that have been made in Terminal Services technology is the addition of the new Remote Desktop client, included with Windows XP and products of the Windows Server 2003 family (Fig. 8.23). This new client is based on the newer version of the Microsoft RDP protocol (Microsoft RDP v. 5.2).

Note

The traditional computing model is based on the TCP/IP protocol stack for transferring data between workstations and servers. Terminal services, however, have very specific needs for network link implementation, since only video information, keyboard, and mouse clicks are communicated, while all data processing takes place on the server. Two main protocols have been developed for this model — ICA (developed by Citrix) and RDP (developed by Microsoft). Windows 2000 Terminal Services uses RDP v. 5, which provides additional functionality to its predecessor, RDP v. 4.0 (implemented in Windows NT 4.0 Terminal Server Edition).

Fig. 8.23. The **Remote Desktop Connection** window

New features implemented by RDP5 included support for:

❑ Windows CE clients
❑ Remote control of user sessions
❑ Bitmap cashing to disk (RDP4 supported caching only to RAM)
❑ Client clipboard mapping

The newer versions of RDP (RDP v. 5.1 in Windows XP and RDP v. 5.2 in Windows Server 2003) additionally provide native support for client drive mapping, audio, enhanced video resolution and color depth, and a new feature — a connection bar that allows the user to "pin" the chosen part of large full-screen display to a specific part of their small PDA-sized screen during full-screen Terminal

Services sessions (Fig. 8.24). Furthermore, the new Remote Desktop client can be used to access both RDP connections to Windows XP and Windows Server 2003 computers as well as for accessing the existing RDP4 and RDP5 Terminal Servers. Finally, the new client allows you to save connection settings to RDP files, thus eliminating the necessity to edit the registry.

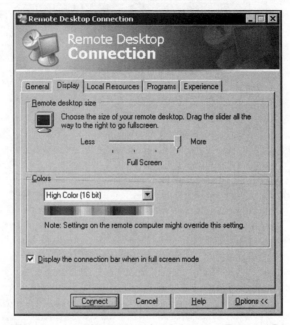

Fig. 8.24. The **Display** configuration tab of the new Remote Desktop client

Note

Windows Server 2003 Enterprise Edition and Windows Server 2003 Datacenter Edition also implement a new technology known as Terminal Services Session Directory, which enhances user ability to reconnect to an active session on a terminal server cluster.

Remote Assistance

Remote Assistance is a feature of Windows Server 2003 and Windows XP that allows remote control over a desktop session. Rest assured that there are controls that you can use to ensure that only authorized individuals and computers can participate in. Let's take a brief tour of the Remote Assistance possibilities, then I'll explain the controls and what I consider to be the best practices.

Note

Notice the difference between Remote Assistance and Remote Desktop! Remote Desktop provides an administrator with the ability to remotely connect to a computer for troubleshooting or management purposes or to access the network remotely. A Remote Desktop session does not allow a user present at the remote system to see the activity on the screen. The machine is locked and cannot be accessed while the remote session is active. Unlike the Remote Desktop, which starts a separate session, Remote Assistance allows the participation in an existing session by an individual logged on to the system (called the novice) and someone (called the expert) from a remote computer. Both novice and expert can see what's happening on the novice's computer, and both can participate. The expert can watch the novice to see a demonstration.

Similar to Remote Desktop, the default security settings in Windows XP and Windows Server 2003 allow you to enable the Remote Assistance feature via the Control Panel. To do so, the user who needs assistance can proceed as follows:

1. Start the System applet on the Control Panel, and go to the **Remote** tab (see Fig. 8.22).

2. Set the **Turn on Remote Assistance and allow invitations to be sent from this computer** checkbox. After you enable this option, the **Advanced** button will become available, allowing you to specify advanced settings for Remote Assistance sessions. A Remote Assistance session can be either "view-only" or allow remote control. Although one can choose to refuse the expert's request for control during the session, this choice and others can be configured via settings on the **Remote** tab of the **System Control Panel** applet. Clicking **Advanced** on this tab presents the following choices (Fig. 8.25):

   • **Allow this computer to be controlled remotely** — Determines whether to allow or deny remote control once connected.

   • **Set the maximum amount of time invitations can remain open** (in days, minutes, and hours).

However useful this function may be, allowing a user to control it via the Control Panel is not realistic. Although many users are capable of choosing good mentors, others have no common sense at all. Likewise, well-meaning but ill-advised "experts" can do a lot of harm.

Group Policy does offer a solution; it allows different degrees of control for different computers and can be centrally managed. By default, Remote Assistance settings in Group Policy are not configured and therefore have no impact on the settings made on the Control Panel. However, like other Group Policy settings, once you set the Group Policy settings, they will override any local settings.

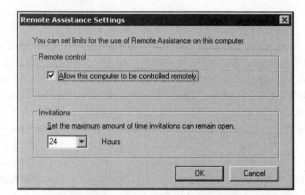

Fig. 8.25. The **Remote Assistance Settings** window

Group Policy controls for Remote Assistance are located under **Computer Settings** | **Administrative Templates** | **System** | **Remote Assistance** (Fig. 8.26). To control Remote Assistance solicitations, select the **Solicited Remote Assistance** node, and select the settings appropriately. In Figure 8.27, Remote Assistance, including remote control, is allowed, but invitations are valid for 24 hours. Notice that a 24-hour interval (the default setting) is rather long, since long-term invitations increase the risk of compromise. Thus, in order to increase security it is recommended that you decrease this setting to, say, 3 hours.

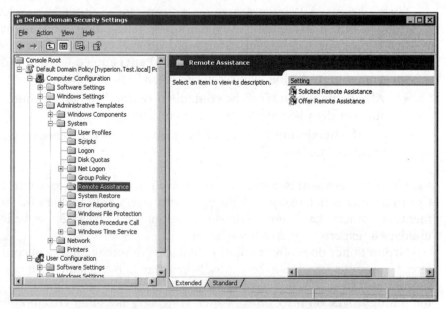

Fig. 8.26. Group Policy controls for Remote Assistance

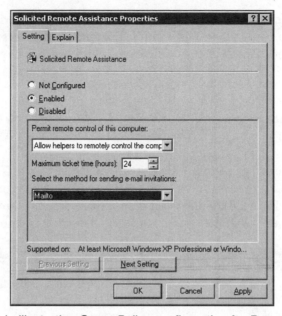

Fig. 8.27. Example illustrating Group Policy configuration for Remote Assistance

Customizing a Network Using the Registry

It's impossible to provide a complete reference for all of Windows NT, Windows 2000, Windows XP, and Windows Server 2003 networking in a single chapter (for example, the Resource Kits usually include a comprehensive volume entitled "Windows NT Networking"). This topic certainly deserves a separate book. However, I hope that this chapter helps you to understand how network settings are stored in the registry, and how these settings are related to the data displayed by Control Panel applets. This topic is one of the most interesting ones, and if you explore it, you'll make many discoveries and invent many new ways of customizing network settings.

The remaining sections of this chapter will describe various methods of customizing network settings using the registry.

Securing DNS Servers against DoS Attacks

During the last few years, Denial of Service (DoS) and, especially, Distributed Denial of Service (DDoS) attacks have become the most serious threats to corporate networks. The number of such attacks is growing steadily with time, and currently no one can feel safe and absolutely secure from encountering this threat. Of course, the tips provided here also won't guarantee absolute security against attacks on DNS servers. However, they will serve as good add-ons to your security policy.

Note

Before introducing the registry modifications described below into the configuration of your production servers, it is recommended that you test them in your lab environment.

All registry settings described in this section are located under the HKEY_LOCAL_MACHINE\SYSTEM\CurrentControlSet\Services\Tcpip\Parameters registry key (Fig. 8.28). Notice that if specific parameters are missing from your registry, this means that the system considers them to be set to default values.

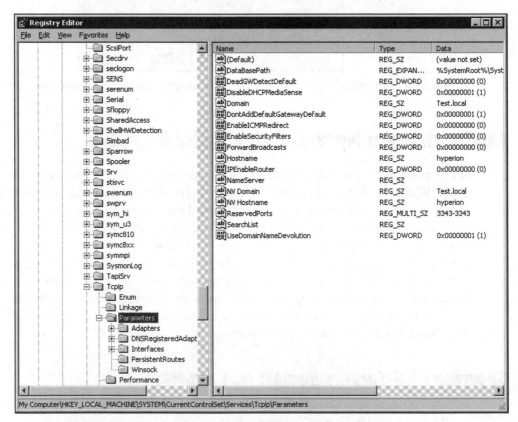

Fig. 8.28. The HKEY_LOCAL_MACHINE\SYSTEM\CurrentControlSet\
Services\Tcpip\Parameters **registry key**

Brief descriptions of these parameters and their recommended values are provided below:

☐ EnableDeadGWDetect (REG_DWORD data type). The default value (1) enables TCP/IP to switch to a secondary gateway if many connections experience problems. However, in cases when you are under a DoS attack, such behavior is undesirable, since all traffic can be redirected to a gateway that is not constantly monitored. Because of this reason, set this parameter to 0.

☐ EnablePMTUDiscovery (REG_DWORD data type). The default value of this parameter enables TCP/IP to determine Maximum Transmission Unit (MTU) that can be transmitted to the system. This feature is potentially dangerous, since it enables the attacker to bypass your security system or cause it to fail by means of transmitting fragmented traffic. For example, many Intrusion Detection Systems (IDS) are still unable to correctly assemble fragmented IP packets. If you set this parameter to 0, the MTU value will always be equal to 576 bytes.

☐ KeepAlive (REG_DWORD data type). This parameter specifies how frequently an idle connection on a remote system should be verified. Set the value for 300000.

☐ SynAttackProtect (REG_DWORD data type). Creating this value will enable you to provide minimum protection against a specific type of DoS attack known as SYN Flood. SYN Flood attacks interfere with the normal acknowledgement handshake between a client and a server. Under normal conditions, this process comprises three stages:

• The client sends the request to establish a connection to the server (SYN message).
• The server responds by sending an acknowledgement (SYN-ACK message).
• The client confirms the reception of the SYN-ACK message by sending an acknowledgement (ACK message).

If your server became a target for a SYN Flood attack, it will receive a flood of connection requests, which will gradually prevent it from receiving acknowledgements from clients. Thus, legitimate users will be unable to establish connections. The recommended value for this parameter is 2 (you can also set this value to 1, but this configuration is less efficient).

Securing Terminal Services Connections

Materials provided in this section will certainly prove useful for those who want to improve security when using Remote Desktop for Administration in Windows Server 2003. As was already mentioned earlier in this chapter, this facility is automatically installed on all servers running Windows Server 2003. However, remote administration with this tool is not enabled by default. After it is enabled (see Fig. 8.22), you can use Group Policy or the Terminal Services Configuration tool to further configure Terminal Services. By default, only members of the Administrators group have permission to connect in administrative mode (but they can only connect two at a time). This default security setting is useful. However, there are several additional settings and tools that can be used to improve security, including Group Policy, the local Terminal Server configuration tool, local client settings and, of course, registry editing.

 Note

In addition to advice and tips provided here, don't forget about regular system hardening practices and security policies adopted by your company. More detailed information on this topic will be provided in *Chapter 9*. Furthermore, carefully weigh the benefits provided by enabling remote access for administrative purposes to potential dangers of exposing the system to additional risks.

To modify the default settings for Remote Desktop, proceed as follows:

1. Open the Control Panel, start Administrative Tools, then select the **Terminal Services Configuration** option. The **Terminal Services Configuration** console will open (Fig. 8.29).

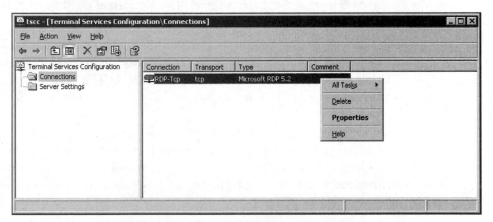

Fig. 8.29. Configuring a RDP-Tcp connection

2. Right-click the **RDP-Tcp** connection, then choose the **Properties** command from the right-click menu.

3. The **RDP-Tcp Properties** window will open. On the **General** tab (Fig. 8.30), change the default encryption level to **High** (the default value is **Client**

compatible). All data that transfers between the client and server will be at the server's highest encryption level. Currently, that is set to 128 bits. The client must be able to use 128 bits or it will not be able to connect.

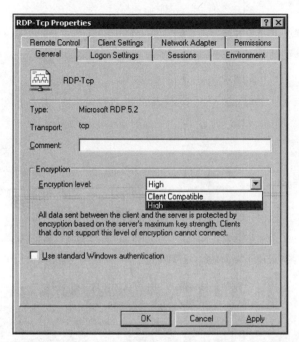

Fig. 8.30. The **General** tab of the **RDP-Tcp Properties** window

4. Next, go to the **Logon Settings** tab (Fig. 8.31) and set the **Always prompt for password** checkbox. The Remote Desktop connection has a setting that allows the user to save his or her password for the connection. This setting would allow anyone who was able to log on to the local computer to access the remote system through the console. This feature is potentially dangerous, since it might provide an attacker with easy access to remote systems. Setting the **Always prompt for password** option ensures that the user logs on each time, regardless of the client setting.

5. On the **Sessions** tab (Fig. 8.32), note that by default, user accounts are set to **Disconnect from session** if a session limit is reached or a connection is broken (the option is grayed out in the figure). This setting is a good idea if system administration tasks are running and a connection is broken as a result of network problems. The task will continue to run while the session is in a disconnected state, and the administrator can reconnect. The alternative, **End session**,

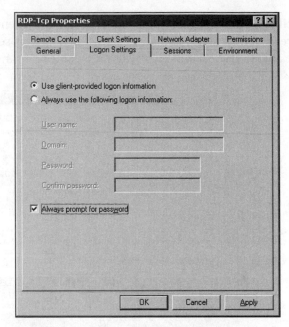

Fig. 8.31. The **Logon Settings** tab of the **RDP-Tcp Properties** window

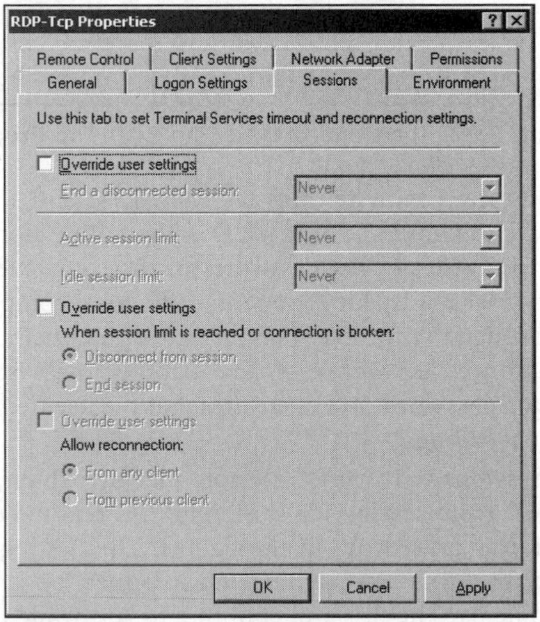

Fig. 8.32. The **Sessions** tab of the **RDP-Tcp Properties** window

would stop the running process with unpredictable results. Figure the values for **Active session limit** and **Idle session limit** parameters according to the usage of these sessions. Limiting active sessions is probably not a good idea, as it will prevent some administrative chores from getting done. Limiting an idle session is useful. If you are engaged in a session and leave your computer, anyone could use the open session to the server — a session open with administrative privileges. Setting an idle time-out may prevent such an occurrence; at least it will limit exposure. This setting will also help in situations where multiple administrators want to connect. If two administrators are connected yet not using the session, the third administrator cannot connect.

Remote Desktop Port Settings

In contrast to the steps described above, the tweak described in this section can only be accomplished by direct editing of the system registry. In order to allow the Remote Desktop use over the Internet, TCP port 3389 must be open on the firewall or an alternative port must be assigned to the service. If possible, configure the firewall to allow the 3389 port connection only to an authenticated user. If you will be limiting the number of computers in use, limit the connections to the port on those specific computers. To block connections to that port on sensitive systems, use IPSec.

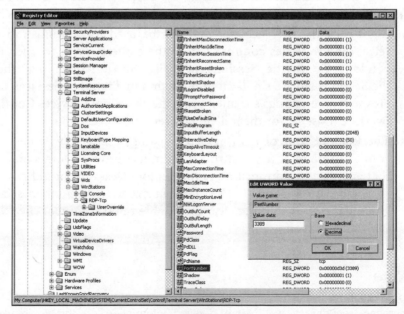

Fig. 8.33. The `PortNumber` value entry under `HKEY_LOCAL_MACHINE\SYSTEM\`
`CurrentControlSet\Control\TerminalServer\WinStations\RDP-Tcp\PortNumber`

To change the port used by Remote Desktop, do the following:

1. Open the registry and locate the `HKEY_LOCAL_MACHINE\SYSTEM\CurrentControlSet\Control\TerminalServer\WinStations\RDP-Tcp` key.
2. Under this key, find the `PortNumber` value entry, which by default is set to `3389` (Fig. 8.33). Change this value as appropriate (for example, to `8098`).
3. Now, to access the server using the new setting, type the new port number after the IP address of the computer to which you want to connect. If the new port is 8098, and the IP address of the server is 192.168.1.8, the new IP address and port combination will be 192.168.1.8:8098.

Client Settings

To configure client settings for Remote Desktop, you need to open the **Properties** window for specific user accounts. To do so, proceed as follows:

1. Open Control Panel, select the **Administrative tools** option, and then start **Users and Computers** or **Active Directory Users and Computers** MMC snap-ins (depending on the role of your computer and whether it participates in a domain).
2. Right-click the user account that will be used for administrative access, and select the Properties command from the context menu to open the properties window. Go to the **Sessions** tab (Fig. 8.34). Notice that the settings on the **Sessions** tab are similar to those found in **Terminal Services Configuration**. However, the settings specified using the **Terminal Services Configuration** tool override those set for the individual user.
3. The **Remote control** tab (Fig. 8.35) settings establish whether or not this account can be remotely controlled. Administrative accounts and user accounts that are used by administrators for Remote Desktop should not be configured to allow remote control. Therefore, in order to strengthen security, it is recommended that the user clear the **Enable remote control checkbox**, as shown in this illustration.

▶ *Note*

In addition to settings that enhance security, strong policies and procedures will increase security as well. More detailed information on this topic will be provided in *Chapter 9*.

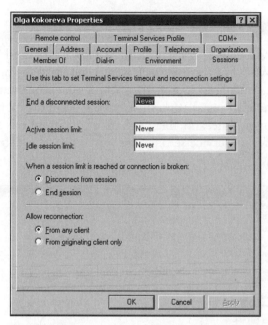

Fig. 8.34. The **Sessions** tab of the user account properties window

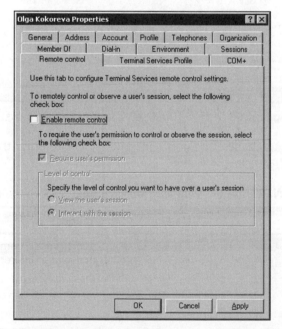

Fig. 8.35. The **Remote control** tab of the user account properties window

Registry Entries for the W32Time Service

One of the most confusing elements in Windows 2000 and Windows Server 2003 domains is the W32Time service, which is integrated into the operating system in order to ensure that date and time are properly synchronized throughout your organization.

Unfortunately, installation instructions don't explain the reliance of user authentication on time, and, therefore, many organizations run into logon problems.

The W32Time service settings are stored in the registry under the HKEY_LOCAL_ MACHINE\SYSTEM\CurrentControlSet\Services\W32Time\Parameters key (Fig. 8. 36).

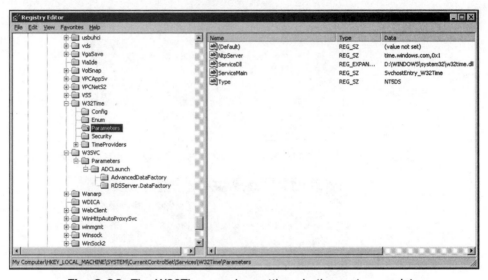

Fig. 8.36. The W32Time service settings in the system registry

The value entries that you can specify here to tune the W32Time service are outlined in Table 8.3.

Table 8.3. W32Time Service Registry Values

Value name	Data type	Description	Values
AvoidTimeSyncOnWan	REG_DWORD	Synchronize with a computer that is at a different site.	0 = Site is ignored [default]. 1 = Do *not* synchronize with a time source that is at a different site.

continues

Table 8.3 Continued

Value name	Data type	Description	Values
GetDcBackoffMaxTimes	REG_DWORD	The maximum number of times to double the back-off interval when successive attempts to find a domain controller fail. An event is logged every time a full wait occurs.	0 = The wait between attempts is at a minimum and no event is logged. 7 = [default]
GetDcBackoffMinutes	REG_DWORD	The starting number of minutes to wait before looking for a domain controller, if the last attempt failed.	15 = [default]
LocalNTP	REG_DWORD	Start the SNTP server.	0 = Don't start the SNTP server, unless this computer is a domain controller [default]. 1 = Always start the SNTP server.
NtpServer	REG_SZ	Stores the value from NET TIME /SETSNTP.	Blank by default. Sample data value: 192.4.41.40
Period	REG_DWORD	Control how often the time service synchronizes.	0 = once a day 65535, every 2 days 65534, every 3 days 65533, every week (7 days) 65532, every 45 minutes until 3 good synchronizations occur, then once every 8 hours (3 per day) [default] 65531, every 45 minutes until 1 good synchronization occurs, then once every day
ReliableTimeSource	REG_DWORD	Does this computer have a reliable time source?	0 = No [default] 1 = This computer has a reliable time source (this is only useful on a domain controller).

continues

Table 8.3 Continued

Value name	Data type	Description	Values
Type	REG_SZ	How does this computer synchronize	Nt5DS = synchronize to domain hierarchy or manually configured source [default] NTP = synchronize to manually configured source NoSync = do *not* synchronize time
Adj	REG_DWORD	Maintains computer clock information between reboots	Change not recommended
msSkewPerDay	REG_DWORD	Maintains computer clock information between reboots	Change not recommended

Note

Period can be a type REG_SZ with special values: Bidaily, every 2 days; Tridaily, every 3 days; Weekly, every week (7 days); SpecialSkew, every 45 minutes until 3 good synchronizations occur, then once every 8 hours (3 per day) [default]; DailySpecialSkew, every 45 minutes until 1 good synchronization occurs, then once every day.

Disabling Dynamic DNS Registration

By default, all computers running Windows 2000, Windows XP, or Windows Server 2003 attempt to dynamically register on the DNS servers specified on the **General** tab of the TCP/IP properties window. To disable this feature, click the **Advanced** button on the **General** tab of the **Internet Protocol (TCP/IP) Properties** window. The **Advanced TCP/IP Settings** window will open. Go to the **DNS** tab and clear the **Register this connection's addresses in DNS** checkbox.

In case you want to perform the same operation using the registry, open the HKEY_LOCAL_MACHINE\SYSTEM\CurrentControlSet\Services\Tcpip\Parameters\ Interfaces key, and set the DisableDynamicUpdate value (of REG_DWORD data type) to 1.

Disabling Persistent Network Connections

To disable the option for restoring persistent network connections, start the registry editor, open the `HKEY_USERS\.DEFAULT\Software\Microsoft\` `WindowsNT\CurrentVersion\Network\Persistent Connections` key, and locate the `SaveConnections` setting. The default value for this setting is `yes` (Fig. 8.37). To disable persistent network connections, set this value to `no`.

Note

To disable persistent network connections for users, set the `SaveConnections` value to `no` in all existing user profiles. This information is stored in the registry under the following keys: `HKEY_USERS\<User SID>\SOFTWARE\Microsoft\WindowsNT\` `CurrentVersion\Network\Persistent Connections`.

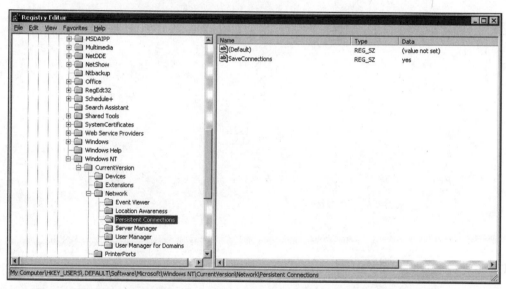

Fig. 8.37. The `HKEY_USERS\.DEFAULT\Software\Microsoft\WindowsNT\` `CurrentVersion\Network\Persistent Connections` registry key

Summary

In this chapter, we briefly discussed the network settings in the Windows 2000, Windows XP, and Windows Server 2003 registries. In the next chapter, we'll discuss important topics concerning registry protection and security.

CHAPTER 9

Protecting
the Registry

*Whatever can be used for good
can also be used for evil.*

Alfred Nobel

This chapter is dedicated to measures that will allow you to protect the registry. At the same time, these security measures won't create any difficulties for you when performing everyday tasks. Notice that while this chapter can't be considered a complete security reference, the measures of protecting the system registry discussed here are important, and each system administrator must know them.

In nearly all the chapters of this book, I've tried to emphasize that Windows XP and products of the Windows Server 2003 family are based on the Windows NT/2000 kernel. And, as a matter of fact, Windows NT/2000 is the first Microsoft operating system where security requirements were taken into account at the earliest stages of development. From the very beginning, Windows NT developers knew they would have to create an operating system that would meet the C2-level requirements for protected operating systems. The set of criteria, developed by the U.S. National Security Agency (NSA) for evaluating the level of security for computer systems and software, was published as a series of books. Each of these books' covers had a different color, and because of this, the set of these security standards became known as the Rainbow Series. The "C2 Security Level" is one of the most commonly used terms in the Rainbow Series. Certification of software for C2 security requirements is performed using the Trusted Computer System Evaluation Criteria (TCSEC). The TCSEC criteria, known as the Orange Book, provides specifications for the procedure of evaluating the security level of information systems for governmental organizations. The C2 security class is considered to be the highest security class, by which any general-purpose operating system can be certified.

 Note

It's also necessary to mention an alternative point of view. The C2 class is regarded as the highest security level for general-purpose operating systems. It can't be regarded as the highest security level, though, if you take into account all of the existing operating systems. Notice that if it's necessary to provide the highest security level, you should use specialized operating systems (and all widely used operating systems such as Novell NetWare, Windows NT/2000, Windows XP, Windows Server 2003, UNIX, and Linux can't be considered as such). For certification of the most secure operating systems used by military organizations (for example, nuclear power stations), there are other higher security classes, the highest being the A class. A lower level of security (in comparison to the C2 level) is provided by the C1 and D classes. Notice that there isn't any certification for the C1 class. As for the D class, it includes all the operating systems that don't meet the requirements of other classes. If you're interested in more detailed information concerning the Rainbow Series, download it from **http://www.radium.ncsc.mil/tpep/library/rainbow**.

Certification and testing of any operating system for the C2 security class includes evaluation and testing the security functions implemented by the operating system. This testing will determine if this function has been implemented satisfactorily and if it works correctly. The C2 security level requirements include the following:

❑ Required identification and authentication of all operating system users. The system must provide the capability to identify each user who has authorized access to the system, and provide access for only those users.

❑ Discretionary access control — users must be able to protect their data.

❑ Auditing capabilities — the system must have the capacity to audit all actions performed by the users and operating system itself.

❏ Protecting the system objects against reuse — the operating system must be capable of preventing user access to the resources released by another user (for example, preventing users from reading and reusing released memory or reading deleted files).

The process of certifying the operating system according to the C2 security class includes the following procedures:

❏ Investigating the source code
❏ Study of the documentation concerning implementation details provided by software developers
❏ Repeated testing in order to eliminate errors discovered during previous phases

Note

A more detailed description of the certification procedure is provided at **http://www.radium.ncsc.mil/tpep**.

Cases of unauthorized access to computer networks are the reality of life today. The most common case of this can be seen when users themselves damage the computer they're working on. This usually happens when a user has just enough knowledge to be dangerous. If such users find one of the registry editors (Regedit.exe or Regedt32.exe), and you didn't take any precautions, they'll only become "worried" when the operating system stops booting.

Methods of Restricting Registry Access

As was already mentioned, Windows GUI was always oriented towards beginners who may need protection from human errors. Starting with Windows 2000, Microsoft began to introduce additional protective measures, practically each of these are also present in Windows XP and products of the Windows Server 2003 family. One such feature is known as "protected operating system files" (which shouldn't be edited, or even seen, by an ordinary user). These files are sometimes called "super hidden". Actually, there's no such attribute. The files simply have a combination of Hidden and System attributes. By default, Windows Explorer doesn't display these files. You may set Hidden and System attributes for the tools that ordinary users should not run, including networking tools, resource kit utilities and, of course, registry editors. Thus, you'll "hide" them from beginners, who may be afraid of command lines such as dir /a.

▶ *Note*

Did you place the Regedit shortcut on the desktop or on the **Start** menu (just for convenience)? Well, don't forget to remove all such shortcuts, otherwise users will be able to find them with the **Search** command. Also, don't forget that the **Start** menu contains the **Run** command, and setting the Hidden and System attributes won't prevent the user from starting Regedit.exe using this command.

Some other methods of preventing users from running potentially dangerous programs include the following approaches:

❑ Removing executable files from users' workstations
❑ Using Software Restriction Policies
❑ Protecting executable files by using file system permissions
❑ Editing access rights to registry keys

Removing Executables

One of the most common ways to prevent users from running undesirable tools is to remove the executables that you don't want them to run. For example, some authors recommend that one "delete Regedit.exe from all workstations". This, of course, will prevent beginners from running it. But what about convenience? A better solution would be to rename the file and move it to another directory. Of course, if you decide to do so, don't forget where you moved the file and what you named it. Besides this, there are other problems associated with this approach:

❑ First, Windows File Protection (WFP) might make it difficult to remove tools that are considered part of the OS and thus protected. Furthermore, patches, system updates, and additional Windows components might reinstall the removed executable without warning.

❑ Second, savvy users and skilled attackers can still provide their own copies of a tool that you want to restrict, not to mention other unauthorized programs, including software pranks, spyware, and keystroke loggers that could enable them to capture passwords or other sensitive information. This has become a primary concern with the arrival of pocket-sized ultra-portable storage media, such as USB Flash drives, which can hold 8 Mb — 1 GB of data that can be instantly accessed from any PC with a USB port. As was outlined in *Chapter 2*, the introduction of these devices into corporate networks offers users a convenient alternative to floppy disks and ZIP drives. At the same time, however, these devices present several security challenges to network administrators. Besides the introduction of harmful software, the threat of data theft is also a possibility. Note that any unattended and unlocked PC with a USB port can become an ideal target for attackers or disgruntled employees.

Note

In order to protect one's computer against the risks posed by ultra-portable USB media, several steps can be taken. First of all, you must educate your users and establish a corporate policy for taking data out of the office and bringing files from home. In order to foil attempts at data theft, it is recommended that you configure all workstations to lock automatically when left unattended for a few minutes. Usually this interval is set from 10 to 20 minutes, but for those desktops holding sensitive data the recommended value is 5 minutes or less. Also notice that recently USB Flash drives with built-in security features have become available. Thus, if you don't want to completely eliminate such a device from being used, consider using only secure devices. Finally, you might wish to restrict USB ports on all desktops. Although USB devices can't be managed using Group Policy, you can use third-party tools such as SecureNT (which can be downloaded from **http://www.securewave.com/products/securent/secure_nt.html**). This software can control access to all I/O devices such as floppy drives, PDAs, USB external storage, CD-ROM, and many other PnP devices.

Using Software Restriction Policies

The ability to use Software Restriction Policies is a new feature of Windows XP and Windows Server 2003. Software Restriction Policies provide a completely new method of preventing unauthorized usage of system tools and other potentially dangerous software. It also helps you to restrict users by allowing them to run only approved software, and prevents attackers from using system tools in an attack on the system.

When using Software Restriction Policies, the system administrator can choose one of the following two approaches:

❑ Create a policy that prohibits all software, then create unrestricted rules, which allow only approved software to run.

❑ Create a policy that allows all software to run, then create a set of rules which prevents specific programs from running.

Software Restriction Policies are based on the following types of rules:

❑ *Path* — Rules of this type explicitly identify a program path; can be bypassed if the user places a copy of the restricted program in a different location.

❑ *Hash* — When a program is selected, a cryptographic hash is built. Any attempt to run the program will result in a check of the hash, and the program will be allowed to run or prohibited from doing so according to the policy type. In contrast to the previous type, rules of this type are not so easy to bypass, since the program can reside anywhere, and the action taken will be the same.

❑ *Certificate* — Rules of this type are built based on the presence of a code publishers' software-signing certificate. Certificate rules apply to scripts and MSI files only. To use them, a code-signing certificate is used to sign the files. Certificate rules are used to identify the code-signing certificates that are valid on this computer or on the computers within the Group Policy Container (GPC) of this GPO.

❑ *Internet zone* — This option enables the administrator to prevent users from running software from a particular Internet Explorer (IE) zone. However, this type of rule cannot prevent users from running software that has already been downloaded from that zone.

To create, examine, or manage local Software Restriction Policies, proceed as follows:

1. Click **Start**, select **Run**, and type `secpol.msc` in the **Open** field, then click **OK**, or, alternately, open the **Control Panel** window, and select **Administrative Tools | Local Security Policy**.

2. Select the **Software Restriction Policies** container. If no policy exists, right-click the container, and select the **Create New Policies** command (Fig. 9.1).

▶ *Note*

To create or manage Software Restriction Polices for a site, domain, or organizational unit (OU), open the Group Policy Object (GPO) for the appropriate container. The **Software Restriction Policy** container is located under **Computer Settings | Security Settings**.

3. After you create a new Software Restriction policy, the console window will look as shown in Fig. 9.2. Enforcement properties include or exclude DLLs and identify whether the policy applies to members of the Administrators group (Fig. 9.3). By default, policies apply to all users and program files except library files such as DLLs. Additional settings include the **Designated File Types**

option (Fig. 9.4) that allows you to edit the list of so-called designated file types, which includes files that by default are considered to be in executable code. Using this option, you can add new file types to that list as well as delete specific files from the list of executables. Finally, the **Trusted Publishers** option opens the **Trusted Publishers Properties** window (Fig. 9.5), where you can determine whether users, computer administrators, or enterprise administrators can select the trusted publishers of the software.

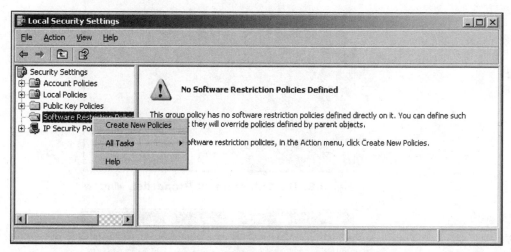

Fig. 9.1. Creating a new Software Restriction Policy

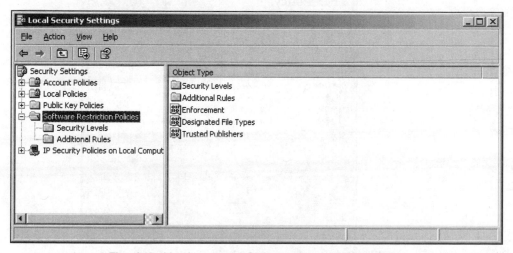

Fig. 9.2. Newly created Software Restriction Policies

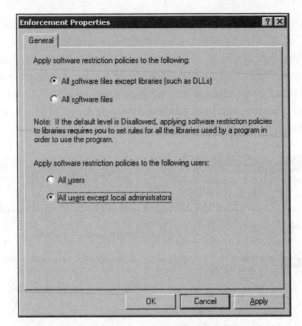

Fig. 9.3. The **Enforcement Properties** window

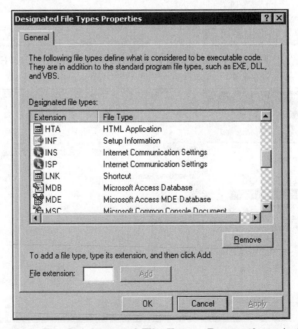

Fig. 9.4. The **Designated File Types Properties** window

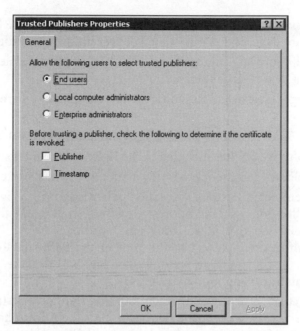

Fig. 9.5. The **Trusted Publishers Properties** window

4. Using the Software Restriction Policies, you can easily create a policy restricting the use of specific software tools. To do so, you have to determine the list of tools that need to be restricted and the type of rule that will be used. Notice that it is up to you to compose the list of restricted tools (as was already mentioned, this list would normally include various networking tools, resource kit utilities, registry editors, and other potentially dangerous tools).

Note

Notice that Software Restriction Policy is itself a potentially dangerous tool that can easily allow you to create such a policy that can wreak havoc on your organization by prohibiting users from running applications they really need or even preventing client systems from running. As a result, it is advisable that you first create a test policy using the Local Security Policy MMC snap-in on a standalone workstation running Windows XP, and then test it on a single machine first. Having created the policy, test it by applying it to a single OU that represents a test computer or computers to make sure that the test policy satisfies your requirements without having a negative impact on other software. After that, you can enforce the policy in multiple systems in your production environment.

5. The best way of creating your first software restriction policy is by starting up with all software allowed to run and then creating rules that prevent individual

programs from running. To illustrate this approach, let us create a simple Software Restriction Policy that will prevent the following tools from running:

- All software located in the D:\Program Files\Resource Kit and E:\Olga\TOOLZ folders
- Regedt32.exe and Regedit.exe tools (no matter where registry editors are located)
- LC3.exe password-auditing tool (no matter where it is located)
- Software on sites included in the IE Restricted Sites security zone
- Solitaire game (sol.exe — no matter where it is located)

The completed software restriction policy is shown in Fig. 9.6.

6. Since this policy should not restrict administrators, the first step to take is to set the policy so that it will only affect ordinary users. To do so, double-click the **Enforcement** object at the root of the **Software Restriction Policy** container. In the resulting window (see Fig. 9.3), set the **All users except local administrators** option, then click **OK**.

7. Next, create a new rule for each tool that should be restricted. For example, in order to create a new path rule, right-click the **Additional Rules** container, and select the **Create new path rule** command from the context menu. The **New Path Rule** window will open (Fig. 9.7). Enter the path (for example, E:\OLGA\TOOLZ), leave the **Security level** option at **Disallowed** and click **OK**. Proceed the same way to create path rules for all the software that you want to restrict using path rules.

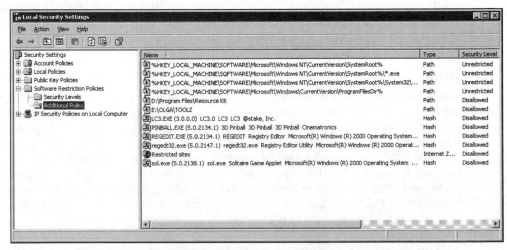

Fig. 9.6. The completed software restriction policy, which lists the policy type and basic information

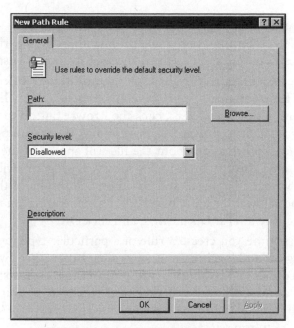

Fig. 9.7. The **New Path Rule** window

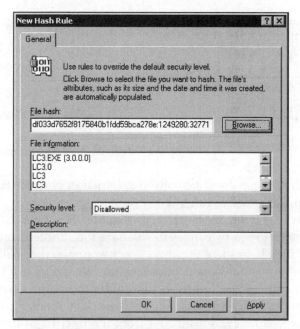

Fig. 9.8. The **New Hash Rule** window

8. To create a new Internet Zone rule, proceed in a similar way, but select the **New Internet Zone Rule** command from the right-click menu. Select the **Restricted Sites** option, leave the security level at **Disallowed**, then click **OK**.

9. To create a Hash rule, right-click the **Additional Rules** container, select **New Hash Rule** command from the context menu, and, when the **New Hash Rule** window appears (Fig. 9. 8), click the **Browse** button to locate a copy of the file that you want to prevent from running. The hash appears in the **File Hash** field, and information about the file will appear in the **File Information** box. Now, any attempt to run the specified program will result in a check of the cryptographic hash, and based on the results of this check, the program will be allowed or disallowed to run depending on the policy type. Leave the security level at **Disallowed**, and click **OK**.

10. The first time you create a rule of a particular type, test it. You can do so by logging off and logging on as an ordinary user, then by attempting to run the tool. You should be refused and receive the message shown in Fig. 9.9. Next, log on as Administrator and attempt to run the tool. You should be able to do so. Test all rules to ensure that they operate as you expect. Any changes to the rules should require a retest.

Fig. 9.9. Error message displayed to the user when attempting to run restricted software

After creating and testing software restriction policies, take some time to investigate them for possible holes. For example, when you create path rules, if a program file type is not covered by the **Designated file types list** (see Fig. 9.4), the program will be allowed to run. Path rules are the simplest to understand and create. However, they have their drawbacks. For example, they will only prevent the user from running restricted tools from within the specified folder and its subfolders. If the user can copy a tool from that folder to another location, that user will be able to run the tool. Furthermore, if the user can obtain a copy of the tool from another source (typically, download it from the Internet or bring it to the office using one of the ultra-portable media discussed above), the user will also be able to run it.

> ### ► Note
>
> Finally, if you are creating path rules to prevent system utilities from running, don't forget to make a path rule that includes %*windir*%\system32\dllcache. A copy of the disallowed program might be available at this location, and if a path rule does not cover it, the program will be able to run.

Thus, if the aim of your policy is to absolutely prevent users from running certain tools, you should create hash rules for each one.

> ### ► Note
>
> Hash rules, however, also do not provide absolute protection against undesirable software. For example, later versions of a restricted program will not be restricted by the hash rules that you have written.

Finally, consider what happens if a program calls another program that calls yet another one — you must carefully investigate what happens in each particular case. Of course, if the program is disallowed, it cannot run, and, therefore, cannot call other programs. On the other hand, if a program is not restricted, it can both run on its own or be called from within another allowed application. The situation is possible, however, when an unrestricted program calls a disallowed one. The disallowed program will not run, of course, but this might result in the failure of some unrestricted programs, which might be required for users to do their jobs. Another important point that you need to consider is situations in which there are multiple policies applied to the same program. In this case, you must be aware of the following order of precedence that exists when processing software restriction policies (the first item in the list has the highest precedence):

- ☐ Hash rule
- ☐ Certificate rule
- ☐ Path rule (if path rules conflict, the most restrictive will take precedence)
- ☐ Internet zone rule

To conclude our discussion of software restriction policies, it is necessary to emphasize several other points, briefly listed below:

- ☐ Before designing and implementing domain-wide software restriction policies, you will have to migrate to Windows Server 2003 domains and upgrade all clients to Windows XP. Remember that Windows 2000 and earlier versions are unable to process software restriction policies.

❏ Be aware that this technology is rather new, and it will take time before it becomes mature and reliable. At the moment of this writing, it was not totally bug-free, and even the simplest local software restriction policies required careful testing before they could be implemented in a Windows Server 2003 domain. Still, this new technology is very promising, and as you migrate to Windows Server 2003 domain controllers, will prove to be rather useful.

Setting Restrictive File Permissions

The easiest way to avoid problems caused by unskilled users who damage the registry is to simply prevent their access to the registry. Setting restrictive file permissions is the best-known and time-honored way of preventing undesirable access to critically important files, including system utilities such as registry editors, registry hives, and user profiles. Unfortunately, this approach is not totally free from drawbacks and limitations, the most important of which are briefly outlined below:

❏ This method of protection can only be used when, according to the recommended security practices, all drives on all Windows NT, Windows 2000, Windows XP, and Windows Server 2003 computers are NTFS-formatted. Unfortunately, using NTFS isn't always possible. Sometimes it's necessary to use the FAT file system in multi-boot systems or because of legacy applications (this reason is the most common one). Thus, if it's necessary to use FAT, you'll need to develop alternative measures of protecting the registry.

❏ Although standard file permission settings on system files and folders are fairly secure when the Windows NT-based system is installed on NTFS drives, and the system administrator might further harden security on network servers and user workstations, there is still no guarantee that for every machine, every permission setting is correct.

Note

More detailed information on the default file and registry key permissions in Windows Server 2003 will be provided later in this chapter.

❏ Finally, this method doesn't prevent savvy users or attackers from placing their own copies of restricted tools in a folder where they have the right to run the program.

Editing Access Rights to the Registry Keys

If you have some previous experience working with Windows NT/2000, you'll certainly notice that many of the security features in Windows XP and Windows Server 2003 will be quite familiar to you.

For example, similar to Windows NT/2000, Windows XP and products of the Windows Server 2003 family identify users and groups using security identifiers (Security Ids, SIDs). Security identifiers are quite long, and are unique for each user (even for user accounts in different systems). If you first delete the user account on the local computer or in the domain, and then create a new user account with the same login name, the system will generate a new security ID for that account. There's no way to have two identical security Ids. SIDs have the following format: S-1-XXXXX1-YYYYY2-....-RID, where: S-1 — security ID, version 1; XXXXX — authority number, YYYYYn — subauthority numbers, RID — relative identifier (Relative ID). Notice that the Relative ID (RID) won't be unique for each computer.

> ### Note
> Also notice that many users, even experienced ones, often think that the system identifies each user by his or her credentials — username (or login name) and the password. This isn't so; it's the SID that uniquely identifies the user to the system. User profiles, which will be discussed in detail in *Chapter 10*, are also identified by their associated SIDs.

As aforementioned, most of the user SIDs are unique. However, there are so-called well-known SIDs, whose values are constant for all systems. For example, such SIDs include the following users and groups:

☐ *Everyone (S-1-1-0).* The Everyone group will be discussed later in this chapter. For now, let us take notice of the fact that on computers running Windows Server 2003, the Everyone group includes Authenticated Users (S-1-5-11) and Guest (S-1-5-*domain*-501). On computers running earlier versions of the operating system, Everyone includes Authenticated Users and Guest plus Anonymous Logon (S-1-5-7). The identifier authority value for this SID is 1 (World Authority), while its subauthority value is 0 (Null RID).

☐ *Creator Owner (S-1-3-0).* This is the Creator Owner user, serving as a placeholder in an inheritable Access Control Entry (ACE). When the ACE is inherited, the system replaces the SID for Creator Owner with the SID for the object's current owner. The identifier authority value for this SID is 3 (Creator Authority). It has only one subauthority value, 0 (Null RID).

Note

A complete list of well-known SIDs in Windows 2000 is provided in the Microsoft Knowledge Base article Q243330 — *"Well-Known Security Identifiers in Windows 2000"*. One of the significant security enhancements in Windows XP and Windows Server 2003 is the introduction of two new built-in accounts — NetworkService (S-1-5-20) and LocalService (S-1-5-19) that are suitable for use by many services. This was done to eliminate the common weakness of Windows 2000 and its predecessors, where most services run under the SYSTEM account (S-1-5-18) and can therefore do anything, whether they need to have such broad privileges or not or not. Thus, if an attacker can break the service, he or she might be able to run code under the security context of the operating system (OS), and fully own that system. By providing two built-in less privileged accounts, Microsoft has significantly improved this situation.

On all computers running Windows NT-based operating systems, including Windows 2000, Windows XP, and products of the Windows Server 2003 family, access to resources is controlled by Access Control Lists (ACLs) and SIDs. Like Windows NT/2000, Windows XP and Windows Server 2003 support Access Control Lists (ACL) for the registry. You can use ACL to protect registry keys. Actually, ACL represents the database supporting information on access rights to individual operating system objects (in our case, the objects are registry keys).

 Note

Notice that in Windows NT/2000, only Regedt32.exe provided access to the ACL for the registry keys. The Regedit.exe version supplied with Windows NT/2000 didn't provide this capability. As compared to Windows NT/2000, Windows XP and Windows Server 2003 also provide an improvement in this area. The Regedit.exe version included with this new release now integrates its traditional strong points with the functionality that was available earlier only in Regedt32.exe, including, of course, access to the ACLs and auditing registry key access. Detailed, step-by-step instructions on setting access rights to the registry keys were provided in *Chapter 3*. In this chapter, we'll concentrate on practical tips rather than on routine administrative operations.

First of all, we'll specify the registry keys to be secured in order to secure and protect the whole registry.

Standard Access Rights in Windows XP and Windows Server 2003

Standard security settings in Windows Server 2003 are defined by default access rights that are set for the following built-in local security groups (Fig. 9.10):

❏ *Account Operators* (S-1-5-32-548). This is a built-in local group that exists only on domain controllers and, by default, has no members. Account Operators can create, modify, and delete accounts for users, groups, and computers in all containers and organizational units (OUs) of Active Directory, except the **Builtin** container and the **Domain Controllers** OU. Account Operators can modify neither the Administrators and Domain Admins groups, nor the accounts for members of those groups.

❏ *Administrators* (S-1-5-32-544). Similar to Windows 2000, members of the Administrators group have full control of the local computer. They can create or delete user accounts and modify permissions for users and resources. Notice that by default, this group will contain two members — the local Administrator account (S-1-5-*domain*-500) and System (S-1-5-18) — an identity that is used locally by the operating system and by services configured to log on as LocalSystem. SYSTEM is a hidden member of the Administrators group, which means that most tools do not list SYSTEM as a member of the group. However, the Administrators SID is present in System's access token. If you are performing an upgrade from an earlier Windows NT/2000 version, this group will include existing members of the Administrators group. If your computer joins a domain, this group will also include the members of the Domain Admins group (S-1-5-*root_domain*-518) to local Administrators. When a server is promoted to domain controller, the operating system adds the Enterprise Admins group (S-1-5-*root_domain*-519) as well. Notice that, if desired, you can remove either Domain Admins or Enterprise Admins groups from the local Administrators group. However, it is impossible to remove either SYSTEM or the local Administrator account (still, the local Administrator account can be renamed).

▶ **Note**

It is strongly recommended that you limit the number of users who belong to the Administrators group, no matter what system you are running — Windows NT/2000, Windows XP, or Windows Server 2003. The reason for this tip is straightforward — the greater the number of members in the Administrators group, the more vulnerable your system will be, because all these accounts (especially if they aren't properly protected with strong passwords) can potentially be used to gain unauthorized access to a computer.

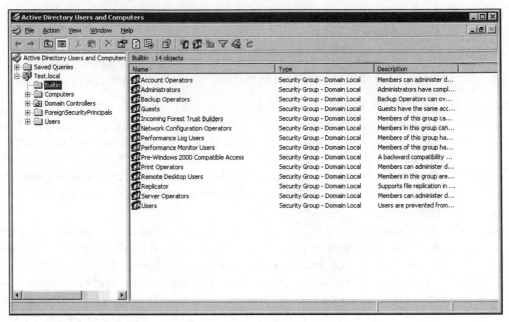

Fig. 9.10. Windows Server 2003 built-in local security groups
(the screenshot is taken on the domain controller)

❏ *Backup Operators* (S-1-5-32-551). By default, this built-in local group has no members. Backup Operators can back up and restore all files on a computer, regardless of the permissions that protect those files. Backup Operators can also log on to the computer and shut it down, but they cannot change security settings.

❏ *Guests* (S-1-5-32-546). By default, this built-in local group has only one member — the local Guest account (S-1-5-domain-501) — an account for people who do not have individual accounts. Guest is a real account, which can be used to log on interactively (by default, however, it is disabled). It does not require a password, but can have one. When a server becomes a domain controller, the Domain Guests group (S-1-5-*domain*-514) becomes a member of the local Guests group. Default security settings in Windows XP and Windows Server 2003 deny access to the application and system event logs for the members of the Guests group. In all other aspects, members of the Guests group have the same access rights as members of the Users group. This allows occasional or one-time users to log on to a computer's built-in Guest account and be granted limited abilities.

❏ *Network Configuration Operators* (S-1-5-32-556). Members of this group have limited administrative privileges that allow them to configure networking features, such as IP address assignment, without having other administrative rights on the computer. By default, the group has no members.

❑ *Power Users* (S-1-5-32-547). This built-in local security group was first introduced with Windows 2000. Similar to Windows 2000, this group has fewer rights than Administrators; but at the same time, they have wider access rights and permissions than the Users group. In contrast to Users, Power Users have Read/Write permissions to other parts of the operating system in addition to their own user profiles. Power Users can create local users and groups; modify and delete accounts that they have created; and remove users from the Power Users, Users, and Guests groups. Power Users can also install most applications; create, manage, and delete local printers; create and delete file shares; and start (but not stop) services. After a fresh installation, this group has no members. On computers upgraded from Windows NT 4.0, it has one member, Interactive (S-1-5-4) — a group that includes all users who have logged on interactively, either locally or through a Remote Desktop connection. The Power Users group does not exist on domain controllers.

❑ *Pre-Windows 2000 Compatible Access* (S-1-5-32-554). This built-in local group exists only on domain controllers running Windows 2000 or Windows Server 2003. By default, its members have read access to user and group objects in Active Directory. This group is intended to facilitate anonymous queries of Active Directory, which might be needed by some pre-Windows 2000 services, such as the Windows NT Remote Access Service. To enable anonymous access to Active Directory, add Everyone (S-1-1-0) and Anonymous Logon (S-1-5-7) to the Pre-Windows 2000 Compatible Access group. To disable anonymous access to Active Directory, do not add any members to the group.

❑ *Print Operators* (S-1-5-32-550). This built-in local group exists only on domain controllers. By default, it has no members. Print Operators can manage printers and document queues.

❑ *Remote Desktop Users* (S-1-5-32-555). Members of this built-in local group can log on to the computer through the Remote Desktop (also known as Terminal Services in Remote Administration mode). By default, the group has no members.

❑ *Replicator* (S-1-5-32-552). This built-in local group only exists on domain controllers. In Windows NT domains, it is used by the File Replication service. Members of this group are allowed to replicate files across a domain. Although this group is present in Windows 2000 and later versions of the operating system, it is not used.

- *Server Operators* (S-1-5-32-549). By default, this built-in local group is empty. Server Operators have no default rights on a member server. On a domain controller, Server Operators can log on interactively, access administrative shares, create and delete shared folders, start and stop services, back up and restore files, manage disks and volumes, and shut down the computer.

- *Users* (S-1-5-32-545). By default, this built-in local group includes only Authenticated *Users* (S-1-5-11) — a group that includes all users and computers whose identities have been authenticated, and Interactive (S-1-5-4). Local user accounts are added to the Users group automatically when the accounts are created. When you install a new copy of the operating system on the NTFS partition, the standard settings of the security subsystem are configured so that the members of this group can't break the integrity of the OS and installed applications. Users can run applications, access local and network printers, shut down or lock the computer, and install applications that only they are allowed to use if the installation program of the application supports per-user installation. Members of the Users group can't modify registry settings that influence the whole configuration or change the operating system files. They have no rights to install applications that can be used by others (this is one of the precautions taken to protect against worms and Trojans), and they also can't install most legacy applications. Microsoft also recommends that you include all end users into the Users group to protect your system integrity.

Standard security settings are applied by Security Configuration Manager during the operating system installation, when the GUI setup starts. For this purpose, the Security Configuration Manager uses security templates located in the *%SystemRoot%*\inf folder.

Naturally, the template used for applying default security settings depends on the OS being installed and the computer's role in your network environment. When you perform a clean installation of workstations running Windows XP Professional, the *%SystemRoot%*\inf\defltwk.inf security template will be used (notice that upgrades from Windows 9*x* platforms are treated as clean installs). If you are upgrading to Windows XP from Windows NT/2000, Security Configuration Manager will use the *%SystemRoot%*\inf\DWUp.inf security template. When you perform a clean installation of Windows Server 2003 member server, default security settings are taken from the *%SystemRoot%*\inf\defltsw.inf security template, while for upgrades — from the *%SystemRoot%*\inf\dsup.inf template. For domain controllers, the *%SystemRoot%*\inf\defltdc.inf template is used. When you upgrade domain controllers from Windows NT 4.0, the Security Configuration Manager will use the *%SystemRoot%*\inf\dcup.inf template.

> ### Note
>
> If you want to affect the security settings that are applied by default during installation, you can modify the above-mentioned security templates in the installation files folder.

As was already discussed, for standalone computers or computers participating in a workgroup, users belonging to the Administrators group have unlimited access to all file system and registry objects. Users and Power Users have a more restricted set of access rights.

> ### Note
>
> Windows XP and Windows Server 2003 include a new root ACL, which is also implemented by `Format` and `Convert` commands. In addition to previous releases, the Security Configuration Manager now secures the root directory during setup, if the current root security descriptor grants the Everyone group Full Control permission. This provides increased security for non-Windows directories. The new root ACL is as follows:
>
> - Administrators, System: Full Control (Container Inherit, Object Inherit)
> - Creator Owner: Full Control (Container Inherit, Object Inherit, Inherit Only)
> - Everyone: Read\Execute (No Inheritance)
> - Users: Read\Execute (Container Inherit, Object Inherit)
> - Users: Create Directory (Container Inherit)
> - Users: Add File (Container Inherit, Inherit Only)

Power Users can write new files into directories (the list is provided below), but can't modify files that were written to these directories during installation. All members of the Power Users group inherit Modify access to all the files created in these directories by a member of their group.

%SystemRoot%	*%SystemRoot%\inf*
%SystemRoot%\Config	*%SystemRoot%\media*
%SystemRoot%\cursors	*%SystemRoot%\system*
%SystemRoot%\fonts	*%SystemDir%*
%SystemRoot%\help	*%SystemDir%\RAS*

Maintaining Proper System File and Registry Permissions across All Windows Server 2003 Computers within a Domain

Although standard system file and registry permissions for Windows Server 2003 seem fairly secure, a wise administrator doesn't assume that the default permissions on system folders, files, and registry keys are always going to be the best possible settings. For example, the installation of new software always adds folders and files, and sometimes services, for which you'll also need to consider permissions set automatically, as well as changes to the inherited permissions.

Note

When a Windows Server 2003 computer is promoted to a domain controller, an additional set of permissions is applied.

If you need to return to the settings applied at install time after having changed the default permissions, proceed as follows:

1. From the **Start** menu, select **Run**, and type mmc into the **Open** field. When the MMC console window opens, select the **Add/Remove snap-in** command from the **File** menu. The **Add/Remove Snap-in** window opened at the **Standalone** tab will open. Click the **Add** button, and select the **Security Configuration and Analysis** option from the list of available snap-ins (Fig. 9.11). Click **Add**, then **Close**, then **OK**.

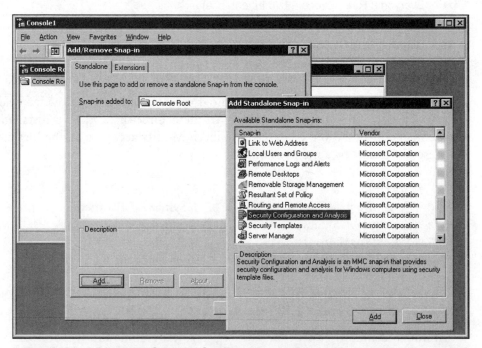

Fig. 9.11. Adding the Security Configuration and Analysis standalone snap-in

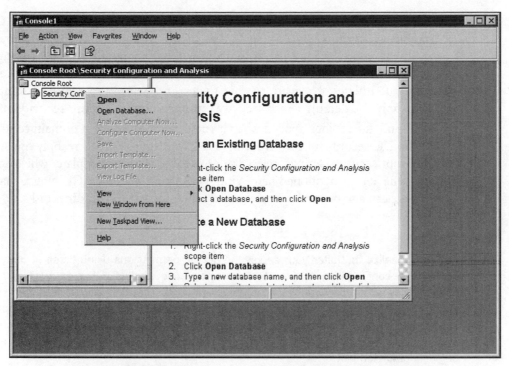

Fig. 9.12. Opening the Security Configuration Database

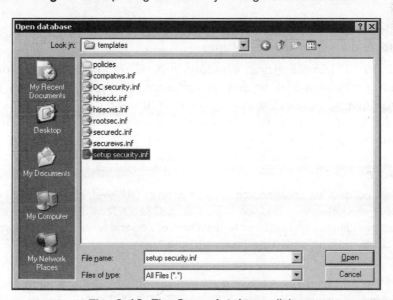

Fig. 9.13. The **Open database** dialog

2. Right-click the **Security Configuration and Analysis** item and select the **Open Database…** command from the context menu (Fig. 9.12). The **Open Database** dialog will appear (Fig. 9.13), where you will be prompted to select a database, and then click **Open**. By default, security templates are stored at *%SystemRoot%\ security\templates*. Navigate to this folder and select the required template. To reapply the default server security settings, select the setup security.inf file.

    To reapply the settings applied when a server is promoted to a domain controller, use the DC security.inf security template. If you only want to reapply the system drive root security settings, select the rootsec.inf security template, which implements the above-mentioned new Windows Server 2003 root ACL. Notice that this template can also be used to apply similar settings to the root of other disks.

Note

You must realize that after you reapply the default permissions using these security templates, any configuration settings that you may have applied either manually or using Group Policy will be overwritten by the default settings. Therefore, if you need to preserve your changes, create a copy of the default template(s), introduce officially approved changes into it, and maintain these copies as well as default security templates. Proceeding in such a way, you'll have a backup of your current security settings as well as the original default template.

Using Group Policy to Maintain File and Registry Permission Settings

Similar to Group Policy in Windows 2000, Group Policy in Windows Server 2003 allows administrators to centrally manage, configure, and push security policy and other administrative settings to an entire site, domain, or organizational unit. Policies, officially named Group Policy Objects (GPOs), are linked to these containers.

Note

Most policies are implemented at the domain or OU level, since it is not practical to implement site policies. In addition to domain policies, a local Group Policy is configured and can be adjusted on individual workstations or servers. More detailed information on Group Policies will be provided in *Chapters 10* and *11*.

File and registry permission settings can only be configured within the **Computer Settings** portion of the Group Policy (Fig. 9.14). To add registry path to the policy, expand the console tree as shown in this screenshot, right-click the **Registry** item, and select the **Add Key** command from the context menu. After you add new registry keys to the policy, the Discretionary Access Control Lists (DACLs) applied to them propagate to the objects on the computer when the policy is applied.

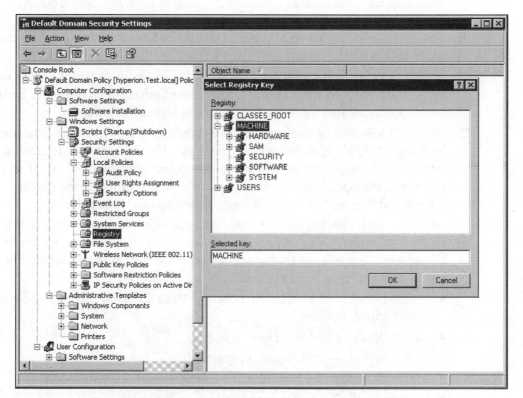

Fig. 9.14. Configuring registry permission settings within the **Computer Settings** portion of the Group Policy

Using Secedit to Maintain File and Registry Permission Settings

Besides Group Policy, you can use the Secedit.exe command-line tool to maintain file and registry permission settings. The Secedit.exe is the command-line version of the Security and Analysis Configuration tool.

The `secedit.exe` tool uses the following command-line syntax:

```
secedit [/configure | /analyze | /import | /export | /validate |
/generaterollback]
```

where:

Secedit /configure — this command configures a system with security settings stored in a database. The syntax used by this command option is as follows:

```
secedit   /configure   /db   db_filename   [/cfg   cfg_filename]
[/overwrite][/areas area1 area2...] [/log log_filename] [/quiet]
```

❏ /db *db_filename* — specifies the *db_filename* database used to perform the security configuration.

❏ /cfg *cfg_filename* — specifies the *cfg_filename* security template that needs to be imported into the database prior to configuring the computer. Security templates are created using the Security Templates MMC snap-in.

❏ /overwrite — this option instructs the secedit tool to empty the database before importing the specified security template. If this parameter is missing, the settings in the security template are accumulated into the database. If this parameter is not specified and there are conflicting settings in the database and the template being imported, the template settings will take priority.

❏ /areas — specifies the security areas to be applied to the system. If this parameter is omitted, all security settings defined in the database are applied to the system. To configure multiple areas, separate each area by a space. The following security areas are supported:

- SECURITYPOLICY — Account Policies, Audit Policies, Event Log Settings, and Security Options.
- GROUP_MGMT — Restricted Group settings
- USER_RIGHTS — User Rights Assignment
- REGKEYS — Registry Permissions
- FILESTORE — File System permissions
- SERVICES — System Service settings

❏ /log *log_filename* — specifies a file in which to log the status of the configuration process (*log_filename*). If this parameter is missing, the configuration-processing information is logged in the Scesrv.log file, which is located in the %*windir*%\security\logs directory.

❏ /quiet — specifies that the configuration process should take place without prompting the user for any confirmation.

Secedit /analyze — this option analyzes current systems settings against baseline settings that are stored in a database. The analysis results are stored in a separate area of the database and can be viewed in the Security Configuration and Analysis snap-in. The syntax for this command is as follows:

```
secedit /analyze /db db_filename [/cfg cfg_filename ] [/overwrite]
[/log log_filename] [/quiet]
```

❏ /db *db_filename* — specifies the database used to perform the analysis.

❏ /cfg *cfg_filename* — specifies a security template to import into the database prior to performing the analysis. Security templates are created using the Security Templates snap-in.

❏ /log *log_filename* — specifies a file in which to log the status of the configuration process. If not specified, the configuration-processing information is logged in the Scesrv.log file, which is located in the s%*windir*%\security\logs directory.

❏ /quiet — specifies that the analysis process should take place without prompting the user for any confirmation.

Secedit /import — allows you to import a security template into a database so that the settings specified in the template can be applied to a system or analyzed against a system. This command uses the following syntax:

```
secedit    /import      /db    db_filename   /cfg    cfg_filename
[/overwrite][/areas area1 area2...] [/log log_filename] [/quiet]
```

❏ /db *db_filename* — specifies the database that the security template settings will be imported into.

❏ /cfg *cfg_filename* — specifies a security template to import into the database. Security templates are created using the Security Templates snap-in.

❏ /overwrite — specifies that the database should be emptied prior to importing the security template. If this parameter is not specified, the settings in the security template are accumulated into the database. If this parameter is not specified and there are conflicting settings in the database and the template being imported, the template settings win.

❏ /areas — specifies the security areas to export. If this parameter is not specified, all security settings defined in the database are exported. To export specific areas, separate each area by a space. The following security areas are exported:

   ● SECURITYPOLICY — Account Policies, Audit Policies, Event Log Settings, and Security Options.

   ● GROUP_MGMT — Restricted Group settings

   ● USER_RIGHTS — User Rights Assignment

- REGKEYS — Registry Permissions
- FILESTORE — File System permissions
- SERVICES — System Service settings

❑ /log *log_filename* — specifies a file in which to log the status of the import process. If not specified, the import-processing information is logged in the scesrv.log file which is located in the %*windir*%\security\logs directory.

❑ /quiet — specifies that the import process should take place without prompting the user for any confirmation.

Secedit /export — allows you to export security settings stored in the database. The syntax of this command is:

```
secedit /export /db db_filename [tablename] /cfg cfg_filename [/areas
area1 area2...] [/log log_filename]
```

❑ /db *db_filename* — specifies the database used to perform the security configuration.

❑ /cfg *cfg_filename* — specifies a security template to export the database contents to.

- tablename — specifies the table to export data from. If no argument is specified, the configuration table data is exported.

❑ /areas — specifies the security areas to export. If this parameter is not specified, all security settings defined in the database are exported. To export specific areas, separate each area by a space. The following security areas are exported:

- SECURITYPOLICY — Account Policies, Audit Policies, Event Log Settings and Security Options.
- GROUP_MGMT — Restricted Group settings
- USER_RIGHTS — User Rights Assignment
- REGKEYS — Registry Permissions
- FILESTORE — File System permissions
- SERVICES — System Service settings

❑ /log *log_filename* — specifies a file in which to log the status of the export process. If not specified, the export-processing information is logged in the scesrv.log file which is located in the %*windir*%\security\logs directory.

Secedit /generaterollback — allows you to generate a rollback template with respect to a configuration template. The syntax of this command is:

```
secedit /generaterollback /cfg cfg_filename /rbk filename [/log log_filename]
[/quiet]
```

❑ /db *db_filename* — specifies the database used to perform the rollback.

❑ /cfg *cfg_filename* — specifies a security template with respect to which a rollback template is generated. Security templates are created using the Security Templates snap-in.

❑ /rbk *filename* — specifies a security template into which the rollback information is written. Security templates are created using the Security Templates snap-in.

❑ /log *log_filename* — specifies a file in which to log the status of the rollback process. If not specified, the rollback-processing information is logged in the Scesrv.log file, which is located in the %*windir*%\security\logs directory.

❑ /quiet — specifies that the rollback process should take place without prompting the user for any confirmation.

In addition, secedit.exe can be used to apply a single node from a security template. Thus, to reapply your preferred file permissions, you can use a single command-line command. To reapply your preferred registry permissions, you can use another line. Put both commands in a batch file or write a simple script, and you can reapply both file permissions and registry permissions across multiple servers. And you can use the scheduling service (schtasks.exe) to periodically refresh these settings without any replication burden. After testing the statements, you can schedule a periodic refresh by putting both commands (or the combination line) in a batch file. Test the batch file. If successful, use the task scheduler or schtasks.exe to schedule the refresh. Table 9.1 provides an explanation of the most useful schtasks.exe command-line switches; additional switches are available.

Table 9.1. The Switches for schtasks.exe

Switch	Description
/create	Create a task
/tn	The name of the new task
/tr	The name of the batch file or command to run
/sc	When to schedule the repetitive event (once, every n times a month, every month, every n times a day, at this time every day, and so on)
/d	Which day of the week; Monday is the default, so I could have left out this switch in the example; /d * runs the process every day

continues

Table 9.3 Continued

Switch	Description
/ru	Under whose authority; if a user account name is entered here (use the *domainname\username* format), the password is entered using the /rp switch; to use a local computer account use the \machine switch and \u and \p parameters (when the SYSTEM account is used, no password is entered)

The Most Important Registry Keys that Need Protection

Microsoft officially recommends that system administrators restrict user access to certain subkeys under HKEY_LOCAL_MACHINE\SOFTWARE. The purpose of this restriction is to prevent unauthorized access to the software settings.

 ### *Note*

Microsoft officially recommends that system administrators restrict user access to the following registry keys:

HKEY_LOCAL_MACHINE\SOFTWARE\Microsoft\Windows NT\CurrentVersion and
HKEY_LOCAL_MACHINE\SOFTWARE\Microsoft\Windows\CurrentVersion.

For all earlier versions of Windows NT-based systems, including Windows 2000, it is recommended that the user restrict the Everyone group (note that in Windows XP and Windows Server 2003 the Everyone group has been restricted by default). For the Everyone group, it's sufficient to have the Query Value, Enumerate Subkeys, Notify, and Read Control rights to the HKEY_LOCAL_MACHINE\SOFTWARE\Microsoft\Windows NT\CurrentVersion registry key and the following subkeys under this key: AeDebug, Compatibility, Drivers, Embedding, Font Drivers, FontCache, FontMapper, Fonts, FontSubstitutes, GRE_Initialize, MCI, MCI Extensions, Ports (and all its subkeys), Type 1 Installer, Windows 3.1 MigrationStatus (and all its subkeys), WOW (and all its subkeys).

The same set of access rights (Query Value, Enumerate Subkeys, Notify, and Read Control) needs to be assigned to the Everyone group for the Uninstall, Run, and RunOnce subkeys under HKEY_LOCAL_MACHINE\SOFTWARE\Microsoft\Windows\CurrentVersion.

Microsoft also recommends that you restrict user access to the HKEY_LOCAL_MACHINE\SOFTWARE\Microsoft\Windows NT\CurrentVersion\Perflib key that stores the data, which governs system performance. In Windows NT 4.0, the Everyone group by default has Read access to this key (it's recommended that you delete this group from the Perflib ACL). As shown in Fig. 9.15, in Windows Server 2003, the Everyone group by default has no access to this key.

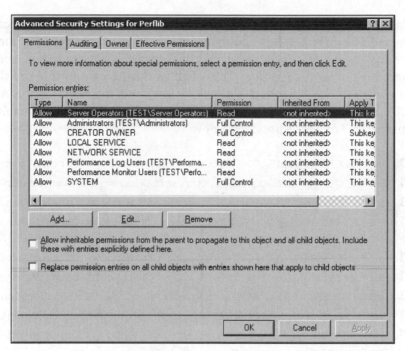

Fig. 9.15. Restricting access to the `HKEY_LOCAL_MACHINE\SOFTWARE\`
`Microsoft\Windows NT\CurrentVersion\Perflib` registry key

The Everyone group has restricted access rights (only Query Value, Enumerate Subkeys, Notify, and Read Control) to other registry keys, including `HKEY_CLASSES_ROOT` root key and all its subkeys, and for the `HKEY_USERS\` `.DEFAULT` key. By protecting these keys, you protect important system settings from changes (for example, this will prevent users from changing the filename extension associations or specifying new security settings for Internet Explorer).

Furthermore, it's necessary to restrict the Everyone group access to keys such as `HKEY_LOCAL_MACHINE\SYSTEM\CurrentControlSet\Services\LanmanServer\Shares` and `HKEY_LOCAL MACHINE\SYSTEM\CurrentControlSet\Services\UPS`. The Everyone group only needs the following rights to these keys: Query Value, Enumerate Subkeys, Notify and Read Control. By setting these restrictions, you'll prevent unauthorized access to shared system resources and to using the `ImagePath` setting under the UPS key for starting undesirable software. Only the operating system (System) and members of the Administrators group need Full Control access to these keys.

Finally, it is necessary to provide a tip, universal for all Windows NT-based systems. Pay close attention to the `Run`, `RunOnce`, and `RunOnceEx` registry keys under `HKEY_LOCAL_MACHINE\SOFTWARE\Microsoft\Windows\CurrentVersion`. For example, the system runs all the programs listed under the RunOnceEx key only once, and then deletes the settings specifying the starting parameters for these programs. It's easy to see that these registry settings may allow users to run undesirable software on the local computer. Thus, Full Control access to this key should only be provided to the operating system (System) and members of the Administrators group. The list of registry keys, which are used most often for installing worms, viruses, and Trojans, is provided below:

❐ HKEY_LOCAL_MACHINE\SOFTWARE\Microsoft\Windows\CurrentVersion\Run

❐ HKEY_LOCAL_MACHINE\SOFTWARE\Microsoft\Windows\CurrentVersion\RunServices

❐ HKEY_LOCAL_MACHINE\SOFTWARE\Microsoft\Windows\CurrentVersion\RunOnce

❐ HKEY_LOCAL_MACHINE\SOFTWARE\Microsoft\Windows\CurrentVersion\
RunServicesOnce

❐ HKEY_USERS\DEFAULT\SOFTWARE\Microsoft\Windows\CurrentVersion\Run

❐ HKEY_CURRENT_USER\SOFTWARE\Microsoft\Windows\CurrentVersion\Run

❐ HKEY_CURRENT_USER\SOFTWARE\Microsoft\Windows\CurrentVersion\RunServices

❐ HKEY_CURRENT_USER\SOFTWARE\Microsoft\Windows\CurrentVersion\RunOnce

❐ HKEY_CURRENT_USER\SOFTWARE\Microsoft\Windows\CurrentVersion\
RunServicesOnce

❐ HKEY_LOCAL_MACHINE\SOFTWARE\Microsoft\Windows\CurrentVersion\RunOnceEx

Therefore, if you suspect that your computer is infected, these registry keys must be checked first. Furthermore, the list of such keys is constantly being supplemented. Since recently, the following keys have been included into this list:

❐ HKLM\Software\Microsoft\Windows\CurrentVersion\App Paths

❐ HKLM\Software\Microsoft\Windows\CurrentVersion\Controls Folder

❐ HKLM\Software\Microsoft\Windows\CurrentVersion\DeleteFiles

❐ HKLM\Software\Microsoft\Windows\CurrentVersion\Explorer

❐ HKLM\Software\Microsoft\Windows\CurrentVersion\Extensions

❐ HKLM\Software\Microsoft\Windows\CurrentVersion\ExtShellViews

❐ HKLM\Software\Microsoft\Windows\CurrentVersion\Internet Settings

❐ HKLM\Software\Microsoft\Windows\CurrentVersion\ModuleUsage

❐ HKLM\Software\Microsoft\Windows\CurrentVersion\RenameFiles

❐ HKLM\Software\Microsoft\Windows\CurrentVersion\Setup

❐ HKLM\Software\Microsoft\Windows\CurrentVersion\SharedDLLs

❐ HKLM\Software\Microsoft\Windows\CurrentVersion\Shell Extensions

☐ HKLM\Software\Microsoft\Windows\CurrentVersion\Uninstall

☐ HKLM\Software\Microsoft\Windows NT\CurrentVersion\Compatibility

☐ HKLM\Software\Microsoft\Windows NT\CurrentVersion\Drivers

☐ HKLM\Software\Microsoft\Windows NT\CurrentVersion\drivers.desc

☐ HKLM\Software\Microsoft\Windows NT\CurrentVersion\Drivers32\0

☐ HKLM\Software\Microsoft\Windows NT\CurrentVersion\Embedding

☐ HKLM\Software\Microsoft\Windows NT\CurrentVersion\MCI

☐ HKLM\Software\Microsoft\Windows NT\CurrentVersion\MCI Extensions

☐ HKLM\Software\Microsoft\Windows NT\CurrentVersion\Ports

☐ HKLM\Software\Microsoft\Windows NT\CurrentVersion\ProfileList

☐ HKLM\Software\Microsoft\Windows NT\CurrentVersion\WOW

▶ *Note*

It's necessary to mention one more registry key, which is also very important in terms of security. When you work with the Remote Access Service (RAS), the system sometimes displays dialogs prompting you to enter a login name and password. These dialogs often contain checkboxes, which allow you to save the password (for example, **Save This Password** or **Remember This Password**). Although this feature is very convenient for end users, it can possibly be very dangerous, because the passwords are stored in such a way that they can be easily retrieved by the system (and, for that matter, by anyone else). This is especially important for those of you working with laptops and other portable computers, because if your machine is lost or stolen, the person who finds (or steals) it will have access to all your networks.

The easiest way to protect yourself against this risk is to disable the feature for saving RAS passwords on RAS clients. Open the HKEY_LOCAL_MACHINE\ SYSTEM\CurrentControlSet\Services\RemoteAccess\Parameters key and add the REG_DWORD setting named DisableSavePassword. Now the system won't prompt you to save your RAS password.

Protecting the Registry against Unauthorized Remote Access

Remote access to the registry is very convenient when the system administrator needs to support end users from his own workplace. Furthermore, some services must also have access to the registry in order to function correctly. For example, on a system that runs directory replication, the Directory Replicator service requires access to the remote registry. The Spooler service also requires this access, when it is connecting to a printer over the network.

However, in some cases, this capability may be potentially dangerous, that's why remote access must be authorized.

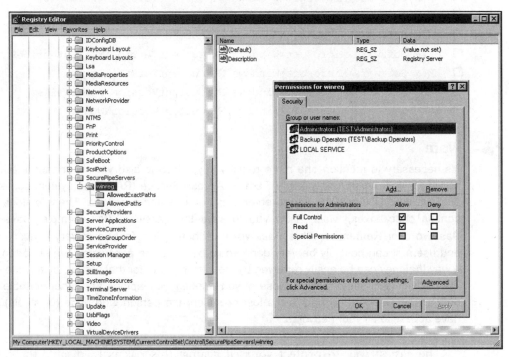

Fig. 9.16. Configuring the Access Control List for HKEY_LOCAL_MACHINE\SYSTEM\ CurrentControlSet\Control\SecurePipeServers\Winreg

When you attempt to connect the registry of the remote Windows NT-based system, the Server service will check if there's an HKEY_LOCAL_MACHINE\ System\CurrentControlSet\Control\SecurePipeServers\Winreg key in that registry (Fig. 9.16). Getting remote access to the registry is made possible with the following factors:

❑ If there isn't a \Winreg subkey key in the registry that you want to protect, then any remote user will have access to the registry. This user will be able to manipulate your registry within the limits defined by its ACL.

❑ If there's a \Winreg subkey, then the Access Control List defined for this key will specify who can access the registry remotely. (But remember that Back

Orifice 2000, or BO2K, allows remote access to the registry, despite the presence of a \Winreg subkey and its access permissions. However, someone must install its server part on your system).

This means that to protect your system from unauthorized remote access, you need to configure the ACL for the following registry key: HKEY_LOCAL_MACHINE\ System\CurrentControlSet\Control\SecurePipeServers\Winreg. If the ACL for \Winreg key provides the remote user's read or write access (explicitly or through group membership), the user will be able to connect to the registry remotely. After establishing the connection, the user rights will be restricted only by his or her access rights to individual keys. Thus, if the user has Read access to the Winreg key, this will provide him or her access to other registry keys (if this is allowed by their ACLs).

Thus, to manage remote registry access, proceed as follows:

1. If your registry does not contain the HKEY_LOCAL_MACHINE\System\ CurrentControlSet\Control\SecurePipeServers\Winreg key, create it by following the procedure described in step 2.

▶ *Note*

You only need to create the \Winreg key on those computers running Windows NT 4.0 Workstation. Windows NT 4.0 Server, Windows 2000 Professional, Windows 2000 Server, Windows XP, and Windows Server 2003 systems contain this key by default (unless someone has deleted it), and system administrators have Full Control access to this key.

2. Start Registry Editor (if you are running Windows 2000 or earlier, use Regedt32.exe), and then locate the HKEY_LOCAL_MACHINE\SYSTEM\ CurrentControlSet\Control registry key and create the SecurePipeServers subkey. Under this key, create the Winreg subkey. Next, under the Winreg subkey, create a new value entry of the REG_SZ data type, and name it Registry Server.

3. Edit the current permissions for the Winreg subkey or add users or groups to whom you want to grant access. The default permissions on this key are different for different operating systems:

   - On Windows 2000 systems, remote access to the registry is provided to the members of the Administrators group and to the SYSTEM built-in account.

   - On a Windows XP Professional, network access to the registry is provided to the members of the Administrators and Backup Operators built-in groups, and to the Local Service built-in account. Administrators have Full

Control access, and Backup Operators have Read access. On a Windows XP Home Edition, by default only the Administrators group can gain access to the registry over the network. Administrators have Full Control access.

- On Windows Server 2003 systems, network access to the registry is provided to the Administrators and Backup Operators built-in groups, and to the Local Service built-in account. Administrators have Full Control access, and Backup Operators have Read access.

Note

Notice the usage of the Local Service built-in account on Windows XP and Windows Server 2003 systems in contrast to the usage of the SYSTEM built-in account on Windows 2000. As was already mentioned, the Local Service account is less privileged than the SYSTEM built-in account.

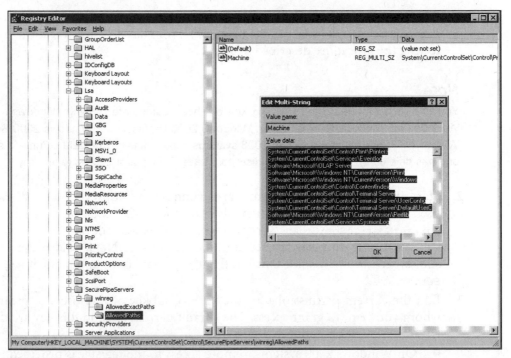

Fig. 9.17. The `Machine` value of the `HKEY_LOCAL_MACHINE\System\CurrentControlSet\Control\SecurePipeServers\Winreg\AllowedPaths` registry key

4. If you have restricted remote registry access, and therefore, some services that require it to function correctly begin to experience problems, you can either

add the account name of the service to the access list on the `Winreg` subkey. Alternately, you can configure Windows to bypass the access restriction to certain keys. To do so, you will need to list the keys for those services in the `Machine` (Fig. 9.17) or `Users` values under the `HKEY_LOCAL_MACHINE\System\CurrentControlSet\Control\SecurePipeServers\Winreg\AllowedPaths` key.

> ### Note
> The `Users` value does not exist by default. You might have to create the value.

Under the `Machine` value (`REG_MULTI_SZ` data type), you can add any valid path to a location within the registry to the default value which you want to allow remote access to, provided that no explicit access restriction exists for that location. For the `Users` value (`REG_MULTI_SZ` data type), use the following information to add keys for which you want to bypass restrictions — a valid path to a location in the registry to which you want to allow user access, provided that no explicit restrictions exist for that location.

Protecting SAM and Security Hives

Windows NT/2000, Windows XP, and Windows Server 2003 security information is stored in the SAM (Security Accounts Manager) and Security registry hives.

> ### Note
> Although starting with Windows 2000, Microsoft has introduced the Active Directory (AD) — arguably the most complex of new technologies, which in some ways represents a further extension of the system registry, the SAM database has retained its importance. In contrast to Windows NT 4.0 domain controllers, where SAM used to be simply a registry hive, on native-mode Windows 2000 and Windows Server 2003 domain controllers, the directory services database is stored in the Ntds.dit file. The SAM is now part of the Active Directory, which serves as a kind of "super-registry", storing all user and machine information, as well as a whole host of other types of objects, including group policies and applications. However, the SAM database continues to store local accounts (required to log on locally). Furthermore, if your computer that is running Windows 2000, Windows XP or Windows Server 2003 does not participate in a domain, the SAM database remains the main storage of the user and group accounts information. Among other things, it is important to notice that the Directory Service Restore Mode Administrator password, which is separate from the Administrator password that is stored in the Active Directory, resides in the local SAM (%*SystemRoot*%\System32\Config\SAM).

The SAM hive contains user passwords as a table of hash codes; the Security hive stores security information for the local system, including user rights and permissions, password policies and group membership.

 ### *Note*

The SAM information is encrypted. However, there are many utilities that allow you to crack the SAM hive. The most common examples are PWDUMP, NT Crack, and L0phtCrack (at the time of this writing, the latest version was LC4).

How to Protect the SAM Hive

Microsoft officially states that the best way to protect Windows NT/2000, Windows XP, and Windows Server 2003 is to protect administrative passwords. This, however, isn't enough. Many users can access the SAM and Security hives, including members of the Backup Operators group, whose responsibility is registry backup.

By default, no user (not even the Administrator) has the necessary access rights that would allow them to access or view the SAM database using the registry editor. However, the SAM and Security hives are stored on the hard disk, the same as all the other files. All you need to do is to get the copies of these files. Of course, you can't do this by simply copying the registry of the running Windows NT/2000, Windows XP, or Windows Server 2003 system. If you make such an attempt, you'll get an error message (Fig. 9.18).

Fig. 9.18. When an attempt to copy the registry of the running
Windows NT/2000, Windows XP, or Windows Server 2003 operating system
is made, the system displays an error message

However, there are tools such as Regback included with Windows NT 4.0 Resource Kit and REG included with newer releases of the Resource Kit. By using these tools, members of Administrators or Backup Operators groups can obtain copies of the registry even if the system is up and running.

If Windows NT-based operating system is installed on the FAT volume, then anyone who can reboot the system and has physical access to the computer can copy the system registry. They need only to reboot the system, start MS-DOS or Windows 9*x*/ME, and copy the SAM and Security hives from the *%SystemRoot%*\System32\Config folder.

▶ *Note*

If Windows NT/2000, Windows XP or Windows Server 2003 is installed on NTFS volume, you can use the NTFSDOS utility for copying the SAM and Security hives (you can download it from **http://www.sysinternals.com/ntfs30.htm**). NTFSDOS mounts NTFS volumes under DOS. This utility and its clones (for example, NTFS for Windows 98) cause different, and sometimes negative, reactions (because of the potential risk to the security subsystem). When the first version of NTFSDOS appeared, Microsoft had to state officially that "true security is physical security". NTFSDOS, though, is one of the most useful tools for registry backup and recovery and may be very helpful when performing emergency recovery (especially if this has to be done very quickly). After all, whatever can be used for good, can also be used for evil.

To summarize, in order to protect the SAM and Security files from unauthorized copying, you need to provide true physical security for the computers you need to protect. Also, don't assign every user the right to reboot the system.

▶ *Note*

By default, this privilege is assigned to Administrators, Backup Operators, Power Users, and Users on Windows 2000/XP workstations. On member servers, it is assigned to Administrators, Power Users, and Backup Operators. On domain controllers, it is assigned to Administrators, Account Operators, Backup Operators, Print Operators, and Server Operators.

To edit the user permissions in Windows 2000, Windows XP, or Windows Server 2003, log onto the system as a member of the Administrators group, open the **Control Panel** windows, start **Administrative Tools** and select the **Local Security Policy** option. Expand the MMC tree and select the **User Rights Assignment** option. The list of user rights will appear in the right pane of this window (Fig. 9.19).

Now, can we say that the Windows NT-based system is secure? No, we can't, because there are backup copies of the registry. In Windows NT 4.0, backup copies of the registry are created immediately after a successful setup or whenever you start the Rdisk/s command. The backup copies of the registry are stored in the *%SystemRoot%*\Repair directory. Backup copies of the Windows 2000/XP/ Windows Server 2003 registry are created whenever you backup the System State Data. As you may recall, all this information is stored in the *%SystemRoot%*\

Repair\Regback folder. These files aren't in use by the system, and any user who has appropriate access rights can copy them. In Windows NT 4.0, system's NTFS access rights don't protect the *%SystemRoot%*\Repair directory. Every user has Read access to this directory, and that's enough to copy the files. In Windows 2000, Windows XP and Windows Server 2003, the Users group by default only has the List permission for this directory, and this permission doesn't allow you to copy the files. If you installed your system as an upgrade from earlier versions of Windows NT, though, access rights to the registry and file system objects might be inherited from the previous system.

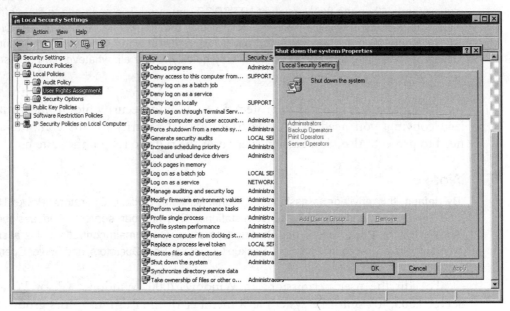

Fig. 9.19. The list of user groups allowed to reboot the system
(Windows Server 2003 domain controller)

Thus, to prevent unauthorized copying of the SAM and Security files, you need to do the following:

❏ Don't assign end users permission to log on locally on the servers.

❏ Whenever possible, use NTFS file system.

❏ Provide physical security for all servers.

❏ In Windows NT 4.0 and in Windows 2000/XP systems upgraded from earlier Windows NT versions, restrict access rights to the *%SystemRoot%*\Repair folder.

❏ Secure the backup copies of the registry and emergency repair disks (Windows NT 4.0) or System State Data (Windows 2000, Windows XP, and Windows Server 2003).

You may ask "But what happens if someone steals my SAM and Security hives?" The answer is very simple: You don't need serious hacking skills to crack the stolen SAM. If you have these files at your disposal, you can make any number of dictionary or brute-force attacks. And if you have LC4 at your disposal (which can be downloaded from **http://www.atstake.com/lc4** and represents a new version of the well-known L0phtCrack password-auditing tool), your success mainly depends on the quality of the dictionary you use (Fig. 9.20).

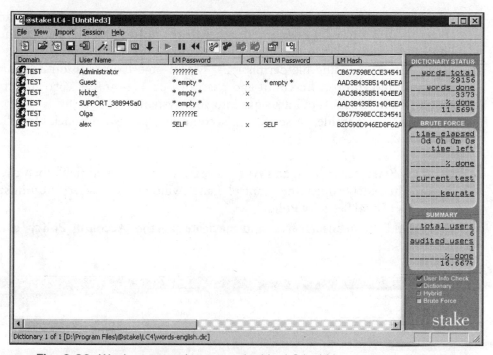

Fig. 9.20. Weak passwords are cracked by LC4 within a matter of minutes

Note

Imagine that you want to hack your own SAM hive (and then try to do it). Remember, your tasks are significantly easier than those of a hacker, because you don't need to plan a remote attack to steal the SAM and Security hives. If you can crack some passwords automatically, explain to the users who've specified these passwords that they're compromising system security.

Thus, to protect the system, you need to:

❑ Ensure a strong account policy (or, at least, prevent users from setting blank passwords and require that passwords be at least 8 characters long, use arbitrary combinations of letters and digits, and specify the system policy in relation to password complexity).

❑ Pay special attention to protecting the local Administrator account from misuse.

Ensuring Strong Account Policy in Windows Server 2003

An *account policy* is a collection of settings that influence user accounts and their ability to authenticate the system. In other words, the account policy sets the standards for initial access to the system and includes every setting that controls access in any form (including file permissions, system objects permissions, dial-up permissions, and so on). If account and password policies are set correctly, this will prevent many attempts of intrusions into your system.

To create, examine, or set strong account and password policies in Windows Server 2003, proceed as follows:

1. Click **Start**, select **Run**, and type secpol.msc in the **Open** field, then click **OK**, or, alternately, open the Control Panel window, and select **Administrative Tools | Local Security Policy**.

2. Expand the console tree and navigate to the **Account Policy** container (Fig. 9.21).

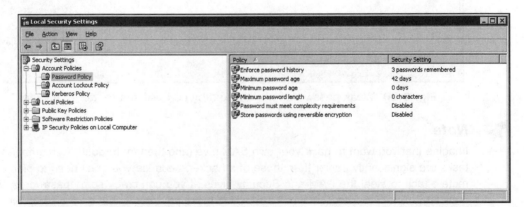

Fig. 9.21. The default settings of the account policies in Windows Server 2003

Notice that default account policies are far from perfect, and most security professionals recommend that they be strengthened. The recommended settings are summarized in Tables 9.2 and 9.3.

Table 9.2. Recommended Settings for the Password Policy

Setting	Description	Recommended setting
Enforce password history	Unfortunately, most end users just hate having to remember their passwords. Even if the administrator encourages them to change passwords frequently, they try to bypass this limitation by changing the password and then immediately returning to an old and familiar one. Enforcing this policy will prevent them from reusing their passwords. Note that this policy alone won't work, because it must be supported by the **Minimum password age** policy.	13 passwords remembered (the default setting instructs the system to remember 3 passwords).
Maximum password age	Setting the **Password never expires** checkbox in the user account properties when creating or editing user accounts is not a good idea. In order to minimize chances that an intruder will use a password that has been guessed or cracked, it is necessary to have users periodically change their passwords.	The default value is 42 days, but in sensitive environments it is recommended that users reduce this value.
Minimum password age	As was already mentioned, this setting supports the **Enforce password history** policy. If you don't change the default value (0), then the user will immediately be able to change the password in order to return to the original one.	At least 5 days.
Minimum password length	As was shown by the example presented in Fig. 9.21, password-cracking tools crack weak passwords in a matter of minutes. Although there is no common opinion about what password length is best, it is still recommended that you make the password at least 8 characters long. Note that in Windows Server 2003 the default UI can handle more than 14 characters. Although with the original LAN Manager password hashing, a 14-character password was no harder to crack than two 7-character parts, the introduction of NTLMv2 and Kerberos management of password-hashing has eliminated this shortcoming. Also notice that recently published security reports state that most contemporary password crackers use the 8-eight character standard as a starting point.	At least 8 characters.

continues

Table 9.2 Continued

Setting	Description	Recommended setting
Password must meet complexity requirements	Although this setting does not prevent users from using dictionary words as their passwords or including numbers at the end and upper-case letters at the beginning of the passwords (all these habits simplify brute-force attacks), it is recommended that the user enable this policy. When this setting is enabled, the newly-created password must satisfy three out of four of the following requirements: upper- and lower-case letters, numbers, and keyboard special characters. This is important, since password-cracking utilities are gradually becoming more and more advanced. For example, the newest version of L0phtCrack, LC4, implements an improved hybrid cracking mode that can both append and prepend characters to dictionary words, and look for common substitutions — if the dictionary word is "password", it will also crack "password!", "!password", or even "#$p@$$w0rd^%".	Enabled.
Store password using reversible encryption	If you want to tighten security on your server, don't turn this setting on. It is available for a single purpose — to provide compatibility with non-Microsoft clients that do not support newer Windows authentication process (therefore, such clients must be able to decrypt passwords). Use this setting only if necessary (i.e., if you have such clients in your network environment).	Disabled.

 Note

A good password policy is essential to network security, but, unfortunately, it is often overlooked. Here are several tips about the worst practices that you should avoid under all circumstances:

- Do not create local Administrator accounts (or common domain-level administrator accounts) using a variation of the company name, computer name, advertising tag lines or dictionary words, such as *%companyname%*#1, win2k*%companyname%*, etc.

- Do not create new user accounts with simple passwords that aren't required to change the password after the first logon.

Be aware that none of the above-described settings can force your end users to create strong passwords. Similarly, even the strongest password policy can prevent users from writing down their passwords and attaching a note to their monitors, sharing passwords with other users, or complaining to management when they have to get help to reset a password they have forgotten.

Table 9.3. Recommended Settings for the Account Lockout Policy

Setting	Description	Recommended setting
Account lockout duration	The number of minutes a locked-out account will stay locked out. If this is set to 0, the account will have to be unlocked by an administrator or someone who has been given the right to do so.	30 minutes
Account lockout threshold	The number of incorrect attempts at guessing a password that can be made before the account is locked out.	5 invalid logons
Reset account lockout counter after	The number of minutes after which the count of invalid logon attempts will be reset. If the number of minutes between one invalid logon and another is greater than the number of minutes to which this setting is configured, the previous invalid logon attempts won't matter.	10 minutes

Protecting the Local Administrator Account

When your Windows NT-based system is joined to a domain, the local Administrator account is still present (as was already mentioned, it resides in (%*SystemRoot*%\System32\Config\SAM). Actually, members of the Domain Admins group can administer the local system only because this group is added to the local Administrators group. Hence, it is necessary to protect the local Administrator's account from unauthorized use or misuse. This goal could be achieved by taking the following protective steps:

❑ As aforementioned, physical security is essential. Although this recommendation might seem elementary, you must not overlook such obvious things. As statistics have shown, most security incidents in corporate environments occur from the inside. Therefore, it is necessary to physically secure all servers (they should be placed in a physically secure room with monitored access) and critical workstations (consider locking the cases or using removable hard drives that are locked up at night). On physically unsecured systems, disable the ability to boot from a CD or floppy. Also, for extra security, disable AutoRun functionality for CD-ROM drives on physically insecure systems. Finally, when considering physical security, do not forget about securing your backup media.

❑ Use NTFS on all partitions. For Windows 2000, Windows XP, and Windows Server 2003, enable EFS (Encrypting File System) — a built-in powerful encryption system, which adds an extra layer of security to drives, folders, or files. Be sure to enable encryption on folders, not just files. All files that are placed in that folder will be encrypted. In particular, it is recommended that the user encrypt the TEMP folder, which is used by applications to temporarily store copies of files being modified (notice that applications do not always clean that folder after closing the files).

❑ Restrict the number of unnecessary user accounts, such as any duplicate user accounts, accounts created for testing purposes, shared accounts, etc. Most generic accounts have weak passwords and provide lots of unnecessary access rights. In Windows NT 4.0, disable the Guest account. Although Windows 2000 and its successors disable the Guest account by default, it is still recommended that you make sure that someone has not enabled it. For additional security, assign a complex password to the account anyway, and restrict its logon hours.

❑ Restrict the addition of local accounts to the local Administrators group, and require a strong password for the local Administrator account. Rename the Administrator account. Although this won't stop qualified intruders (they will use the SID to find out what is the name of the Administrator account), it will still result in a time delay. When renaming the local Administrator account, try to avoid using the word "Admin" in its name. Also, consider creating a dummy account named "Administrator", having a long, rather complex password and no privileges. Enable auditing on this account to get information when someone is tampering with it.

❑ Shut down and disable unnecessary services, since they take up system resources and can open holes into your operating system. IIS, RAS, and Terminal Services have security and configuration issues of their own, and should be implemented carefully if required. You should be aware of all the services that run on your servers and audit them periodically. Also, on Windows 2000 systems, it is recommended that you remove OS/2 and POSIX subsystems if you do not use them (and, in fact, they are used quite rarely). Removing these subsystems will improve performance and reduce potential security risks. To remove the OS/2 and POSIX subsystems, delete the \%*SystemRoot*%\system32\os2 directory and all of its subdirectories, then use the Registry Editor to remove the following registry entries: HKEY_LOCAL_MACHINE\SOFTWARE\Microsoft\OS/2 Subsystem for NT key with all its subkeys, the Os2LibPath entry under

HKEY_LOCAL_MACHINE\SYSTEM\CurrentControlSet\Control\Session Manager\ Environment, the Optional entry and all entries for OS2 and POSIX under HKEY_LOCAL_MACHINE\SYSTEM\CurrentControlSet\Control\Session Manager\ SubSystems. The changes take effect the next time the computer is started. You might want to update the emergency repair disk to reflect these changes.

❑ Disable DirectDraw. Here one should notice that disabling DirectDraw will impact the programs that actually require it (mainly, these are modern games), but it will not influence most business applications. Furthermore, this will prevent direct access to video hardware and memory, which is required by the basic C2 security. To do this, go to the HKLM\SYSTEM\CurrentControlSet\ Control\GraphicsDrivers\DCI registry key and set the Timeout value (REG_DWORD data type) to 0.

❑ Disable the default hidden shares. Windows NT-based systems create hidden shares that are used by the SYSTEM account (also hidden). All Windows NT-based operating systems open hidden shares on each installation for use by the system account. However, you can view all shared folders on your computer by typing the net share command from a command prompt. There are two methods of disabling the default shares — first, you can stop or disable the Server service, which removes the ability to share folders on your computer. To use the second approach, edit the HKEY_LOCAL_MACHINE\SYSTEM\ CurrentControlSet\Services\LanManServer\Parameters registry key. For server platforms, create the AutoShareServer value (REG_DWORD) and set it to 0. For workstations, create the REG_DWORD value named AutoShareWks and set it to 0. Keep in mind, however, that this security measure might cause problems with applications.

❑ Restrict anonymous access to the computer. Anonymous users or services that log on anonymously are automatically added to the Anonymous Logon built-in security group (S-1-5-7). In earlier versions of Windows NT, such users or services were able to access many resources (sometimes in cases where access should have only been granted to authenticated users). Starting with Windows 2000, Microsoft introduced stricter security settings which prevent anonymous access to all resources, except for those who have been explicitly assigned access. You can do this by using the Local Security Policy MMC snap-in or by editing the registry directly. To achieve this purpose using Local Security Policy, one had to select the **Additional restrictions for anonymous connections** option under **Security Settings | Local Policies | Security Options**, and then setting the **No access without explicit anonymous permissions** option. To do the same thing by editing the registry directly, it was necessary to create the `REG_DWORD` value named `RestrictAnonymous` under `HKEY_LOCAL_MACHINE\` `SYSTEM\CurrentControlSet\Control\LSA` registry key and set this value to `0x2` (Hex).

In addition to these standard protective measures, Windows XP and Windows Server 2003 include a set of powerful new security features, which will be briefly considered in the following few sections.

Windows XP and Windows Server 2003 Enhancements and Compatibility Issues

Windows XP and Windows Server 2003 have gone even further than Windows 2000 in tightening the security system, and introduced a range of additional protective steps. However, it is necessary to mention that if you decide to use them, this might cause some administrative inconvenience, especially in mixed environments. Therefore, you must test them carefully before deploying them.

Restricting Anonymous Access

In contrast to previous versions of Windows, the access token for anonymous users no longer includes the Everyone security group. Therefore, the access token for anonymous users contains SIDs for:

❑ Anonymous Logon
❑ The logon type (usually Network)

When an anonymous user tries to access a resource on a computer that is running Windows XP, he or she is not granted permissions or group memberships that are available to the Everyone security group. The SID for the Everyone security group is present in the anonymous user's access token. It should be noted that in most cases this restriction is desirable and appropriate. However, in some situations, for the sake of backward compatibility, you may need to include the Anonymous Logon security group into the Everyone group. For this very purpose, Windows XP and Windows Server 2003 have introduced a new registry value, `EveryoneIncludesAnonymous`, which can be set using the methods described below.

To enable anonymous access via MMC, proceed as follows:

1. Start the Local Security Policy MMC snap-in, expand the **Security Settings** tree, then select **Local Policies | Security Options**.
2. Double-click **Network access: Let Everyone permissions apply to anonymous users.** By default, this policy setting is disabled (Fig. 9.22).

3. To enable anonymous users to be members of the Everyone security group, click **Enabled**. To prevent the inclusion of the Everyone security group SID in the anonymous user's access token (the Windows XP and Windows Server 2003 default), **click Disabled**.

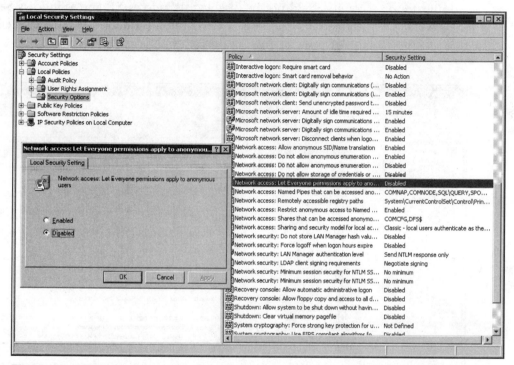

Fig. 9.22. Setting `EveryoneIncludesAnonymous` registry value via Local Security Policy

To set the `EveryoneIncludesAnonymous` registry value by using Registry Editor, proceed as follows:

1. Start Regedit.exe and locate the following registry key:

   HKEY_LOCAL_MACHINE\SYSTEM\CurrentControlSet\Control\Lsa

2. Right-click `EveryoneIncludesAnonymous`, and then click **Modify**.

3. To enable anonymous users to be members of the Everyone security group, in the **Value data** box, type 1. To prevent the inclusion of the Everyone security group SID in the anonymous user's access token, type 0.

4. Quit Registry Editor.

Disabling the Administrator Account

This security option is only available in Windows XP and Windows Server 2003 and lets you disable the local Administrator account. To do so, simply right-click the local Administrator account, and select the **Disable account** command from the context menu. In contrast to previous Windows NT-based systems, where local Administrator accounts could not be disabled, Windows XP and Windows Server 2003 will allow you to do this (Fig. 9.23). This option is rather useful, since it eliminates the possibility of misusing the Administrator password.

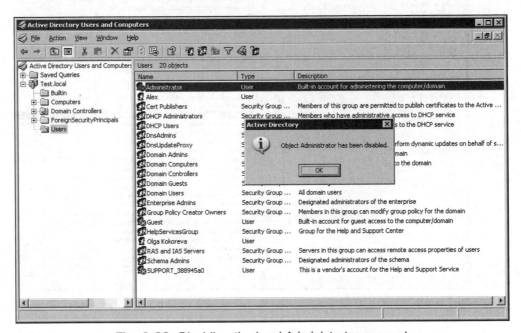

Fig. 9.23. Disabling the local Administrator account

Note

Because members of the Domain Admins group have administrative authority on computers joined in their domain, you still maintain the ability to administer the system. Also, the Administrator account will remain enabled when booting in safe mode.

Selecting this feature, however, can have some interesting side effects. For example, if you change the password policy after disabling the Administrator account, and this account no longer meets the policy requirements, your attempt at re-enabling it will fail. In this case, another administrator must log on and reset the Administrator account password. If there are no other administrative accounts, you will have to reboot to the safe mode to fix the problem.

Limiting Local Account Use of Blank Passwords to Console-Logon Only

Admittedly, the password policy should prevent the use of blank passwords entirely. However, you should recall that someone who has the password to the local Administrator's account (or other account with membership in the local Administrators group) could modify the local account and password policy to permit blank passwords and modify an account in order to use it. When the use of blank passwords is limited to console logon only (an option for only Windows XP and Windows Server 2003 systems), an account with a blank password cannot be used for network logon. The user must work on the Windows XP or Windows Server 2003 system in which the account exists. You have effectively prevented an intruder from using the local Administrator account (or any other privileged account) to access files, folders, registry keys, and so on, on this machine. This configuration also prevents applications such as FTP, Telnet, and terminal services from using an account with a blank password. However, Microsoft advises that applications requiring remote access be written to bypass this setting.

Security Through Obscurity

Of course, security through obscurity will not work, if obscurity is your only line of defense. However, making things more difficult for attackers is a useful practice, especially when it comes to protecting the local Administrator account. The option allowing one to rename this account existed already in Windows 2000, and remains a part of Windows XP and Windows Server 2003. However, as was mentioned earlier, it won't stop a qualified intruder, since the task of determining which of the accounts is the local Administrator's account would not be too difficult. Being well aware of this weak point, Microsoft has introduced several new protective measures, intended to make this harder. They can be enforced via Group Policy (under **Local Policy | Security Options**). The list of these new policies includes:

❑ **Network access: Allow Anonymous SID and Name Translation.** When this setting is enabled, the system will answer anonymous requests for the name of the account associated with SID belonging to the local Administrator account. Since the local Administrator account is associated with the well-known SID, the task of determining the new name of this account becomes trivial. If you disable this setting, such an anonymous request will be denied. It is recommended that the user enable this setting for all domain-level accounts via the Default Domain Group Policy MMC snap-in. Local account settings can be different and may be set by changing this security option within a group policy linked to the specific organizational unit within which the machine account resides.

❏ **Network access: Do Not Allow Anonymous Enumeration of SAM Accounts.** This Windows XP and Windows Server 2003 security option prevents anonymous access to a listing of Security Accounts Manager (SAM) accounts.

Note

This option is useful in obscuring information about the domain, especially if your organization uses naming conventions for user accounts. If the attacker knows that your organization uses naming conventions, he or she can deduce the rules used in these conventions, and thus easily guess the correct account name for some employees. On the other hand, it has implications for trusts, because some functions require the ability to anonymously list accounts. For example, the administrator of a trusting domain must be an authenticated user of a trusted domain in order to perform administrative tasks such as accessing the list of accounts of the trusted domain when assigning access to resources to trusted domain users. Actually, when performing such tasks, Windows Server 2003 prompts for and account and password for the trusted domain.

Summary

When writing this chapter, I didn't intend to provide you with detailed, step-by-step instructions on the methods of cracking Windows NT/2000/XP or Windows Server 2003 (this information wouldn't be sufficient, anyway). Rather, this chapter is addressed to those of you who are interested in security in general (and in Windows NT security in particular) and want to restrict the security of their networks. Remember: "The person who's been warned, is armed."

Of course, this chapter isn't a complete reference on computer security. This topic deserves a separate book. Additional information sources are provided in the bibliographical reference at the end of this book.

CHAPTER 10

Managing the User Environment

Let every hour be in place
Firm fixed, nor loosely shift,
And well enjoy the vacant space,
As though a birthday gift.

Lewis Carroll
Punctuality

In today's competitive business environment, the distributed office model is quickly replacing the traditional model of the corporate network. And, in today's distributed office, all users and co-workers, regardless of where they are working, require a reliable computing environment, which, generally, comprises the following factors:

❐ Reliable equipment, seamlessly operating, well-managed, and properly maintained

❐ A reliable, well-configured, and properly secured operating system on their client desktops

❑ Compatible, up-to-date applications required for end users to perform their jobs

❑ Consistently available user data

To meet these rather stringent requirements, system and network administrators must work hard. If you are an administrator, you know only too well what I mean. You're personally responsible for all security incidents, hardware malfunctions, software failures, or cases of data loss that might happen. Therefore, you are the person who stays late to ensure that the backup job has been completed successfully, sometimes you have to work weekends setting up or troubleshooting servers, and you are the earliest to come to work and the last to go home. You're the person who supports and educates end users, maintains software installations running from machine to machine, travels to remote offices (sometimes only to reboot the server), and so on. If something goes wrong, you are the first to blame. Of course, all above-described horrors are mainly seen in weak administrative settings. They mainly are due to poor planning and even worse implementation of change and configuration management features.

With the introduction of the system registry, Microsoft has addressed the administrative need for efficient management of the user's work environment, which includes various desktop settings, such as color scheme, mouse settings, size and position of the windows, network connections and printers, environment variables, registry settings, available applications, etc. Even the earliest versions of Windows NT provided the following conventional methods for managing user work environments:

❑ *User profiles*
User profiles contain all the settings for a user-specific Windows work environment, including user documents, mail messages, application configuration settings and preferences, screen settings, network connections and so on.

❑ *Scripts*
The logon script is the batch (BAT) or executable (EXE) file that runs any time you log on to the network from any of the workstations connected to it. Logon scripts can contain various operating system commands; for example, ones that restore network connections and start applications, or set environment variables (such as set paths using the PATH variable or specify the folder to store temporary files using the TEMP variable).

Starting with Windows 2000, Microsoft has implemented a whole range of new technologies called IntelliMirror (as a part of the Zero Administration Initiative), which in Windows XP and Windows Server 2003 was further improved and enhanced. When these new features are properly implemented, many of the administrative nightmares can be significantly reduced. Newer technologies simplify the process of network administration and improve its efficiency. This set of functions allows system administrators and users to create mirror copies of the user profile data stored on the server, thus protecting critically important user data stored in the local system. The main idea of IntelliMirror technologies is that all information on the user profile and the software installed by the user is stored on the server in a personal cache. Using IntelliMirror, the system administrator may install and support application software on the user workstations without interrupting their everyday work. Because the server always has a mirror of the user's working environment, the administrator can quickly replace the user workstation and restore the working environment, including data, installed software, and the administrative policy.

Having spent some time on studying and then carefully planning and implementing these built-in features of Windows Server 2003 will allow you to achieve the following goals:

❑ Reducing downtime and costs associated with disaster recovery
❑ Reducing labor costs associated with inefficient client installation and configuration
❑ Reducing data loss due to hardware failure
❑ Increase productivity by providing data availability even when network resources are unavailable
❑ Allowing applications to be remotely installed and upgraded
❑ Having users' applications, data, and settings available to them regardless of where they work

Basic Information on the User Profiles

All users of modern Windows NT-based operating systems have many customizable settings at their disposal, including wallpapers and screen savers, desktop settings, and many application settings, which can be customized. These settings are only a small part of a large variety of the customizable settings. There are many reasons users may need these customizations (after all, individual preferences are always different).

Before the registry concept was introduced, there was always one common problem: any time you logged onto the network from another computer, you always needed to customize its settings.

A new user profile is created automatically each time a new user logs onto a Windows NT-based operating system for the first time. By default, user profiles in Windows NT, Windows 2000, Windows XP, and Windows Server 2003 support desktop settings for the user environment on the local computer.

 Note

It is necessary to distinguish user profiles from their policies. Profiles are not user policies, and each user has a profile even if they don't use Group Policy.

Advantages of the User Profile

User profiles provide the following advantages:

☐ After a successful logon, users start working with their own working environment (including desktop settings) that existed at the time he/she last logged out.

☐ Many users can share a single computer, and each user will get individual settings for their working environment.

☐ User profiles can be stored on the server; they may be used independently from the workstation where the user logs on to the network. These user profiles are called roaming user profiles.

From the administrator's point of view, user profiles provide specific advantages and are capable of:

☐ Creating customized user settings

☐ Specifying common settings for each user group

☐ Assigning mandatory user profiles which can't be changed by the users and don't allow them to change the system's configuration

As was already mentioned in *Chapter 1*, Windows XP and Windows Server 2003 provide the following types of user profiles:

☐ *Local User Profiles*. User profiles of this type are stored on the local computer's hard disk. Any changes that you might introduce to the local user profile are computer-specific and only apply to the computer on which these changes are made.

☐ *Roaming User Profile.* Roaming user profiles are stored on the server, and are available any time the user logs onto a network. Any changes made to a roaming user profile are updated on the server.

☐ *Mandatory User Profile.* This type of user profile can be created or updated only by system administrators. Any changes the user makes to this type of profile are lost when he or she logs off.

▶ *Note*

Mandatory user profiles are included with Windows XP and later only in order to provide backward compatibility with existing Windows NT 4.0 domains. If you have Windows 2000 domains in native mode or have even migrated to Windows Server 2003 domains, and need to provide managed desktop configurations for users and groups, it is recommended that you use Group Policy rather than mandatory user profiles. Group Policy basics will be discussed later in this chapter.

The Settings Stored in the User Profile

Each user profile contains configuration settings and options customized for each individual user. In practice, the user profile can be considered a "snapshot" of the user's working environment.

Main settings stored in the user profile are listed in Table 10.1.

Table 10.1. User Profile Settings

Working environment item	User profile settings
Windows GUI (Windows Explorer or My Computer)	All user-specified settings of the Windows Explorer application
Taskbar	All personal program groups and their properties, all personal programs and their properties, all individual settings of the taskbar
Printer settings	All connections to network printers
Control Panel	All individual user-specific settings specified using Control Panel applets
Accessories	All user-specific customized settings of the applications that influence Windows NT/2000, Windows XP, or Windows Server 2003 working environments, including individual settings for Calculator, Notepad, Paint, HyperTerminal, etc.

continues

Table 10.1 Continued

Working environment item	User profile settings
Application settings	All Windows applications allow individual settings in relation to each individual user. If this information exists, it's stored in the user's registry hive (HKEY_CURRENT_USER)
Bookmarks in the online Help system	All Help bookmarks set by the user
Favorites registry key	All registry keys marked by the user as Favorites

User Profile Structure

Each user profile consists of a registry hive (Ntuser.dat file, which is mapped to the HKEY_CLASSES_ROOT registry key when the user logs on) and a set of folders in the file system of your computer. Since the release of Windows NT 4.0, the default location of user profiles has changed in order to allow administrators to provide better security for the operating system folders without affecting user data. Let us consider the default location of user profiles in more detail.

All Windows NT user profiles are stored in the *%SystemRoot%*\Profiles folder. When you log onto the system for the first time, the system creates a new profile for you based on the Default User profile, present on each Windows NT Workstation or Windows NT Server computer. The \Default User folder and profile folders for individual users contain the Ntuser.dat and Ntuser.dat.log files (user profile hive and its log) together with the desktop shortcuts.

The naming conventions for the user profile folders have changed with Windows 2000. In general, the location of Windows 2000, Windows XP, or Windows Server 2003 user profiles depends on the method used to install the operating system:

❑ If Windows 2000, Windows XP, or Windows Server 2003 was installed fresh, the Setup program will create a new folder for storing user profiles: *%SystemDrive%*:\Documents and Settings (for example, C:\Documents and Settings).

❑ If the system was installed as an upgrade from the previous Windows NT versions, user profile folders will be located in the *%SystemRoot%*\Profiles folder (like in Windows NT 4.0).

► **Note**

Later in this chapter, we'll use the *%ProfilePath%* variable to specify a path to the folder that contains user profiles.

The locations of user profiles for each of the possible types of OS installation are briefly described in Table 10.2.

Table 10.2. User Profile Locations

Installation type	User profiles location
Clean installation of Windows 2000, Windows XP or Windows Server 2003 (no previous operating system)	%*SystemDrive*%\Documents and Settings; for example, C:\Documents and Settings
Upgrade from Windows 2000	%*SystemDrive*%\Documents and Settings; for example, C:\Documents and Settings
Upgrade from Windows NT 4.0	%*SystemRoot*%\Profiles; for example, C:\WinNT\Profiles
Windows 2000 or Windows XP systems upgraded from Windows 9*x*/ME	%*SystemDrive*%\Documents and Settings; for example, C:\Documents and Settings

Like the previous versions of Windows NT/2000, Windows XP and Windows Server 2003 automatically create a user profile when the new user first logs onto the system. To store this profile, the system creates a new nested folder named after the login name of the new user and located under the %*ProfilePath*% folder. The path to this folder will be saved in the system registry and associated with the user's security identifier (Security ID, SID).

Note

Also notice that many users, even experienced ones, often think that the system identifies each user by his or her username (or login name) and the password. This isn't so; it's the SID that uniquely identifies the user. User profiles are also identified by their associated SIDs (Fig. 10.1).

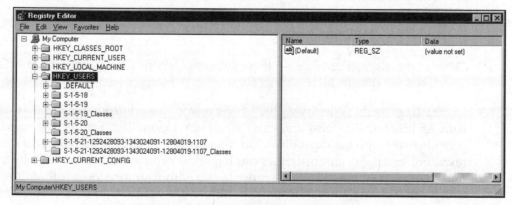

Fig. 10.1. The HKEY_USERS registry key

The HKEY_USERS registry key contains the default user profile as well as profiles for all user accounts currently logged on to the computer. The HKEY_USERS\.DEFAULT key contains parameters that the system applies before any user logs on to the system. Other subkeys represent SIDs of the currently logged on user accounts:

❑ HKEY_USERS\S-1-5-18 — This subkey contains parameters for the LocalSystem, an identity used locally by the OS and by services configured to log on as Local-System. Notice that this identity is a hidden member of the Administrators group. That is, any process running as LocalSystem has the SID for the Administrators built-in group in its access token.

❑ HKEY_USERS\S-1-5-19 — This subkey contains parameters for the LocalService, an identity used by services that do not need such extensive local privileges as Local System, and do not need authenticated network access.

❑ HKEY_USERS\S-1-5-20 — This subkey contains parameters for the NetworkService, an identity used by services that do not need extensive local privileges, but do require authenticated network access.

Note

All three above-listed SIDs are well-known SIDs (more information on well-known SIDs was provided in *Chapter 9*). Also notice that NetworkService (S-1-5-20) and LocalService (S-1-5-19) are newly introduced built-in accounts, only existing in Windows XP and Windows Server 2003 in order to reduce the number of services running in the SYSTEM context. Therefore, the HKEY_USERS registry key in Windows 2000 or earlier does not contain subkeys identified by these SIDs.

❑ HKEY_USERS\CURRENT_USER_SID (in the example shown in Fig. 10.1, the CURRENT_USER_SID is S-1-5-21-1292428093-1343024091-12804019-1107). This subkey contains parameters that correspond to the current user, who has logged on locally.

❑ HKEY_USERS\SID_Classes — these subkeys contain file associations and COM classes for specific SIDs

Starting with Windows 2000, Microsoft has introduced the so-called **Run As** functionality, also known as secondary logon. This feature is designed to provide users with the capability of starting programs under different security contexts. For example, administrators can log on as ordinary users, and invoke a secondary logon (administrative) in order to run administrative tools without needing to log off. To start a program under a different security context, it is sufficient to right-click the file that you want to start, and then select the **Run As** command from the context menu. The **Run As** dialog will open (Fig. 10.2), where you will be able to select the user account with administrative rights.

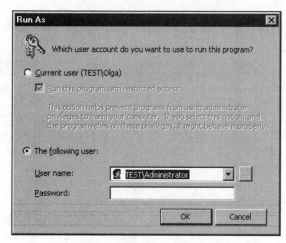

Fig. 10.2. Using a secondary logon

▶ *Note*

Secondary logons represent a security enhancement, which protects the system against unintended actions, attacks on the local Administrator account and Trojan Horse attacks while accessing non-trusted sites using Internet Explorer.

After the user invokes a secondary logon and provides credentials for the administrative account, Windows will load additional settings for the secondary logon, and new subkeys will appear under HKEY_USERS registry key (Fig. 10.3).

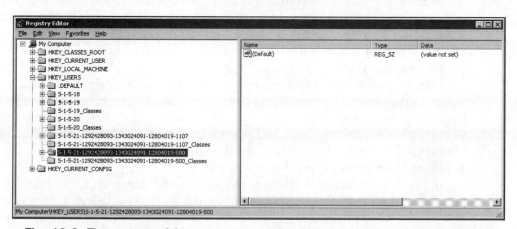

Fig. 10.3. The contents of the HKEY_USERS registry key after invoking a secondary logon

Note

If **Run As** functionality is unavailable, check if the Secondary Logon service is started (Fig. 10.4).

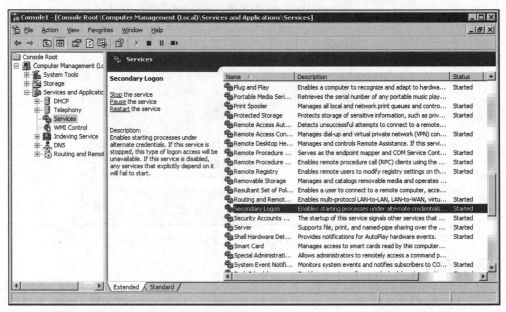

Fig. 10.4. The **Run As** functionality depends on the Secondary Logon service

When the user logs into the local system using a local or domain user account, and the *%ProfilePath%* folder doesn't contain a subfolder with a name like the user's login name, the system will create such a folder. The path to this folder will be saved in the registry and associated with the user's SID. For example, if "Olga" logs into the Windows 2000/XP or Windows Server 2003 system, the system will create a folder named *%SystemDrive%*:\Documents and Settings\Olga to store a new user profile (Fig. 10.5).

Later, if a user from another domain, having the same login name, attempts to log on to the network from this computer, the system will create another user profile folder for them. The folder will be named using the following format: *%SystemDrive%*:\Documents and Settings\Olga [*DOMAIN_NAME*], where [*DOMAIN_NAME*] is the name of the domain to which the user account with the duplicated user name belongs to.

If both the login and domain names are the same, but the SIDs of two user accounts are different (this may happen when you delete a user account, and then create another one with the same name belonging to the same domain), the system will create a new user profile folders named as

follows: %*SystemDrive*%:\Documents and Settings\Olga [*DOMAIN_NAME*].000,
%*SystemDrive*%:\Documents and Settings\Olga [*DOMAIN_NAME*].001, etc.

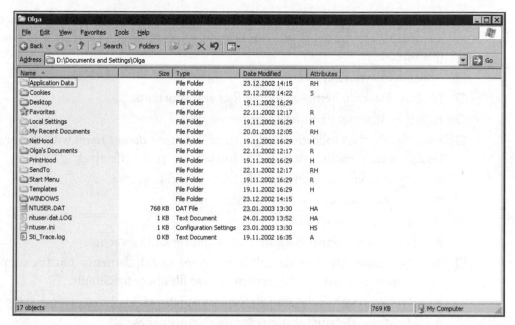

Fig. 10.5. Typical contents of the user profile folder

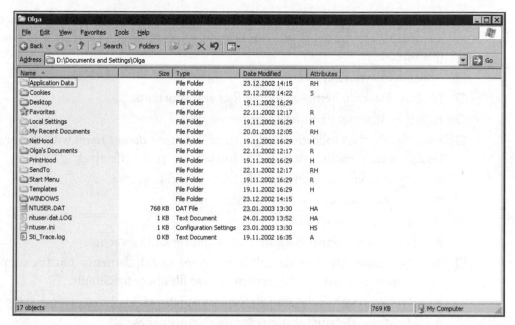 ***Note***

As I mentioned before, Windows NT 4.0 stores all locally cached user profiles in the
%*SystemRoot*%\Profiles folder. If you've installed the newer version as an upgrade from
Windows NT, the system will continue using this folder for storing user profiles. If you've
installed a new copy of Windows 2000, Windows XP, or Windows Server 2003, the Setup
program will create a new "Documents and Settings" folder for storing user profiles. This
folder will be located on the same partition with the Windows 2000/XP or Windows Server
2003 operating system. Notice that some legacy applications use hard-coded pathnames
to access locally cached user profiles. This may cause a problem in mixed environments.
For example, if the path to the user profile is coded "%*SystemRoot*%\Profiles", the program
may behave as expected in Windows NT 4.0, but it will fail to find the user profile in Windows 2000, Windows XP, or Windows Server 2003.

Now let us consider in more detail the preferences stored in the profile directories. The screenshot shown in Fig. 10.5 illustrates the typical structure of the user

profile, which in Windows XP and Windows Server 2003 contains the following folders:

❑ *Application data**. Application-specific data, such as a custom dictionary for a word processing program. Application vendors decide what data to store in this directory.

❑ *Cookies*. Internet Explorer cookies.

❑ *Desktop*. Desktop items, including files and shortcuts.

❑ *Favorites*. Internet Explorer favorites.

❑ *Local Settings**. Application settings and data that *do not roam* with the profile. Usually either machine-specific, or too large to roam effectively.

- *Application data*. Computer-specific application data.

- *History*. Internet Explorer history.

- *Temp*. Temporary files.

- *Temporary Internet Files*. Internet Explorer offline cache.

❑ *My Documents*. The new default location for any documents that the user creates. Applications should be written to save files here by default.

- *My Pictures*. Default location for user's pictures.

- *My Music*. Default locations for user's music files.

❑ *NetHood**. Shortcuts to Network Neighborhood items.

❑ *PrintHood**. Shortcuts to printer folder items.

❑ *Recent*. Shortcuts to the most recently used documents.

❑ *SendTo*. Shortcuts to document storage locations and applications.

❑ *Start Menu*. Shortcuts to program items.

❑ *Templates**. Shortcuts to template items.

> ### Note
>
> By default, the **Local Settings** folder and its subfolders do not roam with the profile. This folder contains application data not required to roam with the user, such as temporary files, non-critical settings, and data too large to roam efficiently.

---

* These directories are hidden by default. To see these directories, change the **View | Options**.

The Ntuser.dat File

The Ntuser.dat file is the part of the registry that actually supports the user profile. This file is the cached copy of the local HKEY_CURRENT_USER subtree (Fig. 10.6). It stores the settings, which define the working environment for the currently logged on user.

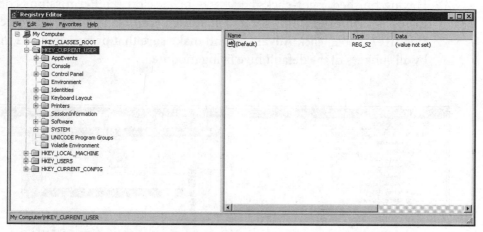

Fig. 10.6. The settings defining the working environment for the currently logged on user are stored under HKEY_CURRENT_USER

Defining Initial Settings for New Users

Many tips and registry hacks that specify "how to" modify the settings related to specific users recommend that you log on to the system as that user and then modify specific parameters under the HKEY_CURRENT_USER registry key. However, this approach seems impractical when you need to apply the setting to multiple users (just consider how many times you would need to log on, start the registry editor to introduce the same modification, then log off). If this is the case, the small tip provided here will help you to specify unified initial settings for all new users who log on to the system for the first time. The main idea here is, that any modification that you can introduce to the HKEY_CURRENT_USER registry key can also be made to the default user hive.

To modify the default user profile hive, do the following:

1. Start Regedit.exe, highlight the HKEY_USERS key and select the **Load Hive** command from the **File** menu.

2. Select the Ntuser.dat file from the %*SystemDrive*%\Documents and Settings\ Default User folder.

3. Enter the name for the hive to be loaded (for example, NTUSER) into the **Key Name** dialog. Now introduce any desired modification to any key or value entry within the newly loaded NTUSER hive.

4. Having finished, right-click the NTUSER hive, select the **Permissions** command from the context menu, and assign Read permission to the Everyone group (Fig. 10.7). Then click **Advanced** and make sure that permissions are inherited by all subkeys of the default hive being modified.

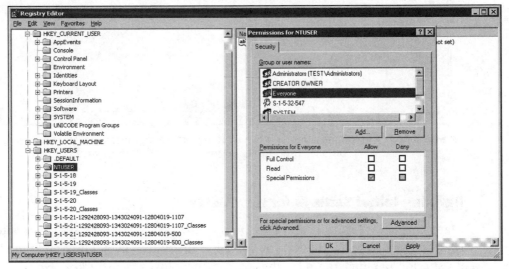

Fig. 10.7. Setting permissions for the modified default user hive

5. Unload the hive and close registry editor. Now all new users will have the settings that you specified.

Note

This tip also works for Windows 2000 and previous versions. However, in this case, you'll need to use Regedt32.exe, and edit the default Ntuser.dat hive file, which is usually located in the %*SystemDrive*%\Documents and Settings\Default User folder (Windows 2000) or under %*windir*%\Profiles\Default User directory (Windows NT 4.0).

Fixing a Corrupt User Profile

If you have a misbehaving user account, this might be due to a corrupt user profile. To determine if the profile is corrupt, proceed as follows:

1. Create a new temporary account and assign it the same rights and group membership as the suspect account.
2. Log on to the system as a new temporary user. The new profile for that user will be created.
3. Log off, then log on with administrative privileges. Start the System applet in Control Panel, go to the **Advanced** tab, and click the **Settings** button in the **User Profiles** group. The **User Profiles** window (Fig. 10.8) will open. Select the suspected profile and click the **Copy To** button.

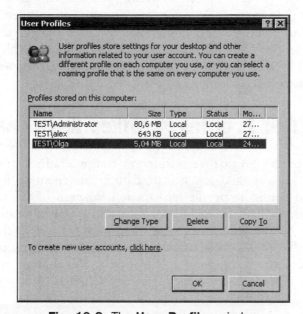

Fig. 10.8. The **User Profiles** window

4. The **Copy To** window will open (Fig. 10.9). Click the **Browse** button, select the newly created temporary account under the %*SystemDrive*%\Documents and Settings folder and click **OK**.
5. Click the **Change** button in the **Permitted to use** option group and set the appropriate permissions, then click **OK**.

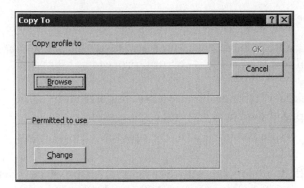

Fig. 10.9. The **Copy To** window

6. Log off, then log on as a new temporary user. If you experience the same problem, then the user profile is actually corrupt. In this case, locate the corrupt user profile in the %*SystemDrive*%\Documents and Settings folder, and delete the whole user profile folder. When the user logs on, the system will create a new user profile. If the problem has been eliminated, this means that it was not caused by a corrupt user profile. Most probably, the user account itself is corrupt and must be deleted and recreated.

Roaming User Profiles in Mixed Environments

Roaming users move between different computers in a mixed network environment. To achieve this, you will need to create roaming user profiles, and then enable and configure profile information for each of the roaming users in your organization. When you enable roaming and specify a network share for roaming files, some files and folders automatically roam with the users. This makes the user files available to roaming users, regardless of the client computer from which the user logs on to the domain. Creating and enabling a roaming user profile is a two-step procedure:

1. Create and configure a test user profile.
2. Copy the test user profile to a network server.

▶ Note

Before enabling roaming user profiles, it is recommended that you consider the important point of application compatibility. The underlying reason is straightforward, although, strangely enough, overlooked. The problem is that some new features and functionality available in newer versions of applications might be unavailable to users who have earlier versions of the same applications. This, of course, becomes a source of confusion in networks that use a mix of different versions of the same application. One such example is Microsoft Outlook 2002, since some of its features are unavailable to the users of Outlook 2000. Therefore, if you are using Microsoft Outlook as a mail client, it is recommended that you ensure that the same version of the application is used in a single area (such as a domain), or at least perform a centralized upgrade.

To create a test profile for a roaming user on a client computer running Windows 2000, Windows XP, or Windows Server 2003, follow these steps:

1. Log on as Administrator, open the Administrative Tools applet and click the **Computer Management** icon.

2. In the console tree, expand **Local Users and Groups**, right-click **Users** and select the **New User** command from the right-click menu.

3. When the **New User** window opens (Fig. 10.10), type in a name and password for the user, then clear the **User must change password at next logon** checkbox. Click **Create**, and then click **Close**.

4. Quit the Computer Management snap-in and log off the computer.

5. Log on as the test user account that you have just created. A user profile is automatically created on the local computer in the %*SystemDrive*%\Documents and Settings*Username* folder (where *Username* is the name of the new user account that you have just created).

6. Configure the desktop environment, including appearance, shortcuts, **Start** menu options, etc.

7. Log off, and then log on as Administrator.

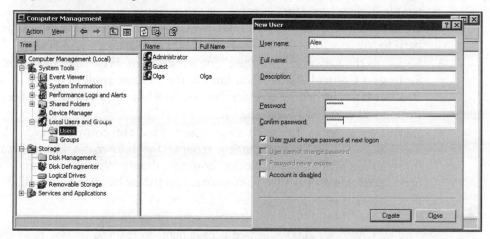

Fig. 10.10. Creating a test user account

After creating a test profile, you need to copy it to a network server. To achieve this goal, proceed as follows:

1. Create an account for the administrative user on the Windows 2000 Server or Windows Server 2003 PDC (use Active Directory Users and Computers for this purpose). This user will be the administrator of the user profiles. Also create a shared directory for storing user profiles, for example: *Server_name*\Profiles. Within this shared folder, create a *user_name* folder for each user.

2. Copy the roaming profile that you have created and configured, to the *user_name* folder(s) on the network server. To do so, log on as Administrator on the client workstation, open the **User Profiles** window (see Fig. 10.8), select the profile that you want to configure as roaming from the **Profiles stored on this computer** list, and click the **Copy To** button. In the **Copy To** dialog (see Fig. 10.9), click the **Browse** button and specify the path using the UNC (Universal Naming Convention) format (for example: \\`Server_name`\Profiles\ `user_name`). If the folder doesn't exist, it will be created.

3. On the Windows 2000 Server or Windows Server 2003 PDC, start the Active Directory Users and Computers MMS snap-in. In the console tree, expand the *Domain* node, and then click the folder where users are located (typically, the **Users** folder). In the list of user names, right-click the name of the user whom you are going to configure for roaming, and then click **Properties**. Go to the **Profile** tab (Fig. 10.11).

4. For clients running Windows NT, Windows 2000, Windows XP, or Windows Server 2003, go to the **Profile Path** field in the **User Profile** group. Type in the full path to the user profile folder that you have created for the roaming profile of that user (for example, \\`Server_name`\Profiles\`user_name`. For clients running Windows 9*x*/ME, set the **Connect** radio button and type the full path to the user folder into the **To** field.)

5. Logon to the network from the client workstation. From the **Start** menu, select **Settings | Control Panel**, then launch the System applet and go to the **User Profiles** tab. The profile type for the user to whom you've assigned the roaming profile will change to **Roaming**.

6. Repeat these steps for each user whom you are configuring for roaming. To make this profile mandatory, rename the Ntuser.dat file as Ntuser.man in the user's profile folder. Notice, however, that in Windows XP and Windows Server 2003, mandatory user profiles are supported for backward compatibility only.

Note

Starting with Windows 2000, standard access rights to roaming profiles have changed in comparison to those in Windows NT 4.0. For example, administrators no longer have Full

Control access to all user profiles. Consequently, if an administrator needs access to the contents of the user profile, he or she will need to take ownership for the appropriate file system objects (if the user profiles are stored on the NTFS partition) and also to take ownership for the respective registry hives. From a security point of view, this is a wise thing to do, because the operation of taking ownership is an event that can be audited. Also notice that Windows Server 2003 does not support the use of encrypted files with roaming user profiles.

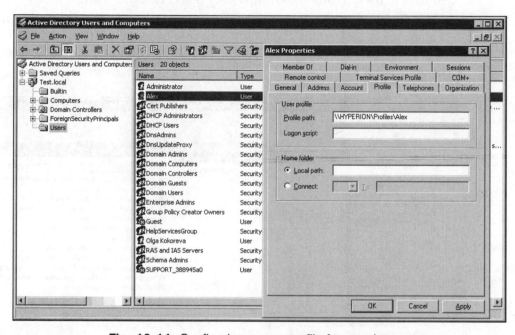

Fig. 10.11. Configuring a user profile for roaming

Windows XP and Windows Server 2003 Enhancements to Roaming User Profiles

Windows XP and Windows Server 2003 introduce several enhancements to user settings management, including more reliable roaming, an improved user profile merge algorithm and several new group policy settings. Let us consider these enhancements in more detail.

First of all, user profile policies in Windows XP and Windows Server 2003 have their own node in Group Policy Editor (Fig. 10.12). Furthermore, there are three new policies. To view these policies, proceed as follows:

1.   Click **Start**, click **Run**, type mmc, and then click **OK**.

2. From the **File** menu, select the **Add/Remove Snap-in** command, go to the **Standalone** tab and click **Add**.

3. From the **Available Standalone Snap-ins** list, select the **Group Policy** option and then click the **Add** button. When the **Select Group Policy object** window opens, select the **Local Computer** option to edit the local Group Policy object, or click **Browse** to find the Group Policy object that you want.

4. Click **Finish**, then **Close**, then **OK**. The Group Policy snap-in opens the Group Policy object for editing. Expand the console tree in the left pane of this window as follows: **Computer Configuration** | **Administrative Templates** | **System** | **User Profiles** (Fig. 10.12).

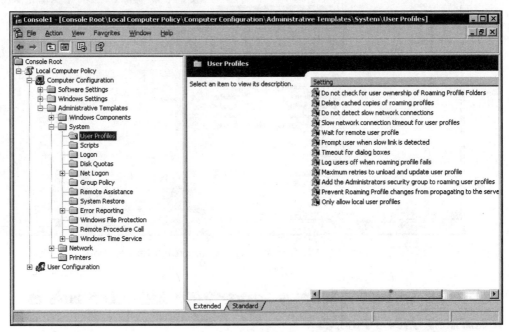

Fig. 10.12. User Profile Policies have their own node in Group Policy Editor

The three new policies that have been added with Windows XP are the last ones in the list of the available policies in the right pane of the Group Policy window:

❑ **Prevent Roaming Profile Changes From Propagating to the server**. As its name implies, this policy specifies whether the changes made by the users to their roaming profiles are merged with the copies of their roaming profiles stored on the server. If you set this policy, the users at login will receive the copies of their roaming profiles, but the changes they introduce will not be merged with their roaming profiles.

❏ **Add the Administrator security group to the roaming user profile share.** As was aforementioned, starting with Windows 2000, the default permissions for newly created roaming profiles provide full control permissions for the user and no access to the Administrators group. If you want to reset this behavior in a way compatible to Windows NT 4.0, where the Administrators group has full control of the user's profile directories, you should set this policy.

❏ **Do Not Allow users to change profile type.** Allows an administrator to control whether a user is allowed to change their profile type from a Roaming Profile to a Local profile.

Note

Besides new policies, Windows XP and Windows Server 2003 provide other improvements to roaming profiles management. For example, in Windows 2000 there may be situations in which applications and services keep registry keys open during logoff. This prevents Windows from unloading the user's registry hive and saving the user profiles modifications to the server. As a result, such "locked" user profiles never get unloaded, and take up a large amount of memory on a server that has many users logging on. If such a profile is marked for deletion at logoff in order to clean up the disk space on the server, it also never gets deleted. In Windows XP this problem was not an issue. Now Windows saves the user's registry hive at the end of the 60-second delay and roams the profile correctly. In contrast to Windows 2000, when the application or service closes the registry key that locks the user profile, Windows XP and Windows Server 2003 unload the hive and free the memory consumed by the user profile. In cases where an application or service never releases the registry key, Windows XP will delete all profiles marked for deletion at the next reboot.

Non-Roaming Folders and Quotas on Profile Size

The way the users get their profiles depends on the profile type configured for them. Let us consider this process in more detail. For local profiles the procedure comprises the following steps:

❏ The user logs on. The operating system checks the list of user profiles located in `HKEY_LOCAL_MACHINE\SOFTWARE\Microsoft\WindowsNT\CurrentVersion\ ProfileList` (Fig. 10.13) to determine if a local profile exists for the user. If an entry exists, then this local profile is used. If a local profile is not found, and the computer is part of a domain, the operating system checks if a domain-wide default profile exists (it must be located on the domain controller's NETLOGON share in a folder named Default User). If a default domain-wide user profile exists, it will be copied to the following subfolder on the local computer: %*SystemDrive*%\Documents and Settings*Username*. If a default domain-wide user profile does not exist, then the local default profile is copied from the %*Systemdrive*%\Documents and Settings\Default User folder to the %*SystemDrive*%\Documents and Settings*Username* subfolder on the local computer.

❏ The user's registry hive (Ntuser.dat) is mapped to the HKEY_CURRENT_USER portion of the registry.

❏ When the user logs off, a profile is saved to the local hard disk of the computer.

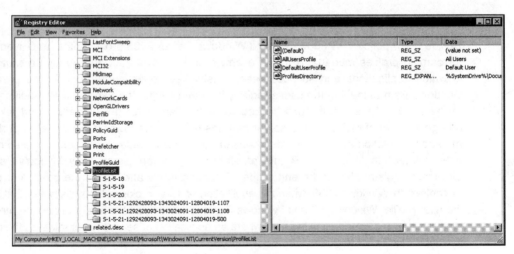

Fig. 10.13. The list of user profiles is stored in the registry under the HKEY_LOCAL_MACHINE\SOFTWARE\Microsoft\Windows NT\CurrentVersion\ ProfileList **key**

For roaming profiles this process is as follows:

❏ The user logs on, and Windows checks the list of user profiles stored in the registry under HKEY_LOCAL_MACHINE\SOFTWARE\Microsoft\WindowsNT\ CurrentVersion\ProfileList key to determine if a cached copy of the profile exists. If a local copy of the profile is not found, and the computer is part of a domain, Windows checks to determine if a domain-wide default profile exists in the Default User folder on the domain controller's NETLOGON share. If a default domain-wide user profile exists, it will be copied to the following subfolder on the local computer: %*SystemDrive*%\Documents and Settings\ *Username*. If a default domain-wide user profile does not exist, then the local default profile is copied from the %*Systemdrive*%\Documents and Settings\ Default User folder to the %*SystemDrive*%\Documents and Settings*Username* subfolder on the local computer.

❏ The user's registry hive (Ntuser.dat) is copied to the local cached copy of their user profile, and is mapped to the HKEY_CURRENT_USER portion of the registry. The contents of the local cached profile are compared with the copy of the profile on the server, and the two profiles are merged.

❏ The user can then run applications and edit documents as normal. When the user logs off, their local profile is copied to the path configured by the administrator. If a profile already exists on the server, the local profile is merged with the server copy.

Note

In Windows NT 4.0, the merge algorithm was based on the Xcopy command with full synchronization support. That means that there is only one master copy of the profile at any given time. When the user is logged on, the master profile is on the local computer, and when the user is not logged on, the master copy of his or her profile is on the server. This algorithm works fine in most cases, where a user logs on to only a single computer. However, a user who logs on to multiple computers at the same time might experience unexpected behavior. Windows XP and Windows Server 2003 eliminate this problem by introducing the profile merging at the file level. When a document or file is updated, the new algorithm compares the timestamp of the destination file with the timestamp of the source file. If the destination file is newer, it is not overwritten.

As was mentioned earlier, roaming user profiles are copied from the server to the client when the user logs on, and copied back when the user logs off. However, Windows 2000, Windows XP, and Windows Server 2003 include the per-user Local Settings folder within the user profile that is not copied during log on or log off sessions. Operating system components and other applications can store non-roaming per-user data in this folder. On the other hand, the IntelliMirror technology includes the Folder Redirection feature that allows administrators to redirect the location of specific user profile folders to a network location (from the user's point of view, this looks just like roaming, but in this case the user settings actually remain on the network share). Folder redirection can be used with all types of profiles, including local, roaming, or mandatory. Combining Folder Redirection with roaming profiles allows you to get all the benefits of roaming profiles and at the same time to minimize network traffic.

Table 10.3. lists the folders that roam with the profile by default, and indicates whether they can be redirected using Group Policy.

Table 10.3. Folders that Roam with the Profile

Folder Name	Description	Roams with Profile by default	Redirect with Group Policy
Application Data	Per-user roaming application data	Yes	Yes
Cookies	User's Internet Explorer cookies	Yes	No
Desktop		Yes	Yes
Favorites	User's Internet Explorer favorites	Yes	No
Local Settings	Temporary files and per-user non-roaming application data	No	No
My Documents	User's documents	Yes	Yes
NetHood		Yes	No
PrintHood		Yes	No
Recent	Shortcuts to recently used documents	Yes	No
Send To		Yes	No
Start Menu	User's personal start menu	Yes	Yes
Templates	Per-user customized templates	Yes	No

Scripts

Scripts represent powerful and handy administrative facilities that allow automating most routine tasks. As a matter of fact, most system administrators use logon and logoff scripts, which represent batch (BAT) or executable (EXE) files that run any time the user logs on or off from any of the networked workstations. Such scripts may contain operating system commands (for example, the ones that restore network connections or run applications), specify environment variables, such as PATH or TEMP, and many more.

Starting with Windows 2000, several enhancements have been added to this area. To remain compatible with earlier Windows NT versions, Windows 2000,

Windows XP, and Windows Server 2003 continue to keep the logon script that was used in Microsoft Windows NT 4.0. As you remember, already in Windows NT 4.0 logon scripts were assigned to individual user accounts. In Windows 2000, Windows XP, and Windows Server 2003, you assign logon scripts to individual users by typing the path to the logon script file in the **Logon script** field of the **Profile** tab in the **UserName Properties** dialog (see Fig. 10.11).

Note

For local users in Workgroup environment, use Computer Management MMC snap-in for this purpose. When your computer joins to an Active Directory domain, the same task is performed on domain controllers using Active Directory Users and Computers MMC snap-in.

When a user logs on with an account to which a logon script has been assigned (i.e., a path to the logon script for the user account appears in the **Logon script** field), the server locates and runs the script. Note that the entry in the **Logon script** box only specifies the file name (and optionally the relative path) of the logon script. The actual logon script is located on the server.

Windows 2000/XP and Windows Server 2003, in addition, provide a set of policy-driven scripts, including user logon, user logoff, computer startup, and computer shutdown scripts, which you can manage using the Group Policy snap-in (Fig. 10.14). In contrast to logon scripts assigned at the **Profile** tab of the *UserName* **Properties** window, which apply to individual users only, scripts assigned using the Group Policy apply to all the users and computers for which a particular Group Policy object applies.

Note

Microsoft assumes that on a Windows 2000 Server or in a Windows Server 2003 environment, Group Policy is the administrator's primary tool for defining and controlling how programs, network resources, and the operating system behave for users and computers in an organization. In an Active Directory environment, Group Policy is applied to users or computers on the basis of their membership in sites, domains, or organizational units. More information on Group Policy will be provided later in this chapter.

To run the Group Policy MMC snap-in, click **Start**, select the **Run** command, and type `gpedit.msc` into the **Open** field.

Note

You must be an administrator to add Group Policy to a Microsoft Management Console (MMC) and to use Group Policy in a saved console.

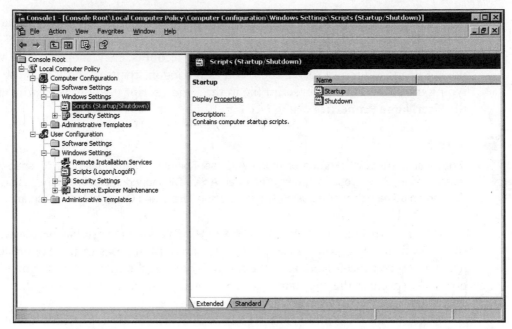

Fig. 10.14. In addition to Logon/Logoff, Windows 2000/XP and products of the Windows Server 2003 family provide Startup/Shutdown scripts

The Group Policy snap-in includes the following two extensions for script deployment:

☐ **Scripts (Startup/Shutdown).** After opening the Group Policy MMC snap-in, you can find these policies under **Local Computer Policy | Computer Configuration | Windows Settings**. Use this extension to specify the scripts that run when you start up and shut down the computer. To assign a startup or shutdown script, navigate to the **Scripts (Startup/Shutdown)** node in the console tree, go to the right pane and then double-click the script that you want to configure. Note that the script that you assign using this method will run on the LocalSystem account.

☐ **Scripts (Logon/Logoff).** Use this extension to specify the scripts that run when a user logs on or off the computer. To configure the user logon and logoff scripts, start the Group Policy snap-in, expand **Local Computer Policy | User Configuration | Windows Settings**, then click **Scripts (Logon/Logoff)**, go to the right pane and double-click the script that you want to configure. These scripts run on the User account and not on the Administrator account.

Also starting with Windows 2000, yet another improvement was made in the scripting area — Windows Script Host (WSH) 2.0 — a language-independent scripting host that includes support for Microsoft Visual Basic Scripting Edition (VBScript) and JScript scripting engines. WSH 2.0 is capable of creating simple but flexible and powerful scripts to automate network administration. Because WSH is language-independent, you're free to select any scripting language you prefer: Visual Basic Scripting Edition (VBScript), JScript, and Perl. WSH also supports COM, allowing you to enjoy the advantages of new technologies such as Windows Management Instrumentation (WMI) and Active Directory Services Interface (ADSI). Since Windows 2000 and its successors include Windows Script Host (WSH), all above-mentioned scripts can use it. This means that you can run the script when you click it on the Windows desktop or when you type the name of the script at the command prompt, and then press <Enter>.

Using WSH in Logon Scripts

We won't dive into the details here; instead, let's look at a small example of the logon script which edits the registry (after all, this is a book on the registry). Most end users are afraid of registry editing procedures. Because of this, you can write a small logon script for these users that customizes the system registry. WSH provides a convenient and easy technique for manipulating the registry using the following methods: regRead, regWrite, and regDelete.

An example of the code provided below changes the proxy settings stored in the registry under HKCU\Software\Microsoft\Windows\CurrentVersion\Internet Settings\ProxyServer. First of all, you need to read these settings using the regRead method. Then, using the regWrite method, you can overwrite the existing value (for example, replace the existing value by NEWPROXY:80). Finally, you need to make sure that the changes you've introduced are correct. This is done using the regRead method:

```
...
sub regProxy
   prefix = _
      "HKCU\Software\Microsoft\Windows\CurrentVersion\Internet Settings\"
      WScript.Echo "Old ProxyServer settings: " & wshShell.regRead(prefix & _
      "ProxyServer")
   wshShell.regWrite prefix & "ProxyServer", "MYPROXY:80"
```

```
        WScript.Echo  "New ProxyServer settings: " & wshShell.regRead(prefix & _
            "ProxyServer")
    end sub
    ...
```

Group Policy Overview

The System policies provide another instrument to help system administrators control user access to the network and manage desktop settings, including data sharing and configuring system settings. The system policy represents registry settings that are automatically loaded when the user logs on to the system. The main difference between system policies and user profiles is that the system policy is applicable to users, user groups, and individual computers. Administrators can specify, modify, and support registry settings for each of the components just listed. By combining system policies for individual users, specific computers from which the user logs on, and for user groups, to which the user may belong, the administrator can get complete control over the types of user environments and user rights and permissions. To define the system policy settings, the administrator simply creates system policy templates.

The System Policy Editor tool was first introduced in the Windows NT 4.0 operating system. It allowed administrators to specify configuration settings for users and computers, and store these settings in the Windows NT registry. Using this utility, administrators could manage user work environments and specify configuration settings for all Windows NT 4.0 computers (both Workstation and Server). Starting with Windows 2000, this tool was replaced by the Group Policy MMC snap-in, which extends the capabilities of the System Policy Editor (SPE) and provides many additional options for managing client computer configurations, including registry based policies, security settings, scripts, and folder redirection. Group policy settings specified by the administrator are stored in the Group Policy Object (GPO), which, in turn, is associated with one of the Active Directory objects (site, domain, or organizational unit).

Group Policy implemented in newer versions of Windows NT-based operating systems has many significant advantages over the Windows NT 4.0 system policy (not to mention Windows 95/98). These advantages include:

❑ The possibility of associating with Active Directory objects (sites, domains, or organizational units). The policy associated with the Active Directory container influences all other computers and all the users within that container (site, domain, or organizational unit).

❑ Extended configuration capabilities. Both users and computers may be joined into groups.

❑ Improved security in comparison to Windows NT 4.0.

❑ Windows NT 4.0 policies were stored in the user profiles (this was sometimes called "*tattooing* the registry"). The specified registry setting using the System Policy Editor retained its value until it was changed by the administrator for the given policy, or manually changed by the user who edited the registry directly. This situation represented a problem (for example, when you decided to change group membership). This problem has been solved with Windows 2000, because registry settings specified by the group policy are written to the protected registry keys (\Software\Policies and \Software\Microsoft\Windows\CurrentVersion\ Policies). When the group policy object (GPO) is no longer applicable, these settings are cleared.

Administrative Templates

The System Policy Editor utility included with Windows NT 4.0 Server uses administrative templates (ADM files). These templates allow you to define which registry settings are available for editing using the System Policy Editor.

Windows 2000 ADM files also specify registry settings that can be modified using the UI provided by the MMC Group Policy snap-in. The policy settings related to the user who logs on are written to the registry under the HKEY_CURRENT_USER root key (HKCU). The policy settings that relate to the software installed on the computer, and to the computer itself are written to the registry under the HKEY_LOCAL_MACHINE root key (HKLM).

ADM files are text files containing the hierarchy of categories and subcategories. These categories and subcategories define fully qualified registry settings that can be modified using the Group Policy user interface. The term "fully qualified registry setting" means that these settings also specify registry paths to the settings that will be modified using the Group Policy snap-in when you select the appropriate option.

Security Settings

The Group Policy MMC snap-in allows you to specify the security configuration applicable to one or more security areas. The security configuration specified using Group Policy is then applied to all computers within the Active Directory container.

Group Policy, which allows administrators to specify security settings, extends the existing operating system functionality. For example, the following capabilities are provided:

❑ *Account Policies.* These are security settings related to passwords, the account lockout policy, and Kerberos-related policy (within Windows 2000 domains).

❑ *Local Policies.* This is a group of settings that specify the auditing policy, user permissions, and other security settings. The Local policies allow administrators to configure access to the computer both locally and through the network, and specify the events that should be audited.

❑ *Event Log.* These are security settings that control the security of the system event logs (Application, Security, and System), accessed using Event Viewer.

❑ *Restricted Groups.* These settings allow you to specify the users who belong to restricted groups. Thus, the administrator can enforce the security policy in relation to groups like Enterprise Administrators, for example. If another user is added to this restricted group (for example, when there's an emergency and it's necessary to perform an urgent job), the user will automatically be deleted from this group when the group policy comes into force next time.

❑ *System Services.* These options manage the starting mode and security handles for the system and network services.

❑ *Registry.* Used for configuring the security settings for registry keys, including access control, auditing, and owner rights. Security settings for the registry keys are specified according to the same inheritance modes that are used in all Windows 2000 hierarchical structures. Microsoft officially recommends using access rights inheritance when defining security settings for top-level objects, and that users redefine security settings for child objects only when necessary.

❑ *File System.* Used for configuring security settings related to file system objects, including ACLs, auditing, and owner rights.

Incremental Security Templates

Windows 2000, Windows XP, and Windows Server 2003 include incremental security templates. By default, these templates are stored in the *%SystemRoot%*Security\Templates folder. These predefined templates may be further customized using the Security Templates MMC snap-in, and then imported into the Security Settings extension of the MMC Group Policy snap-in.

Incremental security templates have been developed for step-by-step modifications of the standard security settings.

Note

Incremental security templates may be applied only if you've installed a new copy of the operating system, and only when you've installed it on the NTFS partition. If you've installed the OS on the NTFS partition as an upgrade of Windows NT 4.0 or an even earlier Windows NT version, use the standard security template (Basic). The Basic security template is used to configure the system according to the standard security requirements applied by default. Windows 2000/XP and Windows Server 2003 systems installed on FAT partitions can't be protected.

Incremental security templates are listed in Table 10.4.

Table 10.4. Incremental Security Templates

Configuration	Computer Type	Template	Description
Compatible	Workstations and servers	Compatws.inf	Intended for organizations where most users don't need to be included in the Power Users group.
Secure	Workstations, servers, and domain controllers	Securews.inf and Securedc.inf	This configuration provides a higher level of security, including account policy, auditing, and access rights to certain registry keys that directly relate to the system security.
High Secure	Workstations, servers, and domain controllers	Hisecws.inf and Hisecdc.inf	This configuration is intended for computers that work in a pure Windows 2000 or Windows Server 2003 environment. It requires that all network communications be signed by a digital signature and encrypted. Thus, computers that are configured using the High Secure template can't interact with computers running earlier versions of the OS.

How Group Policy Is Stored

Group Policy Objects (GPO) store their information in the Group Policy Container and in the Group Policy Template. The Group Policy Container (GPC) is an Active Directory container that stores Group Policy Object (GPO) properties. It can include nested containers for storing information of the group policy related to both users and computers.

Group Policy Templates

Group Policy Objects (GPOs) store their policy information in the folder structure called Group Policy Template (GPT). GPTs are stored in the \Policies subfolder within the \Sysvol folder on domain controllers.

When modifying the GPO, the template is assigned a directory name, which is actually a Globally Unique Identifier (GUID) of the Group Policy Object that was modified. An example of the name of the Group Policy Template folder is shown below:

```
%SystemRoot%\sysvol\<SYSVOL>\<Domain_Name>\Policies
    \{47636445-af79-11d0-91fe-080036644603}
```

 Note

Notice that the \<SYSVOL> folder becomes a shared directory named SYSVOL.

The Gpt.ini File

The root level of each GPT folder contains the Gpt.ini file, which keeps the following information for all valid group policy objects:

❑ Client extensions of the Group Policy snap-in that contain the user or computer data within the group policy object
❑ Whether or not the settings specifying the user or computer policy are disabled
❑ Version number for the Group Policy snap-in extension used to create the Group Policy Object

Local Group Policy Objects

Local Group Policy Objects exist on each computer. By default, they only contain the security policy. Local Group Policy Objects are stored in the %SystemRoot%\System32\GroupPolicy folder, and users only have Read access to the folder (administrators and the operating system have full control access to this folder).

Group Policy Template Folders

The Group Policy Template folder contains the following subfolders:

❑ \Adm — contains all ADM-files used by the Group Policy Template (GPT).
❑ \Scripts — contains all the scripts used by the GPT.

❑ *User* — contains the Registry.pol file, which lists all registry settings that should be in force in relation to the users. When the user logs on, the system reads this file and loads it to the HKEY_CURRENT_USER registry key. The folder contains the following subfolders:

- *Apps* — contains all files used by Windows Installer
- *Files* — contains a list of files that need to be installed

❑ *Machine* — contains the Registry.pol file that lists all the registry settings, which should be in force in relation to the computers. When the computer is initialized, the Registry.pol file is loaded into the HKEY_LOCAL_MACHINE root key. This folder contains the following subfolders:

- *Apps* — contains all the files that are used by Windows Installer
- *Files* — contains a list of files that need to be installed
- *Microsoft\Windows NT\SecEdit* — stores the file that contains security settings (Gpttmpl.inf)

The \User and \Machine subfolders are created automatically during installation, and all the other folders are created when you install the group policy.

The Registry.pol Files

The Administrative Templates extension of the MMC Group Policy snap-in contains information about the group policy templates such as ASCII formatted files like the one named Registry.pol. These files contain individual registry settings specified by the system administrator using the Group Policy snap-in. As I discussed earlier, these settings must be loaded into the registry under HKLM and HKCU keys.

For each group policy template, there are two Registry.pol files: one for computer configuration in the \Machine folder, and another for user configuration in the \User folder.

▶ *Note*

Format of the Registry.pol files in Windows 2000/XP is different from the Registry.pol format in Windows NT 4.0 and Windows 95. Notice that you need to use Registry.pol files only with the operating system for which these files were created.

The Registry.pol files created in Windows NT 4.0 using the System Policy Editor tool were binary files. In contrast, Registry.pol files created by the Group Policy snap-in in Windows 2000 are text files that contain binary strings.

Registry.pol files created in Windows 2000/XP contain the header and registry settings. The header contains version data and a signature, and it has a DWORD format. Registry settings are specified in the following format:

```
[key; value; type; size; data]
```

where:

key — the path to the registry key (notice that you don't need to specify the root key; for example, HKEY_LOCAL_MACHINE or HKEY_CURRENT_USER). That's because the file location itself (in the \User or \Machine folders) specifies the root key where this key should be loaded.

value — list of the registry keys to be deleted (semicolon used as a separator), for example: **DeleteKeys NoRun;NoFind*.

type — data type. Notice that the file format supports all registry data types (see *Chapter 1*). However, the Administrative Templates snap-in only distinguishes between REG_DWORD, REG_EXPAND_SZ, and REG_SZ.

size — the size of the data field (in bytes).

data — this is the data itself.

Summary

In this chapter, we discussed the user profile files and system policies. The necessary instructions (a survival guide) on how to use system policies to introduce registry modifications were also provided were.

CHAPTER 11

Active Directory Settings in the Registry

*Nature, it seems, is the popular name
for milliards and milliards and milliards
of particles playing their infinite game
of billiards and billiards and billiards.*

Piet Hein
Grooks. Atomiriades

Nature, in general, and contemporary computing technologies, in particular, are extremely complex. When you dive into the details, your corporate network — comprising hundreds of servers and thousands of client workstations with their individual configurations — will seem like "milliards and milliards and milliards of particles". These particles can take on lives of their own, interacting with one another (sometimes in unpredictable ways) as if playing an infinite game of "billiards and billiards and billiards". This can drive to despair even the most dedicated and qualified system administrator! As outlined in *Chapter 1*, the introduction of the system registry was mainly intended to eliminate this administrative nightmare. The registry concept was an attempt to improve system manageability from a single source — the *registry database,* which provides a foundation for all system-wide hardware and software parameters and all custom user settings that exist in Windows. The registry's advantages and disadvantages were discussed in depth, and in the end, this approach proved successful. Today, the Windows-user community takes for granted the existence of the registry and its presence in all operating systems of the Windows family.

Gradually, however, it became evident that the registry alone is not sufficient. Although some difficulties were eliminated, other problems arose. New types of applications appeared, such as Enterprise Resource Planning (ERP), which required directory services to be implemented. For the moment, nearly every company has at least one directory service, and, in many cases, several directories of information. Traditional directory services were based on the X.500 standard for a hierarchical, extensible data store. Today, many other types of directories can be found that don't fit the X.500 model. In addition to ERP, typical directories within companies include network operating system (OS) directories such as Novell Directory Services (NDS) and Microsoft Windows NT 4.0's Security Account Manager (SAM) database.

As far back as 1996, Microsoft began asking its largest enterprise customers which improvements were most needed in the next release of its OS. It became evident that corporate clients had two urgent needs: implementation of the global directory service and reduction of the cost of managing and maintaining Windows NT desktops and servers in large enterprise environments.

To address these needs, Microsoft has implemented Active Directory (AD), a new global directory service that could be considered an extension of the machine-based registry. It is the most significant addition introduced with the release of Windows 2000 into the Windows NT product line. Perhaps most noticeably, AD replaces the SAM database as a repository for domain security principals, such as users and computers. But it does much more than that. Being an extensible, hierarchical directory service, AD provides a solid foundation for developing directory-enabled applications (i.e., applications that use the directory as a store and a source of information to facilitate many types of value-added computing).

Note

As outlined in *Chapter 9*, although the SAM database has been replaced by the Active Directory (AD) database, it still retains its importance. First, the SAM database is now part of AD, and AD serves as a kind of "super-registry", storing all user and machine information as well as a host of other objects, including group policies and applications. Second, SAM continues to store local accounts, and, if your computer is running Windows 2000, Windows XP, or Windows Server 2003 and does not participate in a domain, the SAM database remains the main storage of the user- and group-account information. Among other things, it is important to note that the Directory Service Restore Mode Administrator password, which is separate from the Administrator password stored in Active Directory, resides in the local SAM (%*SystemRoot*%\System32\Config\SAM).

In Windows 2000 and Windows Server 2003 domains, AD now serves as a central repository of all types of user and machine information, as well as of all other objects, such as printers, shared volumes, group policies, and, of course, applications. So, what about the registry? Did it retain its importance? How does it fit within this new pattern? The best way to understand these new concepts is to think about the system registry as a non-replicated database present on any local machine running Windows NT/2000/XP or Windows Server 2003. Then, think of AD as a centralized, replicated registry extension, providing the following enhancements and advantages:

- ❑ New capabilities for managing domain users and client computers.
- ❑ Active Directory-based Group Policies that make it possible to create centralized security templates to control Registry security on all computers and devices in AD domains.
- ❑ Software installation features that allow the administrator to centrally manage application installations and thus manage how registry modifications are made to computers and users. Application deployment through the Windows Installer technology provides a new way of distributing registry changes to computers and users.
- ❑ The Class Store — a set of AD objects that acts like a centralized version of the HKEY_CLASSES_ROOT key of the local registry.

These new features come with some challenges. They directly affect the system registry and influence your ability to modify the registry or troubleshoot registry problems. In this chapter, I will concentrate on these new interrelationships, including AD features that help you modify and manage the local registry on a computer running Windows 2000/XP or Windows Server 2003.

Active Directory Emergency Recovery

Similar to the system registry, which is often referred to as the "heart and soul" of any local computer running Windows NT, Windows 2000, Windows XP, or Windows Server 2003, Active Directory is the "heart and soul" of a corporate Windows-based network. This essential network component must be available to applications and users at all times. There are other similarities between the system registry and the AD, but this is the most important one. In contrast to the registry, which is a local configuration database, AD is a replicated database, and as such, it is vulnerable to the same problems that can damage any distributed database, including:

❏ A corrupted or invalid database schema (defines the structure of the database — what type of data it contains and how that data is arranged)
❏ Missing DNS records
❏ Damaged or corrupted information
❏ Human errors, including accidental errors of the system administrator

Consequently, if you have implemented AD domains in your organization, it is imperative that you develop disaster-prevention and disaster-recovery procedures for your AD infrastructure.

Physical AD Structure

As previously mentioned in this chapter, the Active Directory information, which now replaces the SAM registry hive, is physically stored as an on-disk database. The actual database file is called Ntds.dit, and by default, it resides under *%SystemRoot%*\ntds folder.

Note

On Windows 2000 Server or Windows Server 2003, a pristine copy of the AD database is stored in the *%SystemRoot%*\system32\ntds.dit file. This copy is used when a member server is promoted to a domain controller using the DCPromo utility.

In *Chapter 1*, I introduced mechanisms implemented by Microsoft to ensure that changes to the system registry are consistently and successfully written and are not easily corrupted by system crashes or hard-disk problems. Since AD is a centralized registry storing all user- and computer-related information for an entire organization, it would be logical to expect that similar mechanisms are implemented for the Ntds.dit database. The Ntds.dit is a database file that uses Microsoft's Extensible Storage Engine (ESE) technology, also known as Jet. All changes to AD are transactional, which means that each discrete change is committed to the database individually. For example, if a system administrator resets the password for one AD user, the administrator would be making a single, discrete transaction.

To ensure that all database transactions occur consistently, AD implements a circular log. When a change is made to the AD database, it is written first to the copy of AD running in memory on the domain controller on which the change was made. The change is also written to a change log file stored on disk. If you look in the directory where the Ntds.dit file is stored on a given domain controller (Fig. 11.1), you'll see several files in addition to the database file:

❏ Three log files — Edb.log (the main log file for the AD database), Res1.log, and Res2.log. Each log file is roughly 10 MB. Res1.log and Res2.log files serve as reserves in case the disk partition that stores these log files runs out of disk space. If this happens, reserve log files ensure that there is enough space on the disk to write any uncommitted transactions to the database before shutting down the server.

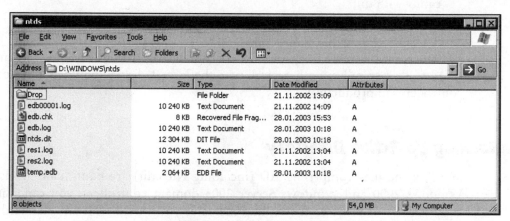

Fig. 11.1. The contents of the %*SystemRoot*%\ntds folder on
a given domain controller

❏ Transaction checkpoint file — Edb.chk. This file keeps track of the last transaction successfully committed to the Ntds.dit file. If the domain controller crashes before all in-memory changes are committed to the Ntds.dit file, the checkpoint file would allow a quick and easy replay of any transactions in the log that hadn't been committed before the crash.

▶ *Note*

The checkpoint file isn't required for AD to recover itself after a crash. But recovering without it takes much longer because the system must scan the entire transaction log to determine which changes were committed to the database file.

When designing and implementing AD infrastructure, it is essential to take into account performance, fault tolerance and disaster recovery. While promoting a member server into a domain controller using the DCPromo utility, you're given the choice of where you want to store the Ntds.dit file (the AD database), the SYSVOL directory (a required shared directory that exists on domain controllers), and the AD log files. Note that there are lots of recommendations for choosing the right configuration for servers that you plan to promote to AD domain controllers. In general, the ideal configuration of a domain controller must have several physical disks. Most authors, including those of Microsoft's official documentation, recommend the following disk configuration for an AD domain controller:

❑ One physical disk for the operating system files and page files
❑ One physical disk for the Ntds.dit database file, which tends to grow significantly with time
❑ One physical disk for AD log files

At a minimum, try to ensure that the system page file and AD log files are on separate disk spindles; both typically see the largest disk activity when a domain controller is in production.

Backing Up Active Directory

Since all the files comprising AD (including Ntds.dit) are continually in use on Windows 2000 and Windows Server 2003 domain controllers, you can't simply copy the AD database to the backup media as you would with any standard user data file (Fig. 11.2). Note that in this respect, the AD database behaves similarly to the SAM registry hive. (This was shown in *Chapter 9*.)

Fig. 11.2. During an attempt to copy the AD database of the running Windows 2000 or Windows Server 2003 domain controller, the system displays this error message

As explained in *Chapter 2*, the built-in Backup utility enables you to perform an online backup of Active Directory. A backup of AD is performed whenever you include System State data as part of a backup on a Windows 2000 or Windows Server 2003 domain controller.

Note

Although the built-in Backup utility supplied with Windows 2000 Server and Windows Server 2003 can perform an online backup of the Active Directory database, some organizations may prefer to use more robust third-party applications. If you want a third-party backup solution, chose a product compatible with your OS (Windows 2000 or Windows Server 2003). The product must be able to backup Active Directory or provide a separate add-on component capable of performing this task. Note that legacy versions of backup products cannot understand the AD format and are unable to back it up. Several leading manufacturers in the field of Windows Servers backup and recovery already supply the products supporting Windows Server 2003. For example, VERITAS (**http://www.veritas.com**) has released the BackupExec 9.0 for Windows Servers, which includes support for Windows 2000 and Windows Server 2003.

Restoring Active Directory

Physically restoring the Active Directory database on the domain controller from a backup is a straightforward procedure. However, there are some important issues that need to be taken into account when performing any AD restore operation, including:

- On networks with more than one domain controller, the AD database is automatically replicated and updated among domain controllers. Therefore, the AD database exists in several locations.
- You can perform AD backup only in its entirety, using a full backup. It is impossible perform an incremental backup of AD.

For example, if you decide to restore the AD database from the backup, you will need to make the following decisions:

- Do you need to restore AD on a local domain controller only? If the problem is limited to the local domain controller, and if other domain controllers contain valid replicas of the AD database, you can perform a non-authoritative restore. After you regain functionality on the failed domain controller, it will receive updates from other domain controllers using AD replication to bring its data store up-to-date.

❏ Have other domain controllers also failed, or do you think their AD replicas may contain invalid or undesirable data? In either situation, you'll need to perform authoritative restore. To do so, you must manually designate the copy of the AD database that you want to restore. The local domain controller will be authoritative, and the "master" copy of the AD database from this domain controller will be replicated to other domain controllers.

Performing a Non-Authoritative Restore

It makes sense to perform non-authoritative restore if only the local domain controller has failed; other domain controllers on your network should be up and running, and AD replicas on those domain controllers should be intact and valid. In this case, you will have two options:

❏ Simply reinstall the OS (Windows 2000 Server or Windows Server 2003), join the newly installed server to a domain, and promote it to a domain controller. The normal AD replication process will then repopulate the domain controller with current directory information.

❏ Start the failed domain controller in Directory Services Restore Mode, and then restore the AD database from the backup copy.

To use the second approach:

1. Start the failed domain controller and press <F8> at the **Boot Loader** menu.
2. When the **Windows Advanced Options Menu** appears, select the **Directory Services Restore Mode (Windows domain controllers only)** option.
3. Once you select **Directory Services Restore Mode,** Windows will start in a safe mode and ask you to log on. Log on as a member of the Administrators group.

▶ *Note*

The processes that take place when any Windows NT-based operating system (including Windows 2000, Windows XP, and Windows Server 2003) is starting up, as well as the Boot Loader menu and the Windows Advanced Options Menu, were covered in detail in *Chapter 6*.

4. After successful logon, run your backup application and use the option to restore AD. For example, using the built-in Backup utility, you must select the backup media and then set the **System State** checkbox (Fig. 11.3).

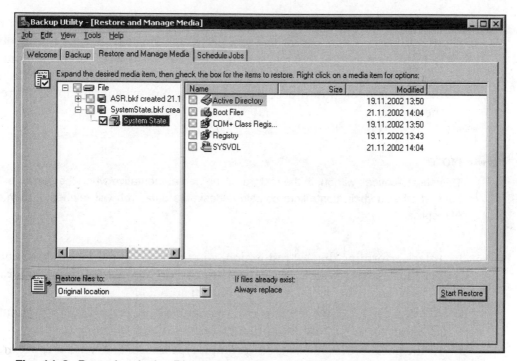

Fig. 11.3. Restoring Active Directory as part of the System State data restore process

Note

If you restore System State data to restore AD and don't designate an alternate location for the restored data, you'll overwrite all System State data in the current installation with that from the backup.

5. Having set the required restore options, click the **Start Restore** button. Once the restore procedure is accomplished, Backup will display a dialog prompting you to restart the domain controller. Click **Yes**.

Once the restored domain controller restarts, it should begin participating in AD replication and receiving directory updates from the other domain controllers.

Performing an Authoritative Restore

Authoritative restore is required when other domain controllers fail or if their replicas of the AD database contain corrupted or invalid data. In either case:

1. Manually designate the copy of the AD database that you restore.

2. Perform an authoritative restore of AD. This is similar to performing a non-authoritative restore except that it requires an extra step after the restore operation (using either the built-in Backup utility or a third-party tool) is complete. Therefore, proceed as though performing a non-authoritative restore, until the last step of this procedure — answer **No**, when prompted to restart the server.

Note

This step is critical; without it, the restore will be non-authoritative when the server restarts. Thus, if other domain controllers contain undesirable data, you will reinherit it from other AD replicas.

3. After performing the AD restoration, you will need to tag the restored copy of the AD database as an authoritative copy. To do so, open a **Command Prompt** window and issue the following command: `ntdsutil`.

4. At the `ntdsutil:` prompt, type `authoritative restore` and press <Enter>. This puts `ntdsutil` into Authoritative Restore mode.

5. At the `authoritative restore:` prompt, type `restore database` to set the entire database you just restored as authoritative. Alternately, you can tag as authoritative any subtree of the restored AD database (for example, an individual organizational unit). To do so, type in the LDAP (Lightweight Directory Access Protocol) string identifying the portion of AD being authoritatively restored, for example: `restore subtree OU=managers,DC=Alist,DC=com`

6. Answer **Yes** when prompted to confirm authoritative restore.

7. Select the **Quit** option, then press <Enter> twice to exit back to a command prompt.

8. Close the Command Prompt session, then restart the computer.

When the system restarts, all other domain controllers in this domain will designate the AD database (or a portion of it) as the authoritative "master" copy and use it to reinitiate the contents of their own AD replicas.

Note

When you perform an authoritative restore of AD, you'll lose any object and schema configuration data created after the AD backup was created (or in the branch of AD being authoritatively restored).

Resetting the Recovery Console Administrator Password on a Domain Controller

When you promote your computer running Windows 2000 Server or Windows Server 2003 to a domain controller, you enter a Directory Service Restore Mode Administrator password, which is used by the Recovery Console. This password is required to login to Directory Services Restore Mode; without it, you will be unable to perform the AD restore procedures. This password is separate from the Administrator password stored in Active Directory. As previously noted in this chapter, the Directory Service Restore Mode Administrator password is stored in the local SAM registry hive (%*SystemRoot*%\System32\Config\SAM).

To reset this password:

1. Shut down and restart the domain controller.
2. When the Boot Loader screen appears, press <F8> to open the **Advanced Windows Options Menu**.
3. Select the **Directory Service Restore Mode** option and log on as Administrator or as a member of the local Administrators group. (Notice that you already need the password.)
4. Use the Local User and Groups MMC snap-in or issue the following command from the command prompt: net user Administrator *.
5. Shut down and restart.

Note

As previously mentioned, if you have forgotten the password, you will not be able to login. Consequently, you will not be able to use the Directory Service Restore Mode to perform the AD restore operation or to reset the Directory Service Restore Mode Administrator password. However, if you remember (or guess) the original Administrator password used when Windows 2000 Server or Windows Server 2003 was installed, you can resolve this situation by following these steps:

1. Perform an alternate installation of Windows 2000/XP or Windows Server 2003 to a different drive. During installation, specify a new computer name.
2. Access the files of the Windows installation for which you need to reset the password, and replace the %*SystemRoot*%\System32\Config\SAM registry hive with the SAM registry hive created during the original installation (this will be the %*SystemRoot*%\ Repair\SAM file).

If you don't remember the original Administrator password of your Windows 2000 Server or Windows Server 2003 installation, demote the domain controller and repromote it.

Group Policy Objects

Starting with Windows NT 4.0, Microsoft introduced System Policy, a mechanism for using the registry to "lock down" specific portions of user desktops to prevent users from tweaking the configuration. System Policy was a significant step forward in centralized administration. However, it didn't completely address most enterprise issues related to reducing the Total Cost of Ownership (TCO), such as:

❏ Software distribution
❏ Configuration management
❏ Security management

Because of this, Microsoft continued its research and developed Group Policy Objects (GPOs), which, starting with Windows 2000, have replaced System Policy.

▶ *Note*

Group Policy is implemented only on Windows 2000 and later. Windows NT 4.0 doesn't support the storage or processing GPOs. However, Windows 2000 and its successors can process the old-style Windows NT 4.0 System Policies (such as Ntconfig.pol) when a user logs on to a Windows NT 4.0 domain from a computer running Windows 2000, Windows XP, or Windows Server 2003.

A local GPO exists on every workstation or server running Windows 2000, Windows XP, or Windows Server 2003. By default, a local GPO is stored in the folder %*SystemRoot*%\System32\GroupPolicy. The local GPO is a standalone object; you must manage it on each computer running Windows 2000 or later using the MMC Group Policy snap-in. Except for its prominence on individual computers, Group Policy shows its power in the AD infrastructure. For example, some of the GPO capabilities available in an AD-based domain environment (centralized software deployment, folder redirection, etc.) are not available on local GPOs. For GPOs to fulfill their real promise, it is necessary to deploy Active Directory and start migrating all workstations and servers to Windows 2000 or later.

One of the key features in Microsoft's Change and Configuration Management (CCM) strategy is the ability to use AD as a kind of application repository. For example, in AD infrastructure you can "advertise" applications such as Word, Excel, or Visio as AD objects. These can be distributed to and installed by end users, depending upon where the objects related to the users or their computers reside in the directory. The name of the feature you use for this advertisement function is Software Installation.

Specifically, Software Installation is defined within a Group Policy Object (GPO). GPOs are AD objects that can be applied to a local machine, site, domain, or organizational unit (OU). Similarly to Group Policy in Windows 2000, Group Policies in Windows Server 2003 can be applied to "containers": entire sites, domains, or OUs. A GPO is linked to a container and applied only to the computers or users whose accounts exist within it. It is rarely efficient or practical to implement site policies, so most policies will be implemented at the domain or OU level. In addition to domain policies, a local Group Policy is configured and can be adjusted on individual workstations or servers.

▶ *Note*

The acronym LSDOU (Local, Site, Domain, OU) is used to describe the cumulative order in which GPOs are applied to users and machines. Each policy is applied during boot or logon. The local policy is applied first, then the domain policy, then the OU policy. Even within these containers, GPO application is cumulative. For example, if we have three OUs — OU1, OU2, and OU3 — the policies linked to OU1 are applied to the users and computers listed in OU2. Policies in OU1 and OU2 are applied to OU3. If a setting is not configured in a previous GPO, the new GPO's setting will be applied. If the new GPO and the old GPO have a conflicting setting, the conflict is resolved by applying the new GPO's setting. But if this setting is not configured, the previous one will remain.

It is important to understand the affect GPOs have on the system registry and how they interrelate and interact with it. GPOs are multifunction AD objects, which comprise multiple "nodes" (Fig. 11.4). Each node within a GPO provides a different kind of control over computers (**Computer Configuration** node) or users (**User Configuration** node).

Table 11.1 summarizes the most common per-computer and per-user nodes available in GPOs.

Table 11.1. Available Functionality Nodes in Group Policy Objects

Computer or user: Node name	Description
Computer: Software Settings: Software Installation	Computer-based deployment of applications
Computer: Windows Settings: Security Settings	Computer-based configuration of security (includes items such as account policy, audit policy, and event log configurations)
Computer: Windows Settings: Scripts-Startup & Shutdown	Specification of computer startup and shutdown scripts

continues

Table 11.1 Continued

Computer or user: Node name	Description
Computer: Administrative Templates	Windows NT 4.0-style System Policy, which enforces changes to the HKLM registry key
User: Software Settings: Software Installation	User-based deployment of applications
User: Internet Explorer Maintenance	Used to set Internet Explorer preferences and "branding" settings per user
User: Windows Settings: Security Settings	Configuration of user-specific IP Security and public-key usage policies
User: Windows Settings: Scripts-Logon and Logoff	Specification of user-specific logon and logoff scripts
User: Remote Installation Services	Configuration options for people using Remote Install Service to install Windows 2000/XP or Windows Server 2003
User: Administrative Templates	Windows NT 4.0-style System Policy, which enforces changes to the HKCU registry key

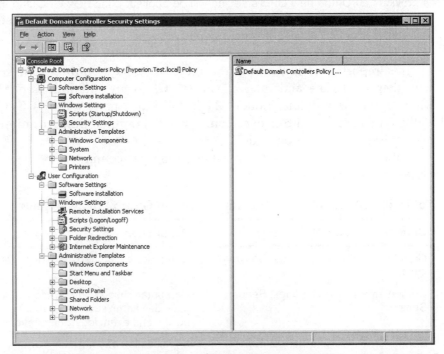

Fig. 11.4. GPOs are multifunction AD objects composed of multiple "nodes", each providing a different control over computers or users.

Concerning our discussion of AD and Group Policy interrelationship with the registry, the most interesting nodes to us are **Software Installation** and **Administrative Templates**.

Note

GPOs are applied to user objects and computer objects only. They are not applied to security groups. However, the effect of a GPO can be filtered by security groups. That is, you can have a GPO *assigned* to a particular OU (all of its users and computers) but restrict how that GPO is *applied* based on the particular security group to which those users or computers belong.

One more thing to note about GPOs is their physical makeup. As outlined in *Chapter 10*, GPOs are composed of two physical "pieces": the Group Policy Template (GPT) and the Group Policy Container (GPC). The first piece, the GPT, is composed of a set of files and folders that are replicated to all domain controllers in an AD domain. By default, GPOs are replicated as part of the SYSVOL share, which is created automatically on all Windows 2000 and Windows Server 2003 domain controllers. Files contained in the SYSVOL share are automatically replicated on the same schedule as the Active Directory replication. The NT File Replication Service (NTFRS) is responsible for replicating SYSVOL. The SYSVOL share resides in *%SystemRoot%*\sysvol\sysvol for a given domain controller. The source files for SYSVOL, however, are kept in the *%SystemRoot%*\sysvol\domain folder. If you expand this folder, you see a Policies subfolder. In this Policies subfolder, you see several folders with names that look like GUIDs (Globally Unique Identifiers) which they are — for the corresponding GPOs in the directory. To view a GPO's GUID using the Group Policy MMC snap-in, right-click the required GPO name and select the **Properties** command from the context menu. The GUID is listed as the "Unique name" for that GPO on the **General** tab or the GPO properties window (Fig. 11.5).

There are a couple of ways to bring up the Group Policy tool, but perhaps the easiest is to load the Active Directory Users and Computers MMC snap-in. Right-click on a Domain or OU name and select **Properties** from the context menu. You'll see a **Group Policy** tab (Fig. 11.6), which lists all available GPOs at that level and lets you edit them. You can also load the Group Policy tool by typing gpedit.msc from a command line. However, when you launch the tool this way, it is automatically focused on the local GPO for that computer, rather than a domain, OU, or site-based GPO.

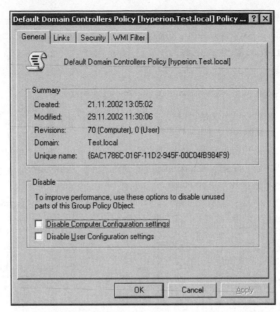

Fig. 11.5. The GUID is listed as the "Unique name" for a specific GPO on the **General** tab or the GPO properties window.

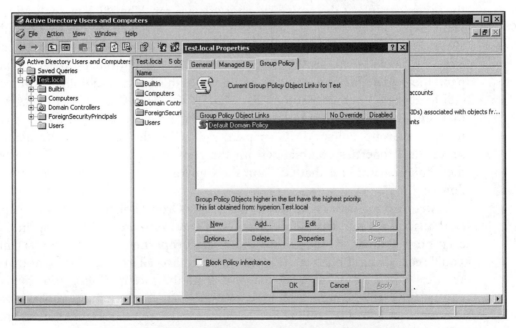

Fig. 11.6. The **Group Policy** tab of the GPO properties window

The example illustrating a directory structure for one of the GPOs in the SYSVOL folder (Fig. 11.7) shows that a typical GPO contains a lot of nested directories. Files in each of these nested directories are replicated to each domain controller within a given domain. For the purposes of this chapter, we'll explore only those pieces of GPO that directly relate to registry, namely, the following subdirectories and their contents:

❑ \Adm
❑ \Machine\Applications*.*
❑ \User\Applications*.*

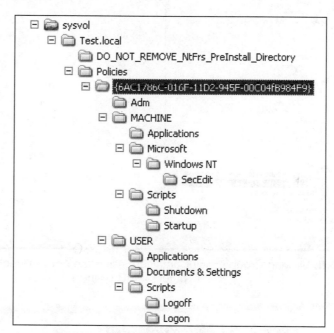

Fig. 11.7. The example directory structure for one of the GPOs stored in the SYSVOL folder

In addition to the Group Policy Template, a GPO is composed of a Group Policy Container (GPC). The GPC, in contrast to the Group Policy Template, represents the part of the GPO that resides in Active Directory itself. Thus, the GPC is a set of Active Directory Objects that are generated when you first create a GPO. To view the GPC structure within Active Directory, proceed as follows:

1. Start the Active Directory Users and Computers MMC snap-in, and select the **Advanced Features** command from the **View** menu.

2. Expand the console tree, drill down to your Active Directory domain, and it locate the folder named System within. The System folder contains a subfolder named Policies, within which you will find GUID-based folders corresponding to Group Policy Objects existing within your domain (Fig. 11.8).

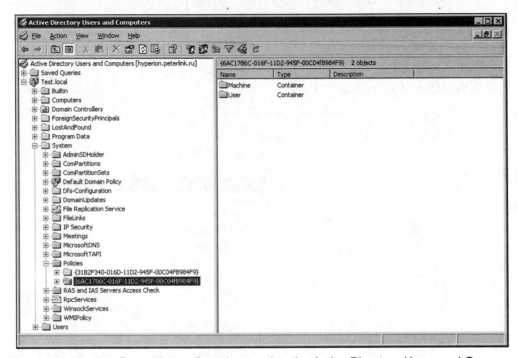

Fig. 11.8. Viewing Group Policy Containers using the Active Directory Users and Computers MMC snap-in

Windows Server 2003 Improvements to Group Policies

As might be expected, computer-specific nodes and their settings are applied to computer objects only when the computer processes the GPO — usually at system startup and periodically thereafter. (These can be configured via Group Policy.) However, user objects process user-specific settings only at time of user logon. These settings also can be updated manually in intervals configured via Group Policy. Hence, a user could log on to a particular computer processing *different* GPOs — if the computer account is in one OU and the user is in another.

Note

You also can trigger computer and user policy manually. In Windows 2000, this could be done by using the `secedit.exe` command with the `/refreshpolicy` option. However, note that `secedit.exe` does not trigger any software installation policy you may have defined. In Windows XP and Windows Server 2003, use the `gpupdate` command to refresh Group Policy. This command replaces the Windows 2000 `secedit /refreshpolicy` command. If you choose not to use the `gpupdate` command, Group Policy will still refresh; it will just take longer.

In the first implementation of Group Policies in Windows 2000, calculating effective policy for a given user or computer was challenging. This was especially true when there were many different GPOs at various levels within a given domain. At that time, Microsoft did not provide helper tools that would allow administrators to model the results of policies applied to a given computer or user. Thus, before undertaking a massive deployment of Group Policies within a corporate environment, it was imperative to carefully test all new policies.

Note

Many administrators used a command-line tool called `GPResult.exe`, which was supplied as part of the Windows 2000 Server Resource Kit. This tool generates a list of current GPO settings for a given user logged onto a given Windows 2000 computer.

With Windows Server 2003, Microsoft introduced several Group Policy management improvements, including:

- *Software Restriction Policies.* The rapid growth of the Internet increases security threats to a network, both from worms or viruses and from attacks. A network also could face internal threats, such as human errors. With software restriction policies, organizations can protect their networks from malicious software or even suspicious code by identifying and specifying the applications that are allowed to run. Unfortunately, Windows 2000 and earlier versions of Windows NT are unable to process software restriction policies. To use such policies, all domains must be migrated to Windows Server 2003 domains in native mode and all clients must be upgraded to Windows XP. (For more information on software restriction policies, refer to *Chapter 9.*)
- *Enhanced User Interface in the Group Policy Object Editor.* Policy settings are more easily understood, managed, and verified with Web-view integration in the Group Policy Object Editor. Clicking on a policy instantly shows the text

explaining its function and supported environments such as Windows XP or Windows 2000.

❑ *Group Policy Management Console.* Expected to be freely available as an add-in component, the Group Policy Management Console (GPMC) provides a new framework for managing Group Policy. With GPMC, an administrator can backup and restore Group Policy Objects (GPOs), import/export and copy/paste GPOs, report GPO settings, and more.

❑ *New Policy Settings.* With Windows Server 2003, Microsoft introduced more than 200 new policy settings that let administrators easily lock down or manage configurations. These settings also enable or prohibit most new features, such as Remote Assistance, AutoUpdating, and Error Reporting.

❑ *User Data and Settings Management Enhancements.* Administrators can automatically configure client computers to meet specific requirements of a user's business roles, group memberships, and location. Improvements include simplified folder redirection and more robust roaming capabilities. These were addressed briefly in *Chapter 10.*

❑ *Cross-Forest Support.* Although GPOs can only be linked to sites, domains, or organizational units (OUs) within a given forest, the cross-forest feature in Windows Server 2003 enables several new scenarios that Group Policy supports.

❑ *Resultant Set of Policy (RSoP).* The Microsoft RSoP tool is probably the most important improvement, since it allows administrators to plan, monitor, and troubleshoot Group Policy. These capabilities in Windows 2000 were limited; only a GPResult.exe command-line Resource Kit utility was available. With RSoP, administrators can plan, preview, and verify policies and their effects on a specific computer or user. Unfortunately, RSoP is unavailable for Windows 2000 and earlier.

Using Resultant Set of Policy

Resultant Set of Policy (RSoP) is a long-awaited tool that allows system administrators to determine which Group Policy settings are being applied to a particular user or computer account. This tool can be used both for planning Group Policies before deploying them in a production environment and for troubleshooting problems with specific Group Policy settings. It implements one of the newest mechanisms for managing and troubleshooting Group Policies, and, therefore, deserves special attention. Unfortunately, like many improvements recently introduced by Microsoft, it is not available for Windows 2000 and earlier versions of Windows NT, nor for other legacy operating systems.

On Windows Server 2003, RSoP can operate in two modes:

❑ Logging mode, which displays Group Policy settings for a specific user or computer. This mode is applicable for standalone computers running Windows Server 2003. At the time of this writing, it also could be used on Windows XP computers joined to Windows 2000 or Windows Server 2003 domains.

❑ Planning mode, which allows administrators to evaluate the affect of applying different Group Policy Objects

Where does RSoP get information on the resulting Group Policies? To gather this data, it queries the Common Infrastructure Management Object Manager (CIMOM) database through Windows Management Instrumentation. The CIMOM database contains information on computers' hardware, software installation settings, scripts, folder redirection settings, security settings, and Internet Explorer maintenance settings. The CIMOM database is refreshed with the current information each time a computer logs on to the network.

▶ *Note*

The Common Infrastructure Management (CIM) model, now known as the Web-Based Enterprise Management (WBEM) initiative, was adopted by the Distributed Management Task Force (DMTF). This emerging standard, intended for all computer systems, offers a common way of describing and managing systems. Windows Management Instrumentation, which is built into Windows 2000, Windows XP, and Windows Server 2003, is the Windows-specific implementation. It can be used to discover information about Windows systems as well as manage them.

To obtain results using RSoP:

1. Start MMC console, then select the **Add/Remove Snap-in** command from the **File** menu. Click the **Add** button on the **Standalone** tab, and select the **Resultant Set of Policy** from the list of available standalone snap-ins. Click **Close,** then click **OK**.

▶ *Note*

To request RSoP, you must either be logged on to the machine as the user whose policy you want to see, have local Administrator privileges on the machine you are querying (membership in the local Administrators, Domain Admins, or Enterprise Admins group is required), or have been delegated control over RSoP.

2. After adding the **Resultant Set of Policy** snap-in, select **Generate RSoP Data** from the **Action** menu. RSoP Wizard will start. Click **Next**.

3. RSoP Wizard will display the **Mode Selection** window (Fig. 11.9). To see Group Policy settings applied to a specific user or computer, select the **Logging mode** option and click **Next**. Note that logging mode might be the only mode available.

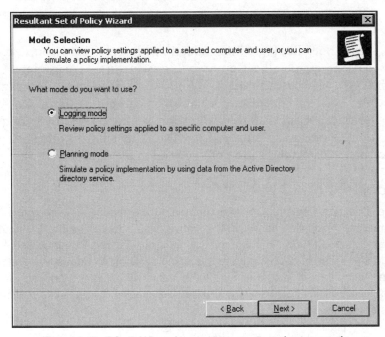

Fig. 11.9. RSoP Wizard prompts you to select a mode

4. Next, the wizard will display a window prompting you to select a computer. You can either display Group Policy settings for the local computer or click the **Browse** button and select a remote system. Make your selection and click **Next**. You will be prompted to select a specific user for whom you need to display policy settings (Fig. 11.10). Select a user and click **Next**.

5. The wizard will display the next window summarizing your selections. To change your selections, click **Back**. To confirm the selected options and proceed with the query, click **Next**, and RSoP will start the query. When the query completes, the wizard will display the final window, where you need to click **Finish**.

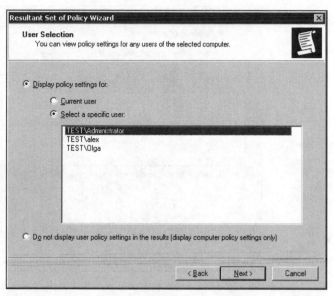

Fig. 11.10. The **User Selection** window displayed by RSoP Wizard

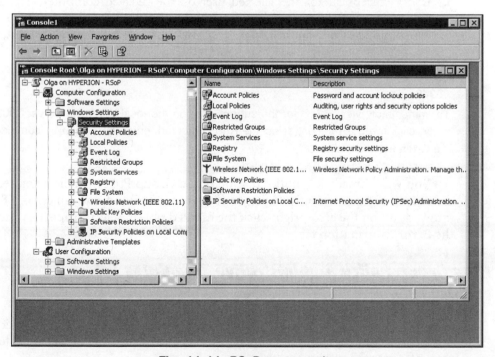

Fig. 11.11. RSoP query results

Fig. 11.12. The **Precedence** tab displays the order of policy application

6. RSoP will appear for the selected user on the selected computer (Fig. 11.11). Click the RSoP folder to view data. Note that you can also set the order in which policies are applied. Simply right-click on the policy element, select **Properties**, then click the **Precedence** tab (Fig. 11.12).

Note

To immediately view RSoP for the current user on the local Windows Server 2003 computer, click the **Start** button, select the **Run** command, enter the `rsop.msc` command into the **Open** field, and click **OK**.

You will immediately notice that there is a Group Policy problem if a red × on the user or computer configuration level appears. (This indicates an error.) To view information on the error, right-click the marked object, select **Properties** and go to the **Error Information** tab.

How Group Policy Administrative Templates Affect the Registry

Now that I have introduced some theoretical foundation required for understanding Group Policy Objects (GPOs), it is time to present some of the GPO features that influence the system registry.

As previously emphasized in this chapter and in *Chapter 10*, both Windows NT 4.0 and Windows 9*x* supported so-called System Policies, which were simply special types of registry files delivered to users at logon time. These registry files (their default names were Ntconfig.pol and Config.pol) were used to centrally modify HKEY_CURRENT_USER and HKEY_LOCAL_MACHINE registry root keys. For example, within a given policy file, it was possible to specify different registry modifications for different users, computers, or global groups. The template ADM files controlled which registry keys and values could be modified and what the possible values could be. These template files represented text files using special macro language to specify which key or value was to be modified and how. Most savvy administrators customized ADM files to enforce the desirable policy. In particular, the following two keys became the primary targets for enforcing system policies:

☐ HKEY_LOCAL_MACHINE\Software\Microsoft\Windows\CurrentVersion\Policies

☐ HKEY_CURRENT_USER\Software\Microsoft\Windows\CurrentVersion\Policies

However, System Policies were limited and difficult to use. Starting with Windows 2000, the situation has improved.

If you refer back to *Table 11.1*, you'll notice that old-style System Policies used in legacy versions of Windows have become part of Group Policy Object (GPO). In Windows 2000 and its successors, the **Administrative Templates** portion of GPO performs functions identical to those of old system policies. Furthermore, GPO-based administrative templates still use the ADM file format.

The default templates, such as System.adm and Inetres.adm, are stored under the \ADM folder within the Group Policy Template (GPT). If you carefully study the format of these files, you will notice that the structure of ADM files in Windows Server 2003 is similar to that of Windows 2000 and even of Windows NT 4.0. The main difference is that each new version supports additional macro keywords to provide new functionality. For example, the EXPLAIN keyword, introduced with Windows 2000 and supported on all later versions, lets the developer of a specific ADM file create Help text associated with a given policy item. The SUPPORTED keyword, introduced with Windows XP and Windows Server 2003, allows the developer to specify supported OS versions. This is an important point, since, as multiple examples have shown in this chapter, not all new features introduced with the release of Windows Server 2003 are supported on Windows XP, to say nothing of earlier Windows versions.

Each GPO can have a different set of ADM files, and each machine or user can process multiple GPOs. Flexibility in the area of desktop and application control and lockdown is as granular as you want to make it.

Having looked at the mechanics of how administrative templates are used, let's move on to what administrators see when they edit a GPO using these templates. Start up the Group Policy tool MMC snap-in, focused on a GPO. Every Windows 2000 or Windows Server 2003 domain contains a Default Domain Policy when first installed, so if you haven't created any other GPOs, you can start by editing that one. To do so:

1. Start the Active Directory Users and Computers MMC snap-in, right-click the name of the domain of interest, and select the **Properties** command from the context menu.

2. Go to the **Group Policy** tab. Highlight the GPO of interest. (Note that if you haven't created any GPOs, only the Default Domain Policy will be available.) Click the **Edit** button.

3. The Group Policy Object Editor will launch, and it will be focused on the se- lected GPO. Under the GPO name, you see two nodes: **Computer Configuration** and **User Configuration**. To demonstrate administrative templates, let's focus on the **User Settings**. Expand the **User Configuration** node, then expand the **Administrative Templates** node. You'll see a tree of folders representing the available areas for administrative template controls (Fig. 11.13).

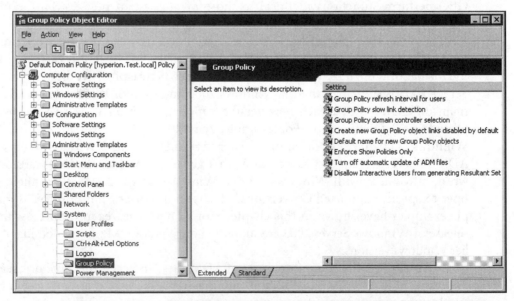

Fig. 11.13. The Group Policy Object Editor focused on the Default Domain Policy

4. What you see is a graphical representation of the ADM files that are loaded by this particular GPO. The ADM files dictate which folders, registry keys, and values are presented here. Each folder, such as Control Panel, Network, and System, represents ADM categories. Within each category are sets of policies that you can specify. For example, if you expand the **System** folder, you will see a subfolder named **Power Management**. After you expand a specific subfolder, the right pane of the Group Policy Object Editor window will expose the list of all available registry limitations that can be set in relation to the selected feature. For example, the **Power Management** folder contains the **Prompt for password on resume from hibernate / suspend** policy. (When you configure this policy, the appropriate setting will be created or modified in registry.)

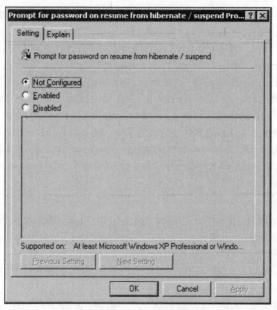

Fig. 11.14. Policy items in Windows 2000, Windows XP or Windows Server 2003 can have one of three states: **Not Configured**, **Enabled**, or **Disabled**

5. To configure a specific policy, simply double-click it to open the respective **Properties** window (Fig. 11.14). Previously in this section, when discussing the ADM file structure, I pointed out the new keywords appearing with each new Windows version. Now, notice the effect they have on the GPO Editor user interface. For example, the EXPLAIN keyword appears in the **Properties** window's **Explain** tab, which you can click to read Help text associated with the selected

policy item. Also notice the **Supported on: At least Windows XP Professional...** string at the bottom of this dialog. It appeared because the SUPPORTED statement was included in the ADM file. Despite these changes to the GPO Editor user interface, the template offers familiar choices. For example, like in Windows NT 4.0 policies, policy items in Windows 2000, Windows XP, or Windows Server 2003 can have three different states (Fig. 11.14), as follows:

- **Not Configured** — The particular registry value behind this policy item is not changed, regardless of its state.
- **Disabled** — This particular policy item is disabled. That is, if the policy is **Prompt for password on resume from hibernate / suspend** — when it is disabled, each user can decide whether to automatically lock his or her computer after performing a resume operation.
- **Enabled** — This policy item is enforced at all times.

6. If multiple GPOs are applied to a user or machine, two identical policy items from different GPOs could contradict each other (i.e., one enables an item and the other disables it). In this case, it's the "last-writer-wins" approach that resolves the conflict. The last writer may not always be obvious because GPOs can reside at the site, domain, or OU levels, and each of level can have multiple GPOs. I already mentioned the order of precedence in the Directory (Local, Site, Domain, OU). In addition, a set of up/down buttons next to the list of available GPOs allows the order of precedence to be set within a container. The higher a GPO is in the list, the later it is processed. Later settings override previous ones.

Once you set all of the policy items within a GPO, where is this information kept? As previously mentioned, it is replicated in the SYSVOL directory in the Group Policy Template for that GPO. Both machine- and user-based administrative template settings are stored in a file called Registry.pol. However, each is stored in its own folder. For example, user-specific Registry.pol is located in %*SystemRoot*%\sysvol\domain\policies\<*GPO_GUID*>\User. Registry.pol replaces the Ntconfig.pol and Config.pol files, which were used in Windows versions earlier than Windows 2000. However, unlike Ntconfig.pol, Registry.pol is not a valid registry hive file. You can't load it into a temporary hive, nor can you view it. It is a text file, but it contains non-printable characters and cannot be edited using a text editor, such as Notepad.

However, one drawback of Windows NT 4.0 policies was the effect of tattooing. When you remove a policy from the domain, the entries are left in the registry for the affected user or machine. This is not the case in Windows 2000 and later. In these newer versions, if you disable or remove a GPO that has made registry changes, the corresponding changes are also removed from the registry.

In Windows NT 4.0, the default path for policy restrictions was in HKCU or HKLM, under the `Software\MS\Windows\CurrentVersion\Policies` keys. (See the full path previously given in this section.) Starting with Windows 2000, the default path for policy settings has been changed to HKCU and HKLM under the `Software\Policies` key. As long as your ADM templates make changes to either of these policy keys, any tattooing is cleaned up when you remove a GPO. Of course, you are not limited to these keys. You could easily create an ADM file that enforces registry policy on `HKLM\Software\Myapp`. However, if a custom ADM file has been created that strays from the well-known keys, those custom keys won't be cleaned up when the GPO is removed.

How Software Installation Works

Another important GPO feature that directly affects the system registry is Software Installation. Any application carrying the label "Designed for Windows" must use registry. Any time a setup program runs, it reads the registry information to determine if all the components necessary to complete the installation procedure successfully are present in the system. It then adds new configuration data to the registry. For this reason, Setup programs — including Windows Setup and setup utilities that install third-party software and/or device drivers — always hold the first position in the list of components using the system registry.

At this point, we come to an important issue. Software installation and distribution technology has undergone significant advances in recent years. Before proceeding with a discussion of these technological improvements, ask yourself a simple question: How are you installing software today? If you're still running from machine to machine with the CD-ROM media and forcing users to take a coffee break for 30 to 60 minutes while you install and test the required application, your method may be inefficient. For a home office or small network (about 10 machines), this may be acceptable. When the number of computers, users, and applications increases, this method quickly becomes a "poor administrative experience". Massive deployments today involve thousands of computers, most of which are administrated remotely. Therefore, it was necessary to develop management software that can remotely deliver most standard software packages to a client.

Understanding this, Microsoft introduced the Software Installation feature, a tool that enables software distribution and desktop configuration management via Active Directory. Using this feature, you can present the required applications for installation to users or machines within specific domain, site, or OU by adding that application to a GPO in Active Directory. The effect of this action is that users subject to that GPO have the required applications installed for them. Of course, the installation does not happen all at once; this would render the machine useless under the weight of simultaneous application installations. Rather, the applications are installed in a "just-in-time" fashion, depending on the configuration within the GPO.

The Windows Server 2003 family includes several improved technologies and features that significantly ease the task of OS and add-on software deployment:

❏ *Remote Installation Services (RIS).* Administrators can use RIS servers to deploy all editions of Windows 2000, Windows XP Professional, and Windows Server 2003 (except Windows 2000 Datacenter Server and Windows Server 2003, Datacenter Edition.) Automated deployment is enhanced with tighter security, improved performance to major components in RIS — such as Trivial File Transfer Protocol (TFTP) — and Hardware Abstraction Layer (HAL) filtering to ensure that images are recognized only by machines with a compatible HAL.

❏ *User State Migration.* Migrating files and settings for multiple users in a corporate environment is easier with the User State Migration Tool (USMT). USMT gives administrators command-line capabilities when they customize specific settings or make unique modifications to Registry. In addition, Windows Server 2003 includes a Files and Settings Transfer Wizard designed for individuals or small-office users. The wizard is also useful in a corporate network environment for employees who receive a new computer and need to migrate their own files and settings without the support of an IT department or help desk.

❏ *Windows Installer.* Managing software applications in a corporate environment has traditionally burdened organizations with high costs. With Windows Installer, administrators can greatly simplify the process of customizing installations, updating and upgrading applications, and resolving configuration problems. Windows Installer can also manage shared resources, enforce consistent file version rules, and diagnose and repair applications at run time.

To deliver an application to users or machines, you normally use the Group Policy Object Editor MMC snap-in focused on the desired GPO. When you are ready to deliver a specific application to users:

1. Place the installation package on the network share. Make sure that it is accessible to the clients.

2. Start the Active Directory Users and Computers MMC snap-in, right-click the name of the domain or OU of interest, and select the **Properties** command from the context menu. Then go to the **Group Policy** tab, highlight the required GPO, and click the **Edit** button.

3. The Group Policy Object Editor will launch, and it will be focused on the se-lected GPO. Expand the console tree and locate the **Software installation** nodes both under **Computer Configuration | Software Settings** and **User Configuration | Software Settings** (Fig. 11.15). The Software Installation fea-ture allows you to deliver applications to computers and users. For example, you can make applications A and B available to computers within a given do-main and make applications C and D available to users within that domain. The effect of this setup will be as follows: Applications A and B will be installed for all users who work on computers subject to that GPO. Additionally, applications C and D will be installed for all users subject to that GPO who logon at the same machine. The example presented in Fig. 11.15 shows several applications published for domain users.

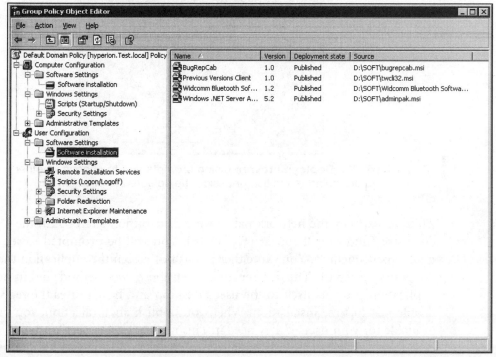

Fig. 11.15. Publishing several applications using the Group Policy Editor MMC snap-in

4. Right-click the **Software installation** node under **Computer Configuration | Software Settings** or **User Configuration | Software Settings**, depending on whether you want to make the application available to computers or users within a given domain or OU. From the right-click menu, select **New | Package**

commands. You will be prompted to specify the network path to the application's distribution package.

Note

The Software Installation feature supports a new package setup format called the Windows Installer. (Windows Installer technology will be covered in more detail later in this chapter.) Application setups packaged using the Windows Installer have an MSI filename extension. The Software Installation feature also supports a down-level format, known as Zero Administration Packaging (ZAP). ZAP files are simple text INI files that let you publish (not assign) your existing application setups without having to convert them to the MSI format.

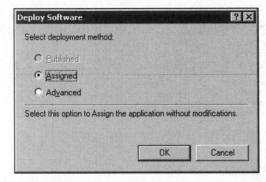

Fig. 11.16. The **Deploy Software** dialog prompts you to choose whether you are going to publish or assign the selected application

5. After you specify the network path to the distribution sharepoint, the **Deploy Software** window will appear (Fig. 11.16). You will be prompted to select the deployment method. You can either publish or assign the application that you are going to deploy. The difference between these two methods lies in how an application presents itself to the user's desktop and how it uses the registry to enable just-in-time installation. When you publish an application, you make it available for your users if they need it. This means it will be an "optional" application available to the user via the Control Panel's Add/Remove Programs applet (Fig. 11.17). Conversely, when you assign an application, you take the first step toward installing that application for a user or machine. An application will be "advertised" in the user's environment and Windows Explorer shell. An icon for that application will be placed to the user's **Start** menu or Desktop, and filename extension association for that application will be created in the registry under HKEY_CLASSES_ROOT.

Note

The option of publishing an application is only available within the **User Settings** portion of GPO. It is impossible to publish an application to a computer. (Notice that the **Published** option is grayed in Fig. 11.16.) Thus, when deploying applications on a per-computer basis, you can only assign applications.

Let's briefly review what happens to the system registry when you publish or assign an application.

As previously mentioned, when you publish an application, it will show up as an option in the Add/Remove Programs Control Panel applet after the user (or machine) logs on to the network. Note that to display the list of published applications, the client needs to query Active Directory. After that, if the user chooses to install the published application and clicks the **Add** button (Fig. 11.17), the setup routine for that application will start to install it on the local computer.

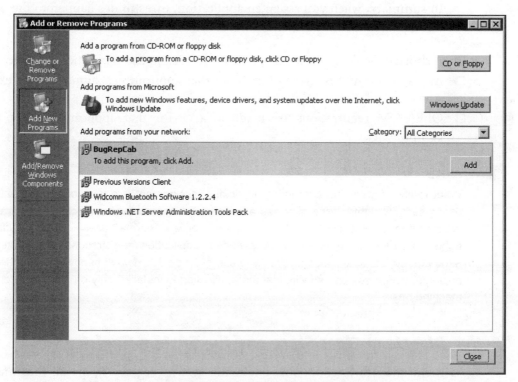

Fig. 11.17. Published applications are available to the user via the Add/Remove Programs applet in Control Panel

On the other hand, when you assign an application, an icon for that application will be placed to the user's **Start** menu or Desktop, and filename extension association for that application will be created in the registry under HKEY_CLASSES_ROOT. Then, even if the application has yet to be installed, the user can invoke the installation process by simply accessing a file that has such an extension type. Suppose Microsoft Word has been assigned to the user but has not been installed. After the user double-clicks a file that has the DOC filename extension, the installation procedure will start.

Note

When you assign an application to a machine, that application is actually installed at system startup. This lets you deliver application installations in an unattended way to a workstation or server.

In summary, when you assign an application, three things happen to the user's environment:

❑ A shortcut is placed on the desktop (if specified in the application package).
❑ An association(s) is made in HKCR for that application's supported file extensions.
❑ OLE/COM registrations are made in HKCR for that application's supported components.

Note

What really happens in HKCR during application assignment is a function of the particular user's security rights. If the user has administrative access over a machine, registrations are made in HKLM\Software\Classes. If the user is a "normal" user — without sufficient rights to write to HKLM — then assigned application registrations are written to HKCU\Software\Classes. However, you can override this default behavior within the MSI package, where you can specify that the application is installed only on a per-user or per-machine basis.

Active Directory Class Store and the System Registry

As mentioned throughout this book, the system registry keeps all information about applications and COM (Component Object Model) components installed on a local system. All information related to how, and from what location, machines and users run installed applications resides under the HKEY_CLASSES_ROOT key. As a result, this key is often viewed as the registry of applications. However, as previously outlined in this chapter, HKEY_CLASSES_ROOT, as well as other parts of the system registry, have one common limitation: they represent the local configuration database. The number of local registries equals the number of Windows-based computers within a network, and there is no easy way of ensuring that application information in all local registries is up-to-date. In previous Windows versions, there also was no easy method of pushing a change to all local registries on client workstations.

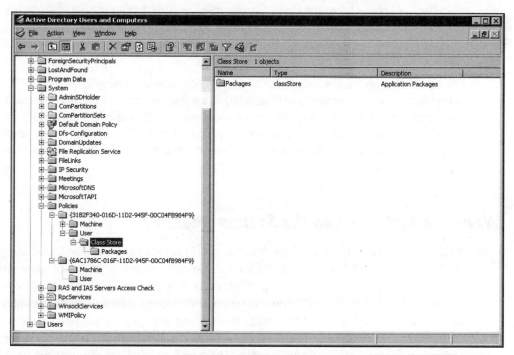

Fig. 11.18. When you publish or assign an application within specific GPO, a Class Store is created

When Active Directory was introduced with Windows 2000, the situation improved. Active Directory serves as a global repository of various objects, such as computers, users, and groups. It includes Class Store, which is associated with Group Policy Objects (GPOs). When an application is published or assigned within specific GPO, a Class Store is created that reflects the COM classes that the application has registered (Fig. 11.18). To view Class Store information, start the Active

Directory Users and Computer MMC snap-in, then select the **Advanced Features** command from the **View** menu. You'll find Class Store information nested within **System | Policies** container, which stores all GPOs (identified by their GUIDs) defined for a specific domain. Under a specific GUID, there are two more subcontainers: Machine and User. Class Store can be either machine- or user-specific, depending upon how application deployment has been defined. After an application is published or assigned, the Microsoft Installer (MSI) package is queried to determine all COM classes defined within that package. These classes are stored by GUID in Class Store.

Thus, Active Directory Class Store serves as a sort of centralized HKCR, or a repository for shared components accessible by all users.

▶ *Note*

Since MMC snap-ins are actually COM servers, usually comprising one or more DLL files with their related HKCR registry entries, MMC is a good example of how this new feature can be used to benefit system administrators. Now, with MMC, you can create MSC files with a set of predefined snap-ins and publish or assign them in a Group Policy. This will give all system administrators a set of powerful tools to perform specific tasks without exposing other administrative areas.

Windows Installer and the System Registry

Previously in this chapter, when discussing GPOs and the Software Installation feature, I mentioned Windows Installer technology, which implements the mechanisms used to deliver and install published or assigned applications. Now, consider in more detail how the Windows Installer technology interacts with the operating system and, more importantly, with the system registry. Windows Installer technology plays a key role in the process of software distribution; it customizes installations, updates and upgrades applications, and resolves configuration problems. In addition to saving time and effort, this new technology provides the following benefits:

❑ The application is installed via OS service. There are two sides to software installation: the application-install package itself and the Windows Installer service, which is installed by default on every computer running Windows 2000, Windows XP, or Windows Server 2003. On Windows 2000 and later, this allows for the installation of applications in an administrative context.

❑ Microsoft Installer (MSI) provides a standard package format. The MSI format represents the new standard for communicating with the Windows Installer technology. The install package is an integral part of software installation. Installation files that are not packaged using the MSI format (with the exception of down-level ZAP files) cannot be published or assigned via Active Directory.

▶ *Note*

MSI is a standard API that defines how software is configured and,installed. Software vendors such as Microsoft, InstallShield, and Wise provide packaging tools that are capable of building MSI files according to the MSI standard. These application packages then can be published or assigned within a GPO.

❑ Transactional install and rollback. This feature helps guarantee that the MSI package is fully installed in the way its vendor intended. If the installation process fails, the transaction rollback function can be used to undo all the changes made up to that point in the installation. Thus, the system — including Registry entries created by the install process — will return to the state that existed before installation began.

❑ Self-repair of corrupt or deleted critical files. MSI format provides the capability of marking certain files for detection of failure. If such a file (usually, a DLL or EXE file) in the distribution is corrupt or deleted, the user will be prompted to repair the installation by presenting the original MSI distribution. If the installation media is available (for example, on a network share), the repair happens automatically.

❑ Install on demand and Just-In-Time (JIT) installation. Previously in this chapter, when discussing procedures of publishing or assigning applications via GPOs, I mentioned that applications deployed using Windows Installer technology can be offered to clients at any time. Once the application is offered (for example, via the Add/Remove Programs applet in Control Panel), users can install the application by simply clicking the **Add** button. The installation of applications assigned to users or machines can be triggered when a user clicks a corresponding registered extension. Applications installed in a JIT fashion are ready to use in a few moments.

❑ Packages can use transform files. An application's package can be developed such that a base or administrative install is prepared for general distribution. A transform file can overlay the base, letting you customize specific installations. Furthermore, MSI packages can use patch files. For example, after a package is on the machine, you might need to fix the source files if a bug is found and apply a patch file to the package.

Note

Like most software products, Windows Installer has versions associated with it. There are major revisions (such as 1.0) and minor revisions (such as 1.1). Windows Installer is unique in that it is versioned for each platform. That is, Windows NT, Windows 9x, Windows 2000, Windows XP, and Windows Server 2003 have their own Windows Installer version numbers. To find out which version of Windows Installer is on your machine, navigate the %*SystemRoot*%\System32 directory, right-click the msi.dll file, select the **Properties** command from the context menu, and go to the **Version** tab (Fig. 11.19). Note the pattern of version numbers; versions that end with ".0" are built in the OS (Windows Server 2003, in this example), while those that end otherwise are downloads.

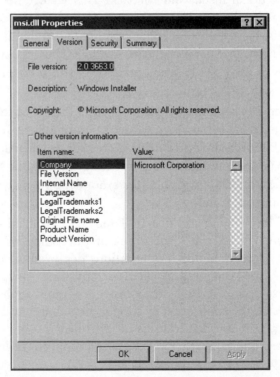

Fig. 11.19. Discovering your Windows Installer version number

An MSI file is itself a kind of database. An MSI file is referred to as Object Linking and Embedding (OLE) Structured Storage. OLE Structured Storage (OSS) is a way of putting intelligence into a file that is otherwise a series of bits read sequentially. OSS files are composed of streams and storage objects. Streams correspond to files; storage objects correspond to directories. In a way, an OSS file is a file system within a file system. That is, the MSI file is a single file on the NTFS partition, but applications using that file can access different objects (e.g., streams and storage) within the file in an organized way. The advantage of OSS files is they can be used to keep rich information in a file. In the context of MSI, OSS provides a database of information within the file that describes an application. The database itself is composed of tables and columns, just like an Access or SQL Server database might be.

Examples of database "tables" within an MSI OSS file include

- Component
- Class
- Registry
- RemoveRegistry
- File
- RemoveFile
- Property
- InstallUISequence

The second side to software installation, the Windows Installer service, is just that — an NT service installed on every Windows 2000 device by default. The executable that comprises the Installer service is msiexec.exe. The Installer service is the piece of code that does all the actual installation work when an application is published or assigned. The Installer service runs in LocalSystem security context by default. As such, it has the ability to perform any system changes that a normal user account would not have sufficient rights to perform. But the Installer service has another unique ability: When a user clicks on a shortcut representing an application that has been deployed using a GPO, the Installer service can not only perform the install on LocalSystem's behalf, it also can perform parts of the install on the user's behalf.

This is especially useful in large environments. In Windows NT 4.0, an application that made changes to the registry in both HKLM and HKCU had to be packaged in two pieces. One piece made the changes to HKLM and those parts of the system to which the normal, non-power, non-administrative user lacks access. That piece was usually delivered to the machine via a system service, such as the AT scheduler, or a third-party tool, such as those included in the Microsoft Systems Management Server. Then, at some later time, perhaps at logon or application startup, the HKCU changes for that application were delivered to the user under their security context using logon scripts, system policies, or application startup "wrappers".

This two-part process was disconnected and difficult to manage in a large environment. With the advent of the Windows Installer service and Microsoft Installer (MSI), you can deliver an application to users as a single event that they initiate when they need the application.

And, as the next section makes clear, you can also define an MSI package so that only certain features within an application — both required features, such as Word functionality, and optional pieces, such as spell checker — need to be installed when the user clicks the icon or activates the extension. I'll talk more about how the Installer service interacts with Registry to install applications later in the chapter.

In addition to installing MSI packages, the Installer service is responsible for determining when an application is broken — and for fixing it. It does this through the use of key files, as I'll explain further on in this chapter. The Installer service also can roll back an application installation if it fails before completion. While an application is installing, temporary files are created in the temporary folder *%SystemDrive%*\config.msi. During a rollback, these files are used to undo steps taken before the failure.

Products, Features, and Components

Microsoft Installer (MSI) and the Windows Installer provide the capability to package an application, so users install only those portions of the application that they need and use. Optional portions, however, are included when users first invoke them. An example of this from the pre-Win2K days is the custom option within most setup routines. The custom option generally let you install only those components that you really wanted. For example, in Microsoft Word, you could have chosen not to install clip art or WordPerfect Help because you didn't plan to use them. If you later decided you wanted those options, you had to find the media and rerun setup to add them.

The MSI way of doing things is more modular and therefore more adaptive to adding and removing components. An MSI package specifies a three-tiered hierarchy to define applications. The three tiers are

❐ Product   ❐ Feature   ❐ Component

A product is the coarsest distinction for an application. (Microsoft Word and Excel are products.) When you install a product, you are installing an application. Products are made up of features, such as Word's spell check and Excel's SQL database access. Features, which are specific to a product, contain components, the lowest and most granular portion of the MSI hierarchy. Components can be shared across multiple products and their associated features.

A component is a set of files and registry entries that define a feature's function. Using our example of the spell-check feature, a component may contain the spell-check DLL and associated registry entries that enable it. The intention is that a component contains only one EXE, DLL, ActiveX Control, or Help file. In that way, you can properly compartmentalize component functions and easily share components across features and products. Likewise, if you have a file that is a DLL, that same version of the file should not occur in more than one component. (If it does, it can be difficult to maintain portability of components across other features and products.)

► *Note*

MSI components can include COM components, but they are not the same things. Transforms (introduced with the Windows Installer technology) are modifications to a base MSI package that let you customize an application installation at install time. For example, you may have purchased a third-party application that already has its own MSI file. To customize the default settings to meet your environment, you can use transforms. If you have ever modified ACME setup STF files that came with older versions of Office, then you can appreciate the functionality that transforms provide. You define a transform when you publish or assign an application within the Group Policy tool. The **Modifications** tab within the application's properties lets you add transforms. Transform files end in MST extensions. Transforms also let you define which product features are installed initially and which are Installed on first use.

The Mechanics of Products, Features, and Components

Now that we have taken a high-level look at how MSI packages are broken down, let's turn to some of the interactions between MSI packages and Registry. The first thing to understand is how products, features, and components are identified. Both products and components are named using a unique 128-bit GUID. Features, however, are given simple names that help identify the function they provide. There are two main keys in Registry, identified below, via which products, features, and components are tracked.

❑ HKEY_LOCAL_MACHINE\Software\Microsoft\Windows\CurrentVersion\Installer — This area contains details about all currently installed products, features, and components, including component names and which components are associated with which features.

❑ HKEY_CLASSES_ROOT\Installer — This area also contains information about installed products, features, and components, including the name of the network or media share from which the MSI product and feature was installed. In addition, this key contains information about COM components that have been advertised by MSI packages but not installed. This information can be used to fault in these components when a calling application needs them.

The Installer service uses these registry keys to determine whether and when an application is incomplete, and if needed, where to find the install media in the event of a reinstall.

The Explorer Shell and the Installer Service

Now that we have looked at the process of packaging and installing applications using the Windows Installer, let's look at how the Explorer shell interacts with the Installer service to know when to fault in your assigned applications. As previously mentioned, when you assign an application, three things (as defined within the MSI file) can happen: A shortcut can be placed on the user's desktop, a file association can be made, and any COM classes included in the application can be registered. When you click on an assigned shortcut or open a document with an assigned file association, how does the Explorer shell know to go to Active Directory and find out where the MSI package for that application is located? It uses "installer tokens," special tags that the shell interprets to discover whether it is dealing with an assigned or published application. Changes in Windows 2000 to the Explorer shell and COM let these applications identify installer tokens. Shortcuts delivered by assignment also contain installer tokens, but if you try to view them by examining a LNK file's properties, you don't see any meaningful information.

The registry value called "command" contains the installer token telling the shell that an application has been assigned. The same method is used on COM objects that have been assigned as part of an application. In this case, the value `InprocServer32` under the `InprocServer32` key contains the token instead of the path to the actual dynamic-link library (DLL) or OCX.

Once the Explorer shell detects an installer token, it passes the token to the Installer service, which is its cue to communicate with Registry to determine where the MSI package for the application physically resides. Once that information is secured, the Installer service begins the install.

Summary

In this chapter, you have seen how new features such as Group Policy-based Administrative Templates and Software Installation interact with and use Registry. The chapter explored how the Windows Installer and MSI packages work together to install applications to the registry and file system in both system and user security contexts. Introduced is the installer token, a new way of representing a path to an assigned or published executable or DLL. The chapter then explained how the installer token works with the Explorer shell and COM to inform the Installer service that AD contains the information needed. Finally, Group Policy-based Class Store was reviewed, a kind of centralized version of HKEY_CLASSES_ROOT that lets you publish COM class registrations in AD.

CHAPTER 12

Troubleshooting Common Problems

Anything that can go wrong, will.

Murphy's Law

We have discussed most aspects of the registry. Let's now consider some problems that frequently arise when working with Windows NT, Windows 2000, Windows XP, or Windows Server 2003 but can be eliminated using the registry.

Where shall we start? It's logical to begin with startup problems and problems that prevent you from logging onto the system. Just imagine the situation: Your work is urgent, but the system stops immediately after rebooting. Now it's impossible for you to do your work right away. You're frustrated and wonder how many tries will it take to troubleshoot this problem?

Detailed instructions on backing up and recovering the system registry were provided in *Chapter 2*. In this chapter, we'll concentrate on several additional but rarely used procedures that may help you get the system up and running after boot failures.

Troubleshooting Startup Problems

Windows Server 2003 is certainly the most reliable version of Windows, possessing a level of robustness that its predecessors lack, even Windows 2000 and Windows XP. Does this mean startup problems cannot occur in Windows Server 2003? No, it doesn't. No existing operating system can be considered crash- or corruption-proof, not even specialized operating systems used by military organizations. Any operating system can be rendered unbootable, and the newest release of Windows is no exception. This issue becomes extremely important in a large-scale corporate network, which depends on the availability of the network operating system (OS) — particularly for network servers. You must be prepared to handle anything that goes terribly wrong and to avoid feeling helpless. A significant part of this chapter is dedicated to troubleshooting startup problems. These, I admit, are the most frustrating ones, especially if your system won't boot when you have a lot of work to do. So, what should you do in an emergency? First, don't panic. Next, try to detect what is preventing the operating system from booting.

Since boot sequence in Windows Server 2003 closely resembles that in Windows 2000/XP, most (but not all) techniques described here can be applied to all three versions. A detailed description of Windows Server 2003 boot sequence was provided in *Chapter 6*. Therefore, I will provide only a short explanation of the boot sequence, and then proceed with problem detection and troubleshooting.

Table 12.1 lists Windows Server 2003 startup phases with brief descriptions of the processes that take place at each stage of the normal boot process.

Table 12.1. Windows Server 2003 Startup Process

Startup stage	Description (*x*86-based systems)
POST routine	CPU initiates the system board POST routines. POST routines of the individual adapters start after the motherboard POST is accomplished successfully.
Initial startup process	The system searches for a boot device according to the boot order setting stored in CMOS. If the boot device is a hard disk, Ntldr starts.
Operating system load	Ntldr switches the CPU to protected mode, starts the file system, then reads the contents of the Boot.ini file. This information determines the startup options and initial boot menu selections.

continues

Table 12.1 Continued

Startup stage	Description (*x86*-based systems)
Hardware detection and configuration selection	Ntdetect.com gathers basic hardware configuration data and passes this information to Ntldr. If more than one hardware profile exists, Windows XP and Windows Server 2003 attempt to use the correct one for the current configuration. Notice that if your computer is ACPI-compliant, Windows XP or Windows Server 2003 ACPI functionality will be used for device enumeration and initialization. (More information on this topic was provided in *Chapter 5*.)
Kernel loading	Ntldr passes the information collected by Ntdetect.com to Ntoskrnl.exe. Ntoskrnl then loads the kernel, HAL, and registry information. A status bar at the bottom portion of the screen indicates progress.
Operating system logon process	Networking-related components (such as TCP/IP) load asynchronously with other services, and the **Begin Logon** prompt appears on screen. After a user logs on successfully, Windows updates the Last Known Good Configuration information to reflect the current state.
New devices are detected by Plug and Play	If Windows XP or Windows Server 2003 detects new devices, they are assigned system resources. The operating system extracts the required driver files from the Driver.cab file. If this file is not found, Windows XP or Windows Server 2003 prompts the user to provide them. Device detection occurs asynchronously with the operating system logon process.

Diagnosing Startup Problems

Fortunately, boot failures in Windows XP and Windows Server 2003 are rare, especially if you perform regular maintenance and take preventive measures against disaster. However, problems still can arise. As with any other operating system, they might be caused both by hardware malfunctions and by software errors. If the problem is severe enough, the system stops booting and displays an error message. A brief list of error messages and their meanings is presented in Table 12.2. Although this list is by no means comprehensive, it covers the most common problems that can cause startup failures of Windows NT-based operating systems, including Windows 2000, Windows XP, and Windows Server 2003.

Table 12.2. Startup Problem Symptoms

Startup problem symptom	Possible cause

The POST routine emits a series of beeps and displays error messages, for example:
 	
`Hard disk error.`
 	
`Hard disk absent/ failed.`
	The system self-test routines stopped because of improperly installed devices.
	
	To recover from hardware problems, carefully review the documentation supplied with your system and perform the basic hardware checks. Verify that all cables are attached correctly and all internal adapters are installed properly. Make sure that all peripheral devices (such as keyboards) necessary to complete the POST without error messages are installed and functioning. If applicable, verify that you have configured correctly all jumpers or dual in-line package (DIP) switches. Jumpers and DIP switches are especially important for hard disks. Run diagnostic software to detect hardware malfunction, and replace the faulty device.
	
	Unfortunately, the topic of troubleshooting hardware problems goes beyond the range of problems discussed in this book. It deserves a separate comprehensive volume. However, I can recommend some resources on the topic that would help you make sense of the BIOS error codes:
	
	BIOS Survival Guide, available at **http://burks.bton.ac.uk/burks/pcinfo/hardware/bios_sg/bios_sg.htm**
	
	Definitions and Solutions for BIOS Error Beeps and Messages/Codes, available at **http://www.earthweb.com**

CMOS or NVRAM settings are not retained	The CMOS memory is faulty, data is corrupt, or the battery needs replacing.

Master boot record (MBR) — related error messages similar to the following:
 	
`Missing operating system.`
 	
`Insert a system diskette and restart the system.`
	The MBR is corrupt.
	
	The easiest method of recovering the damaged MBR is provided by Recovery Console (the methods of starting Recovery Console were discussed in *Chapter 2*). Once you are in Recovery Console, use the FIXMBR command to repair the MBR.
	
	The FIXMBR command uses the following syntax:
	
	`Fixmbr [device_name]`
	
	The parameter *device_name* specifies the drive on which you need to repair the damaged MBR. For example:
	
	`fixmbr \Device\HardDisk0`
	
	If the *device_name* parameter is omitted, the new MBR will be written to the boot device, from which your primary system is loaded. Notice that you'll be prompted to confirm your intention to continue if an invalid partition table is detected.

continues

Table 12.2 Continued

Startup problem symptom	Possible cause

Partition table-related error message similar to the following:
 	
`Invalid partition table.`
 	
`A disk-read error occurred.`
	The partition table is invalid.
	
	You can recover from this problem using the DiskProbe Resource Kit utility or any third-party low-level disk editor. Note that to prevent this problem, you must create a backup copy of the MBR beforehand. (You can use the DiskProbe tool for this purpose.) Detailed information on this topic can be found in the Resource Kit documentation.
	
	If the MBR on the disk used to start Windows is corrupt, most likely you will be unable to start Windows XP or Windows Server 2003 (and, consequently, DiskProbe). Therefore, before proceeding any further, you'll need to start Recovery Console to replace the damaged MBR.

Boot failure caused by disk or file system corruption, not related to damaged MBR or partition table	Start Recovery Console and run the `CHKDSK` command to repair the disk. If this proves to be insufficient, you will need to take additional actions to fully recover the damaged file system.
Windows XP or Windows Server 2003 cannot start after you have installed another operating system	The Windows XP or Windows Server 2003 boot sector was overwritten by the other operating system's setup program. Recovery Console provides the `FIXBOOT` command that enables you to restore the overwritten boot sector.
Missing Boot.ini, Ntoskrnl.exe, or Ntdetect.com files (*x*86-based systems)	Required startup files are missing or damaged, or entries in the Boot.ini are pointing to the wrong partition. Start the Recovery Console and use available commands, such as `REN`, `DEL`, or `COPY`, to restore working copies of boot files.

Bootstrap loader error messages similar to the following:
 	
`Couldn't find loader`
 	
`Please insert another disk.`
	Ntldr is missing or corrupt.
	
	If Ntldr or any other file required to boot the system is missing or corrupt, start Recovery Console and copy the required file.

continues

Table 12.2 Continued

Startup problem symptom	Possible cause

Windows NT-based OS cannot start and displays message similar to the one provided below:
 	
`Windows could not start because the following file is missing or corrupt:`
 	
`\WINNT\SYSTEM32\CON FIG\SYSTEM`
 	
`You can attempt to repair this file by starting Windows Setup using the original Setup floppy disk of CD-ROM.`
 	
`Select 'r' at the first screen to repair.`
	This and similar error messages specifying different file names indicate that the boot failure was caused by a damaged registry hive(s) or by invalid registry settings.
	
	First, try to boot using the safe mode startup option. If your attempt has failed, try the **Last Known Good** boot option. If you still can't boot successfully, start Recovery Console and use the COPY command to restore known good registry files (for example, those located in the *%SystemRoot%*\Repair folder) to the *%SystemRoot%*\System32\Config folder.
	
	If the problem is related to settings for a specific service or driver, you also may be able to use Recovery Console's DISABLE command to disable the offending service or driver.

Boot failure caused by a video display driver problem	Use the safe mode startup option, then repair or replace the driver.
Boot failure caused by service or driver initialization	As a first line of defense, try to boot in safe mode and disable the offending service or driver. If your attempt fails, start Recovery Console and use the LISTSVC and DISABLE commands to identify and disable the service or driver that prevents Windows from booting. If you have a working copy of the system registry, you can use the Recovery Console's COPY command to restore the system registry.
Boot failure caused by invalid file attributes set on system files or folders	Start Recovery Console and use the ATTRIB command to restore the correct attributes.
Boot failure caused by unknown system startup event	Try to boot into the safe mode. If this is not successful, try to use the Boot Logging startup option. Then start Recovery Console and use the TYPE command on the resulting log file to identify the failed initialization event.
Stop messages appear	Many software or hardware issues can cause these messages. In addition to official Microsoft documentation (such as the long list of common STOP messages usually supplied in the Resource Kit documentation), there are other useful resources on troubleshooting STOP messages. One such resource can be found at **http://www.aumha.org/kbestop.htm**

As mentioned in *Chapter 6*, all Windows NT-based systems generate system messages known as blue screens, or "Blue Screens of Death", if they encounter serious errors which they can't correct. If Windows stops loading, the blue screen also may appear to prevent further data corruption. If the STOP message appears during system startup, it's likely that the cause of the problem is among the following:

❑ The user installed third-party software that's destroyed part of the system registry (that is, the HKEY_LOCAL_MACHINE root key). This may happen if the application tries to install a new service or driver. The blue screen will appear, informing the user that the registry or one of its hives couldn't be loaded.

❑ The user incorrectly modified the hardware configuration and, as a result, one of the critical system files was overwritten or corrupted.

❑ The user installed a new service or system driver that is incompatible with the hardware, causing the blue screen to appear after rebooting. Strictly speaking, it's the attempt to load an incompatible file that leads to the corruption of a correct system file.

▶ *Note*

One of the drawbacks of Windows NT 4.0 and earlier versions of the Windows NT operating system was shared system files, which could be overwritten during installation of incompatible third-party software. Starting with Windows 2000, this drawback was eliminated by the addition of appropriate protection for critical system files. This functionality was discussed in *Chapter 6*. If you wish to avoid startup problems, I recommend that you regularly use these tools.

Parallel Installation of the Operating System

What else can be done to provide universal troubleshooting tools for startup problems? A traditional method of increasing the probability of quick and easy recovery became popular among users of Windows NT 4.0 and earlier. This method is known as "parallel installation of the operating system". The parallel installation is another copy of the Windows NT-based operating system installed on the same computer in a different installation folder, preferably on a hard disk different from the primary installation. If the main operating system (the one you use most frequently) fails to boot, an additional copy of the operating system will allow quick access to NTFS volumes, system files, and registry hives. Another method of providing access to NTFS volumes after system failures is to use the NTFSDOS utility, which will be discussed in *Chapter 14*.

Note

Parallel OS installations weaken the system security; like NTFSDOS, parallel installations provide a backdoor to your main operating system. Thus, from a reliability and recoverability point of view, both parallel OS installations and NTFSDOS are beneficial. From a security point of view, they're not ideal methods.

Although the introduction of Recovery Console has significantly reduced the need for parallel OS installation during a system recovery operation, this additional safeguard should not be dismissed altogether. Despite the power of Recovery Console, you may wish to continue using parallel OS installation on the most critical servers running Windows 2000 or Windows Server 2003. For example, it gives you the ability to quickly reset permissions on the primary installation's *%Systemroot%* folder if the permissions are configured incorrectly. This is desirable because Recovery Console does not provide an easy way of resetting such permissions. Furthermore, despite all of its impressive new capabilities and power, Recovery Console remains a limited command-line environment. For example, it doesn't allow you to run a GUI-based registry editor or backup utility, or any other application that requires full GUI-based functionality. If the primary installation becomes inaccessible and you need to access this type of application to restore it, then parallel OS installation will be an enormous relief.

Note

If you need a more advanced, GUI-based version of Recovery Console with built-in Registry Editor, I'd like to draw your attention to ERD Commander 2002 from Aelita Software. This utility will be covered in more detail in *Chapter 14*.

You should install the parallel OS in advance; the procedure is time-consuming, and you may be short of time when problems occur. Note that you can only install the minimum set of options in the parallel OS. To make a parallel installation more useful and the system effective, consider placing the installation on a disk partition other than that where the primary OS is installed. This improves the chances that the parallel OS installation will be accessible if the primary installation's boot partition is damaged severely.

Additional Hardware Profiles

In addition to a parallel installation of the operating system, there's another method of performing quick recovery. If you experiment with various hardware devices and aren't sure if the device you're going to install is listed in Hardware Compatibility List (HCL), you may want to use additional hardware profiles for the system recovery. Proceed as follows:

1. Before installing a new device that may cause a problem, create a new ERD (Windows 2000) or prepare for Automated System Recovery (ASR) (Windows XP and Windows Server 2003). Then back up the system registry using one of the methods described in *Chapter 2*. The ERD (or ASR backup) and registry backup copies will be useful.

2. Create a new hardware profile. Launch the System applet in Control Panel, go to the **Hardware** tab, and click the **Hardware Profiles** button. The **Hardware Profiles** window will open (Fig. 12.1). Click the **Copy** button and create a new hardware profile by copying one of the existing profiles. It's best to name hardware profiles using "speaking names" that explain their purpose (for example, Working — the current hardware profile, free of errors; and Experimental — the new hardware profile, where you'll try solutions to the problem). In the **Hardware profiles selection** group, set the **Wait until I select a hardware profile** radio button.

3. Check if the hardware profiles are working. Try to start the operating system using each of them.

4. Start the computer using the Working profile and try to install the new device and its drivers using the Hardware Wizard. If the system prompts you to reboot the computer, don't reboot the system immediately. Start Device Manager, find the newly installed device in the list, and select the Properties command from the context menu. You'll see the **General** tab of the properties window for this device. If the newly installed device is incompatible, you'll immediately see that "something is wrong" (despite the phrase "This device is working properly" displayed in the **Device status** field, as shown in Fig. 12.2). For example, this device may be marked as an **Unknown** device that may cause problems. To avoid possible problems, disable this device in the current hardware profile by selecting the **Do not use this device in the current hardware profile (disable)** option from the **Device usage** list. The device will be disabled in the current hardware profile, but it will remain enabled in the experimental hardware profile.

5. Now reboot the system and select the experimental hardware profile (where the problem device is enabled). Do you see the "Blue Screen of Death"? Probably not, because the device is disabled in the working hardware profile. In most cases, you'll be able to boot the system using the working hardware profile.

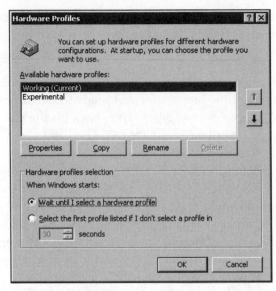

Fig. 12.1. Before installing a new device that isn't listed in the HCL, create an additional hardware profile.

Fig. 12.2. Although the Device Manager states **This device is working properly**, a newly installed device will cause problems. Disable it in the current hardware profile

Note

I recommend that you always have a working hardware profile that contains no errors and enables no problem devices. This profile often provides an easier means of recovering a system with configuration problems than the Advanced startup menu.

How Can I See the "Blue Screen of Death"?

Have you ever seen the "Blue Screen of Death"? If you haven't, most people will consider you a lucky person. What... you're curious to see what it is? Well, here you are!

Windows 2000, Windows XP, and Windows Server 2003 have one undocumented function that allows you to generate an artificial STOP error (blue screen) and manually create a crash dump (Memory.dmp). The STOP screen that appears after using this feature will contain the following message:

```
*** STOP: 0x000000E2 (0x00000000,0x00000000,0x00000000,0x00000000)
The end-user manually generated the crashdump.
```

By default, this feature is disabled. To enable it, you'll need to edit the registry and reboot the computer. Open the HKEY_LOCAL_MACHINE\SYSTEM\CurrentControlSet\Services\i8042prt\Parameters registry key, add the REG_DWORD CrashOnCtrlScroll value, and set it to 1.

After rebooting the system, you'll be able to manually "crash" the system. To view the "Blue Screen of Death," press and hold the right <Ctrl> key, and press the <Scroll Lock> key twice.

How to Recreate a Missing ASR Floppy Disk

If you tried all of these troubleshooting options and nothing happened, you may decide to run the Automated System Recovery (ASR) process. What should you do if the ASR diskette is missing? Does this mean everything is lost? No, it doesn't, not if your ASR backup for storing media works. Using this, you can recreate the missing ASR floppy disk.

The Asr.sif and Asrpnp.sif files contained on the ASR diskette are ASCII files that can be viewed or edited with any text editor, such as Notepad.exe. These files also can be extracted from the ASR backup set and copied to a floppy disk that can be used for an ASR procedure. You can use Backup Utility supplied with Windows Server 2003, Windows XP, or even the version supplied with Windows 2000.

To recreate a missing ASR diskette:

1. Format a 1.44 megabyte (MB) floppy disk and insert the disk into the floppy disk drive of any computer running Windows 2000, Windows XP, or Windows Server 2003.

2. In System Tools, start the Backup program. If it starts in wizard mode, switch to the advanced mode and go to the **Restore and Manage Media** tab (Windows XP and Windows Server 2003) or to the **Restore** tab (Windows 2000). Insert your backup media with the ASR backup set into the backup device and select the **Catalog a backup file** command from the **Tools** menu. When the next window appears, specify the path to the backup copy that you require. (Use the **Browse** button if necessary.)

3. Select the backup media containing the required ASR backup set. Expand the **Automated System Recovery Backup Set** option corresponding to the ASR disk you need to recreate.

4. Expand the *Windows folder*/Repair folder and click the following files from this repair folder: Asr.sif, Asrpnp.sif, and Setup.log (Fig. 12.3). In the **Restore files to** field, select **Alternate location**. In the **Alternate location** field, specify the path to the root of your floppy drive (for example, "A:\").

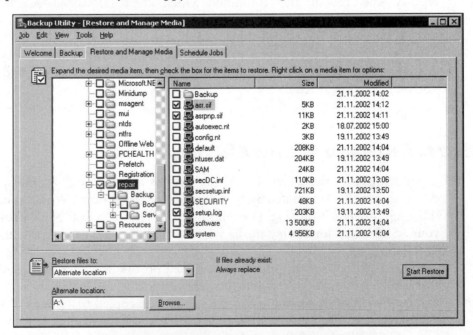

Fig. 12.3. Recreating the missing ASR floppy disk

5. Click **Next**. The other options in this wizard are not mandatory and do not affect the transfer of files to the floppy disk. When the wizard is finished, the files are copied to the specified location. The ASR floppy disk is ready if you need to perform an ASR restore operation.

▶ Note

The Asr.sif and Asrpnp.sif files must reside on the root of the floppy disk drive to be used during ASR restore operation.

Troubleshooting Shutdown Problems

Improper system shutdown can harm any computer. Power failures or fluctuations, and improper system shutdowns caused by them, usually are listed first during discussions about the possible causes of hardware damage and data loss in corporate networks. For network servers, improper shutdown can be disastrous! Furthermore, most system startup problems — such as damaged Master boot record (MBR) or boot sectors, missing or corrupted files, or a damaged registry — are caused by improper shutdown. In general, if you experience problems that prevent your system from shutting down gracefully, you eventually will experience startup problems. As outlined in *Chapter 9*, improper shutdowns also present a serious security threat. Do not overestimate the importance of graceful shutdown.

Performing an Emergency Shutdown

Curiously enough, even experienced users do not know what to do if a computer running Windows 2000, Windows XP, or Windows Server 2003 hangs or does not perform a graceful shutdown. When this happens, they simply power down the system. The best recourse, however, is to perform a so-called emergency shutdown.

The procedure for emergency shutdown described in this section will be helpful if your system stops responding, you cannot shut down normally, or you need to shut down quickly and prevent current information from being saved.

▶ Note

Although this procedure is less harmful than simply turning off the power, it should be used only in emergency situations.

To perform an emergency shutdown:

1. Press <Ctrl>+<Alt>+<Del>.
2. When the **Logon Information** screen is displayed, hold down the <Ctrl> key and press the **Shut Down** button. You will receive the following system message:

   ```
   If you continue, your machine will reboot and any unsaved data will
   be lost. Use this only as a last resort.
   ```

3. Press **OK**.

You can discover which shutdown option was used when you last invoked shutdown, either from the **Start** menu or by pressing the <Ctrl>+<Alt>+<Del> keyboard combination. By default, the system records this information under the HKEY_CURRENT_USER\Software\Microsoft\Windows\CurrentVersion\Explorer registry key. Under this key, you will find the Shutdown Setting value (REG_DWORD data type), which specifies the most recent shutdown method. The Shutdown Setting entry can have the following data values:

- ☐ 0x01 — Log off.
- ☐ 0x02 — Shut down. Ends your session and shuts down Windows 2000, Windows XP, or Windows Server 2003 so that you can safely turn off power.
- ☐ 0x04 — Restart. Ends your session, shuts down, and restarts Windows.
- ☐ 0x10 — Stand by. Maintains your session, keeping the computer running on low power with data still in memory (requires power management support).
- ☐ 0x20 — Stand by (with wakeup events disabled). Maintains your session, keeping the computer running on low power with data still in memory (requires power management support).
- ☐ 0x40 — Hibernate. Saves your session to disk so that you can safely turn off the power. Your session is restored the next time you start Windows.
- ☐ 0x80 — Disconnect. Disconnects your Terminal Server session. You can reconnect to this session when you log on again.

Common Methods of Troubleshooting Shutdown Problems

As outlined earlier in this chapter, shutdown and startup problems are interrelated. In addition, startup and shutdown problems often are caused by similar factors. For example, components that cause startup problems also might interfere with the shutdown process, and vice versa.

Graceful system shutdown is important. In this orderly process, Windows sends specific messages to devices, system services, and applications, notifying them of your intention to shut down the computer. While this process is in progress, Windows waits for applications to close files and allows them a certain amount of time to complete clean-up tasks, such as writing unsaved data to disk. Typically, every enabled device, system service, and application replies to the shutdown message request, indicating to the OS that shutdown can safely occur. The process of safely removing hardware, which I covered in *Chapter 5*, is a good example of such a behavior.

The most common reasons for shutdown problems include:

❏ Device drivers, system services, or applications that do not respond to shutdown messages or send reply messages to the system, informing it that they are busy

❏ Faulty or incompatible device drivers, services, or applications

❏ Hardware changes that cause device conflicts

❏ Firmware incompatibility or incorrect changes to firmware settings

Microsoft recommends the following methods of resolving problems that occur during system shutdown:

❏ Using Task Manager to close an unresponsive application or service

❏ Comparing normal and safe mode Bootlog.txt log entries

To end an unresponsive application or service:

1. Start the Task Manager application by pressing <Ctrl>+<Shift>+<Esc>.

2. Click the **Applications** tab. The **Applications** tab provides status information and displays each application as either **Running** or **Not Responding**. Click the item labeled **Not Responding**, and then click the **End Task** button.

3. To close offending service or driver, go to the **Processes** tab of the **Windows Task Manager** window (Fig. 12.4). To close a specific process, select it from the list and click the **End Process** button.

▶ *Note*

Windows 2000, Windows XP, and Windows Server 2003 have a set of so-called default processes, which are listed in Table 12.3. You cannot use Task Manager to close any of the processes that are marked with an asterisk (*) in this table. The processes that appear in Task Manager, but are not listed in this table, likely caused the problem.

Table 12.3. Default System Processes

Default process name	Description
Csrss.exe*	*Csrss* stands for *client/server run-time subsystem,* an essential subsystem that is always active. It is responsible for console windows and creating or deleting threads.
Explorer.exe	An interactive graphical user interface shell. It provides the familiar Windows taskbar and desktop environment.
Internat.exe	When enabled, Internat.exe displays the **EN** and other language icons in the system notification area, allowing the user to switch between locales. In Control Panel, click the **Regional and Language Options** icon to add keyboard layouts. This tool runs at startup and loads different input locales specified by the user. The locales are determined by the `HKEY_USERS\.DEFAULT\Keyboard Layout\Preload` registry key.
Lsass.exe*	The local security authentication (LSA) subsystem server component generates the process that authenticates users for the Winlogon service. The LSA also responds to authentication information received from the Graphical Identification and Authentication (GINA) Msgina.dll component. If authentication is successful, Lsass.exe generates the user's access token, which starts the initial shell. Other processes that the user initiates inherit this token.
Mstask.exe*	The task scheduler service. It runs tasks at a time determined by the user.
Smss.exe*	The Session Manager subsystem, which starts the user session. This process is initiated by the system thread and is responsible for various activities, including starting the Winlogon.exe and Csrss.exe services and setting system variables.
Spoolsv.exe*	The spooler service. It manages spooled print and fax jobs.
Svchost.exe*	A generic process that acts as a host for other processes running from dynamic-link libraries (DLLs). Multiple entries for this process might be present in the Task Manager list.
Services.exe*	The Services Control Manager starts, stops, and interacts with system services.
System*	Most system kernel-mode threads run as the System process.
System Idle*	A separate instance of this process runs for each processor present, with the sole purpose of accounting for unused processor time.
Taskmgr.exe	The process for Task Manager itself.

continues

Table 12.3 Continued

Default process name	Description
Winlogon.exe*	The process that manages user logon and logoff. Winlogon becomes active when the user presses <Ctrl>+<Alt>+<Del>, after which the logon dialog box appears.
Winmgmt.exe*	A core component of client management. It is a process that begins when the first client application connects, or when management applications request its services.

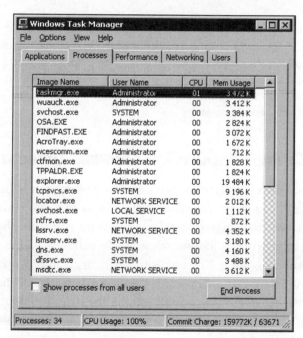

Fig. 12.4. The **Processes** tab of the **Windows Task Manager** window

To compare normal and safe mode Bootlog.txt log entries:

1. Restart the system in safe mode. This causes the system to create a safe mode version of the Ntbtlog.txt file.

2. Copy the safe mode Ntbtlog.txt log to a safe location, and rename the file to prevent it from being accidentally overwritten.

3. Restart the computer in normal mode with boot logging enabled. To enable boot logging, reboot the computer, press the <F8> key when prompted, and

select the **Enable Boot Logging** option from the **Windows Advanced Options** menu.

4. Compare the normal and safe mode versions of Ntbtlog.txt to determine the components not processed in safe mode.

In normal mode, one at a time, stop each application or service that does not appear in the safe mode list or in Table 12.3, which lists the default system processes. Restart the computer until you pin the cause of the shutdown problem. After you identify the problem component, you can disable it and search for an update.

 Note

In addition to these standard methods of troubleshooting shutdown problems, which are also available on Windows 2000, Windows Server 2003 includes Shutdown Event Tracker. This new feature provides a method for tracking why users restart or shut down their computers. This feature was discussed in *Chapter 4* among methods of customizing system startup and shutdown behavior.

Editing the Default Application Cleanup Timeout

Sometimes, when you want to shut down or restart your Windows NT-based operating system, you may see a dialog similar to the one shown in Fig. 12.5. Even worse, this may happen persistently and prevent you from shutting down correctly. This can result from Windows' cleanup default. When the OS shuts down, each running process is given 20 seconds to perform cleanup work. If a process does not respond within this timeout period, Windows displays this dialog.

To solve this problem, you can modify the default timeout by editing the registry. The timeout value is specified by the WaitToKillAppTimeout value under the following registry key:

```
HKEY_CURRENT_USER\Control Panel\Desktop
```

This value is expressed in milliseconds. You can use Registry Editor to modify this value. You must restart the computer for the change to take effect.

 Note

In general, it is not recommended that you increase the shutdown time. In a power failure, your Uninterruptible Power Supply (UPS) may not be able to provide backup power for the computer long enough to allow all the processes, as well as the operating system, to shut down properly.

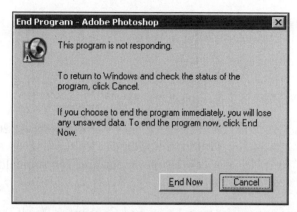

Fig. 12.5. This process didn't respond within the default time-out, preventing Windows from shutting down

Configuring Windows to Clear the Paging File at Shutdown

Some third-party programs may temporarily store unencrypted (plain-text) passwords or other sensitive information in memory. Since Windows XP and products of the Windows Server 2003 family are based on the Windows NT/2000 kernel, this information may be in the paging file, presenting a potential danger to the system security. Users concerned about security may wish to clear the paging file (Pagefile.sys) during shutdown to ensure unsecured data is not in the paging file when the shutdown process is complete.

Note

This tip is applicable to all versions of Windows NT-based systems, starting with Windows NT 3.51. Clearing the paging file is not a substitute for a computer's physical security. Still, it helps to secure data when Windows NT/2000/XP or Windows Server 2003 is not running.

To configure the system to clear the paging file at shutdown, proceed as follows:

1. If you are working with Windows XP or Windows Server 2003, start Regedit.exe. If you are working with Windows NT/2000, start Regedt32.exe.
2. Open the following registry key:

   ```
   HKEY_LOCAL_MACHINE\SYSTEM\CurrentControlSet\Control\Session Manager\
   Memory Management
   ```

3. Find the `ClearPageFileAtShutdown` value (`REG_DWORD` data type) and set its value to `1`. If this value doesn't exist, create it.

Note

This change does not take effect until you restart the computer.

In Windows 2000, Windows XP, and Windows Server 2003, the same task can be accomplished using Group Policy Object Editor (Fig. 12.6). The procedures are slightly different for domain environment and for standalone computers. In the domain environment:

1. Start the Active Directory Users and Computers MMC snap-in. Right-click the container for the domain or the organizational unit to which you want to apply the policy settings. Select the **Properties** command from the right-click menu.

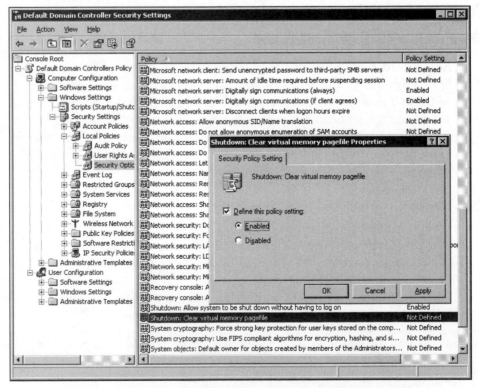

Fig. 12.6. Configuring the system to clear virtual memory pagefile using Group Policy Object Editor

2. Go to the **Group Policy** tab, select the GPO that you want to edit, and click the **Edit** button.

3. The required option can be found under **Computer Configuration | Windows Settings | Security Options**. Double-click the policy named **Shutdown: Clear virtual memory pagefile**, and enable the policy by setting the **Enabled** radio button as shown in Fig. 12.6.

On standalone or single computers, the procedure is similar, but you need to start Local Security Policy MMC snap-in and edit the required policy setting. This is located under **Local Security Policy | Computer Configuration | Windows Settings | Security Options**.

Enabling Verbose Startup, Shutdown, Logon, and Logoff Status Messages

Starting with Windows 2000, you can configure the system to receive verbose startup, shutdown, logon, and logoff status messages. Additional information contained in these status messages may be helpful when you are troubleshooting slow startup, shutdown, logon, or logoff behavior. As usual, this task can be accomplished through different methods — using Group Policies or directly editing the system registry.

To enable verbose status messages for a group of computers in a domain environment:

1. Click **Start**, point to **Administrative Tools**, and start the Active Directory Users and Computers MMC snap-in. When the snap-in starts, right-click the container corresponding to the domain or OU to which you want to apply the policy settings. Select the **Properties** command.

2. Go to the **Group Policy** tab, select one of the existing GPOs, and click **Edit**. Alternatively, you can create a new GPO by clicking the **New** button and providing a descriptive name for the new GPO.

3. When the Group Policy Object Editor window opens, expand **Computer Configuration | Administrative Templates | System** branches of the console tree. Go to the right pane and locate the **Verbose vs normal status messages** setting (Fig. 12.7).

4. Double-click this setting, set the **Enabled** option, and click **OK**.

5. Close Group Policy Object Editor, click **OK**, and quit Active Directory Users and Computers.

Note

Windows ignores this setting if the **Remove Boot / Shutdown / Logon / Logoff status messages** setting is enabled (in Fig. 12.7, this setting directly precedes the **Verbose vs normal status messages** setting).

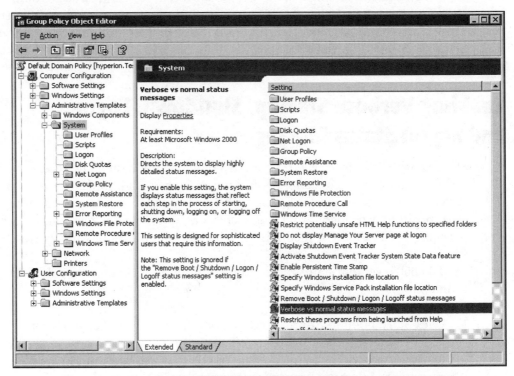

Fig. 12.7. Enabling the **Verbose vs normal status messages** policy in the domain environment

If you are using a standalone computer, or if you want to enable verbose status messages on only one computer, the procedure is similar. In this case, however, you need to edit the **Verbose vs normal status messages** setting under **Local Security Policy | Computer Configuration | Administrative Templates | System** within local GPO. To do so, start the Local Security Policy MMC snap-in. (For example, by clicking **Start**, selecting the **Run** command and typing the gpedit.msc command into the **Open** field.)

As mentioned earlier, you can also enable verbose status messages by editing the registry. To achieve this:

1. Start Regedit.exe (on Windows 2000 systems, use Regedt32.exe) and locate the following registry key: `HKEY_LOCAL_MACHINE\SOFTWARE\Microsoft\Windows\CurrentVersion\Policies\System`
2. Under this key, create a new `DWORD` value named `verbosestatus`, and set this value to `1`.
3. Quit Registry Editor.

► ***Note***

Why would someone directly edit the registry when the same task can be performed safely using the above-described GPO editing procedures, which reduce the chances of human error? Even on the standalone systems and in a workgroup environment, you can edit local security policy, which also reduces the chance of error and Is easier to use. However, direct registry editing retains its importance and can be more convenient. For example, you may need to make changes to many systems in a workgroup environment. Although applying a setting in local security policy is safer than registry editing, this option is not feasible if you have to update several thousands of Windows 2000/XP systems that are not joined to a domain. In this case, modifying the registry makes more sense, especially if you are working remotely.

► ***Note***

Windows does not display status messages If the `DisableStatusMessages` value entry (`DWORD` data type) is present under the same key and its value is set to `1`.

How to Unlock a Windows XP or Windows Server 2003 Computer

In Windows XP and Windows Server 2003, you can lock and unlock a computer either manually (by pressing the <WinKey>+<L> keyboard shortcut) or using a program (such as a screen saver). For example, you can lock your computer at the office then connect to it from another location and continue working with your documents. When you return to your workplace, you can unlock your system.

When a user logs on to a computer, the Winlogon Service stores a hash of the user's password for future unlock attempts. When the user attempts to unlock the system, this stored copy of the password is verified. If the password entered at the unlock-dialog request matches the stored hash, the computer is unlocked. If the password entered does not match the stored hash, the system attempts to perform logon and authenticate the password. If the logon process succeeds, the local hash is updated with the new password. If the logon process is unsuccessful, the unlock process will also be unsuccessful.

Note

For Windows XP Professional, this only happens when you have Fast User Switching disabled. When you join a Windows XP Professional computer to a domain, the Welcome Screen logon (and Fast User Switching) is disabled automatically.

The unlocking process described above was designed to limit network traffic generated by the workstation. However, if you need stringent security, you can edit the following registry setting: `ForceUnlockLogon` (`REG_DWORD` data type) under the following registry key:

```
HKEY_LOCAL_MACHINE\Software\Microsoft\WindowsNT\CurrentVersion\
Winlogon
```

If this value is set to 0 (the default value), the system doesn't force authentication; if it is set to 1, online authentication is required to unlock the workstation, which can force a validation at the domain controller for the user who attempts to unlock the computer.

How to Prevent Applications Listed in the Registry *Run* and *RunOnce* Keys from Starting

As outlined in *Chapter 6*, at logon Windows 2000, Windows XP, and Windows Server 2003 start the programs referenced in the following registry keys:

- ❏ HKEY_LOCAL_MACHINE\Software\Microsoft\Windows\CurrentVersion\RunOnce
- ❏ HKEY_LOCAL_MACHINE\Software\Microsoft\Windows\CurrentVersion\
  Policies\Explorer\Run
- ❏ HKEY_LOCAL_MACHINE\SOFTWARE\Microsoft\Windows\CurrentVersion\Run
- ❏ HKEY_CURRENT_USER\SOFTWARE\Microsoft\Windows\CurrentVersion\Run

Programs listed in the Run registry keys run every time the user logs on. The programs specified under RunOnce key run just once. These entries are generally configured by installation routines. However, Run and RunOnce registry keys also represent the favorite target for attacks and are used most often for installing worms, viruses, and Trojans. For this reason, you may wish to disable the Run and RunOnce lists for your computers.

To accomplish this, enable the **Do not process the run once list** and **Do not process the legacy run list** policies under **Computer Configuration | Administrative Templates | System** or **User Configuration | Administrative Templates | System | Logon** (Fig. 12.8).

If the policies are set to **Not configured**, you can implement them by editing the system registry. Using this method, you can disable the following registry keys that run applications at startup:

☐ HKEY_LOCAL_MACHINE\Software\Microsoft\Windows\CurrentVersion\Run

☐ HKEY_LOCAL_MACHINE\Software\Microsoft\Windows\CurrentVersion\RunOnce

☐ HKEY_CURRENT_USER\Software\Microsoft\Windows\CurrentVersion\Run

☐ HKEY_CURRENT_USER\Software\Microsoft\Windows\CurrentVersion\RunOnce

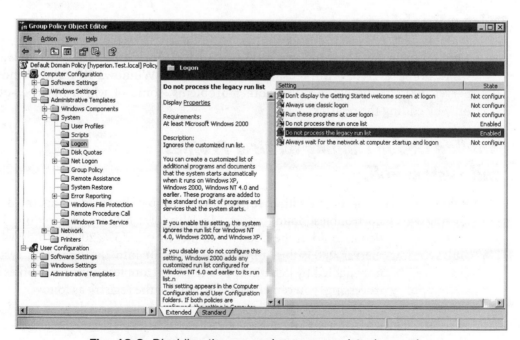

Fig. 12.8. Disabling the Run and RunOnce registry keys using Group Policy Object Editor

To disable any of the above keys, start Registry Editor and locate the following key:

```
HKEY_LOCAL_MACHINE\Software\Microsoft\Windows\CurrentVersion\
Policies\Explorer.
```

Under this key, create REG_DWORD value entries listed in Table 12.4. Set these values to 1. Setting these values to 0 will re-enable respective Run keys.

Table 12.4. Registry Values Disabling Run and RunOnce Keys

Value name	Disables the key
DisableLocalMachineRun	HKEY_LOCAL_MACHINE\Software\Microsoft\Windows\CurrentVersion\Run
DisableLocalMachineRunOnce	HKEY_LOCAL_MACHINE\Software\Microsoft\Windows\CurrentVersion\RunOnce
DisableCurrentUserRun	HKEY_CURRENT_USER\Software\Microsoft\Windows\CurrentVersion\Run
DisableCurrentUserRunOnce	HKEY_CURRENT_USER\Software\Microsoft\Windows\CurrentVersion\RunOnce

Other Problems

Certainly, startup and shutdown problems are the most important ones. However, while doing everyday work using Windows 2000, Windows XP, and Windows Server 2003, you may encounter other problems, some of which may be solved only by editing the registry.

Enabling Debug Logging for User Profiles and System Policy

If you experience problems with user profiles or group policy processing, the debug logging will help troubleshooting efforts. In Windows NT 4.0, this required the user to have a debug build of the Userenv.dll file. In Windows 2000, Windows XP, and Windows Server 2003, this functionality is built into the operating system. However, it is not enabled by default. If you need to troubleshoot user profiles and system policy processing, you can enable it by editing the registry as follows:

1. Start Registry Editor and open the following registry key:

   ```
   HKEY_LOCAL_MACHINE\Software\Microsoft\WindowsNT\CurrentVersion\
   Winlogon
   ```

2. Add the REG_DWORD registry value named UserEnvDebugLevel (or simply modify the value if it already exists). Set the value to 10002 (Hex).

3. Restart the computer. The log file is written to the *%SystemRoot%*\Debug\ UserMode\Userenv.log file.

Configuring the Backup Utility

If you back up your system on a regular basis, you've already noticed that the Backup utility supplied with Windows 2000, Windows XP, and Windows Server 2003 excludes certain files from the backup and recovery processes. To view the list of these files, start the Backup program, select the **Options** command from the **Tools** menu, and go to the **Exclude Files** tab (Fig. 12.9).

By default, Windows 2000, Windows XP, and Windows Server 2003 support the files and folders excluded from the backup and recovery processes preformed using Backup (Ntbackup.exe) and other compatible backup software.

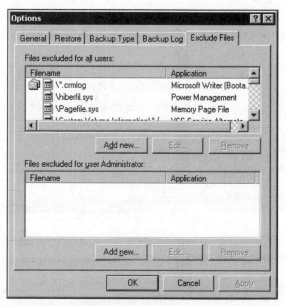

Fig. 12.9. The **Exclude Files** tab of the **Options** window
of the built-in Backup utility

Normally, the exclusion of these files is necessary. However, in some situations the system administrator or advanced user may need to include these files in the backup copy.

The files excluded from the backup and recovery processes are listed in the registry under the following registry key: HKLM\SYSTEM\CurrentControlSet\Control\ BackupRestore\FilesNotToBackup.

Microsoft provides an interface for editing the list of files excluded from backup and recovery processes. The **Exclude Files** tab of the **Options** window in the Backup program has buttons such as **Add new**, **Edit**, and **Remove**. However, all changes entered here will be written into the registry under HKEY_CURRENT_USER, affecting only the user who performed this modification. To change the list of files excluded from backup and recovery procedures for the whole system, the registry must be edited manually.

Default settings listed under the FilesNotToBackup key (they're all REG_MULTI_SZ values) are listed in Table 12.5.

Table 12.5. The List of Default Settings Under the FilesNotToBackup Key

Setting	Data
ASR error file*	*%SystemRoot%\repair*\asr.err
ASR log file*	*%SystemRoot%\repair*\asr.log
Digital Rights Management (DRM) folder*	*%SystemDrive%\Documents and Settings\All Users\DRM* * */s*
Catalog database*	*%SystemRoot%\System32\CatRoot2** */s*
Client Side Cache	*%SystemRoot%*\csc* /s
ComPlus	*%SystemRoot%*\Registration*.crmlog /s
Internet Explorer	*%UserProfile%*\index.dat /s
Memory Page File	\Pagefile.sys
Microsoft Writer (Bootable state)*	*%SystemRoot%\Registration*.clb* *.crmlog /s
Microsoft Writer (Service state)*	*%SystemRoot%*\system32\NtmsData*
MS Distributed Transaction	*%SystemRoot%*\System32\DTCLog\MSDTC.LOG
Netlogon*	*%SystemRoot%*\netlogon.chg
NtFrs	*%SystemRoot%*\ntfrs\jet* /s *%SystemRoot%*\debug\NtFrs* *%SystemRoot%*\sysvol\domain \DO_NOT_REMOVE_NtFrs_PreInstall_Directory* /s *%SystemRoot%*\sysvol\domain \NtFrs_PreExisting___See_EventLog* /s *%SystemRoot%*\sysvol\staging\domain\NTFRS_*

continues

Table 12.5 Continued

Setting	Data
Power Management	\hiberfil.sys
VSS Default Provider	\System Volume Information*{3808876B-C176-4e48-B7AE-04046E6CC752} /s
Temporary Files	*%TEMP%* /s*

* Introduced with Windows XP

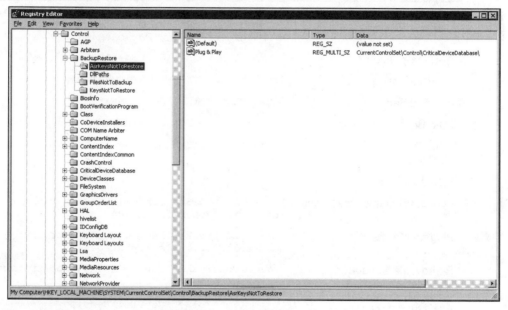

Fig. 12.10. The contents of the HKEY_LOCAL_MACHINE\SYSTEM\CurrentControlSet\ Control\BackupRestore\AsrKeysNotToRestore registry key (new in Windows XP and Windows Server 2003)

Note

The HKLM\SYSTEM\CurrentControlSet\Control\BackupRestore registry key in Windows XP and Windows Server 2003 contains a new subkey, HKEY_LOCAL_MACHINE\ SYSTEM\CurrentControlSet\Control\BackupRestore\AsrKeysNotToRestore, which holds a list of keys that should not be restored by the ASR process (Fig. 12.10). It points to the database of critical devices, which should not be edited because they need to be re-enumerated by the Setup program during ASR process.

Some registry keys are excluded from the backup procedures by default. These keys aren't listed on the **Exclude Files** tab of the **Options** window; consequently, you can't edit this list using the user interface. This list is stored in the registry under `KLM\SYSTEM\CurrentControlSet\Control\BackupRestore\KeysNotToRestore`.

The list of default settings present under this key is shown in Table 12.6.

Table 12.6. Default Settings Stored Under the `HKLM\SYSTEM\`
`Current ControlSet\Control\BackupRestore\KeysNotToRestore` **Registry Key**

Setting	Value
Active Directory Restore	`CurrentControlSet\Services\NTDS\Restore In Progress\CurrentControlSet\Services\ NTDS\Parameters\New Database GUID`
ASR Information*	`CurrentControlSet\Control\ASR\`
Fault Tolerance	`Disk\`
Installed Services	`CurrentControlSet\Services\*`
LDM Boot Information	`CurrentControlSet\Services\dmio\boot info\`
LDM Boot Information (dmboot)*	`CurrentControlSet\Services\dmboot\`
Mount Manager	`MountedDevices\`
Pending Rename Operations	`CurrentControlSet\Control\Session Manager\ PendingFileRenameOperations`
Plug and Play	`CurrentControlSet\Enum\CurrentControlSet \Control\CriticalDeviceDatabase\`
Removable Storage Manager*	`CurrentControlSet\Control\NTMS\ImportDatabase`
Session Manager	`CurrentControlSet\Control\Session`
Windows Setup	`Setup\SystemPartition`

* New in Windows XP and Windows Server 2003

Removing Invalid Items from the List Displayed by the Add/Remove Programs Wizard

The Add/Remove Programs applet in Control Panel is intended for adding, removing, or modifying the applications installed in your system. Starting with Windows 2000, this wizard has significantly improved and has a better user interface.

Despite the improvements, there may be some problems with the wizard. For example, if an application isn't removed correctly and completely, the reference to the application continues to appear in the **Currently installed programs** list. Any attempt to use the Add/Remove Programs wizard to remove the application (by clicking the **Change/Remove** button) results in a series of system messages. These messages say that because some files necessary for the correct removal of the application weren't found, the removal procedure can't be completed. The non-existent application remains in the list.

How can you solve this problem? To remove a non-existent application from the **Currently installed programs** list:

1. Start Regedit.exe and open the `HKEY_LOCAL_MACHINE\SOFTWARE\Microsoft\Windows\CurrentVersion\Uninstall` key.
2. Within this key, find the subkey created by the application you want to remove from the list. If the name of that key isn't evident, browse all the keys and view the `DisplayName` value. This specifies the strings displayed by the Add or Remove Programs wizard in the list of installed applications.
3. When you find the key whose `DisplayName` value specifies the name of the application you want to delete from the list, delete this key with all its contents. Warning: Never try to delete the whole `Uninstall` key!
4. Close Registry Editor. Verify that the Add and Remove Programs wizard no longer displays the incorrectly deleted application.

▶ *Note*

If you proceed according to this recommendation, you'll delete only the reference to the string displayed by the Add and Remove Programs wizard. However, it's possible that some files installed by the incorrectly deleted application will remain in your system. To remove the application completely, you'll need to delete all of its files and all registry entries used by the program. Only an advanced user should do this operation manually. (If you do this, don't forget to backup the registry before proceeding any further.)

Configuring Disk Quota Event Logging

Most advanced users and system administrators have noticed the useful Disk Quota capability, introduced with Windows 2000 and present in later versions. Disk Quota events are written to the event log (if enabled) through the logging option in **Quota** properties for a drive using the NTFS file system (Fig. 12.11).

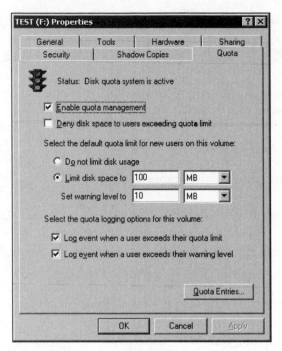

Fig. 12.11. The **Quota** tab of the NTFS drive Properties window

By default, Disk Quota event logging occurs asynchronously (once per hour). If you need to configure the system to log Disk Quota events as soon as a user exceeds one of the threshold values, you must edit the registry. Start Registry Editor, open the `HKEY_LOCAL_MACHINE\System\CurrentControlSet\Control\FileSystem` key, and create the `REG_DWORD` value named `NtfsQuotaNotifyRate`. By default, this isn't present in the registry. Specify the required rate of the Disk Quota event logging. (Specify the value in seconds.)

Summary

In this chapter, we discussed methods for solving some common Windows problems by using the registry. Of course, there are many problems like these. You'll discover numerous methods of using the registry to find solutions. I wish you good luck on this difficult but interesting road.

CHAPTER 13

Advanced Troubleshooting Topics

Just the place for a Snark! I have said it twice:
That alone should encourage the crew.
Just the place for a Snark! I have said it thrice:
What I tell you three times is true.

Lewis Carroll
The Hunting of the Snark

We have discussed the most common problems that can arise when working with Windows NT, Windows 2000, Windows XP, or Windows Server 2003. Let's now consider more advanced customization and troubleshooting topics. It's likely that you already have encountered some of the tips provided here, perhaps even in the previous chapters of this book. However, here we will cover these topics in more detail, and, after all, "what I tell you three times is true".

Interface Customizations

First, I would like to describe some useful user interface (UI) customizations. Most of these can't be set using the GUI tools or administrative utilities.

Registry Values for Configuring Start the Menu in Windows XP and Windows Server 2003

Most users, especially beginners, will prefer to customize the taskbar and **Start** menu using the standard Graphical User Interface (GUI). However, there are lots of capabilities that allow advanced users to customize the Windows XP or Windows Server 2003 interface by using Group Policy Object Editor or by editing the registry directly. Let's cover these settings in more detail.

The most convenient way to edit the taskbar and **Start** menu features is provided by Group Policy Object Editor. To start editing these policies in a workgroup environment or on a standalone Windows XP or Windows Server 2003 computer, proceed as follows:

1. Click **Start**, click **Run**, type mmc, and then click **OK**.
2. From the **File** menu, select the **Add/Remove Snap-in** command. Go to the **Standalone** tab, and click **Add**.
3. From the **Available Standalone Snap-ins** list, select the **Group Policy** option and click the **Add** button. When the **Select Group Policy Object** window opens, select the **Local Computer** option to edit the local Group Policy Object (GPO) or click **Browse** to find the Group Policy Object that you want.
4. Click **Finish**, then **Close**, then **OK**. The Group Policy snap-in opens the Group Policy Object for editing. Expand the console tree in the left pane of this window as follows: **User Configuration** | **Administrative Templates** | **Start Menu and Taskbar** (Fig. 13.1).

▶ Note

In a domain environment, to accomplish the same goal you must open the Group Policy tool MMC snap-in, focused on a specific GPO. To do so, start the Active Directory Users and Computers MMC snap-in, right-click the name of the domain or organizational unit of interest, and select the **Properties** command from the context menu. Then, go to the **Group Policy** tab and highlight the GPO of interest. (Note that if you haven't created any other GPOs, only the Default Domain Policy will be available.) Click the **Edit** button.

Let's choose the **Force classic Start Menu Properties** policy to demonstrate how policies are used to edit features.

1. Go to the right pane of the **Group Policy** window and double-click the **Force classic Start Menu** item in the list of available policies. The **Force classic Start**

Menu Properties window will open (Fig. 13.2). To view the explanation of the policy settings, click the **Explain** tab.

2. To set the selected policy, chose the **Enabled** radio button and click **Apply**.

3. Now, to view the effect of the application of this policy, open the **Taskbar and Start Menu Properties** window and go to the **Start Menu** tab. Notice that the **Start** menu radio button, which is present by default, has become unavailable. The user is now forced to use the classic Windows NT/2000-style **Start** menu (Fig. 13.3).

You can achieve the same result by editing the registry directly. For example, by enabling the **Force classic Start Menu** policy, you create the NoSimpleStartMenu registry value (REG_DWORD data type) under the HKEY_CURRENT_USER\Software\Microsoft\Windows\CurrentVersion\Policies\ Explorer registry key (Fig. 13.4).

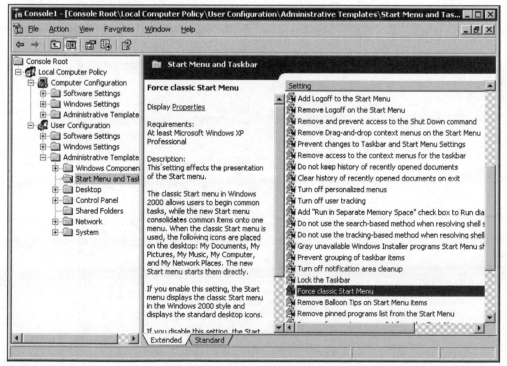

Fig. 13.1. Editing the **Start** menu and taskbar policies using Group Policy Editor

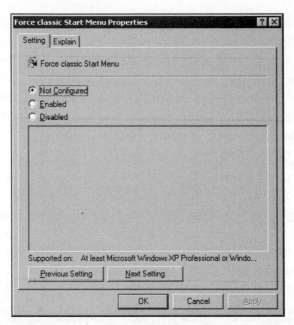

Fig. 13.2. The **Setting** tab of the **Force classic Start Menu Properties** window

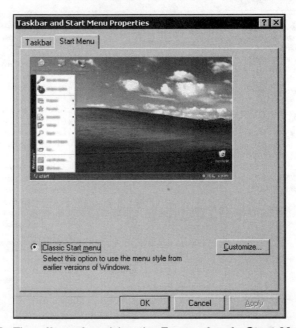

Fig. 13.3. The effect of applying the **Force classic Start Menu** policy

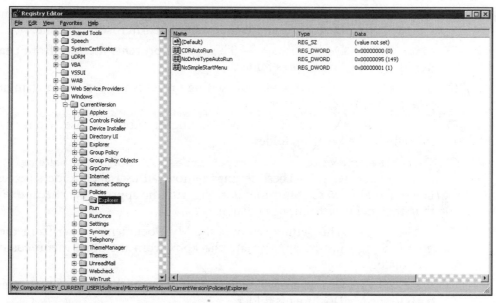

Fig. 13.4. The `HKEY_CURRENT_USER\Software\Microsoft\Windows\CurrentVersion\`
`Policies\Explorer` registry key reflects the effect of applying
the **Force classic Start Menu** policy

Other registry values that you can create to customize the taskbar and **Start** menu are listed below. Except where noted, these values are all of the `REG_DWORD` data type. They reside under the following registry key:

`HKEY_CURRENT_USER\Software\Microsoft\Windows\CurrentVersion\`
`Policies\Explorer`

If the value is set to `1`, the restriction is enabled; when the value is at `0`, the setting is disabled.

☐ `NoStartMenuPinnedList` — This setting removes the pinned programs list from the **Start** menu, along with the **Internet** and **E-mail** checkboxes.

☐ `NoStartMenuMFUprogramsList` — This setting removes the frequently used programs list from the **Start** menu.

☐ `NoStartMenuMorePrograms` — This setting removes the **More Programs** option from the **Start** menu.

☐ `NoCommonGroups` — This setting removes common program groups (items in the All Users profile in the **More Programs** list) from the **Start** menu.

☐ `GreyMSIAds` — This setting displays partially installed programs in gray on the **Start** menu.

❑ NoWindowsUpdate — This setting disables and removes links to Windows Update and locks access to the **Windowsupdate.Microsoft.com** site.

❑ DisableMyPicturesDirChange — This setting prevents the user from changing the path to the My Pictures folder.

❑ DisableMyMusicDirChange — This setting prevents the user from changing the path to the My Music folder.

❑ DisableFavoritesDirChange — This setting prohibits the user from changing the path to the Favorites folder.

❑ NoStartMenuMyMusic, NoSMMyPictures, NoFavoritesMenu, and NoRecentDocsMenu — These settings remove all user shell folders (except My Documents) from the **Start** menu, along with the appropriate checkboxes from the **Start** menu customization dialog.

❑ NoSMMyDocs — This setting removes the My Documents folder from the **Start** menu, along with the appropriate checkbox from the **Start** menu customization dialog.

❑ DisablePersonalDirChange — This setting prevents the user from changing the path to the My Documents folder.

❑ MaxRecentDocs — This setting specifies the maximum number of shortcuts to recently used documents displayed in the **Recent Documents** submenu.

❑ ClearRecentDocsOnExit — This setting clears the history list when the user logs off.

❑ NoRecentDocsMenu — This setting removes the **Recent Documents** folder from the **Start** menu.

❑ NoFavoritesMenu — This setting removes the **Favorites** menu from the **Start** menu, and removes an appropriate checkbox from the **Start** menu customization dialog.

❑ NoNetworkConnections — This setting removes the **Network Connections** item from the **Start** menu. This value also removes the corresponding checkbox that is normally available in the **Start** menu customization dialog.

❑ NoStartMenuNetworkPlaces — This setting removes the **Network Places** item from the **Start** menu and the appropriate checkbox from the **Start** menu customization dialog.

❑ NoRecentDocsNetHood — This setting prohibits the addition of remote shared folders to the **Network Places** item whenever the user opens a document in the shared folder.

❑ NoSMHelp — This setting removes the **Help** item from the **Start** menu. (This will not prevent Help files from running.)

❑ NoFind — This setting removes the **Search** command from the **Start** menu and disables the appropriate option in the **Start** menu customization dialog.

❑ NoRun — This setting removes the **Run** command from the **Start** menu, disables the appropriate checkbox in the **Start** menu customization dialog, and disables the ability to run programs from Task Manager or by pressing <WinKey>+<R>.

❑ MemCheckBoxInRunDlg — This setting adds the **Run in Separate memory Space** checkbox to the **Run** dialog, which allows 16-bit programs to run in a separate VDM (Virtual DOS Machine).

❑ NoSetTaskbar — This setting prevents any changes from being made to the Taskbar and **Start** menu settings. This value also removes the **Taskbar and Start Menu** item from Control Panel and from the **Start** menu.

❑ NoInstrumentation — This setting prevents the system from remembering the programs, paths, and documents used.

❑ NoUserNameInStartMenu — This setting removes the user name from the **Start** menu.

❑ NoResolveSearch — This setting prevents the system from searching the target drive to resolve a shortcut.

❑ NoResolveTrack — This setting prevents the system from using NTFS tracking features when resolving shell shortcuts.

❑ ForceStartMenuLogoff — This setting prevents the user from removing the **Logoff** option from the **Start** menu.

❑ StartmenuLogoff — This setting disables the **Logoff** option in the **Start** menu and prevents users from adding it.

❑ NoClose — This setting removes the **Turn Off Computer** option from the **Start** menu and prevents the user from shutting down the system using the standard shutdown user interface (UI).

❑ NoChangeStartMenu — This setting disables drag-and-drop modifications of the **Start** menu. (Other customization methods remain available unless they are explicitly disabled.)

❑ HKCU\Software\Microsoft\Windows\CurrentVersion\Policies\NonEnum\ {20D04FE0-3AEA-1069-A2D8-08002B30309D} — This setting removes the **My Computer** item from the **Start** menu and disables the corresponding checkbox in the **Start** menu customization dialog.

▶ Note

If the values listed above are created under HKEY_CURRENT_USER, they will be applicable only to the currently logged on user. If you want them to apply to all new users, create them under the HKEY_USERS\.DEFAULT\Software\Microsoft\Windows\ CurrentVersion\Policies\Explorer registry key.

Changing the Behavior of Taskbar Grouping

By default, when you enable the **Group similar taskbar buttons** option at the **Taskbar** tab of the **Taskbar and Start Menu Properties** window (Fig. 13.5), items are grouped only when the taskbar buttons begin to get too small. The item that you opened first is grouped first. Note that the Windows XP and Windows Server 2003 user interfaces allow you to enable or disable the taskbar grouping feature, but they don't provide the ability to change its behavior.

Therefore, registry editing is the most appropriate way to change the default behavior of the taskbar buttons grouping feature. To customize it, create the `TaskbarGroupSize` value (`REG_DWORD` data type) under the following registry key:

```
HKEY_CURRENT_USER\Software\Microsoft\Windows\CurrentVersion\
Explorer\Advanced
```

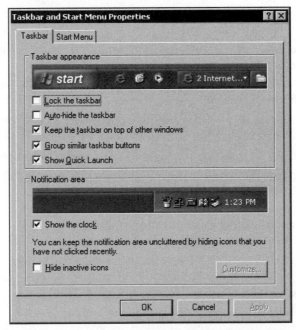

Fig. 13.5. The Taskbar tab of the **Taskbar and Start Menu Properties** dialog

The taskbar grouping behavior depends on the values you assign to the `TaskbarGroupSize` registry value entry. These values are:

❏ 0 — (default) groups by age (oldest group first)
❏ 1 — groups by size (largest group first)

❑   2 — groups any group of size 2 or more

❑   3 — groups any group of size 3 or more

Log off and then back on for this change to take effect.

Disabling Notification Area Balloon Tips

Notification Area balloon tips (Fig. 13.6) are a nice feature, especially for beginners. However, experienced users may become tired of them. For example, if one of your disks is running out of free space, you wouldn't want to be persistently reminded of this fact. Sometimes these tips simply distract you from your work. And, although this feature might be useful on Windows XP workstations, it is redundant for servers.

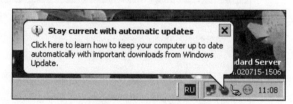

Fig. 13.6. An example of Notification Area balloon tips

To disable the feature:

1. Start Regedit.exe and expand the following key:

   `HKEY_CURRENT_USER\Software\Microsoft\Windows\CurrentVersion\Explorer\Advanced`

2. Create a new `REG_DWORD` value and name it `EnableBalloonTips`. Set this value to 0.
3. Quit Registry Editor, log off, then log back on.

▶ Note

These steps disable all Notification Area balloon tips for the current user. There is no way to disable balloon tips for a specific program.

Preventing a Program from Being Displayed in the Most Frequently Used Programs List

If you like the simple **Start** menu feature, first introduced with Windows XP and also present in Windows Server 2003, you have undoubtedly noticed that it maintains a list of the most frequently used programs. Now, suppose you want to continue using this feature, but you don't want some specific programs to appear in that list. What can you do about it? Of course, you can right-click the required shortcut and select the **Remove from This List** command from the context menu. However, this will not prevent the program from appearing in that list if you use it later. You can also configure the **Start** menu to specify the number of shortcuts in the list of most frequently used programs. You can clear this list by clicking the **Clear List** button (Fig. 13.7). If you don't want the list of most frequently used programs to be displayed, set the value in the **Number of programs on Start menu** field to 0.

This, however, won't prevent a specific application (Regedit.exe, for example) from appearing in the list.

Fig. 13.7. The **General** tab of **the Customize Start Menu** window

The exclusion of specific programs can't be accomplished using the GUI tools. However, if you edit the registry, you can easily achieve the desired result. To do so:

1. Start Registry Editor (Regedit.exe).
2. Add an empty string value named `NoStartPage` to the following registry key (*Program name.exe* is the name of the executable file that is used to start the program):

   `HKEY_CLASSES_ROOT\Applications\Program name.exe`

3. Quit Registry Editor, and restart the computer.

The application will be removed from the list of frequently used programs and will never appear in that list again.

Disabling System Beeps on Windows 2000, Windows XP, and Windows Server 2003

If you or your colleagues in the office care for silence, you might want to disable system beeps. This can be achieved by disabling the Beep driver or by direct registry editing.

To disable the Beep driver using built-in administrative tools:

1. Start Device Manager, select the **Show hidden devices** command from the **View** menu, and expand the **Non-Plug and Play Drivers** branch.
2. Right-click **Beep**, select the **Properties** command from the right-click menu, and go to the **Driver** tab of the **Beep Properties** window (Fig. 13.8).

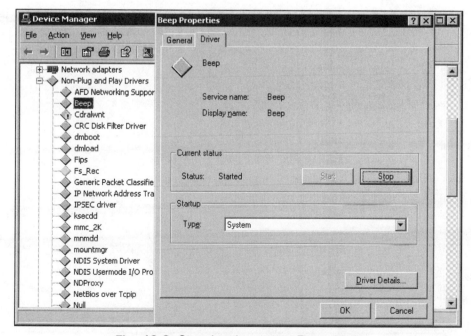

Fig. 13.8. Stopping the system Beep driver

3. Click the **Stop** button to stop the driver. To disable system beeps permanently, you can either change the **Startup Type** to **Disabled** or, if you have several hardware profiles, disable the Beep driver in one of the existing profiles.

Note

The change you have introduced will be applicable to all users who log on to the local system, since it will be saved under the HKLM registry key.

To disable Windows 2000, Windows XP, or Windows Server 2003 system beep for a specific user only:

1. Log on to the system as the user for whom you want to disable system beep.
2. Start Registry Editor and locate the following key: HKEY_CURRENT_USER\Control Panel\Sound (Fig. 13.9).
3. Under this key, locate the Beep value entry (REG_SZ data type) and set it to no.

Note

This time, the change will apply to a specific user, since it is saved under the HKCU registry key. For the change to take effect, you will have to log off and log back on.

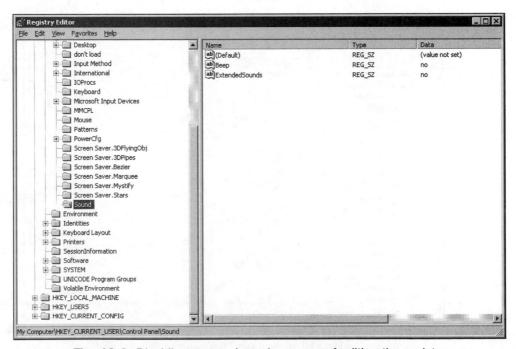

Fig. 13.9. Disabling system beep by means of editing the registry

Troubleshooting Aids

There are many registry-editing tips and tricks that can be used to customize the Windows XP or Windows Server 2003 user interface. Unfortunately, it's impossible to describe them all; even books dedicated to this topic usually only show the top of the iceberg. Some of these registry-editing techniques can be used as troubleshooting aids. In this section, I'll describe those that may be the most helpful.

Customizing System Restore for Windows XP Workstations within Your Domain Environment

System Restore, introduced with Windows XP, is one of the most useful features of this operating system (OS). Unfortunately, some users tend to disable it because it consumes a lot of free disk space (no less than 200 MB). If you are an administrator, you can prevent users from disabling System Restore. To achieve this, simply disable the GUI tools available on Windows XP workstations for configuring System Restore within your domain environment.

 Note

To perform these tasks, log on as Administrator or user with administrative privileges.

There are two ways of performing this task. Let's consider them both.

Using Group Policy Editor to Disable System Restore

To prevent users from disabling or configuring System Restore:

1. Open the Group Policy tool MMC snap-in, focused on a specific GPO. To do so, start the Active Directory Users and Computers MMC snap-in, right-click the name of the domain or organizational unit (OU) of interest, and select the **Properties** command from the context menu. Go to the **Group Policy** tab and highlight the GPO of interest. (Note that if you haven't created any GPOs, only the Default Domain Policy will be available.) Click the **Edit** button.

2. Expand the console tree **Computer Configuration | Administrative Templates | System | System Restore** (Fig. 13.10).

3. Double-click **Turn off System Restore.** On the **Setting** tab, select **Disable**. After you apply this policy, System Restore will be turned on and enforced. Click **Apply**, then click **OK**.

4. Double-click **Turn off Configuration**. On the **Setting** tab, select **Enable**. (For more information about what these settings do, click the **Explain** tab on the **Properties** dialog box.) Click **Apply**, then click **OK**.

5. Open a command prompt and type the `gpudate` command to refresh the policy.

Note

Gpupdate is the command introduced with Windows XP and Windows Server 2003 for refreshing Group Policy. This command replaces the `secedit refreshpolicy` command used in Windows 2000. If you choose not to use the `gpupdate` command, Group Policy will still refresh; it will just take longer. The settings described above are only read at boot time; therefore, it is necessary to reboot.

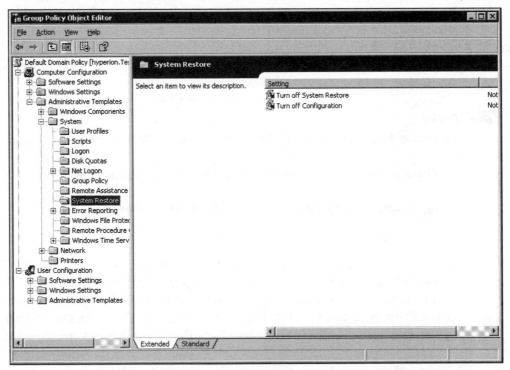

Fig. 13.10. Configuring System Restore using Group Policy Editor

Now, if users try to access System Restore Configuration on their Windows XP computers within your domain environment, the **System Properties** dialog box is present, but the **System Restore** tab is not.

Using Registry Editor to Disable System Restore

On standalone Windows XP computers or within a workgroup environment, you can either apply the setting described above in local security policy or make the registry key modification. As outlined in *Chapter 11*, applying changes via Local Security Policy is easier and much safer. However, direct registry editing might be preferable, especially if you have to update a large number of Windows XP workstations within a workgroup environment. To use Registry Editor for disabling the System Restore Configuration UI on a standalone Windows XP computer or within a workgroup environment, proceed as follows:

1. Start Regedit.exe and expand the following key:

    `HKEY_LOCAL_MACHINE\SOFTWARE\Policies\Microsoft\Windows NT`

2. Under `HKEY_LOCAL_MACHINE\SOFTWARE\Policies\Microsoft\Windows NT`, create a new nested key, named `SystemRestore`.
3. Within this key, create a new `REG_DWORD` value named `DisableConfig`, and set this value to `1`.
4. Close Regedit.exe and reboot the system.

▶ *Note*

You can manage settings by including the modified registry key in a script. More information on this topic will be provided in *Chapter 15*.

Problems with Configuring Encrypting File System in a Mixed Environment

Encrypting File System (EFS), first introduced with Windows 2000, protects sensitive data in files stored on NTFS-formatted disks. Only the user who encrypts a file can open that protected file and work with it. This is especially useful for securing sensitive data on computers shared by several users or on portable computers. For example, if someone else obtains a lost or stolen laptop, that person will be unable to access any of the encrypted files stored on that disk.

Windows XP and Windows Server 2003 include many improvements over EFS implementation in Windows 2000. You now have the option of encrypting the Offline Files database, which could not be encrypted under Windows 2000. To encrypt offline files, select the **Folder Options** command from the **Tools** menu in My Computer or Windows Explorer, go to the **Offline Files** tab, and set the **Encrypt offline files to secure data** checkbox (Fig. 13.11).

Note

Administrative privileges are required to configure how offline files will be encrypted.

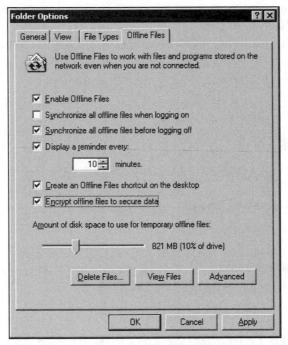

Fig. 13.11. Options for encrypting the Offline Files database

On the other hand, if EFS is not appropriate in your environment, or if you have files that you do not want encrypted, you can use one of several options to disable EFS. There are also numerous ways to configure EFS to meet the needs of your organization.

Unfortunately, this is where problems might arise, especially in a mixed environment. For example, you may have Windows 2000 and Windows Server 2003 domains with client workstations running Windows 2000 Professional. If you decide to upgrade client workstations to Windows XP Professional and want to disable EFS, you will notice that the public key policy, which disables Encrypting File System, has no effect on Windows XP clients.

Note

The same problem exists for Windows 2000 Professional clients joined to a Windows NT domain, since the Windows NT domain administrator cannot be a File Recovery Agent. To disable EFS on a computer running Windows 2000 Professional within a Windows NT domain, you must download Microsoft's hotfix (**http://support.microsoft.com/directory/ article.asp?ID=KB;EN-US;Q288579**). This hotfix adds the registry key, which will be discussed later in this section. Note it is still necessary to change the added registry value to 1 to disable EFS.

The reason for such behavior lies in the difference between the EFS models implemented in Windows 2000 and in its successors (Windows XP and Windows Server 2003). The new EFS model does not require a Data Recovery Agent to be present before files can be encrypted. In Windows 2000, this requirement was mandatory — no recovery agent, no encryption. Because of this limitation, you could prevent file encryption within an entire domain of Windows 2000 clients. You simply had to remove the Data Recovery Agent certificate from the public key policy and delete the recovery policy.

Windows XP Professional and Windows Server 2003 have no such limitation; they allow data encryption regardless of the existence of a Data Recovery Agent.

Thus, if you want to disable EFS in Windows XP or Windows Server 2003, it is necessary to use a different approach. Once again, you have several choices. For example, on standalone systems or within a workgroup environment, you can choose one of the following:

❑ Apply the setting in Local Security Policy
❑ Edit the system registry directly

For Windows XP clients joined in a Windows Server 2003 domain, the preferred method is to use a Group Policy setting. You also could choose to manage the changes by including the modified registry key in a script. For Windows XP workstations joined to Windows 2000 domains, you can add the modified registry key to a security template, and then import that template into Group Policy.

Using Group Policy to Disable EFS in Windows XP and Windows Server 2003

For a standalone Windows XP or Windows Server 2003 system, you can disable EFS using the following procedure:

1. From the **Start** menu, select **Programs | Administrative Tools | Local Security Policy**.

2. Expand the console tree and navigate to **Local Computer Policy | Computer Configuration | Windows Settings | Security Settings | Public Key Policies**.

3. Right-click the **Encrypting File System** folder and select the **Properties** command from the right-click menu.

4. The **Encrypting File System Properties** window will open (Fig. 13.12). Notice that in Windows XP or Windows Server 2003, EFS is enabled by default. To disable it, clear the **Allow users to encrypt files using the Encrypting File System (EFS)** check box. Click **OK.**

5. Open a command prompt and type gpupdate to refresh the policy.

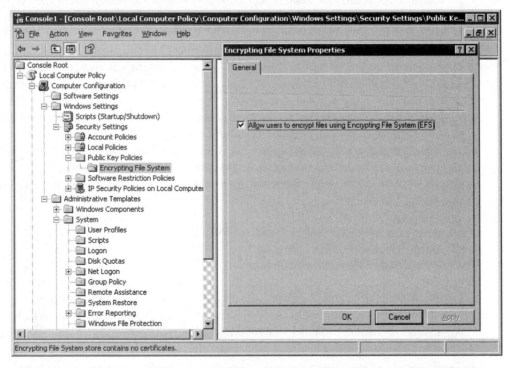

Fig. 13.12. Disabling EFS for a standalone Windows XP or Windows Server 2003 computer through a local security policy setting

▶ *Note*

Disabling EFS in a Windows Server 2003 domain environment is much like the procedure for a standalone system. The only difference is that in a domain environment you need to modify the EFS property page in Group Policy Object Editor focused on specific GPO and applied to a domain or organizational unit (OU).

Disabling EFS Using the Registry

To use the registry to disable EFS on a standalone computer running Windows 2000, Windows XP, or Windows Server 2003:

1. Start Registry Editor (if you are dealing with Windows 2000, use Regedt32.exe), and then open the HKEY_LOCAL_MACHINE\SOFTWARE\Microsoft\Windows NT\ CurrentVersion\EFS subkey.
2. Under this key, create a new REG_DWORD value and name it EfsConfiguration. To disable EFS, assign it a value of 1. If you need to re-enable EFS, simply change the value to 0.

Using Group Policy to Automate the EFS Disable Process

If you would like to add the ability to push the disabled setting through Group Policy on a Windows XP systems joined to a Windows 2000 domain, you can do so by editing the Sceregvl.inf file. This file resides in the *%Windir%*\inf folder and represents a list of registry settings that are exposed in the **Local Policy** | **Security Options** section of security templates (Fig. 13.13).

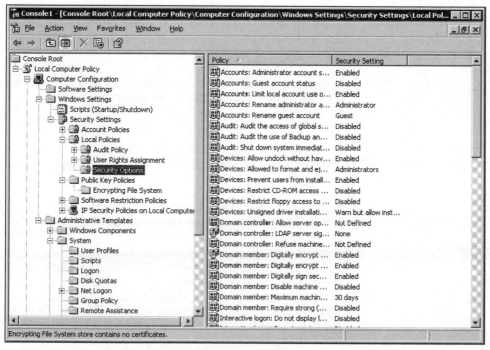

Fig. 13.13. The **Local Policy** | **Security Options** section of security templates

By adding registry information to the file, you can expose additional entries. This extends your ability to manage settings through security configuration and analysis or through Group Policy. The file has two sections: one lists registry keys, [Register Registry Values], and one details what will appear in the security template, [Strings].

First, add the registry information to the file. The following line should be placed within the other registry settings in the [Register Registry Values] section:

```
MACHINE\Software\Microsoft\Windows
NT\CurrentVersion\EFS\EfsConfiguration,4,%EfsConfiguration%,0
```

The syntax for the entries in the [Register Registry Values] section is:

RegistryPath, *RegistryType*, *DisplayName*, *DisplayType*, *Options*

The parameters listed above are briefly explained in Table 13.1.

Table 13.1. Parameters Used in the [Register Registry Values] Section of the Sceregvl.inf File

Parameter	Explanation
RegistryPath	Defines the full path to the registry key and value entry that you want to expose in the Group Policy Editor user interface (UI). Only values that exist under the HKEY_LOCAL_MACHINE root key can be configured. Notice that in the command syntax this root key is referenced by the MACHINE keyword.
RegistryType	Specifies a number that defines the data type of the registry value to be created. The following values are acceptable: 1 — REG_SZ 2 — REG_EXPAND_SZ 3 — REG_BINARY 4 — REG_DWORD 7 — REG_MULTI_SZ
DisplayName	Specifies the string that appears in the Security Options section of the Group Policy Editor UI. This is usually a replaceable parameter that refers to an entry in the [strings] section of the Sceregvl.inf file.
DisplayName	Indicates the type of dialog that should be displayed to allow the user to configure a specific setting. The following values are acceptable: 0 — Boolean: Causes the UI to render two radio buttons, which "enable" or "disable" the registry value. If the **Enabled** option is selected, the registry value is set to 1. If the **Disabled** radio button is chosen, the registry value is set to 0.

continues

Table 13.1 Continued

Parameter	Explanation
DisplayName	1 — `Numeric`: Causes the UI to render a numeric control that allows the user to type in or select a numeric value in the range of 0 to 99999. Numeric display types can specify "unit" strings, such as "minutes" or "seconds", that appear next to the spin control in the UI. These "unit" strings are defined in the **Options** field described below. The registry value is set to the number entered by the user.
	2 — `String`: Causes the UI to render a text box. The registry value is set to the string entered by the user.
	3 — `List`: Causes the UI to render a list box from which the user can select an option. The registry value is set to the numeric value associated with the option chosen by the user. The options presented to the user are defined in the **Options** field described below.
	4 — `Multivalued` (unavailable on Windows 2000): Causes the UI to render an edit control that allows the user to enter multiple lines of text. This display type should be used to define values for `MULTI_SZ` types. The registry value is set to the strings entered by the user; each line is separated by a `NULL` byte.
DisplayName	5 — `Bitmask` (unavailable on Windows 2000): Causes the UI to render a series of checkboxes. Each checkbox corresponds to a numeric value defined in the **Options** field described below. The registry value is set to the bitwise `OR` of the selected values.
Options	Qualifies different *DisplayTypes* as follows:
	If `DisplayType=1` (Numeric), the options field may contain a string that defines the units for the numeric value. The unit string is displayed next to the spin control in the UI. The unit string has no affect on the value set in the registry.
	If `DisplayType=3` (List), the options field defines the list options that are available to the user. Each option consists of a numeric value separated by the "pipe" character '|' followed by the text for the choice. The registry value is set to the numeric value associated with the choice made by the user.
	If `DisplayType=5` (Bitmask), the options field defines the choices that are available to the user. Each choice consists of a numeric value separated by the "pipe" character '|' followed by the text for the choice. The registry value is set to the bitwise `OR` of the choices selected by the user.

Thus, the command that we have added to the `[Register Registry Values]` section (`MACHINE\Software\Microsoft\Windows NT\CurrentVersion\EFS\ EfsConfiguration,4,%EfsConfiguration%,0`) can be explained as follows:

❏ *RegistryPath* = `MACHINE\Software\Microsoft\Windows NT\CurrentVersion\ EFS\EfsConfiguration` — This adds the `EfsConfiguration` value to the HKEY_LOCAL_MACHINE\Software\Microsoft\Windows NT\CurrentVersion\EFS registry key.

❑ *RegistryType* = 4 — The added value must be of the REG_DWORD data type.

❑ *DisplayName* = %EfsConfiguration% — This references the string value in the [Strings] section of the Sceregvl.inf file.

❑ *Display type* = 0 — The dialog represented by the Group Policy Editor UI must have two radio buttons: **Enabled** and **Disabled**.

Now, it is necessary to add a string for display in the GUI to the [Strings] section of the Sceregvl.inf file, for example:

```
EfsConfiguration = "Public Key Infrastructure: Users cannot encrypt files"
```

After the required modifications have been introduced into the Sceregvl.inf file, save it and run the following command at the command prompt:

```
Regsvr32 scecli.dll
```

This command is required to register the changes. If the command is accomplished successfully, a pop-up window will appear.

The list of security options available in the security template now should include your option; your options also should be found in Group Policy Objects (GPOs) examined on this machine. To use the security template, set its value to **Enabled.** Save the template and import it into a Group Policy linked to the organizational unit (OU) in which Windows XP computer accounts reside.

Troubleshooting Windows Installer Issues

In *Chapter 11*, we considered Windows Installer technology and its relationship to the system registry. As outlined in that chapter, the executable file that comprises the Windows Installer service (and is installed on every Windows 2000, Windows XP, or Windows Server 2003 computer by default) is the Msiexec.exe file. By default, the Installer service runs in the LocalSystem security context and can perform any system changes. Besides this, the Installer service can install MSI packages on behalf of the user logged on to the system. The Installer service can determine if the application installation is broken or corrupt and can attempt to fix it. Finally, the Installer service can roll back an application installation if it fails before completion.

Note

While an application installation is in progress, Windows Installer creates temporary files (located in the *%SystemDrive%*\config.msi folder). During a rollback, these files are used to undo steps taken before the failure.

Despite the advantages of Windows Installer, you can encounter problems when installing applications with the technology. In this section, we will briefly consider the most important problems and discuss some troubleshooting techniques.

Using MSIEXEC from the Command Line

As outlined in *Chapter 11*, Windows Installer is a system service. It also can be invoked interactively by the Msiexec.exe command-line tool, which provides powerful capabilities for managing your *.msi packages.

The syntax used by the Msiexec.exe command-line tool is:

```
msiexec.exe /command line option <argument>
```

Here, `argument` must be the path and name of the file. The most common command-line options used with the Msiexec.exe command are:

- `/i <argument>` : Install a product
- `/f <MSI file name>`: Repair a product (*)
- `/a <MSI file name>`: Install a product in "Run from Network" or Administrative mode
- `/x <MSI file name>`: Uninstall a product
- `/j <MSI file name>`: Assign a product (immediately places a shortcut on the desktop or Start menu)
- `/jm <MSI file name>`: Assign a product per machine
- `/ju <MSI file name>`: Assign a product per user
- `/j[u | m] <MSI file name> /t <MST Transform file>`: Assign a product and apply a transform
- `/l <log file name>`: Use in conjunction with one of the above operations to log install (or repair) information to `<log file name>` (*)
- `/p <Patch Package Name>`: Apply a patch to a product
- `/q [n,b,r,f]` : Sets the verbosity of the Install interface to
    - `/qn` = No UI at all
    - `/qb` = Basic UI
    - `/qr` = Reduced UI
    - `/qf` = Full UI
    - `/qn+` = No UI except for completion dialog
    - `/qb+` = Basic UI with completion dialog

Note

Actually, the list of command-line options for the `Msiexec.exe` tool is significantly larger. The options marked here with asterisks (*) have additional suboptions available. A complete list of these options and detailed information about their usage can be found in Microsoft's MSDN Online Library (**http://msdn.microsoft.com**). Furthermore, Microsoft has published a detailed FAQ on Windows Installer, which can be found at **http://www.microsoft.com/ windows2000/community/centers/management/msi.faq.asp**.

Windows Installer is Unavailable on Windows XP and Windows Server 2003

Although the Windows Installer service is installed by default, sometimes it might not be installed correctly. The symptoms of this problem are as follows:

❏ You repeatedly cannot run an installation of an *.msi file successfully.

Note

If you cannot run a single Windows Installer package successfully (but attempts to install other *.msi packages succeed), contact the vendor of that package for support on that particular product's installation. In addition, note that when you invoke an application install from the command line using `msiexec.exe`, you don't, by default, get the elevation of privileges that occurs when you've published or assigned an application via Group Policy. Thus, if you are not a member of the Power Users or Administrators built-in local security groups, the install might fail because of insufficient privileges.

❏ When you attempt to install a program that uses Windows Installer, you receive an error message similar to the following:

```
The Windows Installer service could not be accessed. This can occur
if you are running in safe mode or if the Windows Installer is not
correctly installed.
```

The most probable cause of this problem lies in incorrect or corrupted registration of the Windows Installer engine. To eliminate this problem, you need to unregister and then re-register the Windows Installer service by following these steps:

1. Click the **Start** button, select the **Run** command, and type the `cmd` command into the **Open** field to start the command prompt window.
2. Issue the command `msiexec /unregister` and press <Enter>. This procedure stops the Windows Installer service and unregisters it.

3. Issue the command `msiexec /regserver` and press <Enter>. This command reregisters the service and assures that it is functioning properly.

Note

If this procedure doesn't resolve the problem, you can remove the Windows Installer engine files and do a clean reinstallation.

Enabling Windows Installer Logging

For Windows NT-based applications and systems — including Windows 2000, Windows XP, and products of the Windows Server 2003 family — event logging provides a standard and centralized method for recording important system events related to hardware, software, security, etc. Windows Installer also writes entries into Event Log, which records events such as:

☐ Success or failure of the installation, removal, or repair of a product
☐ Errors that occur during product configuration
☐ Detection of corrupted configuration data
☐ Information about the missing components that cause a repair of an application

Windows Installer 2.0, the latest major release for Windows Installer, provides improved logging options. In previous versions of the service, error codes fell within two or three non-unique event IDs. With Windows Installer 2.0, each error receives an ID, which greatly improves how you can search for and filter Windows Installer events. Besides the OS event log, Windows Installer records errors and events in its own internal error log. The type of logging depends on the options used when enabling the logging mode. You can use various means to enable the logging mode, including:

☐ Issuing the `Msiexec` command with the `/L` option
☐ Editing the registry

When enabling Windows Installer logging from the command line using the `/L` option, you can specify exactly what information is logged and where. To create a log, append `/L<suboptions> Logfile_name` to your `Msiexec` command line. For example, appending the `/L* Logfile_name` command line creates a normal log file with all suboptions except `v` (verbose). To produce a verbose log file, which provides more comprehensive information, use the following syntax: `/L*v Logfile_name`.

Note

If you don't specify a log file name, log files will be stored in your Temp folder under random names starting with the letters Msi.

The list of suboptions available when using the /L command-line switch, is provided below.

- ❏ I — Status messages
- ❏ W — Non-fatal warnings
- ❏ E — All error messages
- ❏ A — Startup of actions
- ❏ R — Action-specific records
- ❏ U — User requests
- ❏ C — Initial UI arguments
- ❏ M — Out-of-memory or fatal-exit information
- ❏ O — Out-of-disk-space messages
- ❏ P — Terminal properties
- ❏ V — Verbose output
- ❏ + — Append to existing file
- ❏ ! — Flush each line to the log
- ❏ * — Log all information except the v option. To include the v option, specify "/l*v"

To enable Windows Installer logging via the registry, start Registry Editor and create a new REG_SZ value entry named Logging under the HKEY_LOCAL_MACHINE\ Software\Policies\Microsoft\Windows\Installer registry key. Set it to a value that could contain the characters from the list above.

Note

You should enable Windows Installer verbose logging only for troubleshooting purposes. After having detected and eliminated the problem, do not leave it enabled because it will have adverse effects on system performance and disk space. Each time you use the Add/Remove Programs tool in Control Panel, a new Msi*.log file is created.

Resetting TCP/IP Settings in Windows XP and Windows Server 2003

If you carefully view the list of networking components for a network interface in Windows XP and Windows Server 2003, you'll notice a strange fact —

the **Uninstall** button is disabled when Internet Protocol (TCP/IP) is selected (Fig. 13.14). In Windows 2000 and earlier versions, it was possible to remove the TCP/IP stack. According to Microsoft, this option is no longer offered because the TCP/IP stack is a core component of the operating system; therefore, it is not possible to uninstall it.

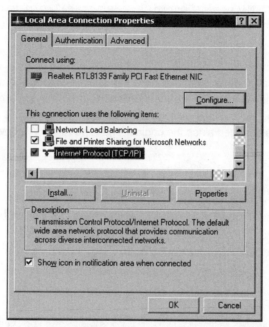

Fig. 13.14. In Windows XP and Windows Server 2003, the **Uninstall** button is disabled when you select TC/IP protocol in the **Local Area Connection Properties** window

What if you want to reset the TCP/IP stack by returning it to its state when the operating system originally was installed? In Windows XP and Windows Server 2003, you can't remove and then reinstall it. However, there is a convenient way to work around this problem. To do so, you must use the netsh (NetShell) utility, which provides a command-line interface for configuring and monitoring Windows XP or Windows Server 2003 networking.

In Windows XP, netsh utility provides a reset command, which rewrites registry keys related to TCP/IP. Consequently, you will get the same result as removing the TCP/IP stack and then reinstalling it.

To reset TCP/IP settings in the registry, go to the command line (**Start | Run**, type cmd, and press <Enter>), then issue the following command:

```
netsh interface ip reset [log_file_name]
```

Instead of *log_file_name*, use the name of the log file where the action will be recorded. If you don't specify the full path to the log file, it will be created in the current directory.

The command will reset TCP/IP settings stored under the following registry keys:

```
HKLM\SYSTEM\CurrentControlSet\Services\Tcpip\Parameters\
HKLM\SYSTEM\CurrentControlSet\Services\DHCP\Parameters\
```

 Note

If a log file already exists, the new log will be appended to the end of existing file. In addition, the contents of the log file depend on the system configuration. There may be times when no actions will be logged. This usually happens if the TCP/IP registry settings have not been changed since the original Windows XP or Windows Server 2003 installation.

Troubleshooting Service Startup Problems

Sometimes, you may encounter a service that can't start because of a logon failure. If this happens, the system might display error messages. Then, the next time you start the system, the following error messages may be in the system event log:

```
Source: Service Control Manager
Event ID: 7000
Description:
The %service% service failed to start due to the following error:
The service did not start due to a logon failure.
```

No information in the **Data** field will be available.

```
Source: Service Control Manager
Event ID: 7013
Description:
Logon attempt with current password failed with the following error:
Logon failure: unknown user name or bad password.
```

No information in the **Data** field will be available (Fig. 13.15).

When you attempt to manually start the service, you will receive an error message informing you that the service could not start because of logon problems. This behavior can occur for any of the following reasons:

❏ The account password the service uses to log on has been changed.

❑ The password data in the registry has been damaged.

❑ The right to log on as a service has been revoked for the specified user account.

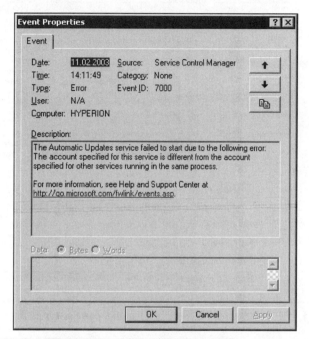

Fig. 13.15. The **Event Properties** window displaying the error message
on the service startup failure because of logon failure

To resolve these issues, you can configure the service to use the built-in system account, change the password for the specified user account to match the current password for that user, or restore the user's right to log on as a service.

If the right to log on as a service is revoked for the specified user account, you can restore this right. The procedure is somewhat different for domain controllers and member servers/client workstations. If the problem takes place at the controller of an Active Directory domain, proceed as follows:

1. Start the Active Directory Users and Computers Microsoft Management Console (MMC) snap-in.

2. Right-click the organizational unit (OU) in which the user right to log on as a service was granted. By default, this is in the **Domain Controllers** OU.

3. Right-click the container, then click **Properties**.

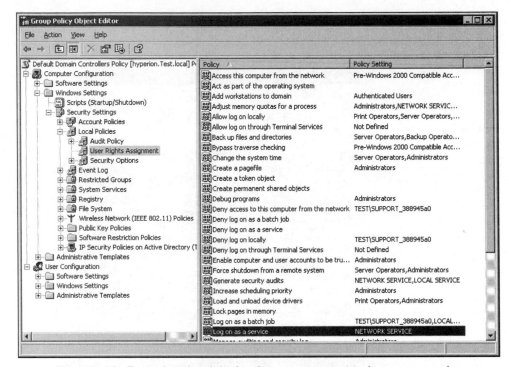

Fig. 13.16. Restoring the right for the user account to log on as service

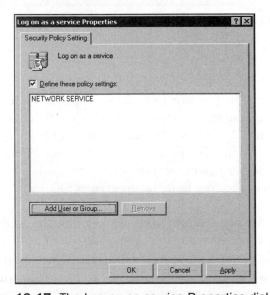

Fig. 13.17. The Log on as service Properties dialog

4. On the **Group Policy** tab, click **Default Domain Controllers Policy**, then click **Edit**. This starts Group Policy Object Editor.

5. Expand the **Computer Configuration** object by clicking the plus sign (+) next to the policy object. Under the **Computer Configuration** object, expand **Windows Settings**, then expand **Security Settings**.

6. Expand Local Policies and click **User Rights Assignment** (Fig. 13.16).

7. In the right pane, right-click **Log on as a service** (Fig. 13.17).

8. Add the user to the policy and click **OK**.

9. Quit Group Policy Object Editor, close **Group Policy Properties**, then close the Active Directory Users and Computers MMC snap-in.

If the problem arises at the member server or a standalone computer, take the following steps:

1. Start the Local Security Settings MMC snap-in.

2. Expand Local Policies and click User Rights Assignment.

3. In the right pane, right-click **Log on as a service**, then click **Properties**. The **Log on as service Properties** window will open.

4. Add the user to the policy and click **OK**.

Configuring Service Logon Information

To configure the password for the specified user account to match the current password for that user:

1. Start the Administrative Tools applet in Control Panel, then double-click the **Services** icon.

2. Right-click the appropriate service, then click **Properties**.

3. The service properties window will open. Go to the **Log On** tab (Fig. 13.18), change the password, and click **Apply**.

4. Go to the **General** tab (Fig. 13.19), and click the **Start** button to restart the service.

If the service starts, you have successfully eliminated the problem. In some situations, the service may not start with the specified user account. In such a case, you may reconfigure the service to start up with the built-in system account.

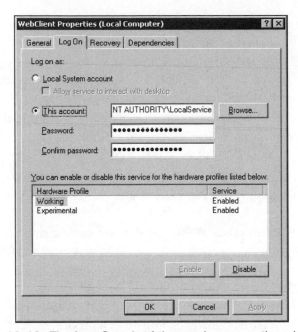

Fig. 13.18. The **Log On** tab of the service properties window

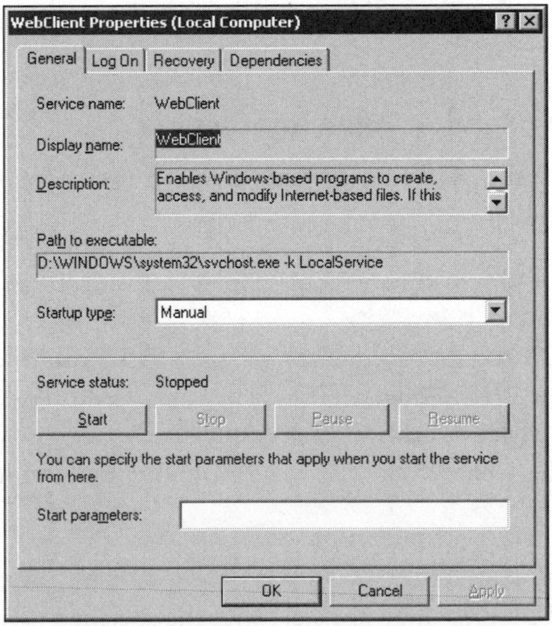

Fig. 13.19. The **General** tab of the service properties window

Configuring the Service to Start Up with the Built-in System Account

To configure the service to start up with the built-in system account:

1. Start the Administrative Tools applet in Control Panel, then double-click the **Services** icon.

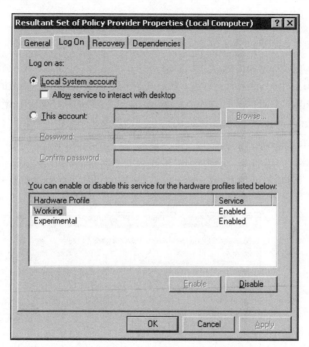

Fig. 13.20. Configuring the service to start up with the Local System account

2. Right-click the appropriate service, then select the **Properties** command from the right-click menu.
3. Go to the **Log On** tab (Fig. 13.20), set the **Local System Account** radio button, and click **Apply**. If the service needs to interact with the desktop, set the **Allow service to interact with desktop** checkbox. (Task Scheduler is an example of a built-in system service that requires interaction with the desktop.) Some third-party services, such as the F-Secure Authentication agent, also need to interact with the desktop. However, as most services don't need this feature, typically you may leave this checkbox unselected.
4. Go to the **General** tab and click the **Start** button to restart the service.

Using Registry Editor to Troubleshoot Service Startup Problems

If you are able to start the Services tool, you can use the procedures described above to troubleshoot service startup problems. Sometimes, however, there may be situations when you are unable to use the Services administrative tool. For example, the computer may hang when you start this tool, and the following message may be displayed:

```
The RPC Server is unavailable
```

It is logical to suppose that the Services tool would not start because of a logon failure with the Remote Procedure Call (RPC) or a dependent service. Some services do not start until their dependent services have connected. For example, the Alerter service depends on the Workstation service (Fig. 13.21). To view the dependencies for a specific service, right-click the required service, select the **Properties** command from the context menu, and go to the **Dependencies** tab. As you can see, the dependencies list for the RPC service is quite long (Fig. 13.22).

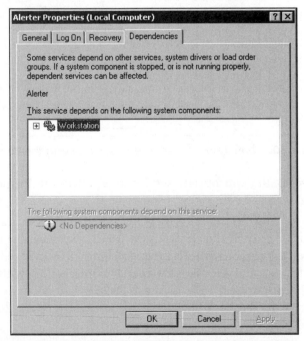

Fig. 13.21. The Alerter service depends on the Workstation service

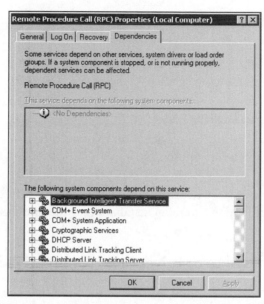

Fig. 13.22. The dependencies list for RPC service is quite long

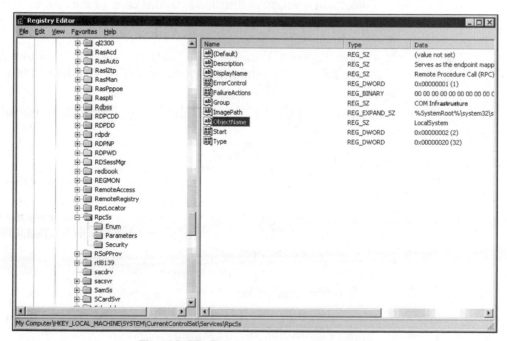

Fig. 13.23. The `ObjectName` value under
`HKEY_LOCAL_MACHINE\SYSTEM\CurrentControlSet\Services\`*`ServiceName`*

If a logon failure with the RPC service prevents you from starting the Services tool and using the safe method of configuring services, proceed as follows:

1. Start Registry Editor and locate the `ObjectName` value under the `HKEY_LOCAL_MACHINE\SYSTEM\CurrentControlSet\Services\ServiceName` registry key.
2. Modify that value entry by setting its value to `localsystem` (Fig. 13.23), click **OK**, and quit Registry Editor.
3. Attempt to restart the service. You may need to restart the computer for some services to restart properly.

If you cannot start Registry Editor, you can modify the service account information by performing a parallel installation of the operating system.

Disabling a Service or Driver that Prevents Windows from Booting

If you have managed to detect the service or device driver that prevents your system from booting, and if you have installed a parallel copy of the operating system that is bootable, you can try to eliminate the problem using the following procedures:

1. Boot into a parallel copy of the system and start Regedit.exe (Windows XP or Windows Server 2003) or Regedt32.exe (Windows NT or Windows 2000).
2. Go to the `HKEY_LOCAL_MACHINE` root key.
3. Use the **Load Hive** command to open the following registry file in the original Windows installation:

   %SystemRoot%\System32\Config\System

   When prompted to assign a name for the hive, assign it a name other than System (for example, System1).
4. Go to the `HKEY_LOCAL_MACHINE\SYSTEM1\Select` registry key and note the value for `Current:REG_DWORD`. (This selects which `ControlSet00x` to load when booting and is the one that needs modification.)
5. Perform the following steps to disable a service:
   - Go to the following registry key:

     `HKEY_LOCAL_MACHINE\TEST\ControlSet00x\Services \<Name of suspected service>`, where x is the value of `Current:REG_DWORD`
   - Change the value of `Start:REG_DWORD` to 0x4.

▶ *Note*

As outlined in *Chapter 6*, valid startup options for the service include 0x2 (Automatic), 0x3 (Manual), and 0x4 (Disabled). Thus, by setting the Start value to 0x4, you disable the service.

To disable a device driver, proceed as follows:

- Go to the HKEY_LOCAL_MACHINE\SYSTEM1\ControlSet00x\Services\<*Name of suspect driver*> where x is the value of Current:REG_DWORD.
- Change the value of Start:REG_DWORD to 0x4.

▶ *Note*

As shown in *Chapter 6*, valid startup options for device drivers include 0x0 (Boot), 0x1 (System), 0x2 (Automatic), 0x3 (Manual), and 0x4 (Disabled).

6. After you have introduced all required modifications, unload the System1 hive, quit Registry Editor, and try to reboot the original versions of Windows NT/2000/XP or Windows Server 2003.

Summary

In this chapter, we briefly considered some advanced customization and troubleshooting topics. I hope that these will help you to get the most out of your Windows operating system (and troubleshoot it, if necessary). All the tricks described here can be performed using the built-in tools of the operating system. However, there are many valuable third-party tools and utilities that may be useful for everyday work with Windows NT/2000/XP or Windows Server 2003. These will be discussed in the next chapter.

CHAPTER 14

Third-Party Registry Utilities

Shall I refuse my dinner because I do not fully understand the process of digestion?

Oliver Heaviside

Each new Microsoft operating-system version, including Windows XP and Windows Server 2003, provides a number of new configuration or administrative utilities. Each of these tools offers new and more convenient methods of editing the registry than those offered by the built-in registry editors (Regedt32.exe or Regedit.exe). Despite this fact, some of the registry tricks (including those discussed in the previous chapter) cannot be performed without editing the registry directly. Microsoft develops more and more advanced methods of registry editing, and most of these are in the form of Control Panel applets for new administrative utilities and wizards. But Microsoft is not alone. Third-party developers have also been active in this sphere.

If you are an experienced Internet user, you can find a large number of useful and handy freeware utilities to help you maintain and troubleshoot your registry.

In this chapter, we will examine a small list of registry utilities that run on Windows NT/2000, Windows XP, and Windows Server 2003 that are generally the most helpful.

Windows XP PowerToys

Ever since the release of Windows 95, Microsoft has supplied a set of PowerToys for each of the major Windows operating-system. PowerToys are small applications that enhance the operating system's functions in a number of ways, enabling users to boost productivity, configure the system UI in various ways and, generally, to expand the operating system's capabilities. Since the initial release, PowerToys has become a favorite of most users, and the popularity is understandable. It is easy to understand why users began asking whether PowerToys would be included in Windows XP when the operating system was still under development. Microsoft didn't disappoint. You can download PowerToys for Windows XP from either **http://www.microsoft.com/downloads** or **http://downloads-zdnet.com.com**.

 Note

Windows XP PowerToys are mainly intended for Windows XP workstations. However, most of them also run on Windows Server 2003. Further, while they were not intended for network servers, there are some PowerToys that are useful even when installed on computers running Windows Server 2003. Particularly worth mentioning are Open Command Window Here, and Tweak UI.

Open Command Window Here

Open Command Window Here is one of the most valuable PowerToys, allowing you easily to drop to the command prompt from any Windows Explorer folder. This is a PowerToy that should be installed even on network servers. After it is installed, the **Open Command Window Here** menu item will be available in the right-click menu in any Windows Explorer folder. Just right-click on a folder, choose **Open Command Window Here**, and a command prompt session (with the selected folder as the default directory) will open. Additionally, if you right-click on a folder icon in a **Windows Explorer** window, will also have the **Open Command Window Here** command available in the resulting menu.

If you like to work at a command prompt, this toy is a must-have.

Tweak UI for Windows XP

The Windows XP version of Tweak UI is the most valuable of all PowerToys included in the current release. It provides a safe and convenient way of customizing various system settings, which are not available in the default Windows XP/ Windows Server 2003 user interface. To achieve the same result without Tweak UI, you would need to edit the system registry. As was mentioned in *Chapter 1*, this tool provides alternative methods for editing the Registry, which are usually safer than those using Regedit.exe.

In contrast to all of the previous releases of Tweak UI, which were included as Control Panel applets, Tweak UI for Windows XP is a standalone executable file. You can place this EXE file in any folder and start it from there, since it doesn't have to be installed prior to use. Tweak UI for Windows XP displays a hierarchical tree of available options in the left pane. After you select an option in the left pane, the right pane will display the available configuration settings (Fig. 14.1).

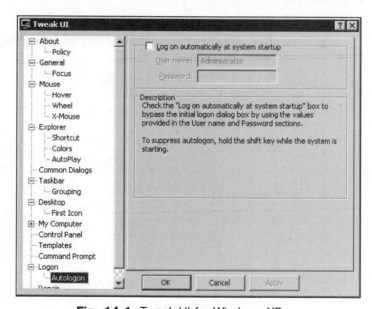

Fig. 14.1. Tweak UI for Windows XP

► **Note**

Before you install Windows XP PowerToys and start playing with this version of TweakUI, make sure that you have deleted any older copies of TweakUI.

The new Tweak UI enables you to do carry out practically any kind of customization, including a number of difficult tasks, such as configuring various UI visual effects, error beeps, cursor shadow, etc.; and configuring the taskbar, shell folders, etc. As was already mentioned in this chapter, to produce the same result without Tweak UI, would have to edit the system registry. For example, the **Colors** category provides you with an easy way of customizing the colors used by Windows Explorer to display compressed and encrypted files (Fig. 14.2). As you may recall, the method for achieving the same effect through editing the system registry was covered in *Chapter 4*. In addition to changing the color for compressed and ecnrypted objects, TweakUI provides the **Hot-tracking** option, which enables Windows to display names in a different color when you point to them with the mouse (provided that you have enabled the single-click user interface). In contrast to customization of the colors used to display compressed and encrypted objects, which, as you should remember, modify the `AltColor` and `AltEncryptionColor REG_BINARY` values under the `HKEY_CURRENT_ USER\Software\Microsoft\Windows\CurrentVersion\Explorer` registry key, the **Hot-tracking** option modifies the `HotTrackingColor` string value under `HKCU\Control Panel\Colors` registry key.

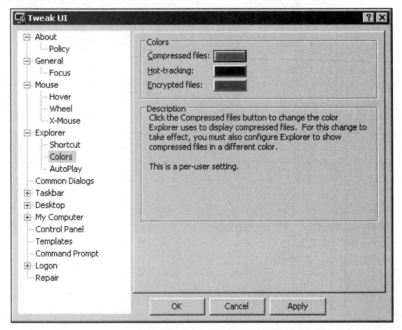

Fig. 14.2. The **Colors** subcategory of the **Explorer** category in TweakUI

In concluding our discussion of PowerToys for Windows XP, you should understand that installing these tools is your choice. Furthermore, we didn't cover all of the Toys included in this collection in this chapter. Instead, we paid particular attention to the tools that seem to be the most useful and convenient. If you like the new Windows XP user interface, you will probably like many of the other Toys not covered here.

RegMaid Utility – Cleaning Your Registry

RegMaid is a utility developed by Microsoft to help track down and clean up problematic OLE entries in the Registry database. RegMaid is quite easy to use and, at the same time, provides the user with as much information about problematic registry entries as possible (Fig. 14.3). This information can then be used to decide which entries you want to delete and which you want to repair.

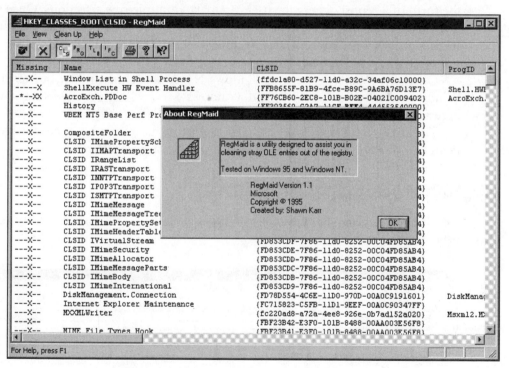

Fig. 14.3. The RegMaid utility main window

Information on the OLE components is stored in the registry under the HKEY_CLASSES_ROOT registry key, where you typically find subsections such as CLSID, TypeLib, Interface, and ProgId.

The RegMaid utility considers CLSID entries to be problematic if they contain a handler or server entry for a file that cannot be found. There are several ways in which this situation may arise. A few of the most common include: deleting or moving a file or a broken network path.

`ProgId` entries will be identified as broken when the associated `CLSID` cannot be found in `HKEY_CLASSES_ROOT\CLSID`. As a result, deleting `CLSID` entries will cause related `ProgId` entries to be listed.

`TypeLib` entries are identified broken when the associated file cannot be found.

`Interface` entries are considered broken when the `TypeLib` entry cannot be matched to one in `HKEY_CLASSES_ROOT\TypeLib`. Consequently, deleting `TypeLib` entries will allow RegMaid to identify the associated problem.

RegMaid provides information about the entries believed to be problematic in the form of a report, where the user can make multiple row selections. Once selections have been made, the user can then delete them from the registry. Although RegMaid does not currently have **Archive** or **Restore** capabilities, it does provide a printed report mechanism for each of the four views.

Officially, Windows 9*x* and Windows NT support this utility, but testing on Windows 2000, Windows XP, and Windows Server 2003 revealed that it works here as well and is rather useful.

This freeware utility is essential for advanced users, and can be downloaded from the Microsoft Download Center (**http://www.microsoft.com**).

Regmon – Registry Monitoring

Developed by Mark Russinovich and Bryce Cogswell, this registry utility is truly brilliant.

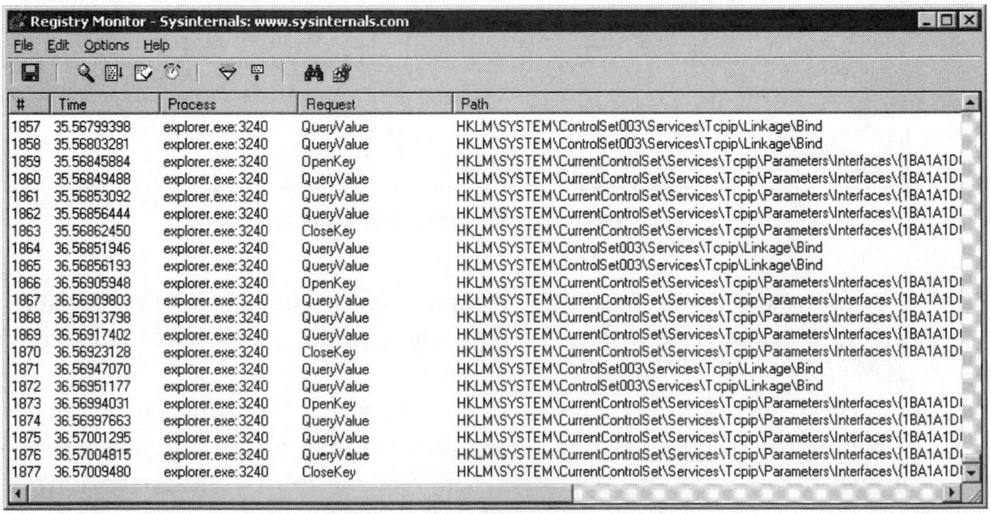

Fig. 14.4. Regmon at work

Regmon monitors the registry and displays all information concerning system-wide registry access. This unique tool is implemented as a combination of a device driver and GUI and is a must for anyone who studies Windows internals or troubleshoots problems caused by an inconsistent registry (Fig. 14.4).

The Regmon utility supports process filtering, allows you to save its output in the ASCII file and even monitors boot-time registry activity.

The authors not only provide it as freeware but also supply technical information on the details of implementation, and even provide the source code.

Supported operating systems: Windows 95/98, Windows NT 4.0, and Windows 2000. It also works well with Windows XP and Windows Server 2003.

Download from: **http://www.sysinternals.com**.

NTFSDOS Professional

This is another popular utility from Mark Russinovich and Bryce Cogswell. Although NTFSDOS isn't a registry-editing tool, it deserves mentioning here because it is a valuable tool for the quick recovery of missing or corrupt files needed to load Windows NT/2000 (these files, of course, include registry hives). NTFSDOS Professional is a small utility and can be started from system disks.

NTFSDOS Professional also contains the NTFSCHK tool for checking NTFS disks under DOS. It will allow you to check the hard disk and perform recovery processes if boot problems are caused by corruption of the NTFS disk structures.

Download the trial version of NTFSDOS Professional from **http://www.sysinternals.com**.

Note that although NTFSDOS Professional isn't freeware, the authors do provide a freeware utility of this type — NTFSDOS (which is provided with the source code).

RegSafe Professional from Imagine LAN

If you edit the registry on a regular basis, you might not be satisfied with the standard functions provided by the built-in registry-editing tools supplied with Windows NT/2000, Windows XP, and Windows Server 2003. If so, then RegSafe Professional from Imagine LAN is just for you!

RegSafe Professional Edition 2.0 is a suite of tools designed to provide Network Administrators, IS/IT professionals, and Power Users with the ability to carry out advanced Registry management on 32-bit Windows PCs. RegSafe provides comprehensive Registry editing and management capabilities not found in other professional-level Registry-editing tools, all from within a protected environment (Fig. 14.5).

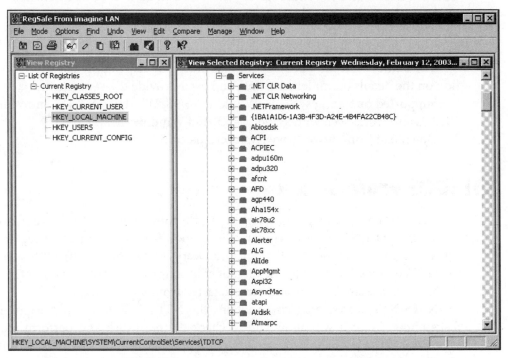

Fig. 14.5. RegSafe is a powerful registry editor with extended functionality

The most attractive features of RegSafe are listed below:

❑ *Protected Environment.* RegSafe automatically saves a copy of the Registry *before* you introduce any modifications. In *Chapter 3*, where we discussed new functions of the Regedit.exe utility supplied with Windows XP and Windows Server 2003, we noted that despite all of its advantages, the new Regedit version lacks the Read-Only mode (which, as you remember, was present in Regedt32.exe). Well, RegSafe has this useful function, which is particularly appropriate for beginners who have only just begun to study the registry structure. Furthermore, in contrast to standard registry-editing tools (Regedit.exe and Regedt32.exe), it has an Undo function, which is available when editing the registry. Unlike other Registry-editing tools, if you make a mistake while editing with RegSafe, you won't trash your system. Even if you mistakenly delete something from your registry, the first thing RegSafe does is take a registry snapshot. It then prompts you to confirm the operation (Fig. 14.6). If you realize later that you have made an error, you can easily undo it (Fig. 14.7).

❑   *Registry Comparison.* RegSafe goes far beyond simple Registry Editing. Consider, for example, its powerful Comparison features. You can compare Current or Snapshot Registries, compare keys/values within the same Registry, compare access control lists (ACL) on Windows NT/2000, Windows XP, and Windows Server 2003 systems. It's fantastic!

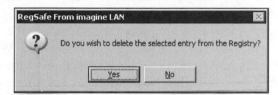

Fig. 14.6. RegSafe prompts the user to confirm
the deletion of registry entries

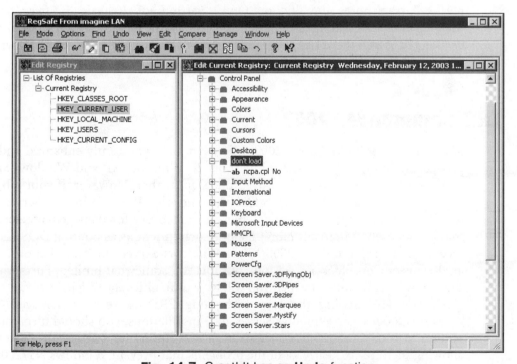

Fig. 14.7. Great! It has an **Undo** function

❏ *Powerful export features.* Administrators and other advanced users will appreciate RegSafe's export feature, which allows portions of a Registry or Registry-comparison-results tree to be exported to a REG file (Regedit4 format).

❏ *Partial or full registry restoration.* If an unwanted change to the Registry was made or a problem with the Registry is detected, RegSafe can perform a *partial* or *full* restoration of a Registry snapshot to the current ("live") Registry.

❏ *Registry restoration for non-booting systems.* I am a big fan of restoring unbootable systems (it just became my favorite hobby). If you are like me, you'll appreciate the capabilities provided by RegSafe in this field. The developers of this magnificent program have implemented so-called Command Prompt SOS technology, which helps to restore the registry on all existing Windows versions (yes, on all of them, including Windows 9*x*, Windows ME, Windows NT/2000/XP, and Windows Server 2003 systems with FAT, FAT32, and NTFS-formatted drives). In addition, RegSafe provides Recovery Console restoration on Windows 2000/XP.

All this makes the registry editor of choice for anyone, from beginners to experts. Furthermore, the "Editor Only" version of RegSafe is *free* (despite the fact that its functions are limited in comparison to the fully-functional retail versions, it is still the most powerful registry-editing tool I have seen). Download this indispensable tool from **http://www.imaginelan.com**.

ERD Commander 2002

Since the release of Windows 2000, Microsoft has significantly enhanced and improved the built-in system-reliability tools. In Windows XP and Windows Server 2003, these tools have been improved one step further. However, if your job is to support and maintain Windows NT/2000, Windows XP, and Windows Server 2003 installations, including performing emergency recovery for damaged systems, you may wonder why Microsoft didn't include such functions as booting DOS disks to recover damaged Windows 2000/XP or Windows Server 2003 installations. After all, Recovery Console is a great tool, but it is still somewhat limited. Furthermore, there may be situations in which you will have difficulties starting it.

If you are missing the ease of booting ERD to recover damaged Windows NT/2000/XP or Windows Server 2003 installations, you should turn your attention to ERD Commander 2002. It is an ideal utility for system administrators, allowing them to fix nearly all of the problems that prevent Windows NT/2000/XP or Windows Server 2003 from booting.

To install and use ERD Commander 2002, you'll need to satisfy the following requirements:

❒ Target system must be equipped with a bootable CD-ROM device and run one of the following operating systems: Windows NT 4.0 with Service Pack 4 or later, Windows 2000, or Windows XP.

▶ *Note*

You can also use ERD Commander 2002 on Windows NT 4.0 systems that do not have SP 4. However, since ERD Commander 2002 needs to update NTFS volumes to a version that requires the NTFS driver from SP 4 or higher, it will prompt you to perform such an update. Although the current version of this product (v.3.0) is officially supported with Windows NT/2000/XP, it also works fine with Windows Server 2003.

❒ Regardless of the operating system used on the target system, ERD Commander 2002 has the following hardware requirements: at least 64 MB RAM and x86 233 Mhz or equivalent processor.
❒ ERD Commander 2002 software.

▶ *Note*

To obtain ERD Commander 2002, visit visit the **http://www.winternals.com/trynow** to order this product on a bootable CD or download a Boot CD-ROM Wizard executable, which you can use to create a bootable CD-ROM ISO image.

To run the ERD Commander 2002 Boot CD-ROM Wizard, you will need the following:

❒ A computer running Windows 9*x*/ME, Windows NT, Windows 2000, or Windows XP, and equipped with a CD-RW drive. CD-ROM burning software capable of creating a bootable CD from an ISO image must be installed in that system.
❒ A blank CD-R or CD-RW disk.

After you start the ERD Commander 2002 Boot CD-ROM Wizard, it will display a traditional Welcome screen (Fig. 14.8), and then prompt you to accept the license agreement, and, finally, to specify an optional password for your rescue CD-ROM, in order to assure that only authorized users can access your systems (Fig. 14.9).

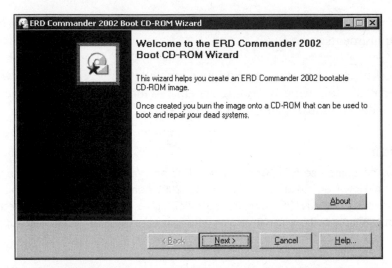

Fig. 14.8. Welcome screen of the ERD Commander 2002 Setup program

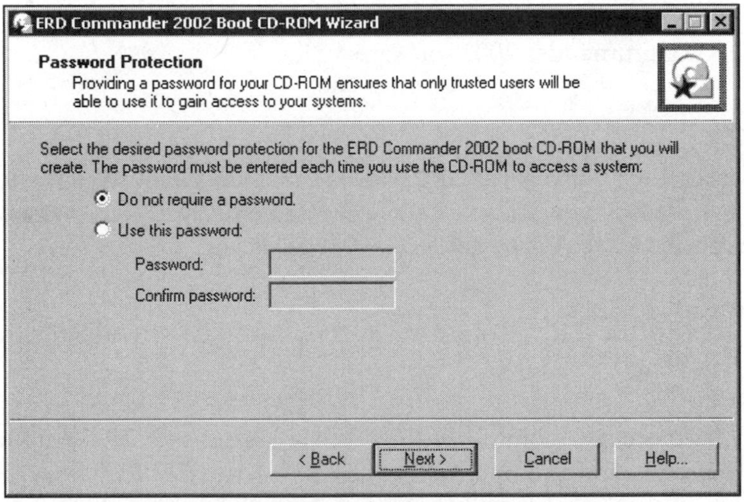

Fig. 14.9. The **Password Protection** screen
of the ERD Commander 2002 Boot CD-ROM Wizard

After you carry out these basic steps, ERD Commander 2002 Boot CD-ROM Wizard extracts all files required to build a bootable CD image (Fig. 14.10). Note that the newest release of this program doesn't require the distribution CD for this purpose (in contrast to the previous version, ERD Commander 2000, which did). After this operation is completed, the Wizard will provide you with the option to include OEM drivers for SCSI devices that Windows XP doesn't support automatically. Finally, the Wizard will provide you with the option of including additional files in the bootable CD image (Fig. 14.11).

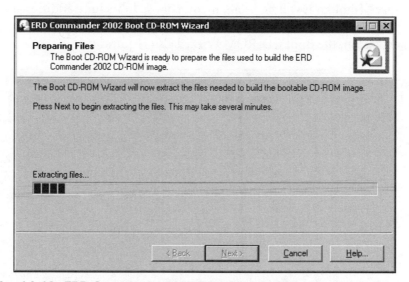

Fig. 14.10. ERD Commander 2002 Boot CD-ROM Wizard extracts files needed to build the bootable CD image

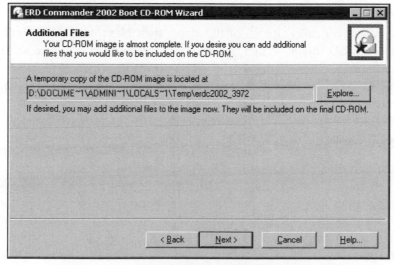

Fig. 14.11. The **Additional Files** dialog of the ERD Commander 2002 Boot CD-ROM Wizard

At the final interactive step, the Boot CD-ROM Wizard will prompt you to specify the destination directory where it will store the generated ISO image (Fig. 14.12). The image usually requires approximately 180 MB of disk storage space (though it will be more, if you choose to include additional files). Since most popular CD-ROM-burning software requires ISO images to have the ISO filename extension, the Boot CD-ROM Wizard also requires that extension.

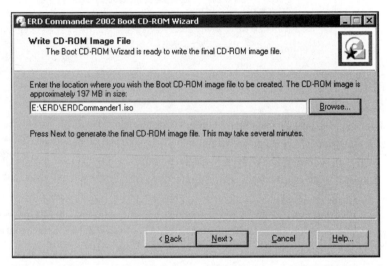

Fig. 14.12. The final interactive step of the Boot CD-ROM Wizard

After you carry out all of the steps, click **Next**, and the wizard will create the bootable CD image. When the Boot CD image has been successfully created, you will need to use your regular CD-ROM-burning software to create an ERD Commander 2002 bootable CD, which you will be able to use when repairing and recovering your damaged systems.

To perform recovery procedures if your Windows NT-based system cannot start, proceed as follows:

1. Insert the ERD Commander 2002 bootable CD into the CD-ROM drive on the target system and reboot the computer. When the message prompting you to press any key to boot from CD appears, press any key, and ERD Commander 2002 will start booting. Once the ERD Commander 2002 boots, it will load a stripped version of Windows XP (Fig. 14.16). Note that, at this stage, it verifies NTFS compatiblity, as shown on the screenshot in Fig. 14.13. As was mentioned earlier, if your target system runs Windows NT 4.0 without SP 4, ERD Commander 2002 will prompt you to update your NTFS volumes.

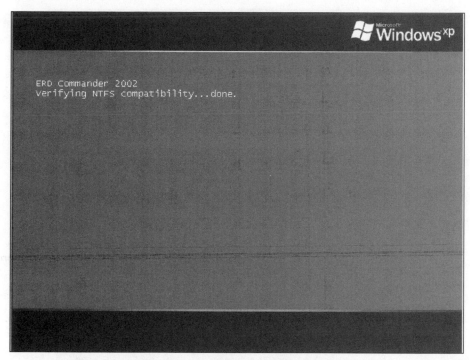

Fig. 14.13. ERD Commander 2002 loads a stripped version of Windows XP

Note

ERD Commander 2002 can access any Windows NT/2000/XP file system, including FAT, FAT32, NTFS, and CDFS. It will also provide you access to the drives of Windows 9x/ME systems (although most of its administrative tools will not function when accessing installations of those operating systems). Also note that ERD Commander 2002 is not intended to solve the problems caused by disk corruption and, therefore, only disks that are consistent enough to be recognized by Windows NT/2000/XP will be accessible. Thus, if your problem is caused by disk corruption, it is recommended that you use other utilities, for example, Disk Commander (also product of Winternals Software).

2. After the stripped Windows XP version loads, ERD Commander 2002 will detect the existing installations (Fig. 14.14). You will likely immediately notice that this function is similar to that of Recovery Console. However, it provides additional capabilities, as well as standard windowing GUI. And, as was already mentioned, although it is officially designed for Windows NT/2000/XP, it also detects Windows Server 2003 installations and works just fine with them.

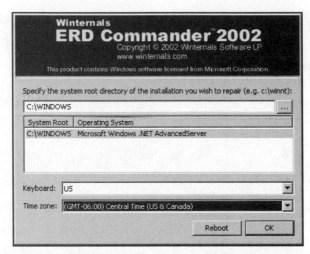

Fig. 14.14. ERD Commander 2002 prompts to specify the installation
that you wish to repair

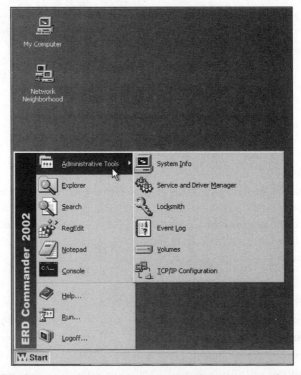

Fig. 14.15. ERD Commander provides a comprehensive set of tools for repairing
damaged installations of all Windows NT-based systems

3. After you choose the damaged installation that you need to repair, ERD Commander 2002 will provide you with a comprehensive set of tools for repairing the damaged system (Fig. 14.15). However, it is important to be aware of the fact that, although it looks similar, this GUI is not the same as the Windows XP code. For example, it is not designed as a general-purpose OS (doing so would be a violation of the end-user license agreement). The environment is designed in such a way as to reboot automatically after 24 hours of continuous usage. Also, do not remove the ERD Commander 2002 CD from the CD-ROM drive while ERD Commander 2002 is running, since doing so will lock-up the environment and make a reboot necessary.

A brief glance at the screenshot shown in Fig. 14.15 confirms that the set of capabilities provided by ERD Commander 2002 would impress even those individuals with the wildest of imaginations.

ERD Commander's built-in tools allow you to perform the following tasks:

❐ Removing or replacing incomatible device drivers.
❐ Updating obsolete system files.
❐ Correcting misconfigured NTFS security.
❐ Updating Locked Files.
❐ Correcting Registry Problems. As outlined throughout this book, a significant number of boot problems are caused by improperly configured registry values. The built-in Registry Editor included with ERD Commander 2002 (Fig. 14.16) has all the capabilities and even the same interface as Windows NT/2000/XP Regedit.exe utility.
❐ Rescuing critically important data from a failed system. Beside the possibility to copy data to removable media, ERD Commander 2002 provides network capabilities, which allow you to copy the data to another system on your network.
❐ Regaining access to the system from which you have been locked out. Have you (or your users) ever forgotten passwords? Or have you ever encountered a situation where you had to administer computers running Windows NT-based operating systems for which you don't know the Administrator password because one of the company's employees has left suddenly? If so, you will appreciate the Locksmith Wizard tool included with ERD Commander 2002 (Fig. 14.17), which provides an easy way of listing all local accounts for a system running Windows NT/2000/XP or Windows Server 2003, and change the password for any of these accounts, including Administrator.

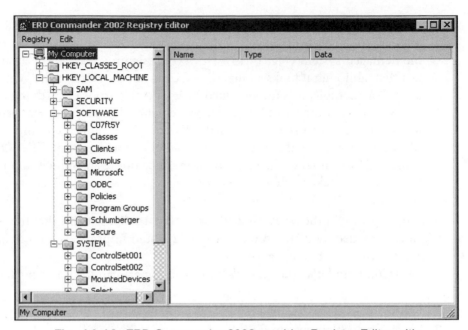

Fig. 14.16. ERD Commander 2002 provides Registry Editor with
the same user interface and the same capabilities
and the Windows NT/2000/XP Regedit.exe tool

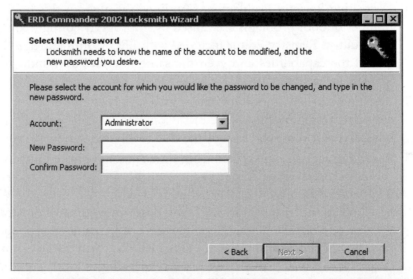

Fig. 14.17. Locksmith Wizard tool included with ERD Commander 2002 provides
the easiest way of changing the password for any user account

Note

Of course, this method of resetting forgotten passwords is not the only one. For example, Windows XP includes a built-in function for resetting forgotten passwords by means of using the password-reset diskette (the procedures are slightly different for Windows XP Professional workstations that are not members of a domain and Windows XP Professional workstations that are joined to a domain). There are other methods of resetting passwords for practically every Windows NT-based operating system, such as replacing SAM, using the system shedule (AT) service, using password-cracking utilities (such as L0phtcrack, which was briefly covered in *Chapter 9*) and so on. There are also many freeware utilities on the Internet (to download one of them, visit **http://home.eunet.no/~pnordahl/ntpasswd/**). The method provided by ERD Commander 2002, however, is the easiest, and has the fewest limitations. Just one final note about ERD Commander 2002 boot CD – store it in a safe place, and remember that there is no security except physical security.

❏ Viewing the Event Logs — ERD Commander 2002 includes the Event Log Viewer tool with the same interface as the Event Log Viewer MMC snap-in. This is a significant advantage over the Recovery Console, since Event Log records often contain valuable clues that will be helpful in detecting the cause of particular problem.

❏ Very powerful recovery capabilities, providing you with access to fault-tolerant drives (including mirror sets, volume sets, and striped sets). And, of course, you can run Chkdsk.exe uitility on corrupt drives.

❏ Enabling and Disabling Services and Drivers.

Freeware Shutdown Stopper

In *Chapter 12*, we briefly discussed the procedures for troubleshooting shutdown problems and performing emergency shutdown (when your system stops responding, when you cannot shutdown normally, or if you simply need to shut down quickly and prevent any current information from being saved). However, situations when you want to prevent your system from being shut down are not uncommon either. Consider, for example, a case where a software installation program doesn't give you any options and reboots the system immediately (although most install programs usually ask the user whether it is desirable to reboot now or wait until later).

If this is the case, consider the Shutdown Stopper freeware utility, which stops your PC from shutting down by aborting the shutdown process. Shutdown Stopper runs in the Windows Notification Tray (Fig. 14.18). To use the program, simply run it and shutdowns will be disabled. You can either right-click on the application's icon to bring up a menu with options or left-click and open the main program window. Either way lets you enable or disable shutdowns, exit the program, or turn off shutdown notifications so you won't be told when a shutdown attempt has occurred. Other options, such as running a command when a shutdown attempt occurs are only available from the main window's **Setup** tab (Fig. 14.19).

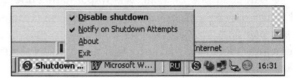

Fig. 14.18. Shutdown Stopper runs in the Windows Notification Tray

Fig. 14.19. The **Setup** tab of the **Shutdown Stopper** window

To download this useful little tool, visit **http://www.otbsw.com**.

Summary

Here, I have only listed the registry utilities that I have tested myself, and can therefore recommend to my readers. You may wish to test other utilities in this class, some of which you can find by visiting the links provided in *Appendix 1 — "Internet resources"*.

CHAPTER 15

Registry Programming

S is for Space.
Ray Bradbury

Although today tools and applications equipped with GUI (Graphical User Interface) really dominate the whole Windows world, including Windows NT, Windows 2000, Windows XP, and Windows Server 2003, most administrators and power users know that automating many routine tasks (for example, such as distributing registry changes to more than 5,000 workstations) cannot be accomplished using GUI tools (such as Registry Editor, in this example). Frankly speaking, when it comes to software development and distributing applications to end users, the Registry Editor is only suitable for testing purposes. Setup programs, REG files, and INF files provide more capabilities for convenient and safe registry modification. Furthermore, if you are going to automate Windows and distribute registry changes to a large number of workstations and servers within your Windows-based network, you will certainly need to consider alternate techniques of accomplishing this task.

Several ways of accomplishing this task already exist in Windows NT 4.0, including system policies and various scripting techniques. With Windows 2000, other new and improved ways appeared to deliver massive registry modifications to multiple workstations and servers. In Windows XP and Windows Server 2003, these methods were enhanced and improved and new mechanisms ensuring that the required registry changes have been delivered. These methods include the following:

❑ Group Policy Objects usage for delivering custom administrative templates and registry security. We briefly covered this topic in *Chapters 10* and *11*.

❑ Using new technologies for massive software distribution and configuration management, including Microsoft's Systems Management Server (SMS), or third-party system mangement packages, as well as using Microsoft Windows Installer Service, which we briefly considered in *Chapter 11*.

❑ Using various shell-scripting techniques, including the usage of Resource Kit command-line tools in your scripts as well as employing the Task Scheduler for scheduled execution of registry scripts.

❑ Using Windows Script Host to modify the registry.

This chapter mainly concentrates on scripting techniques. Any system administrator must possess a reasonable degree of knowledge of built-in scripting, particularly for those who manage large corporate Windows-based networks. Just to illustrate the real power behind built-in scripting capabilities, let us consider some practical situations. For example, let's say you have to introduce configuration modifications to several workstations running Windows NT-based operating systems without going to each machine.

In order to change the local Administrator password on several workstations you would use the following batch file:

```
echo on >password.log
@echo MachineName1 >>password.log
ping MachineName1 >>password.log
if %errorlevel%==0 soon \\MachineName1 cmd /c "net user AccountName1_
NewPassword1" >>password.log
@echo MachineName2 >>password.log
ping MachineName2 >>password.log
if %errorlevel%==0 soon \\MachineName2 cmd /c "net user AccountName2_
NewPassword2" >>password.log
@echo ** end of file ** >>password.log
exit
```

Note

In the above-provided batch file, the Soon command from the Windows 2000 Resource Kit was used. However, the built-in system scheduler (AT) will also work, for example:

```
at \\TargetMachine cmd /c "net user AccountName NewPassword"
```

To illustrate this concept in relation to the registry, let us recall the example with disabling EFS, which we discussed in *Chapter 13*, where we considered the two methods: disabling EFS by direct registry editing, and by means of using Group Policies. Of course, modifying registry keys on a couple of machines is a simple undertaking. However, when you need to introduce this change to hundreds of thousands of machines, this task ceases to be a simple one. In a domain environment where you have implemented Active Directory, it is supposed that you will use Group Policy to distribute the change. Consider however, a situation in which you haven't yet implemented Active Directory, but still need to modify a large number of workstations. This is where scripting techniques will come to your rescue.

There are several ways to modify the registry in an automated fashion, the simplest of which is to create a script that is run locally on the Windows XP systems. Use the following command: reg add "HKLM\SOFTWARE\Microsoft\Windows NT\ CurrentVersion\EFS" /v EfsConfiguration /t REG_DWORD /d 1 /f. You can use a similar command to turn EFS back on, either by simply changing the value to 0 or by deleting the key using the following command:

```
reg delete "HKLM\SOFTWARE\Microsoft\Windows NT\CurrentVersion\_
EFS" /v EfsConfiguration /f
```

 Note

In this example, we have used the REG utility included with the Windows 2000 Resource Kit. This tool allows you to add, modify, delete, and search registry keys and values, perform registry backup and restore, as well as other administrative operations. This command-line utility, which can be successfully used in batch files, can operate over both local and remote registries, and it also works fine with Windows XP and Windows Server 2003. The /f key eliminates the need to prompt the user to confirm the deletion.

Reg.exe supports the following commands:

☐ REG QUERY
Returns information on the keys and values contained within the specified registry key or hive.

❑ REG ADD

Adds a new value into the specified key.

❑ REG UPDATE

Modifies the current state of the registry element. If the registry doesn't contain a specified value, the command is ignored.

❑ REG DELETE

Deletes a registry value, key, or several keys.

❑ REG COPY

Copies a registry element into a new registry key on the local or remote computer.

❑ REG SAVE and REG BACKUP

Save the indicated registry values, keys, or hives to the specified file. These commands are particularly useful for backing up the registry before introducing any changes. The REG SAVE and REG BACKUP commands are identical.

❑ REG RESTORE

Restores the specified value, key, or hive from the file created using the REG SAVE or REG BACKUP commands.

❑ REG LOAD

Temporarily loads the specified key or hive from the file created using REG BACKUP or REG SAVE into the root level of the registry. This command is useful for viewing information, editing registry data, or performing troubleshooting operations.

❑ REG UNLOAD

Unloads the specified key or hive previously loaded using REG LOAD.

The REG SAVE and REG BACKUP commands support the following syntax:

```
REG SAVE RegistryPath FileName [\\Machine]

REG BACKUP RegistryPath FileName [\\Machine]
```

The RegistryPath argument specifies the registry path to the registry key or value in the following format: [ROOTKEY\]Key.

The ROOTKEY parameter specifies the registry root key containing the key to be backed up (the default value of this parameter is HKEY_LOCAL_MACHINE).

The root key may be specified using one of the following abbreviations listed below:

```
HKEY_LOCAL_MACHINE    —  HKLM

HKEY_CURRENT_USER     —  HKCU

HKEY_CLASSES_ROOT     —  HKCR

HKEY_CURRENT_CONFIGURATION — HKCC
```

Note

Only HKLM and HKU keys are available when working with remote systems.

Key — this parameter specifies the complete path to the registry key contained within the root key specified by the ROOTKEY parameter.

FileName — this parameter specifies the file name (without an extension), where the registry data will be saved. (On a local computer, this file will be stored in the current directory; when working with remote systems, in the Windows installation directory.)

Machine — this parameter specifies the name of the remote computer (by default, the local system is used). Use a UNC notation when specifying computer names. For example: \\STATION1.

The REG RESTORE command supports the following syntax:

```
REG RESTORE FileName KeyName [\\Machine]
```

where:

FileName — the name of the file to be restored (without the filename extension). This parameter should specify a file previously created using REG SAVE or REG BACKUP.

KeyName — name of the registry key, in the following format: [ROOTKEY\]Key.

Key — complete path to the registry key contained within the root key specified by the ROOTKEY parameter.

Machine — name of the remote system in UNC format (by default, the local computer will be used).

Main Scripting Challenges

Delivering massive registry changes involves the following challenges:

❑ *Security context under which the script runs.* Security is the most important among all scripting challenges. As you recall, starting with Windows 2000, the security model has undergone some changes, one of which is the introduction of the new built-in Power Users security group. The Users group has limited privileges. Thus, when running a script that delivers changes to a part of the system registry to which a normal user account doesn't have sufficient privileges, you must consider the security context under which that change can be successfully introduced. For example, many keys under HKEY_LOCAL_MACHINE have default permissions, which restrict non-administrative user accounts from modifying them. Only Administrators and Power Users can change these keys (and, consequently, perform such tasks as installing services and applications for all users of the system). One possible answer to this problem would be to reduce normal security to ease the registry change distribution, but this is highly undesirable. A much better approach would be to use the right tools at the right time.

❑ *The timing problem.* To illustrate this problem, consider the following situation. Suppose that you need to make changes to a specific user profile (HKEY_CURRENT_USER). To achieve this goal successfully, either that user must be logged on or, at least the hive of that user's profile must be loaded into a temporary registry key. Now consider a more complicated situation — you need to modify both HKLM and HKCU, and do it simultaneously. Thus, your script will have to operate with two different security contexts at the same time, not to mention ensuring that the target user is currently logged on.

❑ *Logging of changes.* Logging and, possibly, reporting of registry changes is a must, especially in large corporate networks, which need a centralized way to report the result of the changes. Unfortunately, tools such as Regedit.exe are at least inadequate for reporting on the failure or success of the introduced registry changes, and this situation didn't change significantly, even with the arrival of Windows XP and Windows Server 2003.

Now, after discussing the main challenges and pitfalls of registry scripting, let us consider the ways that you can address them using newer mechanisms introduced with Windows 2000 and continuing in later editions.

The Windows Installer uses the Event Log and text log files at each target machine to report on an installation. However, the details are limited, you have to collect them from each machine, and you are unlikely to get the kind of information you need to tell whether a particular value in a particular key failed to register. As a result, I will discuss alternative logging mechanisms that you can include in your registry scripts.

Addressing the Problem of the Security Context

Starting with Windows 2000, Microsoft introduced several ways to resolve the problem of security context when distributing registry changes. The first of these tools is the Secondary Logon service (installed by default on Windows 2000 and in later editions), which we briefly considered in *Chapter 10*. Besides **Run As** GUI functionality, there is a runas.exe command-line tool (somewhat similar to the su command existing in UNIX). This command lets you start a process using the security context of a user other than the one currently logged on.

The `runas` command-line tool uses the following syntax:

```
runas [{/profile|/noprofile}] [/env] [/netonly] [/savedcreds]
[/smartcard] [/showtrustlevels] [/trustlevel] /
user:UserAccountName program
```

where:

`/profile` — loads the user's profile (the default option).

`/no profile` — specifies that the user's profile is not to be loaded. This allows the application to load more quickly, but it can also cause a malfunction in some applications.

`/env` — when used in combination with the `/user` option, instructs the Secondary Logon service to execute the specified command using the environment variables available to the user who initiates the `Runas` command.

`/netonly` — indicates that the user information specified is for remote access only.

`/savedcreds` — indicates if the credentials have been previously saved by this user. This option is not available (and, therefore, will be ignored) on Windows XP Home Edition.

`/smartcard` — indicates whether the credentials are to be supplied from a smartcard.

`/showtrustlevels` — lists the `/trustlevel` options.

`/trustlevel` — specifies the level of authorization at which the application is to run. Use `/showtrustlevels` to see the trust levels available.

`/user:`*UserAccountName* — specifies the name of the user account under which to run the program. The user account format should be *user@domain* or *domain\user*.

`program` — specifies the program or command to run using the account specified in `/user`.

`/?` — displays help at the command prompt.

One of the simplest ways to use runas in scripting is to import a previously exported REG file. For example, you can use it to deliver a REG file to a user's HKCU subtree as follows:

```
Runas /profile /user:test\olga "regedit /s d:\temp\regpatch.reg"
```

Or:

```
Runas /user:test\administrator "reg add HKLM\Software\NewApp\
NewVal=100"
```

Note

When the `runas` line executes, you are prompted to supply the user's password. Once you provide it, the change is made.

Logon/Logoff and Shutdown/Startup scripts provide another way to get around the security context problem when delivering registry scripts. For example, to deliver user-specific changes (`HKCU`), you can use logon and logoff scripts, which run in the security context of the currently logged on user, and for delivering registry changes to `HKLM`, you can use startup and shutdown scripts, which run under the `LocalSystem` security context.

Both logon/logoff and startup/shutdown scripts are part of Group Policies. As was outlined in *Chapter 11*, Group Policies can be applied at the local machine, site, domain, and OU levels, which means that you can assign any number or scripts executing for each machine or user.

▶ *Tip*

Because there can be any number of logon/logoff and startup/shutdown scripts, you can easily run into problems with managing and troubleshooting them. Therefore, try to keep it as simple as possible, and use as few locations as possible to define scripts. Avoid using local GPOs, particularly if your computers are joined to a domain.

The command-line scheduler provides yet another way to deliver changes in the security context other than that of the currently logged on user.

▶ *Note*

In the Windows Server 2003 family, the newer tool, Schtasks.exe, replaces the familiar At.exe scheduler. Although At.exe is still included in the Windows Server 2003 family, Schtasks is the recommended command-line task-scheduling tool.

Addressing the Timing Issues

Generally, the problem of script-timing involves answering the following questions:

- ❑ Do users need to be logged on (or, on the contrary, must they be logged off) for the change introduced by the script to occur?
- ❑ If your script makes changes to the registry, is the key to which the changes are introduced available at execution time?

Similar to script security issues, these problems can be addressed by using Startup/Shutdown and Logon/Logoff scripts. The general rule is as follows: if you need script modifications to HKCU, use logon and logoff scripts, while if you need to make changes to HKLM or HKU, use startup or shutdown scripts.

Note

For the most part, it is possible to use logon and logoff scripts to make changes to HKLM or HKU, but the permissions on the affected keys must be open enough to provide access for the currently logged on user.

Addressing the Logging Issues

Logging and reporting of the changes is essentially important. However, as was already mentioned, tools such as Regedit.exe lack this capability, both in Windows 2000 and in Windows XP/Windows Server 2003. Furthermore, depending on the method that you use to introduce changes, logging mechanisms are different. Therefore, when it comes to registry modifications, including registry scripting, it is advisable to use the following approaches:

❑ If you use simple batch scripts to deliver registry changes, you can use simple redirection. To illustrate this approach, let us return to our example with enabling or disabling EFS. The listing provided below shows how to use simple redirection to enable logging in batch script:

```
@echo reg add "HKLM\SOFTWARE\Microsoft\Windows NT\CurrentVersion\EFS"_
/v EfsConfiguration /t REG_DWORD /d 1 /f >reg.log
reg add "HKLM\SOFTWARE\Microsoft\Windows NT\CurrentVersion\EFS" /v_
EfsConfiguration /t REG_DWORD /d 1 /f >>reg.log
if errorlevel 1 @echo command failed >> reg.log
@echo reg delete "HKLM\SOFTWARE\Microsoft\Windows_
NT\CurrentVersion\EFS" /v EfsConfiguration /f >>reg.log
reg delete "HKLM\SOFTWARE\Microsoft\Windows NT\Current Version\EFS"_
/v EfsConfiguration /f >>reg.log
if errorlevel 1 @echo command failed >> reg.log
```

Note

The Resource Kit comes with the Logevent.exe command-line tool, which you can use to generate custom events and log them into the system event log. In addition to using the Windows 2000/XP/Windows Server 2003 system event-logging, Logevent.exe also supports sending the event to another machine's event log. This capability is especially useful in a corporate environment, where you might need to have a central collection point for the results of this script on many systems.

❑ If you use the Windows Installer to install applications on your workstations, it is recommended that you enable the verbose logging mode (see *Chapter 13*).

❑ Finally, you can use third-party tools providing powerful logging capabilities (one of which is the Regmon.exe freeware tool considered in *Chapter 14*).

Using Windows Script Host to Modify the Registry

In *Chapter 10* we already touched on the problem of using Windows Script Host (WSH) and even provided a small code excerpt, which illustrated its usage. Introduced with Windows 2000, WSH is capable of creating simple, but flexible and powerful scripts to automate network administration. Because WSH is language-independent, you're free to select any scripting language you prefer: Visual Basic Scripting Edition (VBScript), JScript, or Perl. WSH also supports COM, allowing you to enjoy the advantages of new technologies such as Windows Management Instrumentation (WMI).

Now, the time has come to consider this topic in more detail. Of course, it is impossible to provide a detailed description of WSH, WMI, or scripting languages, such as VBScript or JScript, within a single chapter (after all, each of these topics deserves a separate book, and quite a comprehensive one, since I have encountered volumes of JScript and Perl that comprised more than 1,500 pages). Therefore, if you want a detailed language reference, simply buy one of those books at your local bookstore.

However, we will consider registry-related topics, and, in particular, the RegRead, RegWrite, and RegDelete methods provided by WSH. We will also consider their practical usage and provide several simple, but useful scripts.

Basic Information on Microsoft Windows Script Host

WSH is a language-independent scripting host for Windows Script-compatible scripting engines. It brings simple, powerful, and flexible scripting to the Windows 32-bit platform, allowing you to run scripts from both the Windows desktop and the command prompt.

Windows Script Host is ideal for non-interactive scripting needs such as logon scripting, administrative scripting, and machine automation.

The Benefits of Windows Script Host

WSH offers the following benefits:

☐ *Two ways to run scripts, WScript.exe and CScript.exe.* WScript.exe provides a Windows-based properties page for setting script properties; CScript.exe provides command-line switches for setting script properties.

☐ *Support for multiple files.* You can call multiple scripting engines and perform multiple jobs from a single Windows Script (WSF) file.

☐ *Low memory requirements.*

☐ *Mapping of script extensions to programmatic identifiers (ProgIDs).* When you start a script from the Windows desktop or the command prompt, the script host reads and passes the specified script file contents to the registered script engine. Instead of using the HTML SCRIPT tag to identify the script, the host uses file extensions; for example, *VBS* for Microsoft Visual Basic® Scripting Edition (VBScript) files, and *JS* for Microsoft JScript® files. Using extensions means you no longer need to be familiar with the ProgID for a given script engine. Windows Script Host handles this for you by maintaining a mapping of script extensions to ProgIDs, launching the appropriate engine for a given script.

Windows XP includes the latest version of Windows Script Host — version 5.6.0 (Fig. 15.1). Versions of Windows Script Host implemented by Microsoft operating systems are listed in Table 15.1.

Table 15.1. WSH Versions Implemented by Microsoft Operating Systems

Host Application	1.0	2.0	5.1	5.6
Microsoft Windows 98	x			
Microsoft Windows ME			x	
Microsoft Windows NT 4 Option Pack	x			
Microsoft Windows 2000		x		
Microsoft Windows XP				x
Microsoft Windows Server 2003				x

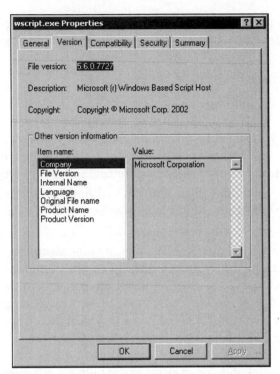

Fig. 15.1. Windows XP and Windows Server 2003 include
the latest version of Windows Script Host — version 5.6.0

In comparison to previous versions, this one provides the following enhancements in functionality.

❑ *Argument-handling has been improved* — handling and documenting command line arguments is simpler. The process of integrating your scripts with other command line scripts has been simplified, and it is easier to create scripts that can supply the user with help information. Refer to the following table for information on the WSH language features that connect you to this new functionality.

❑ *You can run scripts remotely* — you can load scripts onto several remote computer systems, and start them all running simultaneously. While a remote script is running, you can check on its progress, and after it has finished, you can ensure that it has run correctly, or find out what caused it to terminate prematurely. There is a new dispatch object used to create remote WSH objects — the Controller object. In addition, there is a new object that represents an instance of a running script — the Remote WSH object.

❑ *When you start new processes, you can treat them as objects* — you determine the status of spawned processes, and access their standard I/O streams.

❑ *You can access the current working directory* — you can determine/modify the active process' current working directory.

❑ *Security issues unique to scripts have been addressed* — Windows Script Host, a powerful, flexible tool for automating Windows, can at the same time be dangerous if used improperly or with malicious intentions. Windows Script Host 5.6, included with Windows XP and Windows Server 2003, implements a new security model, which enables users to verify the authenticity of a script before running it. Script developers can sign their scripts to prevent unauthorized modifications. Administrators can enforce strict policies that determine which users have privileges to run scripts locally or remotely.

Note

Windows provides a standard mechanism for signing code via signcode.exe. Unfortunately, signcode.exe doesn't ship with Windows, but rather with the Windows SDK. The most useful and interesting article on this important topic can be downloaded from **http://msdn.microsoft.com/library/default.asp?url=/library/en-us/dnclinic/html/ scripting10082001.asp**

Windows Script Host Object Model

As everything in modern Microsoft operating systems, WSH is object-oriented. The Windows Script Host object model consists of 14 objects. The root object is the WScript object.

The Windows Script Host object model provides a logical, systematic way to perform many administrative tasks. The set of COM interfaces it provides can be placed into two main categories:

❑ *Script Execution and Troubleshooting.* This set of interfaces allows scripts to perform basic manipulation of the Windows Script Host, output messages to the screen, and perform basic COM functions such as CreateObject and GetObject.

❑ *Helper Functions.* Helper functions are properties and methods for performing actions such as mapping network drives, connecting to printers, retrieving and modifying environment variables, and manipulating registry keys. Administrators can also use the Windows Script Host helper functions to create simple logon scripts.

Note

For purposes of accessing the registry, the most important object is WshShell, which will be discussed in the next section.

WshShell Object

Provides access to the native Windows shell. The WshShell object is a child object of the WScript object — you must use the WScript method CreateScript to create a WshShell object (i.e., WScript.CreateObject("WScript.Shell")). You create a WshShell object whenever you want to run a program locally, manipulate the contents of the registry, create a shortcut, or access a system folder. The WshShell object provides the Environment collection. This collection allows you to handle environmental variables (such as WINDIR, PATH, or PROMPT).

RegRead Method

The RegRead method returns the value of a key or value name from the registry. This method uses the following syntax:

   Object.**RegRead**(*strName*)

where:

   Object — WshShell object
   strName — string value indicating the key or value-name whose value you want

    The RegRead method can return the values of the following data types: REG_SZ, REG_DWORD, REG_BINARY, REG_EXPAND_SZ, and REG_MULTI_SZ.

    You can specify a key name by ending *strName* with a final backslash. Do not include a final backslash to specify a value name. A value entry has three parts: its name, its data type, and its value. When you specify a key name (as opposed to a value name), RegRead returns the default value. To read a key's default value, specify the name of the key itself. Fully qualified key names and value names begin with a root key. You must use abbreviated versions of root key names with the RegRead method. The five possible root keys are listed in Table 15.2.

Table 15.2. Abbreviations for the Registry Root Key Names

Root Key Name	Abbreviation
HKEY_CURRENT_USER	HKCU
HKEY_LOCAL_MACHINE	HKLM
HKEY_CLASSES_ROOT	HKCR
HKEY_USERS	HKEY_USERS
HKEY_CURRENT_CONFIG	HKEY_CURRENT_CONFIG

RegWrite Method

The RegWrite Method creates a new key, adds another value to an existing key (and assigns it a value), or changes the value of an existing value name. This method uses the following syntax:

Object.**RegWrite**(*strName*, *anyValue* [,*strType*])

where:

Object — WshShell object

strName — string value indicating the key name, value name, or value you want to create, add, or change

anyValue — the name of the new key you want to create, the name of the value you want to add to an existing key, or the new value you want to assign to an existing value name

strType — optional: string value indicating the value's data type

Specify a key name by ending *strName* with a final backslash. Do not include a final backslash to specify a value name. The RegWrite method automatically converts the parameter *anyValue* to either a string or an integer. The value of *strType* determines its data type (either a string or an integer). The options for *strType* are listed in Table 15.3.

Table 15.3. Acceptable Values of the strType Argument for the RegWrite Method

Converted to	*strType*
string	REG_SZ
string	REG_EXPAND_SZ
integer	REG_DWORD
string	REG_BINARY

Note

The `REG_MULTI_SZ` type is not supported for the `RegWrite` method.

Fully qualified key names and value names are prefixed with a root key. You must use abbreviated versions of root key names (if one exists) with the `RegWrite` method. Abbreviated names of the registry root keys used by the `RegWrite` method are the same as those for the `RegRead` method.

RegDelete Method

The `RegDelete` method is used to delete a registry key or one of its values from the registry. This method uses the following syntax:

```
Object.RegDelete(strName)
```

where:

Object — `WshShell` object
strName — string value indicating the name of the registry key or key value you want to delete

Specify a key-name by ending *strName* with a final backslash; leave it off to specify a value name. Fully qualified key names and value names are prefixed with a root key. You must use abbreviated versions of root key names (if one exists) with the `RegDelete` method. There are five possible root keys you can use; they are the same as those for the `RegRead` and `RegWrite` methods.

JScript Example

A simple example written in JavaScript (JScript in Microsoft's implementation), illustrating the usage of these methods is provided in Listing 15.1. This code creates a registry key `HKEY_CURRENT_USER\Software\MyCoolSoftware`, sets its `Default` value (`REG_BINARY` data type) to 1, then creates another `REG_SZ` value entry under this key and assigns it the "`This is a test!`" string value.

Listing 15.1. JScript Example Illustrating Registry Access

```
// The simplest example illustrating registry access using JScript
// Use this module at your own risk

   // Setting variables
```

```
    var vbOKCancel = 1;
    var vbInformation = 64;
    var vbCancel = 2;
    var result;



    // Creating wshShell object



    var WshShell = WScript.CreateObject("WScript.Shell");


    {


    // prompting the user

        result = WshShell.Popup("Do you want to create a new registry setting?",
                                0,
                                  "Registry Access using JScript",
                                  vbOKCancel + vbInformation);
        if (result != vbCancel)
        {


        WshShell.RegWrite ("HKCU\\Software\\MyCoolSoftware\\", 1, "REG_BINARY");
        WshShell.RegWrite
("HKCU\\Software\\MyCoolSoftware\\MySuperProgram",
                          "This is a test!", "REG_SZ");
        var bKey =    WshShell.RegRead ("HKCU\\Software\\MyCoolSoftware\\");
WScript.Echo    (WshShell.RegRead    ("HKCU\\Software\\MyCoolSoftware\\
MySuperProgram"));
```

```
          }

//prompting the user

result = WshShell.Popup("Do you want to delete newly created settings?",
                        0,
                        "Registry Access using JScript",
                        vbOKCancel + vbInformation);
     if (result != vbCancel)
     {
     WshShell.RegDelete
("HKCU\\Software\\MyCoolSoftware\\MySuperProgram");
     WshShell.RegDelete ("HKCU\\Software\\MyCoolSoftware\\");
     }
   }
```

To test this script, enter the code provided in this listing using any text editor (for example, Notepad.exe), and save the file with the JS filename extension. If you double-click this file, WSH server will start and execute the script. Notice that this script prompts the user to confirm adding new registry entries (Fig. 15.2), displays the contents of the newly created registry entry (Fig. 15.3) and then asks the user if the newly created registry key and value entry contained within it should be deleted (Fig. 15.4).

Fig. 15.2. The dialog prompting the user to confirm creating of a new registry setting

Fig. 15.3. Displaying the contents of the newly created registry entry

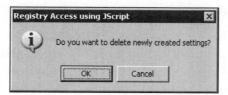

Fig. 15.4. The dialog prompting the user to confirm deletion of
the newly created registry setting(s)

These dialog boxes allow the user to check modifications introduced to the registry at each step, using, for example, Registry Editor (Fig. 15.5).

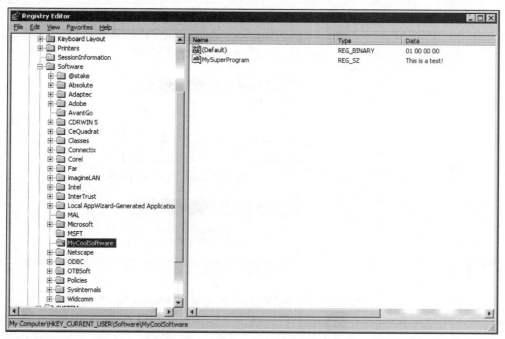

Fig. 15.5. You can use Registry Editor to check modifications introduced to
the registry at each step of the script

VBScript Examples

If you prefer VBScript, you can also use the above-described methods for accessing
the registry (notice the difference in the syntax of JScript and VBScript).

Enabling and Disabling Changes to the Start Menu

A small example is provided below, developed using VBScript, which, in contrast to the previous one, does something useful — it enables or disables changes to the **Start** Menu.

In the previous chapter, we discussed the values that control the **Start** menu. One such value is the `NoChangeStartMenu` under `HKEY_CURRENT_USER\` `SOFTWARE\Microsoft\Windows\CurrentVersion\Policies\Explorer`. When this value is set to 1, one cannot make changes, and when this value is set to 0, changes are allowed. Our small VBScript example first displays the dialog prompting the user to choose whether he or she needs to lock the **Start** menu (Fig.15.6). To manage the **Start** menu via the system registry, the script creates the `NoChangeStartMenu` value, and sets it to 1 if the user chooses to lock the **Start** menu. If the user clicks **No**, the `NoChangeStartMenu` value will be set to 0. Next, the script reads the `NoChangeStartMenu` value from the registry, displays the current **Start** menu status, and prompts the user to change it if desired (Fig. 15.7).

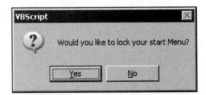

Fig. 15.6. Prompt for the user to lock **Start** menu

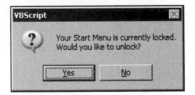

Fig. 15.7. Prompt for the user to unlock **Start** menu

The source code for this example is provided in Listing 15.2.

Listing 15.2. Source Code for the VBScript Example that Enables or Disables Changes to the Start Menu

---

```
Option Explicit

Dim WSHShell, RegKey, NoChangeStartMenu, Result
```

```
Set WSHShell = CreateObject("WScript.Shell")

RegKey = "HKCU\Software\Microsoft\Windows\CurrentVersion\Policies\Explorer\"

Result = MsgBox("Would you like to lock your start Menu?", 36)

   If Result = 6 Then 'clicked yes
      WSHShell.RegWrite regkey & "NoChangeStartMenu", 1
   Else
      WSHShell.RegWrite regkey & "NoChangeStartMenu", 0
   End If

NoChangeStartMenu = WSHShell.RegRead (regkey & "NoChangeStartMenu")

If NoChangeStartMenu = 1 Then 'Start Menu is locked

   Result = MsgBox("Your Start Menu is currently locked." & _
         vbNewLine & "Would you like to unlock?", 36)

   If Result = 6 Then 'clicked yes
      WSHShell.RegWrite regkey & "NoChangeStartMenu", 0
   End If

Else 'Start menu can be changed

   Result = MsgBox("You can change Start menu." & _
         vbNewLine & "Would you like to prohibit changes", 36)

   If Result = 6 Then 'clicked yes
      WSHShell.RegWrite regkey & "NoChangeStartMenu", 1
   End If

End If

' End code
```

Managing System Restore on Windows XP Clients

The example presented in this section illustrates how you can use Windows Management Instrumentation to automate your work with the System Restore feature on client workstations running Windows XP.

Before we proceed any further, let us provide a brief description of WMI scripting capabilities utilization. WMI scripting is a library of automation interfaces. COM-compliant scripting languages use these automation interfaces to access WMI infrastructure. All WMI automation objects, methods and properties are implemented by the Wbemdisp.dll file.

 ### *Note*

To run WMI, you must have administrator privileges.

To access WMI through WMI scripting library, you need to perform three basic steps, which are common to most WMI scripts:

1. Connect to the Windows Management service.
2. Retrieve instances of WMI managed objects.
3. Call a method or access a managed object's property.

Note

To learn more about powerful WMI scripting capabilities, see the Microsoft Windows 2000 Professional Resource Kit or Microsoft Windows 2000 Server Resource Kit, where you can find more than 50 WMI-based scripts, enabling you to manage everything on the target computer, from boot configuration to user accounts.

Enabling and Disabling System Restore on Windows XP Clients

The example in Listing 15.3 automates the task of enabling or disabling System Restore on the specified drive. When it is begun, this code creates WshShell object, then requests user input, prompting the user if it is required to enable or disable System Restore (Fig. 15. 8). To proceed further, the user must enter an appropriate text string (enable or disable) into the text field at the bottom of this dialog and click **OK**.

Next, the script prompts the user to specify the drive on which it is necessary to take the specified action (Fig. 15.9). Specify the drive using the following format: <drive_letter>:\, for example, C:\.

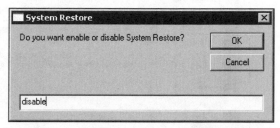

Fig. 15.8. Dialog box prompting the user to specify whether System Restore must be enabled or disabled

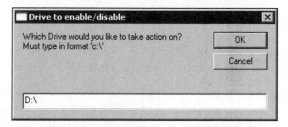

Fig. 15.9. Dialog box prompting the user to specify the drive on which the specified action must be taken

The script runs and performs the specified action on the specified drive. After it is done, it displays a message box, informing the user of the result (Fig. 15.10). To make sure that the specified action was performed successfully, start the System applet in the Control Panel, go to the **System Restore** tab, and check if System Restore is actually turned off for the specified drive (Fig. 15.11).

Fig. 15.10. The message box informing the user of the result of the operation

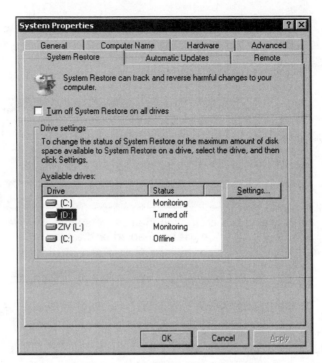

Fig. 15.11. Use the System Restore UI to check if System Restore is actually turned off for the drive you have specified when running the script

Now let us consider the code that implements this series of actions (Listing 15.3).

As was already mentioned, to use WMI scripting the code must connect to the Windows Management service, retrieve instances of the WMI-managed objects, and then call a method or access a managed object's property. In the example presented below, we connect to WMI using the WMI's moniker named winmgmts and SystemRestore class.

Note

A moniker is a standard COM mechanism for binding to a COM object. Detailed information on the WMI moniker syntax can be found at the following address: **http://msdn.microsoft.com/library/psdk/wmisdk/scintro_6tpv.htm**.

Listing 15.3. VBScript Code for Enabling/Disabling System Restore on the Specified Drive

```
' Begin code for enabling or disabling System Restore
Option Explicit
```

```
Dim WSHShell, onoff, drive, SRP, eSRP, Result

'Creating WSHShell object
Set WSHShell = CreateObject("WScript.Shell")
'Requesting user input
onoff = inputbox ("Do you want to enable or disable System Restore?",
"System Restore")
Drive = inputbox ("Which Drive would you like to take action on? Must
type in format 'c:\'", "Drive to enable/disable")
'using WMI moniker and SystemRestore class to access WMI
set SRP = GetObject("winmgmts:\\.\root\default:SystemRestore")
If onoff = "enable"  then
eSRP = SRP.enable(drive)
Result = MsgBox("System Restore is currenly" & _
        vbNewLine & "enabled on the following drive: " &  Drive, 64)
end if
If onoff = "disable" then
eSRP = SRP.disable(drive)
Result = MsgBox("System Restore is currenly" & _
        vbNewLine & "disabled on the following drive: " &  Drive, 64)
end if


' End code
```

Automatically Creating Restore Points on Windows XP Clients

What else can we do with WMI and System Restore? Well, let us try to create a restore point automatically. Now, since we have already created several scripts, this is an easy task. Let us decide what our script must do. First, it must ask the user whether he or she wants to create a new restore point (Fig. 15.12).

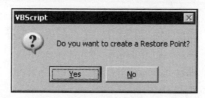

Fig. 15.12. Dialog prompting the user to create a restore point

Next, if the user clicks **Yes**, we must provide the user with the capability to enter the resource point description (Fig. 15.13).

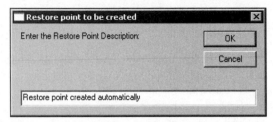

Fig. 15.13. The dialog prompting the user to provide a description for the restore point to be created

After the user provides a restore point description, we use WMI moniker and SystemRestore class to access WMI, and then create a new restore point using the description provided by the user. A very simple code performing these tasks is provided in Listing 15.4.

Listing 15.4. Automatic Creation of the Restore Point

```
Option Explicit

Dim WSHShell, SRP, CSRP, description, Result

Set WSHShell = CreateObject("WScript.Shell")

Result = MsgBox("Do you want to create a Restore Point?", 36)

    If Result = 6 Then 'clicked yes
    description = inputbox ("Enter the Restore Point Description:",
"Restore point to be created")
    'use WMI moniker and SystemRestore class
    set SRP = getobject("winmgmts:\\.\root\default:Systemrestore")

    CSRP = SRP.createrestorepoint (description, 0, 100)

    end if

' End code
```

After running this script, start System Restore and check if the restore point was actually created. The screenshot shown in Fig. 15.14 shows four test restore points, which I created automatically in the process of testing this script.

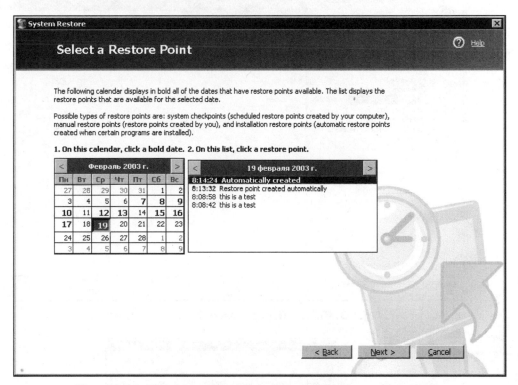

Fig. 15.14. The System Restore window displaying automatically created restore points

Now, after carefully testing the script and making sure that it works, let us consider what practical use we can make of it. For example, wouldn't it be nice if after each successful logon, users (especially those who experiment with the registry) were prompted to create a restore point? As you remember, Windows XP is successfully loaded only after at least one user logs on to the system, and at that point the Clone control set is copied to the **LastKnownGood** configuration. Well, in my opinion, it makes sense if you also create a restore point at that time, just to be on the safe side. This small script can serve this purpose if you assign it as a logon script.

To do so, just copy the script file to the %*SystemRoot*%\System32\GroupPolicy\ User\Scripts\Logon directory (for standalone computers or in a workgroup environment)

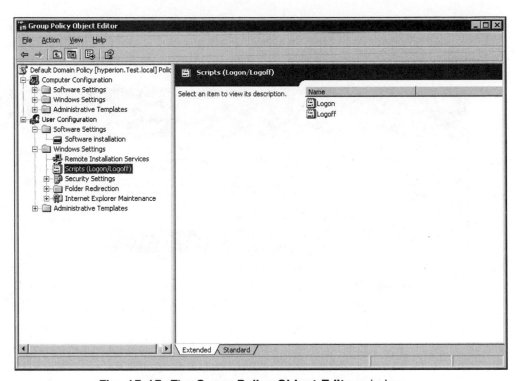

Fig. 15.15. The **Group Policy Object Editor** window

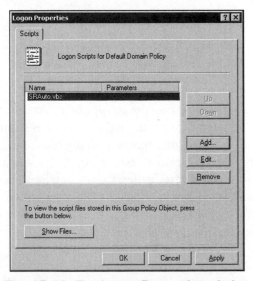

Fig. 15.16. The **Logon Properties** window

or to the *Domain_controller*\Sysvol\<*domain_or_OU*>\Policies\<*GUID*>\USER\ Scripts\Logon directory (for domain environment), then start the Group Policy Object editor, and expand the console tree as shown in Fig. 15.15 (**User Configuration | Windows Settings | Scripts**). Double-click the **Logon** policy to open the **Logon Properties** window (Fig. 15.16), click the **Add** button and add our script to the list of available logon scripts.

Now, each time the user logs on to the local computer, he or she will be prompted to create a restore point.

Summary

Thus, we have created several scripts, starting with the simplest example that can be used for demonstration purposes only, and proceeding further to create a small but useful one. The strongest point of WSH is its simplicity and the ease with which it can be used. Of course, there are certain limitations (for example, the RegRead, RegWrite, and RegDelete methods discussed earlier in this chapter provide no direct way of checking if the registry keys or values which you are going to create, delete, or modify already exist). For this purpose, you'll need to write a special application using any of the development environments available to you (such as Visual Basic, Visual C++, or Delphi).

On the other hand, a Windows script is simply a text file that you can create with any text editor you feel comfortable with — just be sure to save your script file with a WSH-compatible script extension (JS, VBS, or WSF). At the same time, the capabilities of WSH are rather powerful, and if you master it, you'll certainly be able to provide a quick and efficient solution within a matter of minutes.

Internet Resources

Since operating systems are regularly changed to newer versions and various Service Packs are constantly released, practically every book has one common drawback: Once it has been written, revisions and corrections can be made only in a new edition. While writing this book, I faced some difficult conditions with respect to beta versions and Release Candidates of the Windows Server 2003 family of operating systems. I tried to carefully test all the tips and recommendations provided in this book, but...

The best source of information on Windows NT/2000/XP and Windows Server 2003 is the Internet. A list of the most informative and reliable links is provided below. At the time of publication, there were no dead links in this list.

❏ **http://www.wugnet.com**

The site of the Windows Users Group Network (WUGNET) contains lots of information on Microsoft Windows, including Windows 9*x*/ME and Windows NT-based operating systems. On this site, you can find technical support information on various aspects of Windows operating systems, Internet, e-mail, shareware, hardware, games, software development, help authoring, multimedia, Microsoft products, and more.

❏ **http://www.winsupersite.com**

This comprehensive set of resources and breaking news focuses on the newest releases of Windows operating systems. This site covers Windows XP, Windows Server 2003, and even Windows "Longhorn" — the next major desktop Windows release, which will follow Windows XP. You'll find news, FAQs, Tech Showcases, and more concerning current and upcoming Microsoft operating systems and related technologies. This site contains information on exciting new products such as Windows XP Media Center Edition (code-named Free-style), Windows XP Tablet PC Edition, Windows Media 9 Series (code-named Corona), and so on. Interested in Windows 2000 or Windows ME FAQs? No problem; you'll find them under "Retired FAQs". This site is supported by Windows expert Paul Thurrott, the author of many bestsellers covering Windows operating systems, software development, Web programming, and other computing topics.

This site is recommended for advanced Windows users who are interested in new and upcoming versions of Windows operating systems. The author concentrates on new Windows functionality and illustrates how to use most features with practical examples.

❏ **http://www.microsoft.com/**

Windows users certainly know this site; it's among the most reliable and informative sources of information concerning all Microsoft products, including Windows XP and Windows Server 2003. Search the Knowledge Base, and perhaps you'll find the answers to your questions. For assistance with the registry, go to Microsoft's Download Center (**http://www.microsoft.com/downloads/search.asp**), select the operating system you are working with, and search using the **Registry** keyword. You'll find a log of registry patches, tools, and utilities. (Some of them are supplied with the source code.) If you want to understand the working principles of all Windows NT-based operating systems, do not miss Microsoft's Windows Hardware Development site (**http://www.microsoft.com/hwdev/**). This is the most reliable source of hardware information; it provides tools, recommendations, and services for driver developers and hardware designers who create products that work with the Microsoft Windows family of operating systems. The site is updated constantly with the latest news on topics including OnNow design, devices, and drivers. It also provides valuable downloads, such as specifications, white papers, and the newest versions of Windows Driver Development Kit (DDK). I wouldn't call DDK documentation easy reading, especially if you're reading it for the first time. However, there's no other way to become a professional. If you really care about the security of your Windows-based network, you must regularly visit Microsoft Security Advisor (**http://www.microsoft.com/security/default.asp**). This official source of information contains tons of security-related data for IT professionals, software developers, and consumers.

❏ **http://msdn.microsoft.com/msdnmag**

MSDN Journal is the most interesting resource for Windows NT/2000/XP and Windows Server 2003 internals. You'll find articles written by Matt Pietrek, Jeffrey Richter, and other popular authors.

❏ **http://www.ntfaq.com**

This site provides a large collection of FAQs related to contemporary Windows NT-based operating systems. Topics include backup and recovery, Active Directory, registry, security, Windows Script Host, and more. This is an excellent resource if you need to find answers to your questions.

❏ **http://www.winplanet.com/winplanet/**

This site contains a variety of Windows-related news, reviews, tips, tutorials, and downloads, as well as a free weekly Windows newsletter.

❏ **http://www.jsiinc.com/reghack.htm**

This site provides a large variety of registry tips, tricks, and hacks, applicable to practically all existing versions of Windows NT-based operating systems, including Windows NT, Windows 2000, Windows XP, and Windows Server 2003. If you are looking for such things, this is the place for you. It is updated constantly, and hacks arrive daily. No book can compare to it!

❏ **http://www.windowsitlibrary.com/**

As its name implies, this is the Windows IT professional's free online technical reference library. This excellent resource covers nearly all topics related to Windows NT-based operating systems.

❏ **http://www.swynk.com/**

SWYNK.COM is the largest independent resource for Microsoft .NET Enterprise and Windows Server technologies. On this site, you'll find the latest information on Windows NT/2000/XP and Windows Server 2003, SQL, SMS, and Exchange Servers. It provides lots of Windows NT/2000/XP-related resources, including technical articles, Web-based discussion boards, and Windows scripts.

❏ **http://www.osr.com**

This is a site for true professionals! Open Systems Resources, Inc. (OSR) has devoted this entire site to Windows NT/2000/XP customized software development, including the development of file systems and device drivers. You can subscribe to the NT Insider magazine here (free of charge). If you're an NT-programmer, or plan to become one, this site's for you.

❏ **http://www.sysinternals.com**

The Systems Internals site is supported by Mark Russinovich and Bryce Cogswell. These names speak for themselves. In addition to the Regmon and NTFSDOS utilities mentioned in *Chapter 14*, you'll find lots of handy utilities here for Windows 9*x* and Windows NT-based operating systems (most with the source code), as well as valuable technical information. This is my favorite site.

❏ **http://www.winnetmag.com/**
Windows & .NET Magazine is intended for IT professionals specializing in Windows NT-based operating systems, including Windows NT/2000/XP and Windows Server 2003. Subscribers have unlimited access to all materials and archives published in the last five years, but even guest access will give you lots of valuable information.

❏ **http://www.labmice.net/**
LabMice.net offers information on Windows 2000, Windows XP, and more. Visit it, and you won't be disappointed. This portal contains useful links related to all aspects of running Windows 2000 or Windows XP. It holds a large collection of resources on the registry, security, and scripting, including resource centers, online tutorials, and code examples.

❏ **http://www.winguides.com/**
The WinGuides Network provides technical resources and support for tweaking, managing, and securing the Windows operating system using the registry, scripting, and security. It contains a series of technical guides, including Security Guide, Scripting Guide, Driver Guide for Windows, and Windows Registry Guide (formerly Regedit.com), which provide a range of registry tricks and tweaks for optimizing, enhancing, and securing your Windows OS.

❏ **http://www.aelita.com/**
Aelita Software offers of technical information and utilities for Windows NT/2000/XP and Windows Server 2003, including ERDisk for Windows NT/2000 (or simply ERDisk) and ERDisk for Active Directory. ERDisks deliver automated backup and fast, remotely managed recovery of your Windows NT/2000 or Windows Server 2003 enterprise system's configuration and Active Directory. They bridge the gap between native disaster recovery tools, which have limited functionality, and full network backups, which can take hours to retrieve and restore. These utilities are not shareware, but you can download trial versions.

❏ **http://www.radium.ncsc.mil/tpep/library/rainbow/**
This is the "Rainbow Series". In my humble opinion, it doesn't require any comments.

❐ **http://www.windowssecurity.com/default.htm**

This security-related site contains reviews, documents, advisories, and more. It also provides a lot of useful links to other security-related sites, so don't forget to bookmark it.

❐ **http://www.@stake.com**

@stake has assembled the best minds in digital security, including the L0pht Heavy Industries group, to help you understand and mitigate security risks. The LC4 (the latest version of the award-winning password auditing and recovery application L0phtCrack), mentioned in *Chapter 9*, can be downloaded from **http://www.@stake.com/research/lc4/index.html**. You can also download L0phtCrack 1.5, an unsupported command-line version for researchers (not intended for production password auditing). If you want dictionary files, don't forget to download them from **http://packetstormsecurity.org/Crackers/wordlists/indexsize.shtml**.

❐ **http://www.iss.net**

This site is not specific to Windows NT/2000/XP. Still, it offers tons of valuable security information. (Don't forget to visit its security library at **http://xforce.iss.net/security_library/**.) Evaluation versions of security tools are also available for download. They are quite large, so don't forget to free up at least 120 MB of disk space.

❐ **http://www.easydesksoftware.com/**

This is the site dedicated to developing Windows Registry and file system utilities. Here you'll find information and tools required to repair a corrupted registry in practically all Windows operating systems, including Windows 9*x*/ME and Windows NT-based operating systems.

Summary

The list provided here doesn't include all of the Internet resources dedicated to Windows NT/2000/XP and Windows Server 2003. If you're interested in this topic, you'll find many useful resources online. As for me, I've provided the ones I like the best.

Bibliography

A single book can't provide an answer to every question. Often, even an encyclopedia can't provide all the necessary information (and this book certainly isn't an encyclopedia). In this appendix, I list some books that may help you find the answers to your questions.

1. Tim Daniels. *"1001 Secrets for Windows NT Registry"*. NEWS/Four-Hundred Books, 1998, ISBN 1882419685

2. Paul Robichaux, Robert Denn. *"Managing the Windows 2000 Registry"*. O'Reilly & Associates, Incorporated, 2000, ISBN 1565929438

3. Nathan Wallace, Anthony Sequeira. *"Windows 2000 Registry Little Black Book"*, 2nd edition. Coriolis Group, 2001, ISBN 1576108821

4. Kathy Ivens. *"Admin911: Windows 2000 Registry"*. McGraw-Hill Professional, 2000, ISBN 0072129468

5. Jerry Honeykutt. *"Microsoft Windows 2000 Registry Handbook"*. Macmillan USA Publishing, 2000, ISBN 0789716747

6. Kathy Ivens. *"Optimizing the Windows Registry"*. IDG Books Worldwide, 1998, ISBN 076453159X

7. Paul J. Sanna. *"Windows 2000 Registry"*. Prentice Hall PTR, 2000, ISBN 0130300640

8. Weiying Chen, Wayne Berry. *"Windows NT Registry Guide"*. Addison-Wesley, 1997, ISBN 0201694735

9. Don Kiely, Zane Thomas. *"Visual Basic Programmer's Guide to Windows Registry"*. Marbry Software, Incorporated, 1998, ISBN 1890422266

Index